The Japanese Economy

The Japanese Economy: Trade, Industry, and Government

Ryutaro Komiya

UNIVERSITY OF TOKYO PRESS

Publication of this volume was assisted by a grant from The Japan Foundation.

Chapter 1, "Japan's International Trade and Trade Policy," is reprinted from *The Political Economy of Japan, Volume II: The Changing International Context*, edited by Takashi Inoguchi and Daniel I. Okimoto; General Editors, Yasusuke Murakami and High T. Patrick, with the permission of the publishers, Stanford University Press. © 1988 by the Board of Trustees of the Leland Stanford Junior University.

CONTENTS

PREFACE

This work assembles in one volume nine essays which I have written over the last ten years, on the theme of the 1980s Japanese economy, focusing in particular on issues in international economic relations such as trade and direct investment, the Japanese enterprise, and relations between the government and industry.

The book gathers together from the results of my recent research into the Japanese economy those essays which I felt would be most useful in providing a general overview of the contemporary Japanese economy to non-Japanese readers unfamiliar with Japanese-language materials.

Looking back over my career as an economist, I have for the most part been a "user" of economic theory, and participated to only a small extent in the "making" of economic theory. In other words, I feel that my main task as an economist has been to select some important economic problems in the Japanese economy and then, picking out from my toolbox of economic analysis the tools I have felt to be most useful, to analyze those problems, and to point out new approaches and reach conclusions which differed substantially from the hitherto accepted ones. Since about 1980, and particularly over the last five or six years, my interest has come to focus more on Japan's international economic relations, the Japanese enterprise, the relationship of the government to industry and enterprises, and Japan's industrial policy.

Although I make full use of economic theory in analyzing the various problems of the Japanese economy, I believe it is difficult to gain a full understanding of economic problems in the real world solely by reference to economic theory. When I was young I paid little attention to non-economic aspects of an economic problem, and hardly used, or was able to use, any tools other than economic theory—indeed I had a tendency to avoid using other tools as far as possible—but later I gradually came to realize that the legal, political, and administrative aspects of economic problems were as significant as the purely economic aspects. Furthermore, I came to see that when people discuss economic problems they are not only swayed by personal interests but can easily become slaves to ideologies and preconceived ideas. Therefore, although the chapters of this book discuss the problems of the Japanese economy primarily from an economic standpoint, they do not ignore those aspects which are not purely economic.

The book contains a total of nine essays divided into three sections: Part I covers international economic relations, including trade; Part II, the special characteristics of Japanese enterprises; and Part III, industry and government. Let us first look at what sort of problems are dealt with by each of the chapters in turn.

Chapters 1 and 2 give an overview, from the 1950s to the 1980s, of Japan's trade and trade policy (Chapter 1) and Japan's overseas direct investment (Chapter 2), and discuss the nature of the international environment under which they developed and the factors that influenced them. A number of pages are devoted to the legal and political aspects of trade policy in Chapter 1, and to the theory of direct investment in Chapter 2.

Chapter 3 was written with the purpose of assembling the ideas I have come to hold, after many years of reseach and experience, on the theme of present and future world trade system, and the development of the Japanese economy within this system. Here it is pointed out that there is an underlying threat of a "systemic crisis" in the world free trade system, and that the main source of this threat is the rising influence of protectionist political forces within the United States, which is based on a mistaken understanding of the actual state of the American economy and of its international economic relations. Nevertheless I state here that I still remain optimistic about the future of the world trade system.

Within the field of international economic relations, international finance has been among the subjects I have studied intensively. Japan's international monetary and foreign exchange policy between 1971 and 1982 is discussed in the two-volume work *Studies of Contemporary International Finance: Theory, History, and Policy* (in Japanese) which I co-authored with Miyako Suda. I would suggest that interested readers refer to the English translation of the History and Policy volume, to be published under the title *Japan's Foreign Exchange Policy* (Allen and Unwin, 1991).

Chapter 4, the first chapter in Part II, is a discussion of the characteristics of Japanese enterprises in comparison with those of other countries. I was prompted to write the essay which forms the basis of this chapter by two series of lectures I gave at Jilin University in 1984 and at the London School of Economics in 1986. In rewriting my notes for these lectures and in the process of giving them, I came to think that the typical large Japanese enterprise has certain features that are strikingly different from similar European and American enterprises, but has certain aspects and tendencies in common with what are known in economic theory and comparative economic systems as "labor-managed firms."

Chapter 5 is based on a paper I submitted to a symposium of Japanese and Chinese economists, in which I compared Japanese and Chinese enterprises and made some observations on the differences between Japan and China in the individual units of productive activity and their interrelationships which make up the industrial system. I argued there that "in China, the enterprise does not exist, or is almost nonexistent." The paper was translated into Chinese and appears to have been widely read in China: once, when I gave a lecture before a gathering of Chinese managers, I was introduced, with a certain amount of humor, as "Professor Komiya, who said to us Chinese that the enterprise does not exist in China."

Chaper 6 originally appeared as an essay in the book *The Japanese Enterprise (Nihon no kigyo,* 1989), which is the report on a research project by a group of Japanese economists and scholars in management science, with the aim of clarifying the actual nature and characteristics of Japanese enterprises. The book is now being translated into English under the direction of Ronald Dore, and will be published shortly. In this research project we decided to study the characteristics of not only joint-stock companies but also public corporations, agricultural cooperatives, consumer cooperative associations, and mutual life insurance companies. Since nobody in the group at that time was particularly qualified and willing to study mutual life insurance companies, however, it fell to me to write the essay which forms the basis of Chapter 6. Economists, in particular American economists, have a strong tendency to think of enterprises—especially modern, large corporations— solely as joint-stock companies which are "owned" by the stockholders and which attempt to maximize the benefits (in the form of dividends and high share values) to those stockholders; but many of the enterprises that play an important role in the contemporary Japanese economy (and in the European and American economies as well) are in fact cooperative organizations, including mutual life insurance companies. Chapter 6, then, discusses how the mutual life insurance company behaves as an enterprise, how the "surplus" which is the product of its activity is distributed among those concerned with the company, and how the company grows.

"Economic Planning," the first part of Chapter 7, which begins Part III, deals with the "national economic plans," such as the National Income Doubling Plan for the 1960s drawn up by the Economic Planning Agency, and the nationwide "regional plans," while the second part of the chapter, "Industrial Policy," deals with industrial policy as carried out by the Ministry of International Trade and Industry. Many foreigners seem to think that the Japanese government uses economic plans and industrial policy to interfere extensively in the private sector; and those responsible for planning and policy in the Japanese government have a tendency (though it was stronger in the past) to exaggerate the importance of their role as well. Japan's is clearly not a laissez-faire economy with minimal government intervention, but nevertheless the role of economic planning and industrial policy remains limited, and this has been particularly true since the mid-1960s, with the gradual deregulation of trade, licensing of foreign-owned patents and khowhow, and inward foreign direct investment. Chapter 7 discusses these economic plans and industrial policies and explains their content, their role in the Japanese economy, and the decision-making processes that paved the way for them. The latter half of Chapter 7 was originally written as the introductory chapter to *Industrial Policy of Japan* (*Nihon no sangyo seisaku*, 1984; English translation published by Academic Press, Japan, 1987), edited by the author and two collaborators, which brought together the results of a research project conducted over several years. Readers interested in Japan's industrial policy should refer to this work.

Chapter 8 deals with Japan's fiscal and monetary policies, which are most important in the government's macroeconomic management. It gives a brief chronology of Japan's macroeconomic development over the decade beginning with the first oil crisis, which started in autumn 1973, and analyzes why Japan's macroeconomic perfomance in terms of the growth rate, rate of inflation, unemployment rate, growth rate, and rate of rise in productivity was so much better than those of the other major industrialized countries. It examines what factors in the Japanese economy were responsible, and why the economy was much less influenced by the second oil crisis when it had been dealt such a heavy blow by the first.

Chapter 9, the final chapter, turns to a question of a slightly different nature from that of the other chapters, and discusses the recruitment of the government bureaucrats in charge of economic policy making, the training they receive, and their careers, as an exercise in a sort of sociology of learning or sociology of economics. The matters dealt with here are common knowledge to the bureaucrats themselves and to those familiar with Japanese government ministries and agencies, but, as far as I know, few accounts of this kind have appeared in Japanese, let alone in English. I have included this chapter because I feel that knowledge of this field is a considerable help in understanding the working of Japan's economic policy, the organization and behavior of Japanese enterprises, and Japan's labor market.

The chapters of this book thus cover a wide range of problems related to Japan's international economic relations enterprises, industry, and government economic policy. While the various chapters were originally written independently as papers presented at conferences on the themes they discuss, broadly speaking they all reflect interests I have consistently held from around 1980 up to the present, and represent a comprehensive summary of my understanding of the contemporary Japanese economy.

There are various interrelationships among the chapters of the book. For example, the understanding of Japanese enterprises arrived at in Chapter 4 is closely connected to the performance of the Japanese economy in the wake of the first oil crisis, as recounted in Chapter 8, and to the theory of direct investment and the development of direct investment by Japanese enterprises, as discussed in Chapter 3. The relationship of the Japanese government to industry and enterprises, and the change in this relationship from the 1950s down to the present, discussed in Chapter 7, and the development of trade policy, analyzed in Chapter 1, are complementary. Again, it was my understanding of the organization of the Japanese bureaucracy, as discussed in Chapter 9, which prompted me later to think seriously about the distinctive characteristics of Japanese enterprises, and provided a basis for the manuscripts which later became Chapter 4. I believe, therefore, that this book taken as a whole gives an overall picture of the Japanese economy in the 1980s and a coherent view of Japan's international economic relations, its enterprises, and the relationship between government and industry.

A few of the chapters of this book were originally written as papers co-authored with colleagues, and I would like to express my deepest thanks to Motoshige Itoh (Chapter 1), Kazuo Yasui (Chapter 8), and Kozo Yamamoto (Chapter 9), for permitting me to reproduce their joint work in this volume. I would also like to thank the copyright owners of the publications in which the original essays appeared, for allowing me to reproduce them here. Finally, I am deeply grateful to Ms. Susan Schmidt and Ms. Reiko Ose of the University of Tokyo Press for their unstinting help with the publication of the book.

In the process of working on this volume, I have been struck once again by the enormity of the linguistic barrier between Japan and other countries. This barrier prevents communication especially from Japanese into foreign languages, and gives rise to a sharp imbalance in the flow of international or intercultural communication. A very wide range of books, magazines, and newspapers come into Japan in vast quantities, to be read in the original languages or in Japanese translations; whereas very few foreigners understand Japanese, and only a tiny number of publications in Japanese go out from Japan. Again, many Japanese can read books written in foreign languages, but only a few rare Japanese are capable of writing accurately in foreign languages. I myself have great difficulty writing in English. As a result, there is much less information and literature introducing Japan in foreign languages than introducing foreign countries in Japanese. The cost of translation from Japanese into English is astonishingly high compared with that of English into Japanese, and translation into English is often of poor quality. The number of Japanese works translated into foreign languages every year is probably less than 1% of the number of foreign-language works translated into Japanese.

This is why, when the situation becomes a little more complex, as it has recently in the real of Japan-U.S. economic relations, Japan tends to be misunderstood abroad, and misunderstandings lead to unwarranted criticisms and denunciations, which often cause me, as a Japanese, to heave a sigh. I will be gratified, therefore, if this book goes even a little way towards bridging the communication gap between Japan and foreign countries, if it rectifies even slightly the extreme imbalance in the communication flows, and if it contributes to a better understanding by foreigners of the Japanese economy.

September 1990   RYUTARO KOMIYA

Part I

International Trade and Investment

CHAPTER 1

JAPAN'S INTERNATIONAL TRADE AND TRADE POLICY

The purpose of this chapter is to review the evolution of Japan's international trade and trade policy from the time of Japan's accession to GATT (General Agreement on Tariffs and Trade) in 1955 up to the 1980s, to assess their impact on the Japanese economy, and to explore their likely development in the near future. More specifically, we investigate several questions: (1) How has the pattern of Japanese trade evolved, and what types of trade policy measures has the Japanese government taken? What were the theory and philosophy behind such policy measures? (2) How have trade relations developed between Japan and other countries, especially the major developed countries? (3) What role did Japan play in the arena of world policy formation? (4) How did the Japanese government's trade policies and international agreements affect Japan's international trade? After studying these questions, we attempt to assess the future outlook for Japan's trade and for the world trade regime on which Japan's economic development critically depends.

We divide the three decades under review into three periods.

The first period: 1955–67. In 1955, Japan became a member of GATT and thereafter gradually began liberalizing imports (in the preceding period imports had been severely restricted). By the end of this period, a large number of import quotas had been removed. The Kennedy Round of tariff negotiations under GATT was held in the last part of this period, and the tariff rates of developed countries were lowered substantially.

The second period: 1968–75. This was an intermediate, transitional period between the first period, in which Japan was a relatively small country exporting primarily labor-intensive goods, and the third period, in which Japan became a large, dominant actor in the world economy exporting largely sophisticated machinery. During this transitional period, Japan and the United States engaged in prolonged and painful negotiations over their bilateral trade in textiles and apparel. In the second half of this period, the world economy underwent a series of economic upheavals: the collapse of the Bretton Woods regime, the first oil crisis, worldwide inflation, and a deep depression for the first time in the postwar period. Each of these events had a substantial impact on the Japanese economy.

The third period: 1976–84. The second oil crisis broke out in 1979, and the world economy fell into a long stagnation. During this period, Japan's shares of world industrial production and world trade became much larger, and trade frictions with the United States and the European Community became a serious economic policy issue for Japan. In the midst of this unfavorable environment for free trade, the Tokyo Round—another GATT round of multilateral negotiations on tariffs and nontariff barriers initially proposed by Japan in 1971—was successfully concluded in 1979.

Accession to GATT and Trade Liberalization, 1955–1967

Japan's trade during the mid-1950s

In 1955, when Japan joined GATT, its exports amounted to only 2.4% of total world exports (excluding centrally planned economies), and its exports of industrial products amounted to 4.2% of total world

Table 1
Japanese Exports, 1955–1982

(%)

As share of	1955	1960	1965	1970	1975	1980	1982
Total Western exports[a]	2.4%	3.6%	5.1%	6.9%	7.1%	7.1%	9.1%[b]
Total Western exports of manufactures[c]	4.2	5.9	8.1	10.0	11.3	11.8	12.5
Total Western exports of machinery[d]	1.7	3.9	6.7	9.8	12.5	16.3	18.4

Sources: Bank of Japan, Bureau of Statistics, *Kokusai hikaku tokei* (Statistics for international comparison). (Tokyo, various issues).
[a]Japan's exports/Western countries' exports × 100.
[b]Figure for 1983.
[c]Japan's exports of manufactures/Western countries' exports of manufactures × 100.
[d]Japan's exports of machinery/Western countries' exports of machinery × 100.

exports of industrial products (see Table 1). These shares were much lower than in the 1930s: Japan's share in world exports was about 5.3% in 1938.

In 1955, Japan was gradually recovering from the destruction and disorder resulting from the defeat in World War II. It was still a small, latecomer industrializing country, with a GNP per capita and a wage level much lower than those of the developed countries (see Table 2). Its main exports were labor-intensive products produced by cheap labor using out-of-date equipment. Its imports were largely limited to such necessities as industrial raw materials, fuel, and foodstuffs.

Japan's industrial structure was changing rapidly, however, as a result of a high level of investment in plant and equipment and imports of advanced technologies. The capacity of the steel industry had already been sufficiently expanded and the technologies sufficiently advanced to make exports possible. In 1956, the shipbuilding industry had a share exceeding 20% of total world orders, the first place in the world. In the machinery and chemical industries, a large number of new products were being produced, and levels of production were increasing rapidly.

Trade policy in the era of high economic growth

In December 1955, the year of Japan's accession to GATT, the Japanese government announced and implemented the Five-Year Plan for Economic Independence (*Keizai Jiritsu 5-ka-nen Keikaku*), the first of a series of national economic plans. The announced purposes of the plan were: economic independence and full employment. Economic independence meant, first, to achieve a balance-of-payments equilib-

Table 2
GNP, Selected Countries, 1957–1984

(U.S. $ billions)

Country	1957	1962	1967	1972	1977	1981	1984
Japan	$30.8	$52.8	$115.0	$300.1	$693.5	$1,139.2	$1,261.0
	(339)	(554)	(1,148)	(2,806)	(6.095)	(9,684)	(9,917)ª
U.S.	441.1	554.9	785.0	1,155.2	1,899.5	2,937.7	3,662.8
	(2,565)	(2,974)	(3,942)	(5,532)	(8,704)	(12,783)	(14,093)ª
U.K.	62.1	78.9	94.4	146.6	247.2	504.3	465.0
	(1,207)	(1,441)	(1,713)	(2,627)	(4,419)	(9,032)	(8,140)ª
FRG	51.6	88.8	120.9	259.1	515.6	682.8	642.5
	(1,001)	(1,666)	(2,020)	(4,202)	(8,373)	(11,072)	(10,673)ª

Sources: Same as Table 1.
Note: Figures in parentheses are per capita GNP in U.S. dollars.
ªFigure for 1983.

rium without economic aid from the United States and without the help of foreign exchange receipts from "special procurements" (*toku-ju*), the purchases of Japanese goods and services by U.S. forces in Japan, which had increased sharply during the Korean War; and second, to launch the economy on a steady growth path.[1] Since Japan had to import increasing amounts of raw materials once it got on the path of economic growth, a steady expansion of exports was considered vital to economic independence.

The plan specified four principal policy objectives: modernization of industrial plant and equipment; promotion of international trade; an increase in self-sufficiency; and curtailment of consumption. The second and the third goals may appear contradictory to students of the standard theory of international trade. The authors of the national economic plan and policymakers at the time seem not to have understood fully the notion of gains from free trade based on comparative advantage and efficient resource allocation through international trade and the competitive price mechanism. These two apparently contradictory policy objectives may have been behind Japan's persistently large balance-of-payments deficits from the 1950s to the mid-1960s.

The official exchange rate of 360 yen to the dollar set in 1949 overvalued the yen during this period compared with the exchange rate that would have brought the balance of payments into equilibrium without import restrictions and export promotion measures. This substantial overvaluation played an important role in determining trade and other economic policies in the 1950s and the 1960s. Japan had to promote exports zealously and restrict imports in order to balance its international payments. This was no easy task for the government since economic growth was impossible without increasing amounts of imported raw materials and fuel. The slogan "Export or die" was not too much of an exaggeration for Japanese policymakers in this period.

The government apparently did not consider depreciating the yen to balance Japan's international payments. In general, government policymakers and leading businessmen did not believe in the role of the price mechanism in equalizing supply and demand. For example, the Ministry of Finance and the Bank of Japan maintained the so-called low interest rate policy, artificially keeping the interest rate at a much lower level than the one that would equate the demand and supply of funds in the financial markets. Japanese policymakers preferred to operate a disequilibrium system in which there existed either excess demand or excess supply.

One can better understand the intentions of the policymakers if one interprets "promotion of trade" as "promotion of exports." This was the first pillar of the trade policy system from the 1950s until the late 1960s. On the one hand, exports were promoted by such policy measures as subsidies, provision of low-interest loans for promising export industries, and preferential tax treatment of income from exports and for exploration of new export markets. These measures were meant to lower costs for exporters and to give incentives to export.

On the other hand, since imports would naturally increase along with economic growth, they had to be restrained as much as possible. Imports of raw materials and machinery essential for domestic production were given priority, whereas imports of consumption goods and goods that could be produced domestically had to be severely restricted under the disequilibrium system. This is what was meant by the slogan "making the economy more self-sufficient."[2] As a result, the government subsidized imports of raw materials and machinery under the overvalued yen exchange rate since firms purchasing these goods paid less in terms of yen than they would have had to pay under an equilibrium exchange rate.

The second pillar of Japan's trade policy system in this period was to develop in Japan modern manufacturing industries like those in Europe and the United States. Catching up with the West had been Japan's earnest wish since the Meiji era. It was expressed by the two renowned slogans of the Meiji era: *fukoku kyohei* (to enrich the country and to strengthen the army) and *shokusan kogyo* (to foster industries and to promote enterprise). The Japanese people's ambition to have a strong military force resulted in the disastrous defeat in World War II, but their desire to catch up with the West in economic wealth and modern industries was not abandoned but strengthened after World War II. Slogans like "modernization of firms' equipment," "rationalization of industries," and "promotion of heavy and chemical industries" were very popular in the 1950s. In the New Long-Run Economic Plan (*Shin Keizai Keikaku*, 1958–62), and the Plan for Doubling National Income (*Kokumin Shotoku Baizo Keikaku*, 1961–70), which followed the Five-Year Plan for Economic Independence, "strengthening the foundation of industry," "sophistication of the industrial structure," and "heavy and chemical industrialization" (*jukagaku kogyoka*) were the top-priority policy objectives.

Policymakers thought that only those industries that the highly industrialized countries had successfully established and that appeared to have good prospects for development in Japan should be nurtured and protected in their early stages of development. Although the government did not like the term "infant industry" for several reasons, what the government pursued under the slogan of "heavy and chemical industrialization" was essentially the protection of promising infant industries. As a means of protection, the government, on the one hand, granted infant industries various subsidies (although the amounts of the subsidies were generally limited), preferential tax treatment for depreciation and for income from "important new products," and low-interest loans through government-affiliated banks (especially the Japan Development Bank) and, on the other hand, protected them from foreign competition by import quotas and tariffs and by restricting domestic investment by foreign competitors.[3]

GATT and Japan

Japan acceded to GATT provisionally in 1953 and was admitted as a contracting party in 1955. There were several anomalies, however, in the relationship between Japan and GATT.[4]

In 1955, 14 countries, including the United Kingdom, France, the Netherlands, Belgium, Australia, India, and New Zealand, which accounted for about 40% of Japan's exports to GATT members, refused to have GATT relations with Japan by invoking Article 35 (which allows member-states to refuse to have GATT relations with another member-state). Among the major trading nations, only the United States, Canada, West Germany, Italy, and the Scandinavian countries accepted Japan as a full member of GATT and gave it most-favored-nation (MFN) treatment, at least formally. This is one of the rare cases where Article 35 was applied among GATT members: no country besides Japan has ever been so widely discriminated against in the GATT system, whether legally or illegally. Moreover, many countries, mostly former colonies of the United Kingdom and France, that joined GATT later applied Article 35 to Japan.[5]

These countries had bitter memories of the rapid expansion of Japanese exports of textiles, sundries, chinaware, and other labor-intensive products in the 1930s, utilizing "cheap labor" or "social dumping" as a leverage, according to their perception. These countries feared, or argued that they feared, that cheap Japanese products would flood their domestic markets and those of their ex-colonies. "Underlying these [fears] was the knowledge that Japan was a country with a large and talented population relative to its other factors of production, . . . that Japan must import huge amounts of food and raw materials. . . . Japan was therefore seen as almost certain to be a particularly aggressive, international competitor in labor-intensive manufactured goods."[6]

The United Kingdom ceased to apply Article 35 to Japan in 1963, and other European countries followed. By 1972 among Western European countries, only Austria, Ireland, and Portugal still invoked Article 35 against Japan. Many European countries continued to discriminate against Japanese exports, however. Most of them requested Japan, as a condition for their withdrawal of the application of Article 35, to accept their discriminatory import policies against Japan or to agree not to bring the case to GATT even if they violated GATT by impairing Japanese exports. Moreover, Italy, West Germany, and the Scandinavian countries, which had never applied Article 35 to Japan, also practiced discriminatory import restrictions against Japanese exports that were not allowed under the GATT. A large number of European countries still impose discriminatory (nonmultilateral) import quotas and import embargoes against Japan.[7]

The United States was eager to establish a normal GATT relationship with Japan and helped Japan obtain full membership.[8] In fact, Japan's accession to GATT was made possible mainly by the strong leadership of the United States. The United States's support for Japan's accession should be viewed in the broad perspective of the overall U.S. policy toward·Japan.[9] During the Occupation period, one of the United States's basic policies was to weaken Japan's economic power, especially that of zaibatsu groups, in order to prevent Japanese militarism from reviving. But this policy stance soon changed as East-West relations deteriorated. The outbreak of the Korean War in 1950 contributed significantly to this change. After the Chinese Communist Party took over mainland China, the threats of the Soviet Union and China in the Western Pacific evidently increased, and U.S. policy shifted swiftly from weakening the Japanese economy to promoting its reconstruction and development. A strong Japan would not only lessen the burden of economic aid for the United States but also make Japan a bridgehead of Western democracy in the Far East, an area where East-West tension was high. From the United States's point of view, it was necessary to provide Japan with ample opportunities to engage in worldwide trade. For this purpose, it was essential to give Japan a position in GATT equal to that of Western countries.

Given the basic U.S. policy toward Japan in the mid-1950s, it is ironical that the United States has asked Japan to impose "voluntary export restrictions" (VERs) on certain exports to the United States. The request resulted from the U.S. executive branch's compromise with Congress. Japan had occasionally used VERs in the late 1930s. Japan's exports of certain textile products and other light manufacturing products to the United States often increased sharply within short periods beginning from around 1955. Confronted with a sharp increase in such imports from Japan, the United States chose an informal approach of asking the Japanese government or industries to "voluntarily" restrict exports of the products in question to the United States for a certain time period rather than making use of formal procedures such as those under GATT Articles 19 (emergency action on imports of particular products) or 28 (modification of schedules). The Japanese government complied with most of these requests.[10] For one thing, Japan was then strenuously carrying on diplomatic negotiations, with the support of the United States, for the removal of the application of GATT Article 35 to Japan.

Although VERs are currently practiced, at the request of their trading partners, by a number of other countries (mostly by developing countries), few countries besides Japan were asked to institute VERs until the late 1960s. Although no statistics are published even today, Japan undoubtedly has a dominant share of the amount of trade under VERs. After Japan, the newly industrializing countries (NICs) conduct large shares of their trade under VERs. Developed countries other than Japan have rarely practiced VER; the export of steel by the European Community (EC) countries to the United States may be one of the few exceptions.[11]

The Kennedy Round and Japan

The Kennedy Round (KR, 1964–67) of tariff negotiations under GATT was an epochal event in world trade in the postwar period, or, one might say, since the beginning of the nineteenth century. The tariff rates of the major industrial countries, especially those on manufactures, were lowered substantially. As far as the developed countries were concerned, the world entered an era of unprecedentedly low-tariff trade.

It is often thought that the free, multilateral world economic regime of the Western nations after World War II, with the International Monetary Fund (IMF) and GATT at its center, was created and developed under the leadership of the United States and was an important part of the so-called Pax Americana. As far as GATT is concerned, however, this is a doubtful view.

Immediately after the war, there was an ambitious plan to establish an International Trade Organization (ITO), but the U.S. Senate refused to ratify the ITO treaty. After several years of unsuccessful attempts to persuade the Senate, the U.S. government had to accept GATT as an administrative agreement, not as a treaty, because of the strong Senate opposition. The United States's position toward GATT was asymmetric with that of most other GATT members, including Japan, in that other members ratified GATT as an international treaty. The asymmetry has been a frequent source of problems. The U.S. Congress takes the position that it is not restricted by GATT; a large number of bills inconsistent with GATT such as the Burke-Hartke bill, various recent "reciprocity" trade bills, and the so-called local-contents bills on automobiles have been introduced in Congress.[12]

Although it is not quite unambiguous whether the United States has been the foremost leader of GATT, no one would deny that the success of the KR owed much to the initiative of the United States, especially to the leadership of President Kennedy. The United States was forced, so to speak, to embark on the KR by the formation of the European Economic Community (EEC) and the challenge of a market without tariff barriers encompassing a population of over 250 million. At the time, it was thought that the United Kingdom might join the EEC.[13]

The United States, followed by the EEC, played the most important role in the KR. Canada played an important role at the beginning, but it soon retired from the main arena when it decided not to be a "linear cutter." The United Kingdom, after deciding not to join the EEC in the early stages of the KR, was also a leading player, as was the Nordic Group (Denmark, Finland, Norway, and Sweden), which banded together during the KR in order to strengthen their bargaining power. Japan was perhaps the fourth or fifth most important actor.

In the beginning, Japan was not enthusiastic about participating. In hindsight this may appear strange, but the Japanese government was still inclined toward protectionism, especially for manufacturing industries, and its economic policy stance was not close to the principles underlying GATT and the IMF. The Japanese government seems to have felt somewhat uneasy about participating in the KR. Japan had been moving toward strengthening tariff protection for agriculture and some manufacturing industries, in order to cope with an impending liberalization of import restrictions and foreign exchange controls because of a change of Japan's status in the IMF to an Article 8 member (which forbids a member-state from restricting payments and transfers for international transactions on current account). (Japan's tariff policy in this period is reviewed in the next section.) The expectation that Japan's participation in the KR would force Japan to reduce its tariff rates made the Japanese government hesitant to take an active role in the early stages of the KR. Japan presented a large number of exceptions to the linear cutting of tariff rates for manufactures, primarily to protect newly emerging industries.

Since the KR was prolonged by a number of troublesome problems such as those concerning EEC agricultural products, not only did the international competitiveness of Japanese manufacturing industries improve considerably, but also the negative tendency of Japan's balance of payments was mitigated. These changes induced Japan to shift from a defensive stance with an emphasis on protecting domestic industries to a more liberal one of mutually lowering tariffs in the hope of expanding exports.

It is clear that Japan profited from the successful conclusion of the KR. On the one hand, the reduction of tariff rates on manufactured goods by its major trading partners contributed to an expansion of Japanese exports, directly as well as indirectly through the expansion of world trade. On the other hand, there is no evidence that Japan's manufacturing industries suffered much from Japan's own tariff reductions.

Trade liberalization program

Around 1960, the major West European countries reestablished their currency convertibility and became IMF Article 8 and GATT Article 11 members (such states are forbidden to use quantitative restrictions on imports for balance-of-payments reasons). Lagging only a few years behind, Japan embarked on a liberalization of import restrictions and foreign exchange controls. Japan became an IMF Article 8 member in 1964. Before this, in January 1961, the government adopted the Outline of the Plan for Trade and Foreign Exchange Liberalization (*Boeki Kawase Jiyuka Keikaku Taiko*). The plan called for increasing the "trade liberalization rate" (the percentage share of imports not covered by import quotas in total imports) from 40% in 1961 to 80 per cent by June 1963 and for removing all restrictions on foreign exchange transactions relating to the current account and gradually relaxing controls on capital-account transactions as well.

Import quotas were removed or relaxed considerably from 1960 to 1963. Import quotas on 1,837 commodities (BTN four-digit classification) were removed; at the end of 1963, 192 items were still subject to import quotas, among which 155 items were "residual quotas," that is, quotas other than those allowed under various articles of GATT. This was still many more than those of other major countries. From 1964 to 1968, when the KR was in progress, trade liberalization made little headway in Japan; residual import quotas were removed on only 35 items during this period. After the conclusion of the KR, however, trade liberalization once again accelerated: quotas on 88 items were removed between 1969 and 1972.

The "trade (imports) liberalization" program and the "capital (inward direct investment) liberalization" program that followed a few years later constituted an important change in the Japanese government's economic policy.[14] These revolutionary policies transformed the Japanese economy, until then a relatively closed one. The liberalization policy distressed Japanese industries and firms; it was often likened to the visit of Perry's "black ships" in 1853 that led to the opening of Japan to foreign commerce.

Japanese industries and firms had been protected from foreign competition since the late 1930s. Trade liberalization forced them to compete in the open market. Government officials responsible for protective policies, representatives of individual industries, and advocates of protectionism such as some academic economists and journalists were generally opposed to the liberalization measures. The situation was described as *soron sansei, kakuron hantai;* that is, people agreed on the desirability of liberalization in principle and for the Japanese economy as a whole but found it unacceptable for some special reasons in their own industry or the field that they supervised or had a special interest in.

The economic policy dominant in Japan until then was quite different from the ideal of free and multilateral international trade, foreign exchange transactions, and international investment underlying GATT, the IMF, and the Organization for Economic Cooperation and Development (OECD). In Japan the dominant economic policy was to view exports as a virtue and imports as a vice.[15] Also, there was a strong desire to protect manufacturing industries that used sophisticated technologies. It is not an exaggeration, perhaps, to say that in the 1950s and 1960s Japan's policymakers strongly desired to protect most modern manufacturing industries.

Tariff policy

Before the trade liberalization program, the Japanese government revised its tariff schedule extensively in 1961. This revision was mildly protectionist. Japan raised, through the tariff negotiations under GATT, rates on many manufactures, such as machinery, heavy electric machinery, and computers, and on some agricultural products, such as dairy products, beans, and seaweed, in exchange for reductions on certain other commodities. Seven principles were announced as basic guidelines for the revisions:

1. To set low tariff rates on primary commodities (agricultural products and minerals) and increase rates with the degree of processing.

2. To set low rates on producer goods and high rates on consumer goods.

3. To set low rates on those goods that could not be produced domestically or only in limited quantities with no possibility of expanded domestic production in the future, and to set high rates on those goods whose potential domestic supply was elastic and either was or would be competing with imports.

4. To set high rates on the products of those industries with good prospects for development, especially on the products of newly established industries.

5. To set low rates both on the products or raw materials of well-established export industries.

6. To set rates on the products of stagnant industries, industries with no prospects for future development, or declining industries high enough and on their materials low enough to facilitate a smooth and gradual transfer of employment to other sectors.

7. To set low rates on necessities and high rates on luxuries, and to set low rates on imports for such purposes as education, culture, and health.[16]

A policy of protective tariffs and tariff escalation is visible in guidelines 1 through 5 and in the second half of guideline 6.

The Japanese administrative system

The Japanese administrative system was another source of potential conflicts with the free-trade principles of GATT and the IMF. For each industry, there is a corresponding government office, department, or section of a ministry in Japan. Such an office is called a *genkyoku* in Japanese government jargon.

In the heyday of "industrial policy" in the 1950s and 1960s, the *genkyoku* (the bureau or authorities in charge of an industry) was in general strongly biased toward protectionism, particularly in the early postwar years.[17] Each *genkyoku* tended to introduce various measures to regulate new entries in the sector under its supervision and a licensing system to control the activities of firms such as new plants or branch offices, introduction of new products, imports of foreign technologies, and joint ventures with foreign firms. A *genkyoku* was generally considered responsible not only for supervisory matters prescribed by laws and ordinances but also for guidance, suggestions, direction, and consultation on an informal basis (*gyosei shido*) with respect to a wide variety of activities by firms in the industry. In particular, the *genkyoku* generally considered it desirable to eliminate "excessive" competition, making an industrywide plan for production, investment, and sales and, if possible, by regulating (formally and informally) prices (including fares, fees, interest rates, and commissions) when necessary. By these means, the *genkyoku* attempted to establish and maintain an "orderly" system in which each firm could secure a certain stable level of profits. The *genkyoku* further wished that the firms under its jurisdiction did not run into financial difficulties and even tended to dislike a change in the rank order of firms according to the market share.

Genkyoku officials held (and some still hold) such attitudes or policy orientations for several reasons. First, if the industry in question encountered problems, the officials were held responsible or even accused of mismanagement and had to expend much effort to help the industry recover. Second, bureaucrats enjoy authority, and it is natural for them to maintain and expand their authority. Third, paradoxically, when a regulatory system has existed for some time, it is often quite convenient and comfortable for the industry itself, especially for its leading firms.

During the 1930s, the Japanese government not only approved but sometimes promoted and even forced cartelization of industries. During World War II and the immediate postwar period, rigid and extensive controls on production and distribution of a large number of commodities were enforced. Antitrust law was introduced into Japan during the Occupation period, but since it conflicted with Japan's traditional economic policy, it took much time to take root.

Why, then, did the Japanese government want to join international treaties and organizations such as GATT, IMF, and OECD, given its traditional mercantilist philosophy as well as an administrative system for economic policy quite different from the basic philosophy and principles underlying such treaties and organizations? Our view is that it was not so much because the Japanese political leaders and government officials then in charge of economic policy thought that free competition and liberalization of trade, investment, and exchange transactions were the best arrangements for Japan. Rather, these leaders and officials wanted to secure export markets around the world by joining these treaties and organizations. They wished Japan to become a full member of the international economic community and to play a major role there in the future. Furthermore, they expected that Japan could utilize the financial facilities of the IMF and the International Bank for Reconstruction and Development (IBRD). Liberalization of imports, inward direct investments, and foreign exchange controls were thought of as a "necessary cost" or a "sacrifice" that Japan had to pay in order to secure membership in the international club of major industrialized countries.

Summary of the trade liberalization process

The process of trade liberalization and capital liberalization in Japan in the 1960s had several basic features. First, politicians, officials, and businessmen did not quite understand, at least in the early stage, the theory that liberalization would benefit the Japanese economy by improving resource allocation and promoting competition. Rather, they thought that liberalization of imports and inward direct investment were a necessary sacrifice for Japan to become a member of the international economic community and especially of the club of major industrialized countries of Western Europe and North America.

Second, the government took great care not to trigger rapid change in resource allocation, especially in those areas much affected by the liberalization program. Liberalization proceeded in a gradual and piecemeal fashion; liberalization measures were introduced first in those areas where political and social opposition was weak. It took a long time, therefore, for trade liberalization, capital liberalization, and liberalization of foreign exchange controls to be nearly completed or to finish the first stage.

Third, the pace of liberalization was much influenced by the strength of external pressure for liberalization. In those areas where liberalization was requested by a foreign country with a strong negotiating power vis-à-vis Japan, and in periods when such pressures were strong, liberalization proceeded relatively fast. There were strong tendencies in Japanese society to resist foreign pressures and to preserve the status quo as much as possible unless forced to give it up.

Fourth, liberalization was carried out gradually and in a piecemeal fashion in order to avoid disorder in the areas affected. Policy measures were often meticulously designed down to minute details. This was made possible by the *genkyoku* administrative system and the many competent and honest bureaucrats operating it. For example, sometimes the government liberalized only several subgroups of commodities under a BTN four-digit group. Or it introduced a tariff-quota system, a new mechanism adopted in the 1961 revision of the tariff law, when abolishing an import quota, setting a second-stage tariff rate at a quite high level for imports over a given amount. Also, the government gave various forms of adjustment assistance to industries adversely affected by liberalization.

Fifth, there were few cases where liberalization was reversed after implementation. This is because liberalization was cautiously and meticulously prepared and was implemented in stages. To our knowledge, the government has only rarely reversed the liberalization of trade by reintroducing import quotas or other restrictive measures in view of a rapid increase in imports. Japan's liberalization of imports and inward direct investment was slow but steady.[18]

From an Improving Balance of Payments to the First Oil Crisis, 1968–1975

Development of Japan's trade

Throughout the 1960s, the Japanese economy experienced what is called "high growth" and a rapid expansion of both exports and imports. It is not correct to characterize Japan's economic growth as export-led since throughout the 1960s the growth rate of domestic private investment in plant and equipment was much higher than the growth rate of exports. Moreover, including both goods and services, Japan's exports and imports expanded almost at the same pace. There is no room for doubt, however, that the favorable international environment in the 1960s was one of the most important conditions for Japan's high growth: it made possible a higher growth rate of exports (and hence of imports) than that of GNP for Japan, and a much higher rate of economic growth for Japan than the world average (see Table 3).

During the 1960s, three important changes took place in Japan's international trade. First, Japan's share of world trade rose substantially. Second, the composition of Japan's exports changed markedly; the share of products heavily dependent on cheap unskilled labor such as textiles, miscellaneous light industry products, sewing machines, and inexpensive cameras declined, and the share of products of heavy engineering industries such as steel, various kinds of machinery, and automobiles rose substantially (see Fig. 1). As for imports, the share of raw materials for textiles declined, and that of fuel (primarily petroleum and coal) increased, even before the oil crisis. The share of machinery in imports increased slightly during the 1960s (but it declined from 1965 to 1975) (see Fig. 2). Japan was apparently in a transition between the stage of a latecomer, newly industrializing country having a comparative advantage in labor-intensive products and the stage of a highly developed industrial country having a comparative advantage in high value-added engineering products utilizing sophisticated technologies.

The third change was in the balance of payments: Japan's balance of payments in its current account gradually freed itself from persistent pressure toward deficits around 1968. Since then, the current-account balance has generally been positive. This improvement resulted from

Table 3
Ratio of Exports and Imports to GNP, Selected Countries: 1955–1983

(%)

	1955	1960	1965	1971	1976	1981	1983
				JAPAN			
Exports of goods, services, income	11.5%	11.6%	11.1%	12.3%	14.4%	16.6%	15.8%
Exports of merchandise				10.4	12.0	13.3	12.3
Imports of goods, services, income	10.6	11.2	9.9	9.7	13.7	16.0	13.9
Imports of merchandise				8.6	11.6	12.6	10.5
				UNITED STATES			
Exports of goods, services, income	5.0%	5.4%	5.8%	6.4%	9.9%	12.5%	10.2%
Exports of merchandise	3.9	3.9	3.9	4.1	6.7	8.0	5.9
Imports of goods, services, income	4.5	4.6	4.7	6.0	9.7	11.6	10.4
Imports of merchandise				4.2	7.2	9.3	8.1
				UNITED KINGDOM			
Exports of goods, services, income	26.1%	24.5%	23.3%	25.1%	31.3%	31.3%	30.5%
Exports of merchandise				16.1	16.8	20.5	20.8
Imports of goods, services,							

income	26.8	25.2	22.9	22.8	31.4	28.1	28.8
Imports of merchandise				17.3	20.4	20.2	22.5

FRG							
Exports of goods, services, income	20.3%	21.2%	19.0%	22.6%	27.8%	32.1%	32.3%
Exports of merchandise				18.1	22.9	25.8	26.2
Imports of goods, services, income	18.0	18.8	19.0	20.6	25.3	31.4	30.0
Imports of merchandise				10.0	19.8	24.0	23.6

Sources: Same as Table 1.

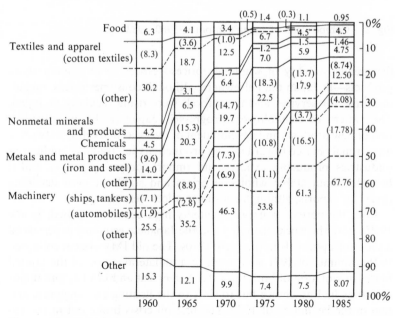

Fig. 1.   Composition of Japan's exports, 1960–1985.

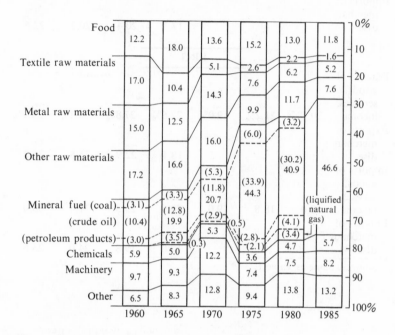

Fig. 2. Composition of Japan's imports, 1960–1983.

the greater stability of wholesale prices—especially of manufactured products—in Japan than elsewhere, although consumer prices, including those for services and fresh food, were rising secularly in Japan. The pattern of technological progress in Japan (including introduction of new products and development of overseas marketing networks) was strongly biased toward raising productivity in "tradable" industries (industries producing exports and import-competing goods), and it brought about stable wholesale prices and stable or even declining prices for exports, although consumer prices were rising.

After the period of unprecedentedly high economic growth in the 1960s, both the world economy and the Japanese economy experienced a series of upheavals in the early 1970s. The old IMF system collapsed in the summer of 1971 as a result of a unilateral action of the United States in violation of both the IMF Agreement and GATT, and major countries had no choice but to shift to the floating exchange-rate system in the beginning of 1973. The first oil crisis broke out in the autumn of 1973, imparting a heavy blow to oil-importing countries and the world economy, which had already begun to become unstable because of simultaneous booms in many countries and worldwide inflation. In the summer of 1974, there arose widespread, though temporary, financial uneasiness in the Eurodollar market as a result of a few bank failures, and for some time Japanese banks had difficulties in rolling over their short-term borrowings. These unexpected events had severe impacts on the Japanese economy, which was heavily dependent on imported oil as a source of energy. Following these events, the world economy fell into the deepest and most prolonged depression and the severest inflation of the postwar period.

In spite of these unfavorable events, Japan was one of the earliest countries to recover from the stagflation following the first oil crisis. Japan succeeded in stabilizing wholesale prices by 1975 and consumer prices by the beginning of 1976. Early adjustments of oil- and energy-related prices and a determined tight-money policy were major factors contributing to the successful price stabilization. Although the rate of growth in real GNP turned negative in 1974, production began to pick up from the latter half of 1974, led by an expansion of exports. By the latter half of 1975, the Japanese economy was launched on a fairly steady growth path, with an annual growth rate of about 5 per cent. Although this was only about half the growth rate of the 1960s, it was still distinctly higher than those of other developed countries.

Foreign requests for import liberalization and Japan's response
After the late 1960s, when Japan's balance of payments began to turn positive, foreign countries, especially the United States, frequently requested Japan to increase imports of manufactures and agricultural products. They have strongly requested the removal of remaining import quotas and reductions of tariff and nontariff barriers, a revaluation of the yen exchange rate, and relaxation of foreign exchange controls.

The Japanese government responded to these requests by removing some import quotas and reducing tariff rates, to the extent that these measures did not create serious difficulties for the domestic producers concerned and did not obstruct the development of important infant industries. But it strongly resisted requests to revalue the yen.

After all, the yen had appreciated from the old IMF parity of 360 yen per dollar before 1971 to 265 yen in 1973. Partly because of this substantial appreciation (approximately 36%) and partly because of the quadrupling of the oil prices, Japan's balance of payments in its current account showed an unprecedentedly large deficit in 1974. Because of this, external pressure for import liberalization subsided from the latter half of 1973 to 1975, and at the same time liberalization halted.

Trade liberalization policy

As already mentioned, few import quotas were removed during the KR period. After the conclusion of the KR, a large number of import quotas were removed: the period from 1969 to 1972 saw a second spate of import liberalization measures. The Japanese government introduced a series of Yen-Defense Policy packages in order to reduce the balance-of-payments surpluses, and the removal of import quotas was part of these packages. As a result of this second spate, the number of items under "residual"—that is, illegal under GATT—import restrictions decreased from 122 in April 1968 to 40 in February 1972, to 33 in April 1972, and finally to 27 at the end of 1975 (see Table 4). Among these 27 items, only four items were manufactures (leather products) and only one was a mining product (coal). The removal of residual import restrictions on manufactures and mining products was practically completed during this period. These figures do not include the quantitative import restriction quotas acceptable under GATT; namely, import embargoes and quotas on (1) rice, wheat, sugar, silk, and certain types of dairy products whose prices were supported by the government or whose trade was controlled by the government, (2) goods such as weapons and gunpowder whose trade was restricted for national security reasons, (3) narcotics and anesthetics, and (4) radioactive substances and atomic hearths. Such items under nonresidual import restrictions numbered 37 in 1968 and 55 in 1975.

Import quotas on the following items were removed between 1968 and 1975: antibiotics and color film (January 1971), automobile engines and soda ash (June 1971), steam turbines and telephone exchange equipment (November 1971), auxiliary equipment for computer systems excluding memory apparatus and terminals, small airplanes (February 1971), high-capability computers and electric cash registers, and integrated circuits with fewer than 200 elements (December 1975). As a result of these liberalization measures, at the end of 1975 products affected by residual import restrictions were mostly agricultural.

Tariff rates

After the tariff reductions agreed on in the KR were implemented, the government further reduced tariff rates in several steps. It put into effect the generalized scheme of preference (GSP) for developing countries in advance of other nations as part of the Yen-Defense Policy package in June 1971. Also, it unilaterally reduced tariff rates on a few commodities in May 1971. In December 1972, it reduced tariff rates on all (with a few exceptions) processed agricultural products, manufactures, and mining products by 20%. These tariff reductions were intended to reduce the current-account surplus. By these measures, Japan decreased its tariff rates substantially and mitigated the tendency toward tariff escalation, lowering the effective rates of protection on processed goods considerably.

It is not easy to compare average tariff rates at different points of time or between different countries. Essentially this is an index number problem, that is, a difficulty in determining the appropriate weights in calculating the average. But judging from statistics on the "import burden ratio" (the ratio of total tariff revenues to the total value of imports, or to the total value of imports on which tariffs are levied), the changes in tariff rates on individual items during the KR and thereafter, and the implementation of the GSP, it seems that (1) the tariff level in Japan was about as high as those of the United States, the United Kingdom, and the EC and slightly higher than those of the Scandinavian countries and Switzerland before the start of the KR; (2) it declined substantially and more than any other country's between 1968 and 1975 (especially from 1973 to 1975); and (3) by the middle of the 1970s, it was lower than those of the United States, the EC, and the United Kingdom. By the early 1980s, officials in charge of the trade affairs of the major countries generally agreed that Japan's tariff rates were the lowest among them (see Table 5 for the average tariff levels of various industrial countries).

Trade conflicts and the Japan-U.S. textile negotiations

Beginning in the late 1950s, the U.S. government occasionally asked the Japanese government to establish VERs on textiles and other labor-intensive, light-industry products. This situation continued into the 1960s. Diplomatic negotiations between Japan and the United States on such bilateral trade issues became prolonged and increasingly difficult in the case of textiles toward the end of the 1960s.

The rapid increases in Japanese exports to the United States of certain textile products and other light-industry commodities in the 1960s tended to induce protectionism in the United States. Generally speaking, this took one of the following forms: (1) the U.S. government acting at the request of private firms or groups adversely affected sometimes applied antidumping regulations, the escape clause, or countervailing duties; (2) VERs or export quotas based on intergovernmental agreement were introduced after diplomatic negotiations be-

Table 4
The Process of Import Liberalization in Japan, 1960–1981

Year	Month	Total number of items under import restrictions	Nonresidual import restrictions (number of items)	Residual import restrictions[a]			Selected items liberalized
				(1)	(2)	Total	
1960	Apr.	1,443	39	55	67	122	
1965	Oct.	161	43	54	68	122	
1968	Apr.	165	54	50	68	118	
1970	Jan.	161	44	39	59	98	
1970	Apr.	141	44	39	59	98	
1971	Jan.	123	44	31	49	80	
1972	Feb.	86	47	12	28	40	Auxiliary equipment for electronic computer systems, radar for aircraft
1972	Apr.	79	47	9	24	33	Ham and bacon, kerosene, fuel oil (reduction in the number of items because of a revision in the Tariff Rate Law)
1973	Apr.	83	52	8	24	32	High-quality desk calculators, electronic computers, integrated circuits (with less than 200 elements)
1974	Dec.	83	55	7	22	29	Integrated circuits (with more than 200 elements)
1975	Dec.	82	56	5	22	27	Electronic computers and auxiliary equipment
1977	Apr.	80	54	5	22	27	Tobacco (An increase of 5 items because of the Washington treaty)
1980	May	78	52	5	22	27	(An increase of one item because of the Chemical Substance Regulation Law)
1981	Dec.	79	53	5	22	27	

[a] (1) Manufactures and minerals, (2) agricultural and fisheries products.

tween the two countries; or (3) the U.S. Congress threatened to pass new laws restricting imports. In Japan, this situation or the process leading to restrictions on trade has been called "Japan-U.S. trade (or economic) friction (or conflict)" (*Nichi-Bei boeki* [*keizai*] *masatsu*). This description applies to friction or conflicts over Japan's exports, but there are other conflicts over Japan's imports.

Among the trade conflicts over Japanese exports to the United States, those concerned with light-industry products like textiles and miscellaneous goods may be termed "old-type trade conflicts," whereas those concerned with color television sets, automobiles, motorcycles, machine tools, and integrated circuits can be called "new-type trade conflict." Trade conflicts over steel and special steel products may be considered an intermediate type.

The earliest round of Japan-U.S. textile negotiations resulted in the Short-Term Agreement (STA) on the cotton textile trade in 1961. The negotiations continued intermittently until the first comprehensive Japan-U.S. agreement on the textile trade was concluded in 1971. This was a typical case of an old-type trade conflict. This was the first serious postwar trade conflict, and the diplomatic negotiations became increasingly troublesome and painful for the two countries. Here it is not necessary to discuss the details of the textile negotiations, but a few remarks from the viewpoint of the history of international trade policy are appropriate.[19]

When Japan and the United States agreed to conclude the STA as an administrative (intergovernmental) agreement in 1961, nobody thought that this was the beginning of widespread, detailed controls on trade in all kinds of textiles covering many countries. The quantita-

Table 5
Ratio of Tariff Revenue to Imports, Selected Countries, 1961—1983

Year	Japan	U.S.	EC[a]	FRG	France	Italy
1961	5.8%	6.7%		7.1%	5.5%	7.4%
1965	8.0	6.8		4.1	6.4	
1970	6.9	5.7	7.4 (3.8)	5.9 (3.3)	5.8 (2.9)	7.5 (4.6)
1974	2.7	3.1	4.2 (2.1)	4.0 (2.0)	2.6 (1.5)	2.8 (1.7)
1979	3.1	3.9	3.9 (1.9)	4.0 (2.0)	2.3 (1.2)	1.8 (1.0)
1983	2.5	3.5	2.7			

Sources: Ministry of Finance, *Zaisei kin'yu tokei geppo* (various issues).

[a]The figures for the EC include the surcharge on agricultural imports. Figures in parentheses are the ratio for total imports including imports from the other EC members; figures without parentheses are for imports from countries outside the EC. The EC includes Belgium, France, Italy, Luxembourg, the Netherlands, and West Germany before 1977, and these countries plus Denmark, Ireland, and the United Kingdom in 1979 and 1983.

tive restrictions on Japan's exports of cotton textile products to the United States was thereafter extended first to exports from Hong Kong, Taiwan, and South Korea and then to exports from all developing countries. On the side of the importing countries, import restrictions spread to European countries, Canada, and Australia.

The bilateral agreement on cotton trade, which was relatively informal in the beginning, became more and more formal, rigid, and multilateral. It also became highly complicated and more or less permanent. The STA on the cotton textile trade (1961) and the Long-Term Agreement (LTA, 1962) were legally recognized by GATT and twice extended (1967, 1970). The United States was then threatened by a rapid expansion of Japanese synthetic fiber and woolen textile exports, and the wave of protectionism in the United States became overwhelming. The negotiations between Japan and the United States were prolonged, and unfortunately, from the viewpoint of economics and world trade, the process became entangled in the U.S. presidential election and the restoration of Okinawa to Japan. Finally, the textile negotiations became so tense that the Japanese government had no choice but to accept the Japan-U.S. Textile Agreement in 1971, covering all textiles. The repercussions were great for all members of GATT. The Multi-Fiber Agreement (MFA) concluded in 1974 covered the worldwide trade of all textiles.

Textile products are important exports for many developing countries. The world trade in textiles today is regulated by rigid quantitative import restrictions under the MFA. Recently, some of the importing countries party to the MFA requested the developing countries exporting textile products to forgo even the modest (5%) annual increase in the quotas agreed on under the MFA. Nobody in favor of free and multilateral world trade would deny that MFA is an unfortunate precedent for formalized worldwide trade control that is strongly detrimental to the economic development of low-income (hence low-wage) developing countries and that it is a serious breach of the basic principles of GATT. It is, however, true that the transfer of the labor force from the textile industry to other industries poses a serious unemployment problem in the developed countries importing textiles since the textile industry is generally labor intensive and textile workers are either relatively unskilled or their skills are not of much use in other industries.[20] Most developed countries, the core members of GATT, felt at the time of the STA and LTA that it was difficult to observe the GATT rules strictly in regard to textile imports. Perhaps something like the STA, LTA, and MFA was necessary to maintain GATT as a more or less effective international agreement. Yet the benefits from these aberrations from free-trade principles are of doubtful value. Although fairly large-scale textile industries still exist in the United States and Western Europe, they have not recovered their international competitiveness. Much of the textile industry in the United States, Western Europe, and Australia is still essentially weak and viable only because of extensive import quotas and high tariffs.

Why did Japan readily accept the request of the United States to institute VERs on textile products at the beginning of the process described above? And why did the Japanese textile industry later strongly resist the U.S. request for export restrictions during the negotiations in 1968–71 for the Japan-U.S. Textile Agreement? The answer to the first question may be that Japanese political leaders felt obliged to accommodate the U.S. request in return for U.S. support for Japan's accession to GATT, as well as for the overall U.S. policy toward Japan. In any case, Japanese political leaders at the time did not want to create troubles in Japan-U.S. relations. Another factor was that VERs, which allowed Japan to control exports, were considered more advantageous for Japan than other U.S. import-restriction measures.[21] VERs were considered the lesser evil and less likely to become permanent than more formal measures such as import quotas, tariffs, or tariff-quotas. The distribution of the rent element inherent in any quantitative restriction measure is more advantageous to the export industry under VERs than under import quotas or tariffs. Furthermore, the industries affected in the early stage—from the late 1950s to the early 1960s—were overwhelmingly small or medium-sized firms with little political power.

The situation in the later years of the Japan-U.S. textile negotiations differed considerably. The leaders of the Japanese textile industry felt that they had long been suffering from the extensive voluntary export restraints since the late 1950s. They thought that the industry could not develop further if export restrictions were further strengthened and that there was no room for accepting an intergovernmental agreement freezing the status quo. Although small or medium-size firms dominated the production of many textile exports, there were large firms in the industry taken as a whole. When a majority of firms in the industry were united, their organizational and political power was considerable. Moreover, the cotton-spinning industry as well as several other major textile industries were centered in the Kansai region (the area around Osaka, Kyoto, and Kobe, and west of these cities) and had a tradition of free-trade beliefs dating from the Meiji period. Many leaders of the major Kansai-based textile companies were more independent and more liberal than the leaders of business circles in

Tokyo, who were closer to the government and tended to favor government regulation.

Despite the industry's resistance, Japanese political leaders judged that it would be unwise to leave a major trade issue unsettled for long. The U.S. government succeeded in ending the long-running negotiations on the textile trade by strong, unilateral actions (including abolishment of the gold convertibility of the U.S. dollar and an across-the-board 10 per cent import surcharge), actions known in Japan as the "Nixon shock."

Since 1971, the Japanese textile industry has been losing its comparative advantage because of the rise in domestic wages and the growth of textile industries in the NICs. The share of textile products in Japan's total exports has been declining rapidly, and some of Japan's export quotas to the United States under the MFA have gone unfulfilled recently. It is even said that the rigid MFA now works to promote exports of Japanese textile products since the MFA restricts exports from the NICs to Europe and the United States, where Japanese exports have to compete with them.

Industrial adjustment in the Japanese textile industry has been relatively easy since its labor force is predominantly young female workers, who usually stay in the labor market only until they marry. Most young women now work in other industries, such as electric appliances, electronics, precision machinery, retail and wholesale trade, and services. Their wages are much higher not only absolutely but also relative to the average wage level for manufacturing or the economy as a whole than the wages young women received in the textile industry two or three decades ago.

Trade conflicts in other areas
From 1968 to 1972, Japanese exports, especially to the United States, expanded rapidly, and Japan's overall balance of payments in its current account showed sizable surpluses. Trade friction tends to become more frequent and serious when the U.S. economy is in recession and Japan's balance of trade is positive, both overall and bilaterally with the United States. The period from 1968 to 1972 was the first such period. Japan experienced then what can be called the "first wave" of the Japan-U.S. trade conflict.

Among the more serious trade frictions were steel exports to the United States. A few years earlier, there had arisen a strong protectionist movement in the United States to restrict steel imports from Europe and Japan. A bill to establish import quotas for steel was introduced in Congress in 1967. Fearing that a formal quota system would be established, the Japanese steel industry set up a voluntary export restraint system in 1966, which was strengthened in 1969. A third VER was enforced from 1972 to 1974. During this period, the EC also introduced a VER on its steel exports to the United States. Meanwhile, Japanese steel exports to the EC increased rapidly from 1969 to 1971, and Japan has enforced a VER on its steel exports to the EC since 1972, with the exception of 1975.

We have characterized trade conflicts in the steel trade as an intermediate type. Japan once had a strong comparative advantage in textiles and other light-industry products based on cheap and efficient labor, whereas the strong international competitiveness of the Japanese steel industry is based on modern and sophisticated technology, locational advantage, and the large size of the domestic market. The steel industry is representative of heavy manufacturing, which policymakers of prewar and early postwar Japan as well as those of many developing countries until recently regarded as having central and symbolic importance in a modern industrial economy. The ability of the Japanese steel industry to compete successfully even in the North American and European markets since the middle of the 1960s indicated that the Japanese economy had reached a new stage of industrialization.

During this second period, trade conflicts arose over footwear and metal tableware (old type), special steel products, sheet glass, and fasteners (intermediate type), and electric and electronic machinery and parts and color television sets (new type). The response of the Japanese color television producers to the trade conflicts is worth noting. They partially replaced exports of their products by direct investment and production in the United States. They also invested in some NICs and exported sets produced there to the United States. The trade conflict over color television sets was solved in this way. This shift to foreign production in response to trade conflicts is becoming common in several other industries such as video tape recorders and motor vehicles.

The Post-Oil Crisis Period, 1976–1984

The economies of many developed countries heavily dependent on imported petroleum as a source of energy were hard hit by the first and second oil crises and experienced serious stagflation. The impact of the oil crises and stagflation soon spread worldwide, including the developing countries and Eastern Europe. Whereas the impact of the first oil crisis was limited mostly to the developed countries, the stagnation following the second oil crisis was more widespread. From 1981 to 1983, the value of world trade dropped from the previous year's level for the first time since World War II. The sharp increase in petroleum prices as well as stagnation following the second oil crisis depressed world demand for petroleum and resulted in a fall in petroleum prices in 1982 and 1983. This contributed to a decline in both the volume and value of world trade since trade in petroleum made up a large portion of world trade by then.

Stagflation hovered over the world economy in the late 1970s and the early 1980s. Unemployment increased annually and led to the rise of protectionism in many countries. The volume of exports of primary commodities and light manufacturing products from developing countries to developed countries generally declined. The international debts of developing countries rose rapidly. Many countries experienced difficulties in servicing their debt and were forced to reduce imports. It thus became increasingly difficult for the world economy to maintain the regime of multilateral free trade.

Despite this unfavorable international environment, the performance of the Japanese economy was good in comparison with that of other major developed countries. Although the inflation rate in Japan during the first oil crisis was among the highest of the major developed countries, the price level stabilized quickly. Inflation during the second oil crisis was well contained and short-lived. Although much lower than in the 1960s, Japan's growth rate was a fairly stable 4 to 6%, a respectable rate much higher and much more stable than that of most other developed countries. The relatively satisfactory performance of the Japanese economy—its containment of inflation, low unemployment, stable growth, and a rapid increase in productivity and technological progress in manufacturing industries—attracted the attention of many developed countries as well as of developing countries such as China. Japan's position in the international economic community improved remarkably. With this rise in status, foreign countries have come to expect much more from Japan than in earlier times, and Japan has received more and more criticism from other countries.

Changes in Japan's structure of trade and balance of payments
An extensive change has taken place in the composition of Japan's trade since the first oil crisis. Because of the rise in energy prices after the first oil crisis, the share of mineral fuel in the total value of Japanese imports increased sharply, from 20.7% in 1970 to 44.3% in 1975, to 49.8% in 1980, and to 50.6% in 1981. This occurred even though the ratio

of energy consumption to real GNP fell substantially because of economizing in energy consumption in individual sectors and the shift in Japan's industrial structure in response to high energy prices. Furthermore, the ratio of domestic supply of food to total consumption has fallen year by year: the share of food in total imports has been in the range of 12–15% since the beginning of the 1970s. In addition, raw materials for manufacturing industries amount to about 20% of total imports. Thus, by the early 1980s, these three groups accounted for some 80% of total Japanese imports. Despite extensive import liberalization, imports of manufactured goods, especially those of finished products, remain low, both relative to GNP and as a proportion of total imports. The low level of imports of finished products has become a focal point of the trade conflict with the European countries and the United States.

The largest change in Japanese exports was a rise in machinery products from 46.3% of all exports in 1970 to 53.8% in 1975, to 67.8% in 1983. The shares of various types of machine goods, automobiles and other transportation equipment, and precision machinery and apparatus all rose conspicuously. Exports of labor-intensive products such as textiles declined sharply. Industries producing intermediate materials such as steel were also losing their comparative advantage as a result of increasing energy costs and a rise in competitors in the NICs.

Japan's terms of trade deteriorated greatly as a result of the two oil crises; from 100 in the base year of 1970, the terms of trade declined to around 60 in 1981. The balance of payments in the current account recorded large deficits of about 1% of GNP in 1974 and 1980, the peak years of the two oil crises. In each case, however, the balance of payments improved promptly. Especially since 1982, Japan has recorded large and increasing current-account surpluses, larger than those from the late 1960s through 1972 and 1976 through 1978, relative to GNP. This has become another major focal point of foreign criticism of Japan.

Comparative advantage in Japan
The change in the structure of Japanese exports since 1975 reflects the changing pattern of comparative advantage of the Japanese economy during the turbulence the world economy has experienced since the beginning of the 1970s. Japan has been strongly competitive in the world market since the latter half of the 1970s in industries with the following characteristics: (1) processing industries, especially the fabricating and assembly-type manufacturing industries with produc-

tion processes consisting of parts production and assembly; (2) use of technology for mass production of standardized products, reflecting the large domestic market in Japan; (3) strict quality control to obtain uniformity of quality, a low proportion of deficient output, and relatively problem-free use; (4) differentiated products, requiring a marketing and service network and "fine-textured" maintenance services for users; (5) fields in which continuous cost reductions are made by accumulating small improvements in production process and product design; (6) product planning and development and accumulation of small improvements of products responding to the needs and preference of users and to changes in their preferences; (7) organizational skills in arranging stages and steps of production and in closely coordinating the timing of production and transportation; and (9) cooperation and coordination among firms in different fields and of different sizes (including the subcontracting system, but not necessarily restricted to it) and among engineers specializing in different areas.

Typical industries with these characteristics are automobiles, electronics, electric machinery, motorcycles, cameras, pianos, audio equipment, communication equipment and apparatus, machine tools, and machinery with electronic controls. These industries are strongly competitive in the world market. The shipbuilding industry lacks the second characteristic, and parts of it also lack the fourth characteristic, yet it satisfies the other conditions, especially 5, 6, and 7. The steel industry does not meet conditions 1 and 4; but it does meet the other conditions. A part of the textile industry producing high-quality products satisfies 4, 6, and 8, and Japan still enjoys a comparative advantage there.

Japan does not have a comparative advantage in all manufacturing industries, especially those with the following characteristics: (1) fields in which R&D plays an important role and R&D itself; (2) industries requiring large-scale fixed plant or apparatus (the exception may be the steel industry); (3) industries closely linked with natural resources; (4) industrial machinery and machine tools based on special technology, especially large-scale machines, with small production runs; (5) industries consuming a large amount of energy;[22] and (6) industries requiring a large amount of unskilled labor.

Airplanes, the chemical industry in general, pharmaceuticals and other specialty chemicals, petrochemicals, paper and pulp, and non-ferrous metals are examples of manufacturing industries that satisfy some of the above characteristics and in which Japan does not have a comparative advantage. Condition 5 became more salient after the two oil crises. Aluminum refining, petrochemicals, and some basic chemicals are now declining industries in Japan. By contrast, although not yet prominent industries, Japan has long traditions in fermented products and in ceramics. Japan may well attain a prominent position in the world market in products based on biotechnology and in new ceramics. The production technologies in which Japan has a comparative advantage have wide applicability, and manufacturing industries based on such characteristics have and will continue to have a strong and quite versatile basis in our view.

Until recently, Japan did not have a comparative advantage in R&D and depended heavily on the United States, the United Kingdom, West Germany, France, and Switzerland for new technologies and new products. Japan's payments of royalties on patents and processes far exceed receipts. Japan receives the major portion of its royalties from developing countries.

Patented technology or the possession of patented technology is not crucial for superior business performance in such industries as shipbuilding, steel, automobiles, electronic products, and machine tools, in which Japan has had or now has a comparative advantage.[23] Japan depends on foreign countries for basic technology and has a comparative advantage in production engineering, control of production processes, improvement of production processes and products, quality control and marketing, all of which depend on the versatile ability characterized by the items in the first list above. This pattern of comparative advantage has resulted in a rapid expansion of machinery exports since 1975.

As many engineering firms in Japan achieved success, however, their R&D expenditures increased steadily, and in recent years many firms have developed their own new technologies. In some firms, receipts of royalties from abroad exceed payments abroad. But it will take some time until Japan's overall balance of payments for technological royalties turns positive.

The second and third waves of the Japan-U.S. trade conflict

The first wave of the Japan-U.S. trade conflict occurred in 1968–72. The second wave took place in 1976–78, and the third has been ongoing since 1981. During each of these periods, Japan experienced a large trade surplus, and the United States a large trade deficit. Many European countries ran trade deficits as well. Exports of manufacturing goods, especially machinery, from Japan to industrialized countries in North America and Europe increased sharply in these periods. In the countries to which imports of specific products increased rapidly from Japan, especially the United States, movements arose aimed at restricting imports from Japan, and the issue of a bilateral trade deficit with Japan became politicized. Because of this, the second and third waves of the trade conflict between Japan and the United States became far more serious than the conflicts of earlier years, as did trade conflicts between Japan and some European countries. It is no exaggeration to say that the Japan-U.S. trade conflict has been a chronic disease since the beginning of the 1980s.[24] The focus of foreign complaints against Japan has shifted from labor-intensive, light manufacturing products, through an intermediate phase, to sophisticated differentiated products of the medium- to high-technology industries, such as color television sets, automobiles, numerically controlled machine tools, integrated circuits, and video tape recorders.

The politicization of trade conflicts also involves Japanese imports. The United States and the European countries have requested Japan to reduce its overall and bilateral trade surpluses and to increase its imports, especially of manufactures from the United States and Europe. The major focal points of discussions on Japanese imports in the third wave have been agricultural products such as beef, oranges, and cigarettes; leather products; the problem of government procurement, especially procurement by Nippon Telegraph and Telephone Corporation; the problem of standards for metal baseball bats and communication equipment; and tariff rates on certain wood products. Foreign countries further criticized the low ratio of imports of manufactures both to total imports and to GNP and the supposedly closed system of distribution and industrial organization, which were considered the cause of the low import ratio.

The diplomatic negotiations on trade conflict issues between Japan and the United States were similar to the earlier textile negotiations in that they were prolonged, complicated, and painful. Unlike usual trade negotiations, in the Japan-U.S. discussions on trade frictions in the second- and third-wave periods the United States simply pressed Japan to liberalize imports in which the United States has interests, primarily in view of Japan's large overall and bilateral balance-of-trade surplus. Usually trade negotiations between two countries take the form of give-and-take, but in these negotiations, which have been going on almost continuously from 1976, the subject matter has been simply how much and how soon Japan would make concessions, with the United States offering little if anything in exchange. Moreover, during this period the United States has been raising its barriers to imports from Japan in various forms; for example, by requesting Japan to introduce VERs on color television sets and automobiles and by raising tariffs on small commercial vehicles and motorcycles.[25]

Japan's VER on automobile exports was one of the most important trade-conflict problems in the third wave. Although Japan had previously agreed to institute VERs on various products, the VER on automobiles was special in several respects. First, automobile exports constitute a large portion of Japan's exports to the United States and elsewhere. Second, the United States has long been the world leader of the automobile industry. Third, this industry has long been a key industry in the United States. Fourth, the automobile market in the United States is highly concentrated, and its products are considerably differentiated. Under such conditions, the VER on Japanese exports enabled U.S. producers to raise prices. Under free trade, U.S. producers must take into account a possible shift of demand to Japanese products when they raise prices, whereas under a VER they can raise prices without fear. Even if the export ceiling under a VER is equal to the level of exports that would be achieved under free trade, the VER leads to a substantial price increase.[26] This change in the behavior of U.S. producers could benefit Japanese producers unless the ceiling under the VER is much lower than the free-trade level.

Automobile prices in the United States rose substantially after the VER was introduced. Although a part of this increase can be explained by the upgrading of the quality of Japanese exports, a considerable portion of the price increase was essentially the result of cartelization. No one would deny that U.S. consumers were hurt by the VER.[27]

The Tokyo Round
Japan played a leading role in the Tokyo Round (TR) of GATT, the first large-scale, multilateral trade negotiation (MTN) after the KR, in which a record number of 99 countries participated. The Japanese government proposed the TR at the general meeting of GATT in November 1971, and its implementation was announced at the Tokyo meeting of the Ministerial Council of GATT in September 1973. However, its actual start had to await U.S. legislation enabling the president to negotiate with other countries on tariffs and other trade policy matters.[28] After passage of the legislation in January 1975, the negotiations began in February of the same year. Since 1974 and 1975 were a very inopportune time, there were many difficulties and the negotiations took much time. The TR was successfully concluded in December 1979. The main results of the TR were as follows.

1. Tariff rates levied by developed countries on manufactures were reduced by about 33 % on the average.

2. Tariffs on agricultural products were substantially reduced. The value of international trade in agricultural products on which tariffs

were reduced amounted to about $15 billion in 1976. The KR had not covered agricultural tariffs.

3. Although the main theme of the KR was tariff reductions, the TR covered both tariffs and nontariff barriers and considered them as equally important subjects. Agreements on nontariff barriers such as antidumping regulations, government procurement, subsidies, countervailing tariffs, and standards were successfully concluded.

4. The principle of not expecting reciprocity from developing countries was carried over from the KR, and several agreements were reached about the legal basis of GSP and other preferences granted to developing countries.

Issues on which agreement were not reached that were left for future negotiations were (1) safeguards; (2) certain special problems of developing countries; (3) further liberalization of trade in agricultural products; (4) dispute-settlement procedures; (5) the trade in services; (6) trade-related international investment; (7) problems related to high-technology industries; (8) illegal products; and (9) adoption of a unified international classification system.

Japan took the initiative in beginning the TR negotiation and was, together with the United States, the most active participant. Japan offered tariff reductions on the largest number of items and was the first state to ratify all the agreements. Moreover, in March 1978 the Japanese government carried out the first round of tariff reductions in advance of the agreed time schedule, partly to express its enthusiasm for the successful conclusion of the negotiations and partly in response to a sharp rise in Japan's trade surplus in 1976–78.

It is clear that Japan held a much more influential position in the international economic community than at the time of the KR. The Japanese recognized much better than in earlier times that Japan benefited from worldwide multilateral free trade and that Japan should play a leading role in preserving and strengthening the multilateral free-trade regime. Such a change in Japanese perceptions was behind Japan's leadership in the TR.

Given the number of participating countries, the list of agreed tariff reductions, the number of the agreements on nontariff barriers, and their contents, one might conclude that the TR was a remarkable achievement. Many would agree that it was epochal in that it furthered the substantial reduction of tariffs achieved during the KR and reached agreement on a wide range of issues concerning nontariff barriers.[29]

On the other hand, the TR took a long time from announcement to conclusion. Many participating countries encountered difficult economic conditions during the negotiations because of the first oil crisis, the ensuing balance-of-payments difficulties, severe inflation, and the deepest depression since World War II. It was natural under such circumstances that protectionism rose in many countries and support for free trade weakened. Despite these problems, however, the TR continued and was successfully concluded, although the participants could not reach agreement on certain issues.

A system for international cooperation like GATT resembles a bicycle: it stops unless efforts are continuously made to keep it going. In this sense, the TR was important in preserving the multilateral free-trade system during a period of severe difficulties for the world economy. The Japanese government apparently realized this and took the initiative in the TR. For the same reason, it has played an active role in opening another new round, the Uruguay Round.

Changing trade policy philosophy
Throughout the 1970s and early 1980s, the international environment surrounding Japan changed drastically, and Japan's industrial capability was strengthened remarkably. The status of Japan in the international community rose substantially. However, the relatively good performance of the Japanese economy after the two oil crises and the success of the Japanese machinery and electronic industries in the world market began to cause an increasing number of trade frictions, and strong tendencies toward protectionism have developed in many major industrialized countries against the expansion of Japanese exports. Foreign requests that Japan open its domestic market have become stronger and more frequent.

In keeping with these basic changes, the dominant philosophy among Japan's economic policy authorities and the Japanese public has changed considerably. The philosophy that free trade is basically the most desirable policy for the Japanese economy, although there could be exceptions such as agricultural protection, has gained recognition among policymakers, leading businessmen, and knowledgeable people. Japan's trade policy, which in the past tended toward mercantilist strategies of promoting exports and restricting imports, began to change toward freer trade. At the same time, Japan's regulation-oriented economic policy philosophy has gradually been evolving toward a free-competition, market-oriented philosophy.

One manifestation of the new free-trade philosophy was the extensive tariff reduction put into effect in March 1978 in advance of the conclusion of the TR. The reduction covered some 125 items, including automobiles and main-frame computers. After the conclusion of the TR, other tariff reductions were implemented in April 1980 in advance of the agreed schedule. The extent of Japan's tariff reductions under the TR was generally greater than those of other countries, and Japan's average tariff level after the complete realization of the TR tariff concessions will be considerably lower than the corresponding levels of other major developed countries. Officials in charge of trade affairs in other major industrialized countries now generally agree that Japan has the lowest import tariffs.

As mentioned above, most of the residual import restrictions on manufactured goods were removed in the previous period. During the third period, partial liberalization (liberalization of import restrictions on some BTN 4-digit items) was put into effect for a number of items in April 1978, and "nonresidual" import restrictions on ten items were removed in January 1980. It is difficult to assess the height of various nontariff barriers in different countries, and the extent of changes in them. Yet Japan completed the necessary procedures for acceptance of all the MTN agreements on nontariff barriers concluded in the TR in advance of all other signatories. As of September 1980, Japan was the only country that had accepted all agreements unconditionally and completed the necessary legal procedures. In addition, Japan simplified customs inspection procedures, sent delegations abroad to promote exports to Japan, and implemented several import promotion measures. Furthermore, after 1980 the Japanese government renewed its effort to liberalize foreign exchange controls and began deregulating domestic financial markets and the telecommunication system.

Another manifestation of the newly emerging free-trade philosophy in Japan is that at the Bonn summit meeting (1985) and in the preparatory meetings for it, Japan jointly with the United States eagerly advocated a new GATT round to further remove trade barriers among the major countries.

Agricultural protection
Japan's trade policy on agricultural imports is a major exception to its newly emerging free-trade policy. Residual import quotas still remain on 22 agricultural products and on a number of items under nonresidual import quotas for the purpose of protecting domestic agriculture. The gap between world prices and domestic prices of cereal products, which is an approximate measure of the strength of protection, is generally higher in Japan than in the EC and in the United States.[30] Japan's dependence on cereals and other food imports is, however, much higher than that of the EC or of the United States.

The political and social forces behind Japan's agricultural protectionism are complex and cannot be explained briefly. Although the policy authorities or agricultural economists who favor agricultural protectionism have rarely stated its purpose explicitly, the principal purposes of Japan's agricultural protection appear to be (1) maintaining a certain degree of domestic self-sufficiency in food supplies or preventing a decline in that degree; and (2) securing opportunities for farmers to earn income, especially those in agricultural prefectures in which there are few alternatives to agricultural employment. The second purpose may be interpreted as serving two further goals: promoting the transmission of basic agricultural technology in farm families in order to maintain some self-sufficiency in food supplies, and sustaining the level of income of farmers, who are now predominantly older persons.

The majority of farmers are now so old that they are reluctant to move to other parts of Japan, and it would be quite costly to move them. Once thrown out of agriculture, they could scarcely work and earn income. Keeping them on the farm may well be a second-best policy, even from a purely economic point of view. Most farmers in agricultural prefectures—the periphery of Japan in relation to the prosperous, industrial center—lack easy access to income-earning opportunities other than agriculture or agriculture-related activities or organizations such as food processing, meat packing, feed mixing, and agricultural cooperatives, which pursue not only agricultural, but also commercial, financial, and political activities. If farmers could gain easier access to alternative income-earning opportunities, the pressure for agricultural protection would be much weakened. It is now much more difficult to provide alternative income-earning opportunities for farmers than in the high growth period, not only for the obvious economic reason, but also for demographic reasons.

Is Japan's domestic market really open?

In the United States and European countries, the notion that Japan's domestic market is very closed remains prevalent, even though it is widely recognized that the average level of tariffs on manufactures is much lower in Japan than in other major developed countries; that, as far as manufactures are concerned, residual import quotas remain on only four items (leather products); and that Japan was the first of the TR signatories to implement all of the codes on nontariff barriers (the Standard Code, Government Procurement Code, Customs Valuation Code, and Import Licensing Code). But has Japan really liberalized imports of manufactures and has Japan's domestic market really become an open one? Or compared with other developed countries do visible and invisible barriers to imports still remain? It is not easy to find the correct answer to these questions. Knowledgeable foreigners cannot deny that Japan's tariffs on manufactures are generally lower than those of other major industrialized countries, and foreign complaints about the closedness of Japan's domestic market are concerned mainly with nontariff barriers.[31] Although tariffs and quantitative restrictions on imports (quotas and embargoes) can be identified readily and compared internationally—with some difficulties—nontariff barriers other than quantitative restrictions are difficult to identify, measure, and compare. Most nontariff barriers are not even objective entities: whether a certain governmental measure or institutional arrangement constitutes a nontariff barrier depends on subjective judgment and can be controversial. For example, from an importing country's point of view, an import quarantine for a vegetable or animal may be absolutely necessary to protect against dissemination of certain diseases; from an exporting country's point of view, it may be an unnecessary nontariff barrier since there is no danger of dissemination, especially when proper care is taken. Various standards and approval systems for safety and consumer protection, importing procedures, and government procurement policies that are necessary for some legitimate purposes and not intended to favor domestic products or domestic suppliers may have characteristics foreigners consider discriminatory against imports. It is exactly in these areas where foreign complaints about Japan's nontariff barriers concentrate. It is difficult to know the facts about what are said to be nontariff barriers, to judge whether they are unnecessary barriers to trade, and to compare them with similar institutions in other countries. Moreover, the actual treatment of imports often differs from the official rules or announced policies in this area.[32]

Since the Meiji period, the Japanese government, as the government of a small, latecomer developing country, has pursued policies to develop domestic industries and modernize the country. From the beginning of industrialization until the late 1960s, Japan's balance of payments has tended toward a deficit, except for a short period around World War I. As a result, government regulation of economic life tends to be pervasive, and institutions tend to give preference to domestic industries over imports and foreign suppliers. It is no wonder that foreigners have had difficulties understanding and dealing with the Japanese economic system. Considering the historical legacy, institutions and a traditional mentality unfavorable to imports and foreigners doing business in Japan remain despite policies since the 1960s to liberalize imports and direct foreign investment.

Since the last years of the 1960s, however, the Japanese government has almost consistently pursued policies of reducing nontariff barriers and promoting imports. In 1981, when the large current-account deficits resulting from the second oil crisis were disappearing, it renewed efforts to reduce import barriers, and from 1982 through 1984 it announced and implemented a series of "packages" of comprehensive import-promoting measures. These include reduction or elimination of tariffs, removal of quotas, improvement of importing procedures and other regulations, dispatch of import promotion missions abroad, and opening of import fairs in Japan.

Beginning in February 1982, the Japanese government reviewed about a hundred rules regarding importing procedures, standards, testing, and so on that had been subject to foreign criticisms and took measures on three-quarters of them. In 1982, the Office of Trade Ombudsman (OTO, later expanded to the Office of Trade and Investment Ombudsman) was established to expedite complaints from foreign and Japanese businessmen about importing procedures and government regulations. The OTO received a total of 159 complaints by the end of August 1984 and instituted improvements or corrected misunderstandings in 117 of them.

Admittedly, these are no answer to the questions posed at the beginning of this section. Yet the serious efforts of the Japanese government to reduce what are thought to be barriers to imports must be taken into account when evaluating the openness—or closedness—of Japan's domestic market.[33]

The low level of imports of manufactures

The low level of manufactured goods in Japan's total imports as well as relative to GNP can be explained as follows. The share of minerals, fuel, raw materials, and food in the total imports of Japan is quite large because of its poor endowments of natural resources and land. Japan has a strong comparative disadvantage in natural resources and agriculture and an equally strong comparative advantage over a wide range of manufactures. Moreover, Japan has no neighboring countries that are similar in language, culture, and income level.[34]

The last condition seems to be an important aspect of the low level of import of manufactures. In order to enjoy a good reputation with consumers and firms in Japan, foreign firms must develop products that conform to the way of living of the Japanese people, the dimensions of their bodies, and their tastes and must provide stable supplies and careful follow-up services. Because of the barriers of language, customs, and distance, few firms have succeeded in taking deep root in Japan's domestic market, although there are now quite a few—and a growing number of—exceptions.

Political background of trade policy

In the post-oil crisis period, it became increasingly obvious that Japan's prosperity depends critically on the world multilateral trade system. In earlier periods Japan was nearly a free-rider on the world trade system, but as it emerged as the second largest highly industrialized free-market economy in the world and as its share in world trade, especially trade in manufactures, became conspicuously large, Japanese policymakers came to recognize the necessity of positive actions to maintain and strengthen the world free-trade system. For that purpose, Japan had to adhere faithfully to the free-trade principles of GATT. But in any country with parliamentary democracy, a move from protectionism or mercantilism toward free trade is politically a rough and rugged path.

Trade policy during the third period has evolved under the balance of power between a group aiming at freer trade and another group trying to maintain the status quo. The former consists of the leaders of the government, the Ministry of International Trade and Industry (MITI), excluding some *genkyoku* sections dealing with specific industries; the Ministry of Foreign Affairs; parts of the Ministry of Finance; and the leaders of the *zaikai* (the industry and business world), who are in a position to consider Japan's overall economic welfare and its position in the international community. The Economic Planning Agency and the Fair Trade Commission are also liberal, free-trade-oriented offices. The other group consists of the leaders of a wide variety of industries (including agriculture) and interest groups that suffer or are supposed to suffer from trade liberalization; *genkyoku* sections in the ministries and agencies that superintend such industries; and politicians, especially in the Liberal Democratic Party, representing the interests of such industries or regions where such industries are located. The government offices that tend to be protectionist are the Ministry of Agriculture, Forestry, and Fisheries, the Ministry of Public Welfare, the Ministry of Transportation, some *genkyoku* sections in MITI, and the Ministry of Posts and Telecommunications. This group often resists implementation of trade-liberalization measures contemplated and planned under the initiative of the first group. The trade policy of Japan during this period evolved as a steady but piecemeal advancement toward freer-trade policies; the advancement was rapid at some times and in some areas and slow in others.[35]

The political background of Japan's agricultural protectionism is illustrative. Japan is similar to other developed countries in that farmers are well organized politically and their representation in the parliament is disproportionately stronger than those of other groups, such as urban residents, consumers, and export industries. This is partly the result of the distribution of parliamentary seats, which has favored rural districts. Urban residents (and, strange as it may seem to foreigners, even consumers' groups sometimes) in Japan are, however, generally sympathetic to farmers. This sympathy is partly based on the general public's uneasiness about Japan's heavy dependence on imported food supplies. Furthermore, most urban families are only one or two generations removed from farming, and they still have strong ties with relatives in rural communities. Thus, urban residents and consumers do not consider their interests as directly opposed to those of farmers, who are often parents, brothers, sisters, or cousins.

In our view, the year 1973 was the turning point in the history of Japan's agricultural protection policy. Until then, a majority of Japanese did not feel uneasy about depending on imported food supplies. This was one factor behind Japan's sharply increasing dependence on imported food throughout the 1960s. (In fact, Japan's current dependence on food imports is markedly higher than that of other major industrialized countries. Although the United Kingdom, Switzerland, and Sweden are also heavily dependent on food imports, the size of Japan's imports of cereals and foodstuffs is strikingly large.) In 1973, a series of events, including the oil crisis, sharp worldwide rises in food prices, and the U.S. embargo of soybean exports to Japan, shook the so-far complacent Japanese. Suddenly they came to realize the vulnerability of the Japanese economy to external shocks and began to think that a further increase in the degree of dependence on food and energy imports would be unsafe and undesirable. This change in attitudes strengthened the political basis of agricultural protectionism.

In regard to import liberalization in other areas, the political power of consumers is weak in Japan, as it perhaps is in other countries. To have a job and to have a position in an organization through which one can exert influence appear to be much more important than small reductions in the prices of some goods.

Intensification of Japan-U.S. economic conflicts

Since 1983, the Japan–U.S. trade conflicts have been aggravated as the U.S. overall current-account deficit, Japan's overall current-account surplus, and the Japan–U.S. bilateral trade imbalance all increased to unprecedented levels. On the Japanese side, the ratio of the current-account surplus to GNP rose to over 1.8% in 1983 and 2.9% in 1984 (the highest figures in the past were 2.3% in 1971 and 2.2% in 1972; it never reached the 2 per cent level from 1973 to 1982); on the U.S. side, the ratio of the current-account deficit to GNP increased to 1.0% in 1983 and 2.6% in 1984 (the highest figures in the past were 0.5, 0.7, and 0.6% in 1972, 1977, and 1978 respectively).

In the United States, the notion spread that such a large balance-of-payments deficit was detrimental to the economy, that the large U.S. deficit was caused by the closedness of Japan's domestic market and the resulting large surplus in Japan's balance of payments, that the Japanese government's trade policy was aimed at increasing the trade surplus or at least keeping imports from increasing, and that if Japan's domestic market were opened by abolishing or reducing artificial trade barriers, U.S. exports to Japan would increase enough to eliminate or substantially diminish the U.S.–Japan bilateral trade imbalance as well as the overall U.S. deficit. These notions arose partly because export expansion in Japan more than compensated the deterioration in Japan's terms of trade. Japan's export expansion tended to be concentrated in a limited number of product areas, and Japanese exports replaced the products of the import-competing industries in the United States.

From an economic point of view, the large imbalance in the balance of payments in the current account reflects the large saving-investment gap between the United States and Japan. Unless gross national saving is increased and investment reduced in the United States, its trade deficit cannot be reduced. The appropriate policy for the United States is to reduce the government budget deficit—that is, to reduce the dissaving in the government sector—and to increase household saving. Also, from 1982 to 1985, the overvalued dollar discouraged exports and promoted imports. This, in turn, suppressed domestic production and reduced income and saving. In order to reduce the U.S. balance-of-payments deficit, it is apparently necessary to reduce the budget deficits. But many U.S. politicians pay no attention to this simple fact and continue to blame Japan for the trade imbalance. The general mood in Washington toward Japan has worsened rapidly since the beginning of 1985.

Initially, Japan–U.S. bilateral negotiations revolved around trade issues, but as time went by they became more diverse. Since around 1976, the U.S. government has extended bilateral negotiations to a wider range of economic policy issues, such as the yen–dollar exchange rate, Japan's macroeconomic policies, liberalization of foreign exchange controls, domestic financial deregulation, Japan's industrial policy, and internationalization of the yen. Thus, since the second half of the 1970s, the Japan–U.S. *trade* conflict has turned into a Japan–U.S. *economic* conflict.

An Overview: The Past and the Near Future

There have been a number of unexpected events in Japan's trade since 1955, and both Japan's trade and the Japanese government's trade policy have changed much over the past three decades. At the beginning of this period, Japan was a small, newly industrializing country that depended chiefly on cheap-labor products to earn foreign exchange. Japan is now one of the largest trading nations in the world and plays a leading role in the arena of international trade diplomacy. In the following, we summarize what we consider some of the most important findings from the previous sections, evaluate Japan's current international trade relations, and speculate on prospects for the future.

Favorable international environment for Japan
The rapid development of Japan's trade since the 1950s was one of the most important factors behind its successful industrialization and high growth rate. World trade developed steadily and fairly rapidly throughout the past three decades except for the past few years. The international economic environment was favorable enough for Japan to achieve a very high rate of growth of imports and exports as well as of real GNP.

The gains from international trade for Japan have not been restricted to gains from a better allocation of already existing productive resources. In the past thirty years, the composition of Japan's exports has changed greatly: many new products unknown at the beginning have emerged in the list of exports. Japan's productivity, technology, the industrial capabilities of the Japanese people, and the managerial capacity of Japanese firms have improved remarkably, and both the level of wages and per capita income have risen greatly. The human resources of Japan (knowledge, technologies, skills, and managerial ability) have expanded greatly through Japan's active participation in international trade.

Changing comparative advantage

At the beginning, Japan had a comparative advantage mainly in labor-intensive products depending on cheap yet high-quality labor and a comparative disadvantage in most primary products closely related to natural resources and land and certain types of machinery and chemicals using sophisticated technologies and requiring large amounts of capital. As time went by, wage levels and technology rose, and the pattern of Japan's comparative advantage shifted toward processing and assembling-type manufacturing industries that depend on mass-production methods and medium to high technologies.

Japan's comparative advantage today is based on such factors as organizational and managerial skills, intelligent and cooperative labor, an efficient use of information, and flexibility in shifting resources from one sector to another. Such technologies in a wider sense are of a versatile character and can be applied over a fairly wide range of manufacturing industries. It appears that Japan will lead other countries in this kind of technology and hence in a fairly wide range of sophisticated manufacturing industries for some time to come.

Since such technologies can be applied to many new industries in which technological innovation is taking place or for which the world demand is increasing rapidly, and since Japan has a severe comparative disadvantage in industries dependent on natural resources and land, free multilateral world trade will be most advantageous for Japan. Thus Japan will remain strongly in favor of free multilateral trade.

Discrimination against Japan within GATT

Japan has been discriminated against in several ways in the GATT system and in trade among the major industrialized countries. The forms of discrimination include the application of Article 35 against Japan, discriminatory import restrictions on Japanese products, and VERs requested by importing countries. Japan is the only member-country of GATT subjected to these forms of discrimination by a large number of other member-countries and over a wide range of products. Gerald Curzon and Victoria Curzon wrote in 1976 that when Japanese wage levels approached European and North American levels, discrimination against Japan would cease.[36] Even today, however, when Japan's wage levels exceed those of several European countries, including the United Kingdom, a wide range of discriminatory practices by European countries against Japanese products still remains. Moreover, discrimination against Japanese exports has intensified in recent years.

Despite this wide range of discriminatory practices, however, Japan's exports increased at a much higher rate than that of the whole world, even in recent years. This implies that although there were barriers and discrimination against Japan, a majority of the countries under the GATT system imported increasing amounts of Japanese products. Thus, Japan enjoyed wide opportunities for trade by participating in the GATT system, despite discrimination against it within the system.

Changing economic policy philosophy
The theory or philosophy of trade policy prevalent among Japanese government officials and leading businessmen has changed considerably during the past three decades. At the beginning, they held a mercantilist philosophy of exporting as much and importing as little as possible and of controlling even the smallest activities of private enterprises. Along with the development of Japanese industry and worldwide trade, however, the philosophy of free trade and free enterprise have become increasingly dominant.

On the one hand, after the two oil crises, the relatively favorable performance of the Japanese economy attracted the attention of many other countries, and the role of Japan in the world economy and in world trade became more prominent. On the other hand, the trade surpluses in 1976–78 and since 1983 have been considered as a major disturbing factor in the world economy, although such a view is doubtful from an economic viewpoint. Hence, the pressure on Japan for trade liberalization became stronger. Moreover, both foreigners and Japanese now expect Japan to play a more active and constructive role in maintaining and strengthening the world free-trade regime. As a result of such changes and pressures, the dominant philosophy of trade policy in Japan has been changing steadily. It was in response to such a change that Japan, together with the United States, played a leading role in the Tokyo Round of GATT and is now eagerly supporting another round.

Of course, the resistance of protectionist groups in Japan has been, and is still, quite strong. Industries and specific regions that are supposed to suffer from import liberalization and market deregulation strongly resist such policy changes. But government leaders, MITI (excluding some *genkyoku* offices), the Ministry of Foreign Affairs, and business leaders now fully recognize the importance of the world free-trade system to Japan and are quite eager to contribute to maintaining the free, multilateral trade system. Japan's trade policy has been evolving under the balance of power between these two groups.

The process of import liberalization

As Japan's balance of payments improved and as requests for import liberalization by foreign countries, especially by the United States, became increasingly strong, Japan's import liberalization proceeded rapidly at some times and in some areas and slowly in others, but it has advanced steadily and more or less continuously since the late 1960s except during the two oil crises. Roughly speaking, the pace of tariff reduction and the removal or relaxation of quotas and other nontariff barriers were directly related to the strength of outside pressure and the size of the balance-of-payments surplus. In contrast, in areas where domestic interest groups strongly resisted, as in agriculture, import liberalization made little progress. The pace of import liberalization also depended on the development of multilateral trade negotiations.

There have been few cases where trade liberalization policy was reversed; that is, where an import quota was reinstituted.[37] This is quite different from the situation in the United States and European countries, where progress toward freer trade has often been reversed, especially since the first oil crisis.

As a result of steady import liberalization, Japan now has perhaps the lowest tariffs among the major countries. Japan's nontariff barriers are also perhaps among the lowest of major industrialized countries, although international comparison in this area is difficult. The barriers to imports of manufactures in the United States and European countries cannot be said to be lower than Japan's if one takes into account import restrictions under the Multi-Fiber Agreement, discriminatory import restrictions against Japan, and VERs that these countries formally or informally ask Japan and developing countries (especially NICs) to implement. But there still remains a myth among politicians, policymakers, and businessmen as well as among the public in Europe and North America that Japan's domestic market is relatively closed and artificially insulated from import competition by tariff and nontariff trade barriers.

Agricultural protection is an important exception to Japan's free-trade policy. Such factors as low agricultural productivity because of the scarcity of land, the rapid aging of the agricultural population, and the Japanese people's strong attachment to their ancestral land have retarded the shift away from agricultural protectionism in Japan.

Moreover, the two oil crises and the worldwide food shortage in the early 1970s made the Japanese people realize their vulnerability to external shocks because of their heavy dependence on imports of energy and food supplies. Considering the domestic political situation and the strength of public opinion in favor of agriculture, there seems no prospect in the near future of a drastic change in this area.

The Japan-U.S. economic conflict

The Japan–U.S. trade conflict began in the period of the textile negotiations in 1968–72 and became more and more serious and expanded into wider areas in 1976–78. In the 1980s, it became the Japan–U.S. economic conflict.[38] Viewed as a series of diplomatic negotiations over trade and economic matters, the Japan–U.S. economic conflict is unusual in several respects. First, unlike usual negotiations over trade or other economic issues in which both parties engage in give-and-take, in the Japan–U.S. negotiations, the United States nearly unilaterally requests Japanese concessions. The main question of the negotiations has been how much and how soon Japan would agree to concede, with the United States' offering little if anything in return.

Second, beginning in 1976 the United States steadily widened the subject matter of the negotiations from trade issues to government policy problems that are thought to affect directly or indirectly trade flows between the two countries. Thus, the United States requested that the agenda include such topics as the yen-dollar exchange, Japan's macroeconomic policies, financial deregulation, internationalization of the yen, and a wide variety of the Japanese government's regulations and standards related to safety, health, telecommunications, and so on.[39]

Third, since most of these subjects are traditionally considered as belonging to the domain of internal affairs of a sovereign state, the attempt by the United States to make these topics the subjects of Japan–U.S. negotiations and to force Japan to take certain policy measures in these areas gave an unfavorable impression that the United States was trying to encroach on Japan's internal affairs.

U.S. pressure on Japan accelerated the liberalization of import restrictions, foreign exchange controls, and regulation of financial markets. Hence, it can be argued that the U.S. pressure has helped make the Japanese economy not only more open but also more efficient and rational. In fact, some Japanese welcomed such U.S. pressure for liberalization. But the unilateral and high-handed way in which the U.S. government demanded concessions from Japan has aroused resentment in Japan.

Why Japan made concessions

In the diplomatic negotiations over economic conflict issues, the Japanese government has made numerous concessions one by one in response to foreign requests regarding both trade and nontrade issues. This passive and piecemeal approach gave the unfavorable impression to government officials and the general public in the United States and other foreign countries that the Japanese government was using delay tactics to evade as much as possible what it should have undertaken by itself.

One might wonder why the Japanese government made concessions at all to such one-sided requests from the United States. First, Japan's overall balance-of-payments surplus and bilateral trade surplus vis-à-vis the United States were especially large when the trade or economic conflict was intense, and the performance of the Japanese economy was relatively good. Japanese government officials perhaps thought that Japan was "guilty" and could afford to accommodate some of the U.S. requests, especially when the United States strongly demanded that Japan cooperate in reducing the large U.S. deficit. But in retrospect this is strange since many members of the IMF with balance-of-payments deficits have been held responsible for mismanaging their economies and have been requested to take corrective actions. No country except the United States has ever requested other countries to take actions to correct its own balance-of-payments deficits.[40]

Second, it may be argued that the U.S. government requested Japan to take actions to correct the imbalance between the two countries to prevent protective legislation. It is a constructive step, therefore, to request Japan to cooperate in countering an incipient rise of protectionism. We think that there is some truth in this view. But if one accepts this view, then a major cause of the Japan–U.S. economic conflict is a lack of political leadership in the United States. Whether such an approach has been successful is a moot question since one could argue that the approach has had at least some effect in fanning the flame of protectionism.

Third, Japanese officials may have feared that the United States would retaliate if Japan did not concede to the United States and thought that concessions were helpful in calming protectionist sentiment in the United States. Although there still remain strong protectionist groups in Japan, the free-trade philosophy has been gaining force among officials and businessmen. More and more Japanese have become convinced that the preservation of the world's free-trade regime is essential for the economic prosperity of Japan. It is not surprising that they thought they should cooperate with the United States as much as possible in eliminating an imbalance they considered detrimental to the maintenance of the free-trade regime.

Fourth, although it has never been mentioned in official documents, the Japanese and American officials in charge of trade negotiations may have considered the bilateral trade and other economic problems as a part of overall—not only economic but also political, security, and cultural—relations. More specifically, Japanese officials felt indebted to the United States for Japan's national security, and U.S. officials were also conscious of the United States' heavy burden as a protector of Japan and as the leader of the Western countries. Such a feeling and perception may have been reflected in Japan's unilateral concessions in trade and other economic relations vis-à-vis the United States.

In this period, the United States strongly requested an expansion of Japan's defense expenditures. Japan acceded to this request to a limited extent, but generally speaking the Japanese government did not want to involve Japan much in defense cooperation because of domestic political considerations. Under these circumstances, the Japanese government tended to consider that it was necessary—and easier—to make concessions on trade and other economic issues.

Economic conflict in a wider perspective
Viewed in a wider and longer-run perspective, several conditions have given rise to the Japan–U.S. economic conflict. First, Japan and the United States have become more and more closely integrated as a result of reductions in tariff and nontariff barriers to trade and in costs of transportation and communication. Not only in merchandise and invisible trade but also in technology, information, finance, and cultural, scientific, and educational exchange, the two countries now depend on each other more heavily than ever before. Second, economic and social forces in the two countries are still very different because of differences in incomes, demography, culture, and customs. These give rise to market forces leading to sudden changes in the pattern and levels of trade flows. Third, both countries are parliamentary democracies, in which decision making on economic policies takes time, with various interest groups participating actively. When a new development is thought prejudicial to a vested interest, the pressure group representing it moves to resist the change, and sometimes such resistance becomes highly politicized.

Fourth, the United States behaves as a superpower and a center country and tends to believe that its social, legal, and administrative institutions are universally superior and should be adopted by other countries. This belief often leads to an imperial or imperialistic manner in economic negotiations with other countries with different cultural traditions. One of the major factors behind the recent flare-up of anti-Japanese feelings in the U.S. Congress is the deficient American understanding of Japan and Japanese culture. Judging from the newspaper reports, U.S. politicians generally seem to have a distorted view of Japan and the Japanese. The extent of Americans' understanding of Japanese culture, language, and social institutions is perhaps much more limited than the Japanese people's understanding of contemporary American culture and social institutions and the English language. This is a great handicap for the United States in marketing its products in Japan and in negotiating effectively with the Japanese.

Fifth, Japan was long isolated from the mainstream of international economic affairs, and Japan's social, legal, and administrative institutions are largely legacies from the time when Japan was a small, latecomer developing country and are not appropriate to Japan's current position in the world economy. The Japanese people's mentality has generally been a small-country one, always thinking about taking advantage of advanced technology and free markets in the outside world, especially in developed countries, but jealously trying to protect their own industries and various vested interests at home. Moreover, the flow of information and exchange of views have been largely one way: that is, from the outside world into Japan. Generally, the Japanese people have made little effort to make themselves well understood by foreigners and to express their own views and ideas. This Japanese failing has been a substantial handicap in Japan's diplomacy.

Of these basic conditions, the first three will remain unchanged in the near future, and the last two will change only slowly. Hence, the Japan–U.S. economic conflict will persist for some time. The subject matter of the conflict will change from time to time, as it has in the past ten years or so, but it is unlikely that the wellspring of friction and tension will dry up in the near future.

Erosion of the GATT system
The GATT system, which is the core of the world's multilateral free trade, has been strengthened since the 1960s by the KR and the TR and by an increase in the number of member-countries. But it has been weakened in some other aspects. In our view, it should be a matter of grave concern that the proportion of the trade among member-countries that is strictly in conformity with GATT declined throughout the 1970s and the first half of the 1980s.[41]

Even in the 1960s, there were some symptoms, such as the agreements on cotton textiles and VERs on certain products, but deviations from the GATT norms became much more visible and numerous in the 1970s. The Multi-Fiber Agreement of 1974 nearly froze the textile trade among GATT members. Bilateral trade in certain products between exporters such as Japan, Korea, Taiwan, and Hong Kong and importers such as the United States, Canada, the United Kingdom, France, Italy, and other European countries has been restricted by formal or informal agreements, such as VERs, the trigger price mechanism (TPM), the basic price system (BPS), and orderly marketing agreements (OMAs). In some sectors such as shipbuilding, world trade has been regulated by attempts at "international coordination" in the OECD. In an effort to protect domestic agriculture, many industrialized countries including Japan, France, and the United States restrict imports of agricultural products by quotas and other administrative measures, some of which are illegal under GATT, although this aberration from the norms of GATT was largely carried over from the beginning of the GATT system.

Apart from these deviations from the principles of free multilateral trade, developing countries have restricted imports of a wide range of products under Article 12 of GATT (which allows import restrictions for balance-of-payments reasons); they have never implemented free-trade policy and hence never participated fully in the GATT system. About the only major obligation they have fulfilled as GATT members is to enforce import restrictions on a nondiscriminatory basis. For GATT members in Eastern Europe (Czechoslovakia, Poland, Romania, and Hungary), the multilateral free-trade principles of GATT or even the tariffs themselves mean little since their trade is under strict state control. Thus, even before the MFA and various VERs, the GATT articles embodying the free-trade principles had real meaning only for a limited number of countries with Article 11 status (West European countries, the United States, Canada, Japan, and a few others). These are the countries that removed, in principle, import restrictions for balance-of-payment reasons. During the 1970s, even among these countries the proportion of international trade under restrictions inconsistent with the basic principles of GATT probably increased.

From the late 1970s to the early 1980s, exports to the United States of textiles, steel, special steel products, color televisions, automobiles, and several others were under restrictions inconsistent with GATT principles. According to some estimates, this proportion reached about a quarter of the total in the case of imports from Japan.

Although some of the arrangements inconsistent with the basic

GATT principles were established under the auspices of GATT (STA, LTA, and MFA), most of them were made outside GATT through bilateral negotiations between the governments concerned. Some of the measures restricting bilateral trade have been negotiated and implemented primarily by industry representatives of the two countries concerned, with government officials participating only marginally. Moreover, some of these are little known to the public. These developments indicate a serious and increasing erosion of the GATT system as a world trade regime. It is no exaggeration to say that the GATT system is now covered with wounds and that the role of GATT as the norm for world trade has diminished substantially.

A repeat of the 1930s?
What is the future of the world trading system and how will it change, say, in the coming five to ten years? It is always difficult to predict the future, but it is particularly difficult to predict the future of the world trading system given the uncertainty about economic, social, and political trends in most major countries. The following is no more than highly speculative conjecture.

In the first half of the 1980s, the dark cloud of stagflation continued to cover a large part of the world economy. Today inflation and unemployment rates are still quite high in many developed countries, and a majority of developing countries are suffering from balance-of-payments difficulties, rapidly accumulating debts, and stagnant exports. It is not surprising that a strong tendency toward protectionism has developed in many countries. Many fear that if current conditions persist, protectionist tendencies will be strengthened and protectionism increased in many countries. The world economy may disintegrate into a few regional economic blocs, each encircled by a wall of trade barriers, as it did in the 1930s.

This is indeed a bleak picture. If this happens, the volume of world trade will dwindle, with disastrous consequences for Japan since it depends heavily on multilateral world trade and has little prospect of forming a largely self-sufficient bloc of its own or joining some regional bloc on favorable terms.

A moderately optimistic view
Yet present conditions in the world economy appear to us considerably different from those prevailing in the 1930s. First, the economies of the industrialized countries are much more closely integrated with each other. Despite the erosion of GATT described above, the major industrialized countries are now generally much more open. The ratio

of imports to GNP has risen substantially in most countries. They are more heavily dependent not only on international flows of merchandise and services, but also on those of technology, information, and knowledge. For industrialized countries, the internationalization of economic and social affairs is an irreversible secular trend.

In such a mutually internationalized world economy, protectionism cannot constitute an advisable permanent solution for any industrialized country to the economic difficulties it now confronts. To protect a medium- to high-technology industry from increasing import competition nearly amounts to defeatism if there is no prospect of getting rid of the protections within a few years. If an industry cannot compete effectively with imports from another country even in its domestic market, it will not be able to compete with other countries' industries in a third country's market. In a world in which colonial empires are a thing of the past, developing countries wishing to import medium- to high-technology products or seeking foreign direct investment in their country for producing such products under joint ventures will turn to those developed countries that produce such products most efficiently. In the case of labor-intensive, low-productivity light industry as well, it is obvious that protectionism fails to provide a solution over the long run. Protecting such an industry from foreign competition means entrapping a larger proportion of the labor force in a low-productivity sector. It will be a burden for the national economy as a whole. It is much better to shift labor and other resources from such a sector to more promising sectors or to any sector that can survive without protection.

Second, from a political point of view, the international relations among the major industrialized countries of the West are basically different from what they were in the 1930s. The world's primary political and military confrontation today is between the two superpowers, the United States and the Soviet Union, and not among Western industrialized countries. In this East-West confrontation, Western countries are by and large tied by common interests and cannot but cooperate in economic and social affairs, although the extent of cooperation may differ in different areas and at different times. The North-South confrontation is also severe at times. In this confrontation, too, the Western countries have common interests in maintaining the liberal, market-oriented economic order and at the same time in assisting the developing countries and mitigating the North-South conflict.[42] In a worldwide political context, it is clear that the major countries of the West have far greater common interests than opposing ones.

The GATT system has been subject to erosion by formal and informal arrangements inconsistent with its basic principles, as pointed out above, yet in the near future there seems to be no international economic system to supersede the free, multilateral, market-oriented economic system of GATT, the IMF, and the OECD. The so-called New International Economic Order proposed by those who profess to represent the interests of developing countries appears to amount to no more than an expression of dissatisfaction with the status quo and of dreary desires. It does not seem to constitute a set of principles for a workable international system in which a large number of countries will participate willingly. It is unlikely that any of the major countries, including the United States, will withdraw from GATT, the IMF, the OECD, or other major international economic organizations or even cease to play an active role in them.

Although its leadership and economic power have been declining, the United States is obviously still the leader of the Western countries in the international economic community and will remain so for many years to come. The role of Japan, which is now perhaps number two, is to cooperate with the United States and other leading countries in maintaining and strengthening the liberal, multilateral world economic order. Japan can never be in a position to contest with the United States or any other country for hegemony over the world economy or some part of it. Japan—or any other country for that matter—would gain little by pursuing such a struggle but would lose a great deal.

Ambition on the part of Japan to be the leader in world affairs is out of the question not only in view of its much restricted military role but also in view of the Japanese economy's high vulnerability to external shocks. If Japan and the United States were vehemently opposed over economic matters and decided to fight an economic war using trade and other economic measures, the United States could inflict severe damage on Japan—of course, at a substantial cost to itself—but Japan could not inflict much damage on the United States. We believe this is well understood by those in charge of international economic affairs in the two countries.

Economic difficulties confronting countries today, such as international payments imbalances, high inflation, unemployment, protectionist tendencies, accumulation of debts, and stagnation cannot be overcome easily. Improvement in these matters will take much time. Yet it seems to us that the world economy is considerably more stable than in the 1930s. It will not as easily disintegrate as it did in the 1930s.

We hope that Japan will adhere to the free-trade principle and play a more active role in maintaining and strengthening the free, multilateral, and market-oriented order of the world economy.

This chapter is co-authored by Motoshige Itoh of the Faculty of Economics, University of Tokyo. An earlier, Japanese-language version was included in Takashi Inoguchi and Daniel I. Okimoto (eds.), *Gendai Nihon no Seiji Keizai*, Vol. 2: *Gendai Nihon no Kokusai Kankei* The Political Economy of Today's Japan, Vol. 2: Japan's External Relations (Sogo Kaihatsu Kiko [NIRA], 1987), and an English version in *The Political Economy of Japan, Volume 2: The Changing International Context*, edited by Takashi Inoguchi and Daniel I. Okimoto (Stanford University Press, 1988); it is reprinted here with the permission of Stanford University Press.

Notes

1. In 1953 and 1954, Japan's imports were about $2 billion, and its exports were only $1.25 billion in 1953 and $1.61 billion in 1954. Thus, Japan had a severe trade imbalance.

2. One might have a more sympathetic view of Japan's trade policy during the 1950s and 1960s if one conceives of the Japanese economy in this period as an Arthur Lewis-type dual economy with surplus labor rather than a Hecksher-Ohlin-type full-employment economy. In the former, the policy of export promotion and import restriction could increase the national income through expansion of employment in the modern manufacturing sector. Even in such an economy, however, the same result could be accomplished more easily by an exchange rate adjustment that makes the foreign exchange dearer relative to wages.

3. It is difficult to determine to what extent Japan's policy of protecting infant industries can be justified on economic grounds and how effective the policy measures undertaken for that purpose were. Economists hold varying views on this issue. For studies attempting to answer these questions, see Komiya, Okuno, and Suzumura, 1984.

4. On the application of GATT Article 35 and other measures of discrimination against Japan by the major European countries and other GATT members until around 1970, see Patterson, 1966, ch. 6; Dam, 1970, and Hazumi and Ogura, 1972.

5. Some of these countries, for example, Central Africa and Chad, discriminated against Japanese products since Japan was a "cheap labor country."

6. Patterson, 1966, p. 275.

7. The facts of discrimination against Japanese exports have not been well known. There have been no official statistics or other publications on this problem, and it is very difficult to obtain factual information. There have been a few well-known cases, however. For example, France, for a long time,

has restricted imports of Japanese automobiles to 3 per cent of the total number of domestically registered automobiles, and Italy allows imports of only 2,000 or so Japanese passenger cars per year. Spain still has discriminatory import embargoes on more than 140 Japanese exports.

8. The difference between the United States and European countries—especially the United Kingdom and France—in their attitudes toward Japan's participation in GATT is partly a result of their different experiences with Japanese exports in the 1930s. In 1951, the Japanese Ministry of Foreign Affairs published the following assessment of the situation in the 1930s: "Japan astonished the world by increasing her exports in 1933 in the midst of the depression . . . , and the future looked bright for the Japanese . . . . But Japan could increase exports only to those countries [or areas] that treated the Japanese goods on more or less equal and free terms, such as England . . . the Near and Middle East . . . Latin America, Thailand, and Manchuria . . . Exports to countries that had adopted a protectionist policy, such as the Soviet Union, the United States, Australia . . . did not increase." Quoted from Kosaka, 1977.

9. See Yamamura, 1967, for U.S. policy toward Japan right after World War II and the way it changed.

10. According to a report Japan presented to GATT in 1968, its trading partners had requested and Japan had imposed VERs on 264 items (by the BTN four-digit classification and by the number of countries). Among them were 51 items requested by the United States.

11. Information and data on VERs are scarce. The governments and the industries concerned generally do not want to publicize their participation since they fear that VERs may spread to their exports to other countries or areas. Furthermore, it is difficult to define what is a VER and what is not. On these points, see Komiya, 1972; Komiya and Amano, 1972.

12. It is perhaps noteworthy, however, that none of these bills have so far been enacted into law or even passed by Congress. On the other hand, the U.S. government sometimes uses the fact of pending congressional consideration of protectionist bills to solicit concessions from foreign governments.

13. "The necessity of new markets for Japan as well as for developing countries" was one of the five reasons given by President Kennedy for the Trade Expansion Act of 1963, which authorized the president to enter the KR negotiations. This indicates that the United States was then still playing, or felt the need of playing, the role of Japan's patron.

14. The first to the fourth rounds of capital liberalization measures were put into effect, respectively, in July 1967, February 1969, September 1970, and August 1971.

15. Such a bias exists more or less in all countries. Even the articles of GATT show influences of such a bias.

16. See Nihon Keizai Kyokai, 1961.

17. For more details, see, Chapters 7 and 9 in this volume, and Komiya, Okuno, and Suzumura, 1984.

18. In recent years, Japan requested South Korea and China to set up VERs on raw silk and certain silk textiles. However, Japan has so far refrained from restricting imports of textile products under the Multi-Fiber Agreement (MFA)—Japan is the only developed country that has not made

use of the import quota system of MFA—and from requesting NICs and developing countries to set up VERs on textile products except the VERs on the silk items mentioned above. See Yamazawa, 1984.

19. For the details of Japan–U.S. textile negotiations, see Destler, Fukui, and Sato, 1979; Inaba and Ikuta, 1970.

20. As pointed out by Neary (1982) the process of shifting resources from labor-intensive industries to other industries tends to cause serious structural unemployment unless wages are flexible.

21. See Komiya, 1972.

22. The price of electricity in Japan is now much higher even than in those other countries that depend on imported petroleum for power generation. The main reason seems to be the high cost of land and the large compensation payments to local residents necessary when building a new power station in Japan.

23. New ceramics, which have been spotlighted recently as one of the high-technology growth industries, also seem to be a field in which patented technologies do not play an important role and in which Japan is likely to have a strong comparative advantage.

24. Since there is a vast literature on the trade conflicts in this period, we do not go into details. For a typical American view, see Subcommittee on Trade, Committee on Ways and Means, U.S. House of Representatives, "Taskforce Report on United States–Japan Trade, with Additional Views (Jan. 1979), and "United States–Japan Trade Report" (Sept. 1980). The literature from Japan's side includes "Nichi-Bei keizai masatsu"(Japan–U.S. economic conflicts), *Kogin chosa*, Nos. 207–8 (1981); Ogura, 1981; Shoda and Sekiguchi, 1983; Uekusa, 1983.

25. Behind this may lie the U.S. perception that the United States has given much to Japan since 1945 economically, including an open domestic market with relatively low tariff and nontariff barriers.

26. See Itoh and Ono, 1984, for a theoretical analysis of this mechanism.

27. See Feenstra, 1984.

28. The attitudes of the U.S. Administration and Congress toward the TR differ to some extent from their attitudes toward previous tariff negotiations. The 1974 Trade Act permitted import restriction measures to mitigate balance-of-payments deficits and relaxed the conditions under which protective measures for the domestic industries can be put into effect.

29. See, e.g., Deardorff and Stern, 1984.

30. Japan's tariffs on certain processed foods also remain high. But this is not necessarily done to protect food-processing industries. Since the domestic prices of raw materials for such industries are high because of agricultural protection, unless the tariffs on such products are kept high enough, the effective rate of protection for food processing might well be negative. Also, unless the tariff rates are high enough, the policy of agricultural protection would be partially undermined by an increase in imports of processed agricultural products.

31. Another criticism is that the Japanese distribution system is so complicated as to make it difficult for foreign manufacturers with strong preferences for traditional business relationships. Here, we simply point out that since WWII the Japanese distribution system and business relationships have been highly competitive, dynamic, and generally efficient and that quite a

few foreign-owned or foreign-affiliated firms and a large number of foreign brands have been quite successful in Japan.

32. Actual administrative practices for imports may differ from the rules prescribed in the law. Many foreign complaints about the closedness of Japan's domestic market concern cumbersome importing procedures, the arbitrariness of the officers in charge, and nontransparency in decisions regarding standards for safety and consumer protection. Some of these complaints may be justified. However, unreasonable administrative practices restricting imports exist in most countries. For example, according to the *Asahi shimbun* (Apr. 18, 1985), in Jan. 1985 President Reagan approved a proclamation under the Agricultural Adjustment Act prohibiting imports of foods containing sugar for the purpose of protecting domestic sugar producers from cheap sugar imports from Canada. This is in itself a substantial nontariff barrier, but it had unexpected restrictive side effects. Traditional Japanese food imports into the United States for consumption primarily by Japanese Americans, their descendants, Japanese businessmen posted in the United States and their families, such as Japanese noodles with soup, Japanese and Korean pickles, *kamaboko* (fishcake) and *tsukudani* (preserved food boiled down in soy sauce) were denied entry at U.S. ports because they contain or were supposed to contain sugar (as a matter of fact they contain from 0.1 per cent to 5 per cent at most). Even Japanese foods containing no sugar at all such as sesame, *mochi* (rice cakes), and *shichimitogarashi* (a kind of mixed spice) could not be imported, whereas candies and *yokan* (a sort of sweet jelly) could be. The treatment differed from port to port. Japanese exporters of these products, most of whom were small businesses, reportedly suffered large losses. Another example was the French government's sudden announcement in Oct. 1982 that customs procedures for video tape recorders could be cleared only at a customs office at an inland town on a small river called Poitiers, about 350 km south-west of Paris. Until then, VTRs could be imported through any major port or airport. Until this unusual restrictive practice was discontinued in April 1983, transportation costs were increased substantially since VTRs had to be trucked to Poitiers, and the limited capacity at Poitiers caused delay and disorder.

33. Since nontariff barriers have recently been highlighted as a focal point of the U.S.–Japan trade conflict and trade negotiation, some people mistakenly think that nontariff barriers are something new. Generally speaking, nontariff barriers have become more apparent since more visible obstacles to trade have been eliminated as a result of the substantial tariff reductions in the KR and TR. Moreover, in the case of Japan, nontariff barriers have consistently been reduced since the middle of the 1960s, unlike in the United States and some other major developed countries, where new nontariff barriers such as quotas, VERs and other trade restriction mechanisms have recently been set up.

34. See Saxonhouse, 1983.

35. The situation is similar to that observed in other parliamentary democracies. For example, in the United States the executive branch is generally internationally oriented and tends to favor free trade, whereas individual industries, labor unions, and congressmen acting for particular industries

and regions are inclined to protectionism, paying little attention to overall national economic welfare and the international commitments of the United States.

36. See Curzon and Curzon, 1976.

37. Although the Japanese government has not introduced any new quotas or strengthened quota restrictions on agricultural imports since the beginning of the 1960s, primarily because of the changing comparative advantage pattern of the Japanese economy, the implicit tariff rates of the quotas (the discrepancy between domestic and world prices for agricultural products) have generally increased in recent years.

38. Trade conflicts exist between Japan and the EC countries as well, and, one might say, even between Japan and the ASEAN countries. But the Japan–EC conflict has been much less serious than the Japan–U.S. one and confined almost entirely to trade issues.

39. The Japanese government, on the other hand, only meekly complained about certain aspects of the U.S. economic policy: high inflation, high interest rates, large government budget deficits, and the policy of nonintervention in the foreign exchange market. Generally speaking, the U.S. government paid little attention to such complaints of the Japanese government or of other foreign governments.

40. Fairly large current-account surpluses or deficits have not been uncommon in the international economy. Generally speaking, they do not present difficulties to other countries. For example, over the 50 years from 1860 to 1910, the United Kingdom ran current-account surpluses averaging 4 per cent of GNP, and in 1909 through 1923 and 1957 through 1975 the United States ran surpluses of 2.0 per cent and 1.1 per cent, respectively, on average. These are much larger than Japan's current surplus relative to the total volume of the world trade at the time. On the other hand, there are many examples of continued current-account deficits. For example, Canada (8.0 per cent of GNP in 1890–1910, 3.5 per cent in 1920–30), Norway (5.5 per cent in 1915–24, 11.4 per cent in 1975–78), Italy (2.2 per cent in 1921–30), and Australia (7.1 per cent in 1812–1910, 2.8 per cent in 1960–83). (Marris, 1987).

41. Cline, 1983, contains a number of papers dealing with this issue.

42. The Japanese government's policy toward North–South trade problems has not been much different from that of other North countries. However, Japan is the only nonwhite country without European and Christian traditions that succeeded in full-scale industrialization, and the shares of the South in Japan's trade and direct investment are much larger than those of other major industrialized countries. Hence, Japan tends to be more sympathetic to the South. Such a stance is perhaps reflected to some extent in Japan's implementation of GSP, in its attitudes to the "safeguard" issue in the TR, and to the Common Fund for price stabilization of primary products. Also, Japan is the only country among the industrialized, high-wage countries that has not yet adopted import restrictions on textiles under the MFA. Other developed countries also requested VERs on various labor-intensive products from low-wage countries, but Japan has rarely done so.

References

Cline, William R., ed. (1983). *Trade Policy in the 1980s*. Washington, D.C.: Institute for International Economics.

Curzon, Gerald, and Victoria Curzon (1976). "The Management of Trade Relations in the GATT," in Andrew Shonfield, ed., *International Economic Relations in Western Countries*. London: Royal Institute for International Affairs, pp. 143–283.

Dam, Kenneth W. (1970). *The GATT: Law and International Economic Organization*. Chicago: University of Chicago Press.

Deardorff, A.V., and M. Stern (1984). "The Effects of the Tokyo Round on the Structure of Protection," in R. E. Baldwin and A. O. Krueger, eds., *The Structure and Evolution of Recent U.S. Trade Policy*. Chicago: University of Chicago Press, pp. 361–88.

Destler, I.M., Haruhiro Fukui, and Hideo Sato (1979). *The Textile Wrangle: Conflict in Japanese-American Relations, 1969–1971*. Ithaca, N.Y.: Cornell University Press.

Feenstra, R.C. (1984). "Voluntary Export Restraint in U.S. Autos, 1980–81: Quality, Employment, and Welfare Effects," in R.E. Baldwin and A.O. Krueger, eds., *The Structure and Evolution of Recent U.S. Trade Policy*. Chicago: University of Chicago Press.

Hazumi, Mitsuhiko, and Kazuo Ogura (1972). "Tai-Nichi Sabetsu Mondai no Ippanteki Haikei" (The General Background of Trade Discrimination against Japan), in Kiyoshi Kojima and Ryutaro Komiya, eds., *Nihon no Hikanzei Boeki Shoheki* (Nontariff Barriers in Japan's Trade). Tokyo: Nihon Keizai Shimbunsha.

Inaba, Hidezo, and Toyoro Ikuta (1970). *Nichi-Bei Sen'i Kosho* (Japan–U.S. Textile Negotiations). Tokyo: Kin'yu Zasei Jijo Kenkyukai.

Itoh, Motoshige, and Yoshiyasu Ono (1984). "Tariffs vs. Quotas Under Duopoly of Heterogeneous Goods," *Journal of International Economics*, 17: 359–73.

Komiya, Ryutaro (1972). "Yushutsu Jishu Kisei" (Volutary Export Restraints), in Kiyoshi Kojima and Ryutaro Komiya, eds., *Nihon no Hikanzei Boeki Shoheki* (Nontariff Barriers in Japan's Trade). Tokyo: Nihon Keizai Shimbunsha, pp. 241–61.

Komiya, Ryutaro, and Akihiro Amano (1972). *Kokusai Keizaigaku* (International Economics). Tokyo: Iwanami Shoten.

Komiya, Ryutaro, Masahiro Okuno, and Kotaro Suzumura, eds. (1984). *Nihon no Sangyo Seisaku* (Japan's Industrial Policy). Tokyo: University of Tokyo Press.

Kosaka, Masataka (1977). "The International Economic Policy of Japan," in R.A. Scalapino, ed., *The Foreign Policy of Modern Japan* (Berkeley: University of California Press)

Marris, Stenen (1987). *Dollars and the Deficits*. Washington, D.C.: Institute for International Economics.

Neary, J.P. (1982). "Capital Mobility, Wage Stickiness, and Adjustment Assistance," in J.N. Bhagwati, ed., *Import Competition and Response*. Chicago: University of Chicago Press.

Nihon Keizai Kyokai (1961). *Boeki Nenkan* (International Trade Yearbook). Tokyo: NKK.

Ogura, Kazuo (1981). *Nichi-Bei Boeki Masatsu* (Japan–U.S. Trade Conflicts). Tokyo: Nihon Keizai Shimbunsha.

Patterson, Gardner (1966). *Discrimination in International Trade: The Policy Issues, 1945–1965*. Princeton: Princeton University Press.

Saxonhouse, Gary (1983). "The Micro- and Macroeconomics of Foreign Sales to Japan," in W.R. Cline, ed., *Trade Policies in the 1980s*. Washington, D.C.: Institute for International Economics, pp. 259–304.

Shoda, Yasutoyo, and Sueo Sekiguchi, eds. (1983). *Nichi-Bei Keizai Masatsu no Kenkyu* (Studies on Japan–U.S. Economic Conflicts). Tokyo: Nihon Keizai Kenkyu Center.

Uekusa, Masu, et al. (1983). *Nihon Sangyo no Seidoteki Tokucho to Boeki Masatsu* (International character of Japanese industry and trade confilcts). Tokyo: Sekai Keizai Kenkyu Kyokai.

Yamamura, Kozo (1967). *Economic Policy in Postwar Japan: Growth Versus Economic Democracy*. Berkeley: University of California Press.

Yamazawa, Ippei (1984). "Sen'i Sangyo" (Textile Industry), in Ryutaro Komiya, Mashiro Okuno, and Kotaro Suzumura, eds., *Nihon no Sangyo Seisaku* (Japan's Industrial Policy). Tokyo: University of Tokyo Press, pp. 345–67.

CHAPTER 2

THE GLOBAL PAYMENTS IMBALANCE, THE "SYSTEMIC CRISIS," AND JAPAN–U.S. ECONOMIC RELATIONS

There is a widespread view today that the world trading system is facing a crisis. While I do not believe that the system is already in a state of crisis, I feel that in recent years there has been an increasing threat of disintegration of the world trading system, and that the potential danger of a "systemic crisis" is growing. The purpose of this chapter is to ask what constitutes this threat of systemic crisis, to consider the factors and conditions which may contribute to this threat, and to discuss how we should cope with it.

I will first discuss what "the world trading system"—or, more accurately, the world trading and monetary system—is, what important changes have taken place in the system from the beginning of the postwar period to the present, and what difficulties the system is now facing (Section I). Next I will discuss the directions in which the world monetary system could possibly be reformed at present (Section II). I will then examine the economic situation in the United States and the current-account imbalance between the United States and Japan, which, in my view, has become the focal point of the threat of systemic crisis (Section III). I will go on to discuss political conditions and international economic relations which have given rise to protectionism in the United States and which have finally been fostering this threat of a crisis (Section IV). Finally, I will discuss prospects for averting the systemic crisis and the role Japan could play in this process (Section V).

I. The Development of the World Trading System

What is the present world trading and monetary system? It is the worldwide economic system of which GATT (the General Agreement on Tariffs and Trade) and the IMF (International Monetary Fund) are the two most fundamental components.

GATT, which came into effect in 1948, developed from bilateral commercial treaties which emerged in the 16th century and proliferated later in the 18th and 19th centuries. GATT represents a multilateral generalization of these treaties. The IMF, established in 1947, is an international agreement and an organization for the purpose of international monetary and settlement arrangements and short-term financing. The IMF developed from the gold standard or the gold exchange standard, which had been the global system for settlement of international payments since the latter part of the 19th century.

There are several other important basic parts of the world trading system, such as the OECD (Organization for Economic Cooperation and Development), IBRD (International Bank for Reconstruction and Development), and other global and regional multilateral financial organizations which were designed to provide official long-term funds. The OECD is an organization whose members are mainly the developed countries of Western Europe, North America, and Japan. It exists chiefly for the exchange of information and cooperation in the area of economic policy. The OECD's codes for liberalization of "invisible trade" and for liberalization of capital movements constitute the important rules of the world trading system. One may say that these institutions and the "summit meetings" and meetings of the finance ministers and central bank presidents of the five to seven major countries (G-5 and G-7) since 1975 form the core of the world trading system.

Basic principles of GATT and the IMF

The three basic principles of the world trading system centered around GATT and the IMF are *multilateralism, free trade*, and *non-discrimination* with regard to merchandise and invisible trade and international settlement. In this context, free trade means abolishing quantitative restrictions on import and other current-account transactions, and making tariff and non-tariff barriers as low as possible. Non-discrimination means that each member nation grants all other member nations most-favored-nation treatment. Although there are rules that are exceptions to these three basic principles, and in practice there are various *de facto* deviations from the rules, the aforementioned three basic principles are the main pillars sustaining the system and have been the fundamental framework of the world trading system.

Japan became a member of the IMF in 1952, and in 1964 its status was changed from an Article 14 country to an Article 8 country. Japan became a provisional member of GATT in 1953, and a full member in 1955.[1] Its status in GATT was changed from an Article 12 country to an Article 11 country in 1963. An Article 12 country of GATT or an Article 14 country of IMF is allowed to maintain quantitative restrictions on imports or exchange restrictions for balance of payments reasons. A GATT Article 11 country or an IMF Article 8 country is a member nation that may not establish quantitative restrictions or exchange restrictions on current-account transactions for balance of payments reasons. While present membership in GATT and the IMF has risen to include a large number of countries, the present world trading system is centered around the twenty or so advanced industralized countries which constitute the OECD. Less developed countries, the Soviet Union, the Eastern European countries, and China participate in the world trading system, but they do so as "periphery" countries. Some of them, such as the Soviet Union, are members of neither the IMF nor GATT. Others are members of the IMF but not GATT. Still others are members of GATT but not the IMF. Furthermore, many of the less developed and East-bloc countries are IMF Article 14 or GATT Article 12 or 18 countries. Thus, the number of countries which have reached full membership status (countries which are both GATT Article 11 and IMF Article 8) is not large. Yet a predominant proportion of the trade and capital movements of these peripheral countries is conducted with the advanced industrialized countries of the West that form the center of the system.

The development of international trade

In the approximately 40 years since the establishment of GATT and the IMF in 1947 and 1948, what major changes have taken place within the world trading system? In discussing this issue, I would like to focus on six points.

First, multilateral merchandise and invisible trade, direct investment, and international capital movement have developed greatly, centered around the Western advanced industrialized nations. This has remarkably accelerated progress toward integration of the world economy. In many countries, international trade has expanded not only faster than the production of tradable commodities but also faster than GNP. The degree of trade dependence (the ratio of export and import to GNP) has risen (see Table 1), and in addition, international economic relations in many areas other than trade have become closer. For example, in the United States, the ratio of imports to GNP was only about 3% around 1960, but has exceeded 9%, approaching 10% between 1984 and 1987. As I will explain later, this trend forms one of the factors that are fomenting the threat of a systemic crisis. While technological progress in the areas of transportation and communication has contributed greatly to the development of global economic integration, this technological progress itself may be viewed as largely brought about by global economic integration.

Many countries, especially those small countries that do not have balanced factor endowments, benefited greatly from the development of the world trading system. Japan, not well endowed with natural resources, was clearly one of these countries.

GATT has increased its membership from the initial 23 countries to 96 countries at present, while the number of member nations of the IMF has risen from 45 countries to 157 countries. After 1970, a number of Eastern European countries became members of GATT or the IMF, and a few Eastern European countries that had been members from the beginning or soon thereafter but had been "idle members" for a long time became active again. China has recently applied for membership in GATT (China is already a member of the IMF), and even the Soviet Union expressed its wish to participate in the Uruguay Round of GATT.

These facts tell the story of the striking growth of the world trading system, and I believe that they demonstrate the success of the three basic principles of the system and the various institutional arrangements embodying them.

Changes in the relative positions of the U.S., Europe, and Japan
In the last 40 years, there have been very significant changes in the relative positions of the major countries and areas that form the "center" of the world trading system. There have also been large changes in relative technological and industrial capabilities. If we take a look at the economies of the U.S. and Japan in the early 1950s, when Japan became a member of GATT and the IMF, the per-capita GNP differential between Japan and the U.S. was somewhere between 1 to 10 and 1 to 15. Considering that the population differential was 1 to 2, the difference in the scale of the two economies was of the order of 20 to 30. At that time, the U.S. economy accounted for over 40% of world production while Japan's share was a meager 1 to 2%. Today, the per-capita GNP level of Japan and the U.S., when converted at the prevailing exchange rate, is about equal. Present rates of GNP growth, when measured in each country's domestic currency, do not differ much, and at a yen-dollar exchange rate of 140 to 150 yen to the dollar, per-capita GNP of the two countries is approximately the same. With the yen higher than that range, Japan's per-capita GNP is more than that of the U.S. Calculations based on exchange rates put Japan's share of world GNP at 15 to 20%, while that of the U.S. has declined to about 30%. Looking at shares of world exports reveals

similar trends. Japan's share fell from a prewar level of 5.3% (1938) to 1.4% in 1950, and in 1955, Japan's share of world exports was still only 2.4%. Nowadays, Japan's share is 13 to 15%.

Western Europe's postwar share in the world economy first grew with the reconstruction of Europe under the Marshall Plan and the creation of the European Common Market and the EC, but thereafter decreased somewhat. The Soviet Union's share and that of the Eastern European countries have followed a similar path.

According to some estimates of China's and Japan's GNP in 1950, their GNPs were then roughly equal. Because China's population at that time was about 6.5 to 7 times that of Japan, the per-capita GNP of China was about one-sixth to one-seventh as large as Japan's. Current figures for China's and Japan's GNP reveal that, at the present exchange rate, China's per-capita GNP is only one eightieth (1/80) or one hundredth (1/100) of Japan's. The gaps between China and the U.S. in terms of both GNP and per-capita GNP have not narrowed much, and may have widened. In contrast, the gains by the East Asian NIEs (newly industrializing economies) and the ASEAN countries in recent years seem quite remarkable.

Japan's rise is not limited to macroeconomic indices like GNP or per-capita GNP. Looking at its level of industrial technology also reveals Japan's remarkable progress. Through the 1960s and 1970s Japanese industry gradually improved its industrial technology, first in such industries as shipbuilding, steel, and household electronics, then in automobiles, machine tools, copying machines, and semiconductors. Initially the U.S. and Western Europe overwhelmingly dominated these industries, but Japan gradually achieved a comparable level of technological capability and then became more advanced in certain areas. Consequently, Japan's export of products of these industries to the U.S. and Europe increased. One of the results was increasing complaints about Japan's exports and "trade friction" between Japan and the U.S. and Europe.

The breakdown of the old IMF system

In the last 40 years significant changes have also occurred in the international monetary system centered around the IMF. It was only for a period of about ten years—from around 1960, when the convertibility of the major West European currencies was recovered, to August 1971, when U.S. President Richard Nixon renounced the gold convertibility of the U.S. dollar—that the initial IMF system, that is, the Bretton Woods System, functioned according to its original design. The adjustable peg system, whereby member countries could occasionally adjust the exchange rates of their currencies, collapsed between 1971 and 1973. At the same time, the tie between gold and national currencies was broken.

As an answer to the question of why the old IMF system collapsed, one can point to three fundamental conditions that could not coexist:

(1) The liberalization of international trade and capital movement, especially the liberalization of capital movement.

(2) Each country independently issuing its own national currency and following its own monetary policy, thereby making inflation and interest ratees different from country to country.

(3) Fixity and/or stability of exchange rates.

As will be discussed later (see Section II), each country can freely choose any two of the above three conditions, but not all three.

The founding members of the old IMF system did not consider requiring member nations to liberalize international capital movement. In addition, the impact of the liberalization of capital movement was not fully understood. During the period when capital movement was severely restricted, even though there were differences in inflation rates, occasional adjustments of exchange rates were sufficient to keep the adjustable peg system working. However, as capital movement was gradually liberalized and international capital flows increased, the basic difficulties of the adjustable peg system gradually became apparent. The old IMF system broke down when the U.S., the key currency country at the center of the system, decided in August 1971 to stop the gold convertibility of the dollar, in breach of the IMF Agreement. If the U.S. had observed the articles of the IMF Agreement and had changed the par value of the U.S. dollar to counteract the "fundamental disequilibrium" in the U.S., the old IMF system might have been able to survive a little longer. However, considering, on the one hand, the increases in international trade and capital movement and, on the other hand, the fact that each country's economic conditions are *always* and *steadily* changing, and sometimes subject to violent fluctuations, the adjustable peg system that allowed for only *occasional* and *jumping* adjustments had an inherent shortcoming leading to an overburdened situation.

The breakdown of the adjustable peg system and the demise of the gold standard did not mean, however, the end of the IMF system. What collapsed was the parity system and the gold convertibility of currencies. The IMF's other basic framework—that is, the principles of non-discrimination, multilateralism in international settlement, the liberalizing of current-account transactions, and official short-term financing for countries needing such assistance to overcome balance of payments difficulties—still remains in place today.

Under the floating exchange rate system which followed the collapse of the parity system, exchange rates of major currencies have been subject to large fluctuations. These fluctuations have been thought to produce undesirable effects on international economic relations, especially in terms of how such fluctuations affect trade and domestic industries, and they have become the sources of dissatisfaction among those who have been adversely affected.

The erosion of the GATT system

GATT has made enormous progress in some respects. The Kennedy Round (1964–1967) of GATT, which was a response to the European challenge in the form of the EEC, was an overwhelming success in promoting the cause of free trade. The Tokyo Round (1973–1979) also proved to be successful. The GSP (Generalized Special Preference), which was implemented after 1971, contributed to the development of trade for less developed countries and furthered global economic integration by encouraging these countries to participate in the world trading system.

On the other hand, however, an erosion of the fundamental principles of the GATT system has been taking place. Trade restrictions that run counter to the fundamental principles of GATT, especially import quotas by the advanced industrialized nations that target exports of manufactured products from latecomer industrializing nations, have increased and proliferated outside the framework of GATT. For example, (1) beginning with the 1957 Japan–U.S. Cotton Textile Agreement, import restrictions on textiles by developed countries were steadily expanded, and eventually this led to the Multilateral Fiber Agreement (MFA) in 1974. Today virtually all major developed countries except for Switzerland and Japan employ quantitative restriction (quota) systems with regard to their textile imports. (2) Trade restrictions, such as "voluntary export restraints" (VER) or the "Orderly Marketing Agreement" (OMA), were first introduced around 1956. In the beginning, these restrictions only applied to U.S.-bound Japanese exports of light-industry, labor-intensive manufactures. As time went on, however, the targets of these restrictions came to include higher-technology industries such as steel, color television sets, and automobiles. The countries involved also came to include Canada and a number of Western European countries on the importing side, and the newly industrializing nations of Asia and a few other developing countries on the exporting side. Furthermore, (3) "grey zone" arrangements such as "moderation" and "monitoring" by the governments of both exporting and importing countries have also increased. (4) Trade restrictions based on special bilateral agreements such as the Japan–U.S. semiconductor agreement have recently been concluded and implemented. (5) As previously mentioned, most of the developing nations and East European countries, who in terms of sheer numbers form an overwhelming majority of GATT members, still remain Article 18 members of GATT. (6) Moreover, many Article 11 countries, including Japan, have continued to impose a number of "residual import restrictions" in violation of GATT.

Global payments imbalance since the 1970s

In the 1970s, following two oil crises (the first in 1973–1974 and the second in 1979–1980), the members of OPEC and some other oil-exporting nations accumulated enormous balance-of-payments surpluses that resulted in a global payments imbalance. In the 1980s some of the "middle" industrializing countries, such as Brazil, Mexico, and Argentina, accumulated staggering current-account deficits leading to the present Third World debt problem. In the wake of these events, after 1983, the current-account surplus of Japan and the current-account deficit of the U.S. increased enormously. Trade and economic "friction" erupted between these two largest "center" countries in the world trading system.

The large current-account surpluses of the OPEC countries did not continue as long as many people had at first feared. In fact, with the fall in oil prices, the OPEC countries' surpluses disappeared. On the other hand, the balance of payments problems of the "heavy debtor" developing countries have yet to improve. The indebtedness of many of these countries has reached unbearable levels and still continues to rise.

For a period of nearly 20 years, until 1982, the United States's balance of payments on current account fluctuated within 1% of the U.S. GNP. That is, for most years before 1982, the U.S. current account registered either a surplus or a deficit of not more than 1% of U.S. GNP. Similarly, Japan's current-account balance remained within 2% of Japan's GNP, on either the plus or the minus side. After 1983, however, the U.S. current-account deficit and Japan's current-account surplus increased dramatically, to levels exceeding 3 to 4% of their respective GNPs. The ratio of Japan's current-account surplus to GNP has been declining since its peak in the middle of 1986, but the Japan-

U.S. trade imbalance in dollar terms has not yet been substantially reduced. In addition, due to its large, continuing current-account deficit, the U.S., which had been a large capital exporting country until 1980, has now become a net debtor nation. In contrast, Japan, whose net foreign asset-liability position had remained within 1 to 2% of GNP until the early 1980s, has suddenly emerged as the world's new giant capital exporting country.

The rise of protectionism
In comparison with the 1960s, the world economy today is nearly stagnant, recording lower growth rates of both GNP and trade. Under these circumstances, the political forces of protectionism are gaining strength in many countries. Since 1980, "trade frictions" between Japan and the Asian newly industrializing economies on the one hand and the North American and West European nations, especially the United States, on the other have become frequent and are escalating. In the 1980s, Japan's domestic economy was in recession and its balance of payments on current account turned into a surplus, based upon an expansion of export of medium-to-high technology manufactured goods coupled with a stagnation in its imports. Complaints and grievances against Japan about trade from the U.S., West European countries, and nearby Asian countries became frequent, and Japan began to feel that it was surrounded on all sides by adversarial criticisms.

The U.S., in particular, has been unable to reduce its large current-account deficits. Protectionism has permeated much more broadly and intensely than in any period of U.S. postwar history, which has seen a number of peaks in protectionism. For the first time since World War II, the U.S. is now experiencing trade or current-account deficits at levels never seen before, with no signs of improvement in the near future. Imports suddenly increased as foreign firms developed a competitive edge over U.S. firms in industries considered important or economically "strategic," such as steel, electronics, automobiles, machine tools, and semiconductors. Japan and the Asian NIEs, which exported these vital products and recorded enormous trade surpluses vis-à-vis the U.S., became the objects of American anxiety, unrest, and complaints. Gradually these responses transformed themselves into criticism and censure, and international trade and economic relations grew to involve more and more political disputes. Today "Japan bashing" is quite popular, and protectionism is an important political force.

What might bring about a "systemic crisis"?

Within the framework of the world trading system that has lasted for over 40 years, the economies of many countries have developed remarkably. Global economic integration has been furthered, and thus we can call this "system" a success. At the same time, however, a number of difficulties have emerged for which there are currently no simple solutions. Most important among these unresolved problems are the high volatility of exchange rates under the floating exchange system, the debt accumulation of some developing countries, large current-account imbalances in Japan and the U.S., "trade friction," and the growth of protectionism in developed nations, especially in the U.S.

Among these problems, which are likely to generate a "systemic crisis" in the world trading system? In the following sections I shall discuss which of the factors possess such potential.

II. The Debt Problem and the Possibility of Reforming the International Monetary System

In the previous section I mentioned a number of difficult problems faced by the world trading system or the GATT–IMF system. In this section I will discuss the debt problem, the reform of the international monetary system, and the policy for coping with large fluctuations in exchange rates.

Change in the LDC problem

When the debt problem first became a serious issue in some of the heavily indebted developing countries, such as in Mexico in 1982, major banks in the U.S., Western Europe, and Japan which had been lending to these countries faced the possibility of bankruptcy or at least serious financial crises due to an inability to reclaim their loans. This created fears of an international financial panic. Now that a few years have passed, the general feeling among financial experts seems to be that the possibility of such a major financial panic is rather remote. American, European, and Japanese banks that lent heavily to these countries have managed to reduce their loans to heavy debtor countries to moderate levels, at least in relative terms. In the case of Japanese banks, the total amount of loans to these heavily indebted nations is now less than 1% of total assets. Consequently, the character of the LDC debt problem has changed from one which involves the possibility of an international financial crisis to one chiefly concerned with how to rehabilitate the individual economies of debtor countries and put them on new growth paths. In other words, while the debt problem of some of the heavily indebted countries is still an unsolved and serious problem for these countries, the possibility that the debt problem will trigger a worldwide systemic crisis has been considerably reduced.

Three national policy goals in an interdependent world
Since the early 1970s, the exchange rates of major currencies have frequently and for no apparent reason undergone large movements under the floating exchange rate system. Many people have suffered and made unforeseen losses and gains. Because these unpredictable exchange rate movements have had significant, unfavorable (as well as favorable) impacts on their domestic economies, it is natural that they have brought about calls for exchange rate stabilization. As I mentioned in Section I, however, in today's world, countries cannot simultaneously achieve (1) liberalization of trade and capital movements, (2) issuance of national currency and pursuit of independent monetary policies, and (3) fixity or stability of exchange rates. Each country can freely choose as many as two of these three goals, but attempts to try to pursue all three will eventually result in failure.

Many of the less developed countries, as well as the Soviet Union, the East European countries, and China, have given up on (1) and have chosen to implement (2) and (3). An overwhelming majority of IMF member nations employ some sort of fixed or managed exchange rate system, and only a few countries use the true floating rate system. Whatever the short-term possibilities may be, it is not easy to fix the exchange rates of a country's currency at some given level over the long run. Among the countries in the European Monetary System, there are countries which rather severely restrict capital movements. Nevertheless, the EMS occasionally has to change the parity rate for their members' currencies.

Among smaller countries, there are examples of countries abandoning (2). Such a country pegs its currency to that of a large neighboring country or to a currency basket. Provided that the real value of the neighboring large country's currency in terms of goods and services is stable, or the value of the currency basket is stable, this may be an advisable choice.

For a major country, however, the best choice is to choose (1) and (2), and to let the exchange rate be dictated by the market. If Japan or Germany were to decide to go under the jurisdiction of the U.S. Federal Reserve System, and the Bank of Japan became the Federal

Reserve Bank of Tokyo and the Deutsche Bundesbank the Federal Reserve Bank of Frankfurt, and each sent a few Japanese or German officials to the Federal Reserve Board as its members, then the exchange rates among the U.S. dollar, Japanese yen, and German mark could be stabilized. Japan and the U.S., or Japan, the U.S., and Germany, would jointly pursue a unified monetary policy. As is the case now among Federal Reserve banks in the U.S., both the Federal Reserve Bank of Tokyo (the Bank of Japan) and the Federal Reserve Bank of Frankfurt (the Deutsche Bundesbank) would follow the policy determined by the Federal Reserve Board in Washington, D.C.

However, Japanese and Germans are unlikely to virtually abandon their national sovereignty over monetary policy, or over the issuance of independent national currencies. All major countries want to maintain the freedom to pursue tight or loose monetary policies in response to macroeconomic policy needs dictated by their own domestic economies. The rates of technological progress and productivity growth differ from country to country. Events such as oil crises and poor and good harvests have varying effects on each country's economy. When external and domestic conditions change and the central banks of individual countries implement independent monetary policies based on separate decisions (not all of which are appropriate), the long-run equilibrium exchange rates are bound to shift. Under such circumstances, it is extremely difficult to maintain a fixed exchange rate over the long run. If long-run stabilization of exchange rates is difficult, then short-run stabilization is also difficult unless capital movements are severely restricted.

Difficulties with the "target zone" approach

People who believe that detrimental effects on domestic economies arise from the high volatility of exchange rates under the floating system have proposed what is called a "target zone" or "reference zone" approach. I believe, however, that under current conditions such an approach is unrealistic. Nowadays, the level of international capital movements has risen to such an extent that firms, individuals, and institutional investors residing in every country hold large amounts of assets, and owe large debts, both denominated in a number of foreign currencies. In view of this, I can find no convincing strategy which will keep the rates in the exchange rate markets within the designated "zone" when these rates reach their upper or lower limit.

Moreover, there is no clear explanation about how to resolve differences between countries over where to set the target zone. The national interests of two countries could easily conflict on this matter. It may be recalled that the old IMF system was constructed extremely skillfully and meticulously with regard to this point.

The best choice given the current situation

In my view, of the above three goals, (1) liberalization, (2) autonomous monetary policies, and (3) stable exchange rates, given the current situation, major countries should clearly choose (1) first, and probably also choose (2). There may be some possibility of effectuating (3), if (2) is somewhat sacrificed. In other words, by pursuing "international coordination" with respect to monetary and other macroeconomic policies among the major industrialized countries, it might be possible to increase exchange rate stability to some extent. I remain highly skeptical, however, about how successful countries will be in achieving international coordination of macroeconomic policies. Moreover, it is difficult to foresee what level of exchange rate stability can be achieved and what degree of autonomy of monetary and fiscal policies will have to be sacrificed in return.

At least in the case of Japan, for example, choosing to stabilize exchange rates at the expense of domestic price stability is definitely not a wise decision. For example, if the Bank of Japan increases the money supply substantially, the appreciation of the yen can possibly be stopped, or the yen may even start depreciating, but there is a high probability that such a policy will give rise to inflation before long.

In conclusion, there seems to be little prospect at the moment for a fundamental reform of the present international monetary system, and especially for a reform of the exchange rate system. Apparently major countries have no choice but to hold on to the current floating system. Even though exchange rates under the floating system are rather volatile, international trade, direct investment, and international lending and borrowing show more vigor nowadays than before the transition to the floating system (see Table 1). This is the result of

Table 1
Trade Dependence of Major Economies[a]: 1962–1985

(%)

	Japan	U.S.	U.K.	F.R.G.	France	E.C.	China
1962	17.9	7.1	30.2	28.4	16.4	30.5	8.8
1970	18.8	8.7	33.5	34.8	20.2	36.6	5.9
1980	26.1	18.5	42.2	46.7	38.3	48.9	15.5
1985	22.5	14.7	44.3	51.3	39.9	51.7	21.9

Source: IMF, *International Financial Statistics*; World Bank (IBRD), *World Bank Atlas*.
[a]Ratio of imports plus exports to GNP.

major industrialized countries choosing (1) and giving up (3). It is hard to believe that changes in exchange rates under the floating system hinder global economic integration significantly more than restrictions on trade and capital movements, which would be necessary under some sort of fixed or "stable" rate system.[2]

III. The Economics of the U.S. Current-Account Imbalance

It appears to me that the rise of protectionism in the U.S. is based on a stylized view of the current U.S. economic situation. The protectionism in the U.S. seems to arise from the perception that the current U.S. economic situation is not satisfactory in many respects and that the difficulties stem from losses the U.S. suffers in international trade and other economic relations. In this section, I will try to discuss six issues: (1) the cause of the current-account imbalance of the U.S. and of Japan, (2) how to evaluate the seriousness of the U.S. current-account imbalance, (3) an assessment of the overall U.S. economic condition, and (4) what steps should be taken to improve the current situation. With regard to these problems, there is a large perception gap between the economists of both nations, on the one hand, and U.S. politicians and journalists as well as dominant public opinion, on the other. There are differences of opinion also among economists, however, in regard to (5) perception of the United States's net foreign investment position and (6) the future of the U.S. dollar.

Evaluation of the current-account imbalance

The U.S. is investing at home more than it is saving as a result of its large government budget deficits, high levels of private investment, and low levels of personal savings. Japan as a whole is saving more than it is investing domestically due to a high level of personal and corporate savings. The large current-account deficit of the U.S. and the large surplus of Japan reflect the macroeconomic situation of these two countries, as outlined above. From a macroeconomic perspective, this is nothing unusual. The size of the current-account deficit of the U.S. or the surplus of Japan relative to these countries' respective GNPs is not particularly large. Even if we look at only OECD member countries in the 1970s and afterwards, we can find many examples of countries which over an extended time period had current-account deficits on a level comparable with, or larger than, that of the current U.S. deficits (see Table 2). From an American point of view, the U.S.

Table 2
Cases of Extended Current Account Deficits[a]

Country	Ratio to GNP (%)	Period (Year)
New Zealand	5.1	1970 – 87
Denmark	3.1	1970 – 87
Greece	5.0	1970 – 87
Iceland	3.8	1970 – 87
Australia	3.3	1970 – 87
Norway	5.5	1970 – 79
Finland	3.8	1972 – 76
Turkey	3.3	1974 – 87
Portugal	5.7	1974 – 84

Source: OECD, *Economic Outlook*.

[a]Examples of countries which had an average ratio of current-account deficit to GNP exceeding 3% for at least 5 years.

current-account deficit is not something to make a great fuss about, although it is quite large from other countries' points of view (compare the list in Table 2).

The striking fact about the current-account deficits of the U.S. and the surpluses of Japan is simply that these two largest economies of the world continuously run large deficits and surpluses. If one considers each of the two countries independently, one finds that their continuing current-account imbalance is not at all a peculiar phenomenon. Although it will not be easy to eliminate or largely reduce the huge current-account imbalance of the U.S. and Japan, the imbalance itself cannot be considered a factor which could lead to a "systemic crisis" in the international trade system. I will offer reasons why this is so.

Whether within a national economy or in a world economy, if economic integration is steadily advancing, and regions within a country or countries within the world are tied more and more closely with each other financially, then interregional capital movements will flourish. It is only natural that international capital moves from countries with excess savings to countries with excess investment, and that the former are accumulating current-account surpluses and the latter current-account deficits.

For 50 years, from 1860 to World War I, Great Britain had an annual average current surplus of about 4% of its GNP. During this period, Great Britain supplied capital all over the world and thus contributed to the growth of underdeveloped countries and regions at that time. Immediately after World War II, U.S. current-account surpluses were also very large. During the periods in which they had record current-account surpluses, both Great Britain and the U.S. had much larger shares of world production than Japan has today.

Relative to the size of the world economy at the time, these countries' current-account surpluses were larger than Japan's present surpluses.

When one looks at the conditions of world economic development today, Japan's current-account surpluses are a very important source of capital supply. From an economic standpoint, it is clearly a mistake to regard Japan's surpluses as a disturbing factor in the world economy.

Since 1982, overall economic conditions in the U.S. have been relatively favorable and sound, in my view. The unemployment rate showed a steady decline from a peak of 10.8% in December 1982 to the mid-5% range by the end of 1988. During this time the U.S. also maintained a relatively high rate of growth. Now the U.S. economy has reached a state of nearly full employment—or, one might say, achieved the natural rate of unemployment. Rises in consumer prices have also declined steadily, to around 4% from more than 10% at the beginning of the 1980s. This condition is partly due to high levels of imports. It is an obvious mistake to believe that the cause of the Japan–U.S. trade imbalance or current-account imbalance lies in the fact that the Japanese domestic market is relatively closed to imports.[3] This can easily be seen from the fact that the bilateral trade balances between the U.S. and nearly all of its major trading partners from 1981 to the present have sharply deteriorated (see Table 3). During this time, there have been a number of countries which have registered relative trade surpluses against the U.S. that are much larger than Japan's surplus in terms of ratio to their GNP.

The U.S. foreign investment position

According to U.S. official statistics, the U.S. net foreign investment position (the difference between U.S. aggregate investments abroad and foreign aggregate investments in the U.S.) was positive for many years but turned negative after 1985 (see Table 3). In view of this, it is said that the U.S. has became a debtor country, and that the debt problem has spread from South and Central America to North America. There is also a growing anxiety in the U.S. that before long the U.S. burden of interest payments on its foreign debt will become rather onerous for the American people. Furthermore, some people think that as the U.S. debt accumulates, there is a possibility of a sharp decline in the dollar exchange rate. Although it would be desirable for the United States to reduce the current-account deficit so as to avoid a precipitous fall into indebtedness, a heavy burden of interest payments for the U.S. is still a very remote possibility, in my opinion. As a matter of fact, the U.S. payments and debt situation is not so urgent as to require immediate and sudden restoration of the current

Table 3
U.S. Bilateral Trade Balance: 1970–1987

(U.S. $ billion)

	1970	1975	1980	1981	1982	1983	1984	1985	1986	1987	1988
World	3.3	4.2	−36.2	−39.6	−42.6	−69.3	−123.3	−148.5	−169.8	−171.2	−139.5
Japan	−1.2	−2.8	−12.2	−18.1	−19.0	−21.7	−36.8	−49.7	−58.6	−59.8	−55.8
Canada	−2.0	−1.0	−6.6	−7.3	−13.1	−14.3	−20.4	−22.2	−23.3	−11.9	−12.2
EC	1.8	5.0	15.7	8.7	3.5	−1.5	−13.3	−22.6	−26.4	−24.3	−12.8
Korea	.3	.2	.3	−.4	−.5	−1.7	−4.0	−4.8	−7.1	−9.9	−9.9
Taiwan	.0	−.5	−3.0	−4.3	−5.2	−7.4	−11.1	−13.1	−15.7	−19.0	−14.1
Hong Kong	−.5	−.9	−2.3	−3.1	−3.4	−4.3	−5.8	−6.2	−6.4	−6.5	−5.1
The 6 ASEAN Countries	.0	−1.5	−4.0	−5.5	−2.1	−4.2	−7.2	−7.5	−6.6	−8.1	−9.0
Central and South America	.9	3.1	4.7	5.4	−3.8	−14.7	−18.0	−17.6	−13.6	−14.9	−11.1
Mexico	3.7	3.5	2.3	3.8	−4.0	−7.9	−6.3	−5.8	−5.2	−5.9	−2.9
Brazil	.2	.0	.3	−1.1	−1.2	−2.8	−5.6	−5.0	−3.5	−4.4	−5.7

Source: U.S. Commerce Dept., Highlights of U. S. Export and Import Trade.

account balance. The current situation is not as aggravated as some people want us to believe.

First, let us examine this problem from the standpoint of the United States's net foreign investment position. U.S. official statistics measure all assets and liabilities in terms of book value. If these statistics were to measure market values, not only the United States's net foreign investment position in 1985 but also that at present would be likely to be positive. This conclusion is consistent with the fact that the difference between receipts and payments in the "investment income" item in the invisibles account of the U.S. balance of payments was still positive in each year between 1985 and 1987 (see Table 3).

According to economic theory, capital stock and income flow correspond to one another. (This idea is expressed, for example, in the concept of "human capital." Education or training which is aimed at obtaining or improving knowledge or skills can be thought of as investment in human capital for the individual or for the nation. Returns from investment in human capital take the form of increases in wages and salaries.) According to this view, receipts of "investment income" exceed payments when U.S. residents' holdings of assets and claims in foreign countries exceed foreigners' holdings of assets and claims in the U.S.

Also according to this view, income from technologies (i.e., patents, royalties, management contracts, copyrights, etc.) is associated with capital assets. Thus, the flow of income from technologies can be thought of as arising from some "intangible" capital stock. The concept of "intangible property" rights reveals the fact that incomes from technologies and other rights come from some sort of capital assets. When these incomes from technologies and other rights are combined with investment incomes, U.S. receipts of investment income still far exceed its payments (see Table 3). If one thinks of the United States's net international investment position in this light, the United States's position is still a large positive figure, and one cannot view the U.S. as a debtor country.[4] It will be some time until U.S. net receipts (receipts minus payments) of investment income plus technologies income become negative.

Secondly, even if the United States's net foreign investment position is now about zero and current account deficits of around 3% of GNP continue for another 10 years, the United States's net international investment position will still be much less than 30% of its GNP. If economic growth during this ten-year period is taken into consideration the ratio of the net negative investment position to the GNP of the U.S. will be in the range of 25–28%. The burden of interest pay-

Table 4
U.S. Foreign Investment Position, Receipts and Payments of Investment Incomes, and Technology and Other Royalties: 1970–1987
(U.S. $ billion)

	Total Assets	Total Debt	Difference	Investment Incomes			Royalties on Technologies etc.		
				Receipts	Payments	Balance	Receipts	Payments	Balance
1970	165.5	106.8	58.6	11.4	5.1	6.2	.6	.1	.4
1975	295.1	221.2	73.9	17.8	11.8	6.0	4.2	.4	3.7
1980	607.1	500.8	106.3	75.9	43.1	32.7	6.8	.7	6.0
1981	719.6	578.7	140.9	85.9	52.9	33.0	7.2	.6	6.5
1982	824.8	688.1	136.7	84.1	56.8	27.3	7.1	.3	6.8
1983	873.5	784.5	89.0	77.0	53.4	23.5	7.8	.4	7.4
1984	895.9	892.6	3.3	87.6	68.5	19.1	8.1	.5	7.5
1985	949.7	1061.1	−111.4	89.9	64.8	25.1	5.8	.8	4.9
1986	1073.7	1341.1	−267.8	88.2	67.3	20.8	6.8	1.0	5.7
1987	116.7	1548.0	−378.3	103.8	83.4	20.4	9.0	1.3	7.7
1988	1253.7	1786.2	−582.5	107.8	105.5	2.2	10.7	2.0	8.7

Sources: Total assets and total debt figures are from *The Economic Report of the President.*
The balance of payments of investment incomes and technology are from the *Survey of Current Business.*

ments on a net debtor position of this magnitude is only a moderate one.[5]

Third, one can subtract fixed capital consumption from the gross domestic capital formation to derive net domestic capital formation in the U.S. national income account. If one then subtracts the current-account deficit from net domestic capital formation, one obtains a figure for annual change in the "net worth" of the U.S. (see Table 4). Although this figure has fallen substantially in recent years, it has remained positive. This figure indicates that the net worth of U.S. citizens as a whole has been increasing every year. When the U.S. current-account balance in the international balance of payments becomes negative, capital funds amounting to that balance are imported from foreign countries. However, capital imports (debt) from foreign countries are used to finance only a portion of U.S. net domestic capital formation.

Financing U.S. current-account deficits
In recent years U.S. current-account deficits have been financed by importing capital from foreign countries. Questions have been raised, however, as to whether this way of financing U.S. current-account deficits can be continued. Fears are entertained in certain circles that with the gradual accumulation of debt owed by the U.S., foreign institutional investors will worry about the possibility of a collapse of the dollar and hesitate to continue to invest in the U.S., especially in the form of portfolio investment in long-term government bonds. In addition, there is anxiety that foreign governments and central banks may reduce the dollar holdings in their official reserves and diversify into assets denominated in other currencies. These developments might result in a situation in which the U.S. would be unable to finance its current-account deficits.

This kind of worry or anxiety is based on a misunderstanding, in my view. It comes from a failure to recognize the peculiar characteristics of the U.S. in the world economy. The U.S. has a special position in the world economy in that its national currency, the dollar, is the key international currency. Almost all U.S. imports and exports of goods and services are denominated and conducted in U.S. dollars. When a country's bilateral current account becomes a surplus vis-à-vis the U.S., its residents as a whole are bound to increase (in the amount of the surplus) their holdings of either liquid or long-term financial assets denominated in dollars. Dollar funds corresponding to the U.S. current-account deficit immediately and automatically flow back to U.S. financial markets. Or more precisely, these funds only circulate within the U.S. banking sector and financial markets, never leaving the U.S. In this way, the U.S. current-account deficit is automatically financed.

When foreign monetary authorities intervene in foreign exchange markets by exchanging foreign currencies for dollars in order to support the U.S. dollar, they invest the dollars that they buy from the exchange market in U.S. treasury bills (and possibly government bonds). Thus, the funds again flow back to the U.S. Some might wonder whether the case might be different if residents of a country (say, Japan) that has a surplus vis-à-vis the U.S. traded dollar-denominated assets for assets denominated in another currency (for instance, German marks) in an effort to diversify the currency composition of their portfolios. This would only mean that now the Germans, instead of the Japanese, would hold the dollar-denominated assets. Moreover, even when residents of a surplus nation purchase U.S. real estate or stocks of U.S. corporations using dollar-denominated liquid assets, dollars automatically return to the U.S. In this case, the U.S. current-account deficit is financed by a capital import of long-term nature. Furthermore, even if U.S. residents borrow funds in financial instruments denominated in currencies other than the U.S. dollar, the dollar funds corresponding to the U.S. current-account deficit still automatically flow back to the U.S.

The fact that even though the current-account deficit continues, all dollar funds automatically return to the U.S. banking sector or financial markets, and the fact that non-residents of the U.S. (foreigners) end up financing the U.S. current-account deficits are special characteristics of the U.S. under the current float system.[6] This is in sharp contrast to the old IMF system or the gold standard, in which flows of private capital movement were limited, and countries with current-account deficits normally had to contract their money supply.

The question of U.S. interest rates

Even though residents of foreign countries automatically finance the U.S. deficit by increasing their investments in the U.S. in an amount precisely equal to that of the U.S. current-account deficit, there still remains the question of how two things will be affected: (1) the U.S. interest rate, especially the long-term interest rate, and (2) the dollar exchange rate. First let us look at the interest rate.

As a result of continued U.S. current-account deficits, the amount of dollar-denominated assets possessed by non-residents of the U.S. rises steadily. This foreign investment itself, however, should not have a significant effect on U.S. interest rates. In my opinion, the percentage of dollar-denominated assets in the U.S. owned by foreigners will remain at a low level in the near future. Moreover, there is no *a priori* reason to suppose that the portfolio preference of non-residents is markedly different from that of residents. Thus, an increase in the proportion of assets held by foreigners should have little effect on the level and the term structure of interest rates in the U.S.

In view of the large depreciation of the dollar since 1985 and the October 1987 stock market crash, there has been a fear that foreign investors, especially Japanese life insurance companies and other institutional investors, will hold back on bidding and investing in long-term U.S. government bonds. If such a retreat takes place, it is feared, U.S. long-term interest rates might rise. Such a fear is entirely unfounded, however. Even if Japanese long-term investors were to refrain from investing in long-term U.S. government bonds, residents of Japan (or non-residents of the U.S.) would make up the difference by acquiring a corresponding amount of liquid dollar-denominated assets. The immediate result would be a rise in long-term interest rates and a decline in short-term interest rates. However, American banks or other financial institutions and intermediaries would, in turn, invest short-term funds in long-term funds. Furthermore, borrowers would shift from borrowing long-term funds to borrowing short-term funds, while those who had surplus funds would shift the funds in the reverse direction. Because short-term and long-term funds are highly substitutable for both borrowers and lenders, if the interest rate gap between long-term and short-term funds were to widen, there would be brisk arbitrage which would work to reduce the gap to the usual level. Consequently, even if Japan's institutional investors were to hold back on investing in long-term U.S. government bonds, it is unlikely that the difference between short- and long-term U.S. interest rates would widen to a noticeable extent.

The possibility of a free-fall of the dollar
There are some people who believe that although dollar-denominated funds amounting to the current-account deficit automatically flow back to the U.S. under the current floating system, if investors, especially non-residents of the U.S., tend more and more to prefer financial assets denominated in currencies other than U.S. dollar, the exchange rate of the dollar vis-à-vis foreign currencies may sooner or later fall as the U.S. accumulates a large amount of debt. There are also people who predict that if the U.S. continues to run current-account deficits, these deficits will sooner or later lead to a "free fall" of the dollar and possibly to its collapse in the exchange market.

According to the theory of portfolio selection, a rise in the percentage of dollar-denominated assets held in the portfolios of non-residents of the U.S. who are normally risk-averse will result in a demand on the part of these investors for a larger risk premium on dollar-denominated assets. It is theoretically plausible that, due to forces such as the pressure of this demand for a larger premium, the dollar will gradually decline in value against foreign currencies.

For the next 5 to 10 years, however, it is hard to believe that the real exchange rate of the U.S. dollar, apart from its nominal exchange rate, will fall by a large margin due to this risk premium factor. It is even harder to believe that this effect or other forces will cause a sudden collapse of the dollar. The most important reason for dismissing both of these possibilities is that, at present, there are no currencies which can replace the dollar as the key currency of the world trading system. No currency is more widely used as the vehicle currency for merchandise and invisibles trading and is better supported by extensive and efficient long- and short-term financial markets than the U.S. dollar. Compared with the dollar, other major currencies have been, and are at present, subject to more extensive exchange controls and financial regulations for both residents and non-residents. In these respects, the present situation differs greatly from the period during which the dollar gradually replaced the British pound sterling. When the pound was devalued in 1949 for the first time since World War II, over 70% of world trade was invoiced in pounds, but the U.S. dollar, as compared with the pound sterling, already possessed several characteristics of a superior international currency. Its value over the long run had been more stable than that of the pound sterling, and it had not been much subject to exchange controls. In contrast to the period immediately after World War II, at present there is no candidate capable of replacing the dollar in the near future.

In addition, if the real exchange rate of the dollar falls substantially against foreign currencies, residents of foreign countries will buy stocks of American corporations and real estate in the U.S.. This investment flow will support the value of the dollar.

Finally, the decline in the real exchange rate of the U.S. dollar over the long run will work to improve the U.S. balance of payments on current account. Then the very real problem of U.S. debt accumulation will come under control, and the situation will improve.[7]

Effective measures to reduce the U.S. trade deficit

Obviously, it is not wise for the U.S. to let its current-account deficit accumulate without limit. The U.S. deficit must be reduced in the near future to a level within acceptable limits. An effective means to this end would be the use of macroeconomic policy. The U.S. must use its own monetary, budgetary, and tax policies to control total domestic expenditure ("absorption") and increase total savings, thereby improving the U.S. savings–investment balance. If such steps are not taken, even if U.S. trading partners lower tariff and non-tariff barriers against imports from the U.S. and let their currencies drastically appreciate, the U.S. current-account deficit will change little. The only change will be in the level and composition of U.S. imports and exports in terms of the kinds of goods and services traded and the countries of destination or origin.

U.S. net foreign indebtedness, and the annual excess of U.S. aggregate investment over aggregate savings, are respectively equal to the sum of the net debts incurred by all economic units in the United States (all U.S. households, firms, and the federal and local governments), and the sum of the annual excess investment over savings of every individual economic unit. In order to reduce the U.S. current-account deficit, the savings and investment balance of these economic entities must be improved. Since investment in the business sector and in infrastructure will contribute to the expansion of productive capacity and improved productivity, generally speaking, reducing investment in these areas may not be wise. In improving the savings and investment balance in the U.S. economy, it is most important that the savings and investment balance of the government sector be improved—that is, that the budget deficit be reduced. It is probably imperative that the U.S. Administration and Congress cooperate to raise taxes and reduce federal spending. Furthermore, it is also probably necessary and desirable to improve the savings and investment balance in the household sector by raising the household savings rate and reducing investment (residential construction) through tax reforms and other measures.

When we think about the future of the U.S. economy, the rate of net U.S. domestic capital formation and the rate of increase in U.S. net worth are perhaps at too low levels in comparison with those of Japan (see Table 5). The U.S. must raise these levels and accelerate domestic capital formation. It is hoped that, by moderating its accumulation of foreign debt, the U.S. will soon make sure that the level of its current-account deficit and foreign debt are kept within acceptable limits relative to GNP.

The U.S. government has often asked foreign governments to pursue macroeconomic policies that will help reduce the U.S. current-account deficit. However, this is not only asking too much of foreign nations;

Table 5
Ratios of U.S. Capital Formation to GNP^a

	Gross Domestic Capital Formation (A)	Depreciation Allowances and Other Capital Consumption (B)	Net Domestic Capital Formation C (A-B)	Current Account Surplus (or Deficit) (D)	U.S. Net Asset Increase E (C+D)
1970	14.6	8.7	5.9 (22.3)	0.2	6.1 (23.6)
1975	13.7	10.1	3.6 (19.6)	1.1	4.7 (19.7)
1980	16.0	11.1	4.9 (18.8)	0.1	4.9 (17.9)
1981	16.9	11.4	5.5 (17.5)	0.2	5.7 (18.3)
1982	14.1	12.1	2.0 (16.2)	-0.3	1.7 (17.0)
1983	14.7	11.6	3.1 (14.6)	-1.4	1.7 (16.3)
1984	17.6	11.0	6.6 (14.2)	-2.8	3.6 (17.0)
1985	16.0	10.9	5.1 (14.0)	-2.9	2.1 (17.4)
1986	15.6	10.8	4.7 (13.6)	-3.1	1.6 (17.7)
1987	15.5	10.8	4.7 (14.6)	-3.2	1.5 (17.8)
1988	15.4	10.5	4.8 (16.1)	-2.6	1.2 (18.4)

Sources: Economic Report of the President.
^{a}U.S. capital formation covers the private sector only. Figures in parentheses in columns C and E are Japan's ratios, including the government sector, for reference, from EPA, Kokumin Keizai Keisan Nenpo (Yearbook for National Income Accounting).

it is also largely meaningless. Every nation has its own macroeconomic policy goals, and it must use its own macroeconomic measures to achieve them. Moreover, every country faces political limitations on the use of macroeconomic policies.

Furthermore, many simulation studies based upon macroeconomic models indicate that favorable "cross effects"—that is, the favorable effects the macroeconomic measures of any one country, say Japan or West Germany, have on macroeconomic targets (such as unemployment and inflation rates, current-account balance, or budget deficit) of another country, say the U.S.—are very small compared with "own effects"—the effects caused by macroeconomic measures of the country itself. For example, when Japan or West Germany expands its domestic demand, this has only a very small effect on U.S. employment, the U.S. current-account balance, or the U.S. government budget deficit.

In order to improve the current-account deficit, it is imperative that the U.S. use its own macroeconomic policy effectively to correct the balance between aggregate expenditure and aggregate output—that is, the balance between aggregate investment and aggregate savings. Without such measures, one cannot expect an improvement in the U.S. current-account deficit.

Improvement in industrial and trade policies
In the areas of industrial and trade policies, it appears to me that it is not wise for the U.S. to pursue current policies which protect domestic industries and firms by imposing import barriers (including voluntary export restraints which the U.S. urged its trade partners to take) for quite a few industries such as all kinds of textiles, steel, automobiles, electronics, semiconductors, and machine tools. Under protectionist policy regimes, profits and wages tend to be inappropriately high. As a result, firms are inclined to neglect improving productivity, and technological progress is often retarded. The U.S. should take steps to remove its protectionist import barriers with the intention of eliminating them soon. It should revive active competition in its domestic market and accelerate revitalization and restructuring of domestic industries and the relocation of the labor force.

IV. Political Conditions Contributing to the Threat of a "Systemic Crisis"

As discussed in the previous section, U.S. economic conditions since the early 1980s have been largely favorable, and U.S. economic performance has been not at all unsatisfactory. The major problems, as I see them, are too high a level of domestic expenditure and the fall in the savings rate, the low level of net domestic capital formation, the large deficit of the balance of payment on current account, and the large government budget deficit. The accumulation of external debt which has accompanied the current-account deficit is far from a level that should cause concern. Nevertheless, since the early 1980s a strong protectionist movement centered around the U.S. Congress has gained power, and this movement has been creating the threat of a systemic crisis in the world trading system.

If the U.S. Congress legislates protectionist trade laws, the U.S. will begin to deviate from the basic rules of the world trading system. There is a great danger that, as such a situation progresses, other countries and regions, especially the EC, might succumb to similar pressures. If this reaction were to occur, barriers to free trade would rise in many countries and proliferate. Violations of, as well as deviations from, the basic rules of the game of the world trading system would become more frequent.

If trade barriers introduced by protectionism and deviations from the basic rule of the game of the world trading system continue to expand beyond tolerable limits, some incident could lead to a breakdown of the basic framework of the world trading system. At this point the "systemic crisis" would become a reality.

The sources of dissatisfaction within the U.S.

The rise of the protectionist movement in the United States may be directly attributable to the rise in U.S. imports since the 1970s, the large-scale U.S. trade and current-account deficits after 1983, and the difficulties in reducing these deficits.[8] The threat of a systemic crisis, however, has been raised mainly by the rise of protectionism within the U.S. Congress. In this particular form of protectionism, I believe that misunderstandings, misperceptions, and feelings of frustration among the public as well as politicians have played important roles.

First, looking at the economics behind the policies undertaken in order to improve the trade deficit, one sees that protectionists have not properly evaluated the current U.S. economic situation, nor understood correctly the causes of the current-account deficit, especially the United States's bilateral deficits vis-à-vis Japan and the East Asian countries. Perhaps some people are using these misunderstandings and illusions for their own political purposes. If American economists could publicize the correct interpretation of the current U.S. economic situation as well as the proper economics to deal with the U.S. balance of payments deficit, then U.S. protectionist rumblings could be stilled considerably.

Second, it appears to me that the U.S. public feels frustrated and discontent with the relative decline in the United States's dominant economic position over the last 40 years as well as the relative rise of Japan. The U.S. bilateral trade balance over the last 10 years has greatly worsened with almost every one of its major trade partners. Despite the fact that relative to their respective GNPs, Canada, Mexico, ASEAN, Korea, Taiwan, and several others have often registered larger trade surpluses vis-à-vis the U.S. than Japan (see Table 3), Japan has borne the brunt of the attacks of protectionists in the U.S., especially in Congress. This is partly because Japanese industries in "key" sectors, such as steel, automobiles, electronics, and machine tools, have been able to achieve superior competitive positions relative to the U.S. industries. In the past, these were industries in which the U.S. competitive advantage had never been challenged. Those that are brought to an inferior position in open competition often question whether their opponents did not do something "unfair."

The American people psychologically do not want to accept the relative decline in the U.S. economic position in the world, the relative rise of Japan over the past 40 years, the decrease in the gap in productivity and technological sophistication between the two countries, and the reversals of dominance in some sectors.

Intertwined, in a delicate and complex way, with the above psychology is the fact that the burden of the U.S. defense budget is quite onerous, whereas that of Japan is very light in terms of defense expenditure relative to GNP.

Third, there is a widespread misperception that Japan's domestic markets are not quite open. It is difficult to measure objectively the relative degrees of openness or closedness of the U.S. or Western European markets. There is no doubt, however, that Japan's markets for both goods and services and for finance and foreign exchange transactions are much more open today than they were in the 1970s. At the same time, the U.S. current account and trade account were more or less balanced in the latter half of the 1970s. It is clear, therefore, that the closedness of Japanese markets cannot logically be claimed to be the "cause" of increases in U.S. current-account deficits.

There are various fragmentary pieces of information and anecdotes which tend to indicate that Japanese markets are more closed than U.S. and West European ones. There are other fragmentary pieces of information and anecdotes, however, that tend to substantiate the opposite claim—that Japanese markets are more *open* than U.S. and European ones. These stories do not possess much persuasive power. The following facts would suggest that the level of openness of Japan's domestic markets is roughly on par with that of the other major industrialized countries including the U.S.

After 1985, with the very large appreciation of the yen, imports of manufactured products to Japan rose very sharply. Imports of manufactured products from countries and areas such as the EC, Korea, and Taiwan more than doubled between 1985 and 1987 (see Table 6). That a price change can cause such a dramatic increase in imports to Japan indicates that Japan's domestic market is sufficiently open.

Another piece of evidence is an index which represents an evaluation of environments for business activities by foreign enterprises. This index is prepared periodically by an American business consultant based on the evaluations of a panel consisting of about 100 businessmen. Based on this index, out of 50 countries for which evaluation is made, in recent years Japan has always been ranked number 2 in openness behind Switzerland. In this ranking, for most years West Germany was rated third, the United States fourth, the U.K. around seventh, and France around twelfth to thirteenth. From these data alone, one cannot definitely conclude that Japan's domestic markets are more open to foreign companies than those of the U.S. and the U.K., but it would be fair to say that this evaluation indicates a fairly high degree of openness of the Japanese market for foreign firms. According to well-informed businessmen who operate in Japan, such as those on the above panel, the Japanese market is a "difficult" one for foreigners because of the language, the differences in culture and social customs, etc. These businessmen evaluated it, however, as a market at least as open as, and perhaps more open than, the domestic markets of other major industrialized countries.

Table 6
Increase in Imports of Manufactured Products to Japan (% increase over the previous year)

(%)

	U.S.	E.C.	Asian NIEs	Korea	Taiwan	ASEAN	Total
1986	23.9	59.7	37.2	39.4	33.8	12.6	31.4
1987	0.2	26.7	56.0	63.0	62.6	47.8	25.0
1988	33.2	37.1	46.4	55.9	38.5	48.9	39.2
1989	19.5	16.7	12.4	12.4	8.2	44.8	15.5

Source: Ministry of Finance, *Gaikoku Boeki Gaikyo* (*Foreign Trade Summary*.)

The politicization of protectionism

Dissatisfaction, frustration, misunderstandings, and misperceptions regarding the causes of difficulties in domestic and international economic affairs exist to a greater or lesser extent in every country. Moreover, protectionism is often an effective means to obtain the support of the electorate in most parliamentary democracies.

In countries other than the U.S., however, the political impact of protectionist movements is more limited, and thus probably will not expand to generate a threat to the world trading system. The threat of a systemic crisis which is embodied in protectionist movements in the U.S. can be attributed to three peculiar characteristics of U.S. international economic relations. These characteristics are described in the next section.

Peculiar characteristics of U.S. international economic relations

1. Being the key currency country. The first peculiar characteristic of U.S. international economic relations arises from the fact that the U.S. dollar is "the" key currency of the world trading system. It is used all over the world as a vehicle currency, a standard of value, and a reserve currency. The status of the dollar as the key currency under both the old IMF system and the present float system stems not from any special legal arrangement in international agreements, but entirely from economic conditions. The special position of the dollar as the key currency is based upon its superior convertibility (absence of exchange controls), long-term stability (over the past 50 to 100 years) of value vis-à-vis goods and services, and the existence of well-developed financial markets for dollar-denominated funds. This last factor is a result partly of the large size of the U.S. economy and partly of good management by U.S. financial authorities. The greatest singularity that arises from the use of the U.S. dollar as the worldwide key currency is that nearly all the United States's international trade and capital movements are conducted in U.S. dollars, and that U.S. current-account deficits have no potential to give rise to difficulties for the U.S. in international settlements, even if they result in cumulative deficits. Consequently, no pressure arises from within the country to improve its own current account.

Countries other than the U.S. keep official international reserves consisting mainly of dollar-denominated liquid assets which can be readily used for international settlements. While one might point out that in recent years proportions of German marks and Japanese yen in the official reserves of various countries have gradually increased, the U.S. dollar is still predominant as a reserve currency. Currencies other than the dollar such as the German mark, Swiss franc, Japanese yen, and the ECU have become more widely used in merchandise and invisible trade and in the issuance of international bonds. However, the U.S. dollar is still predominant as vehicle, reserve, and intervention currency. When a country other than the United States accumulates current-account deficits, except in the case in which there is a steady inflow of long-term capital, the country's official international reserves are reduced. In such a case, the country will have to change its macroeconomic policy in order to improve the current account and/or to look for short-term financing from the IMF or elsewhere. The IMF then asks the deficit country's government to tighten its monetary and fiscal policy so as to reduce the current-account deficit and turn it into surplus within a few years.

In the case of the U.S., however, even though large current-account deficits persist, short- and long-term capital funds denominated in dollars flow into the U.S. Thus, the U.S. faces no difficulty in international settlement. Moreover, since almost all of U.S. trade, investment, and financial transactions are carried out in its own currency, fluctuations of the dollar exchange rate cause relatively little immediate inconvenience to U.S. firms. Today, as the dollar is no longer convertible to gold, there is no need for the U.S. government to borrow funds from the IMF. Thus, even if the U.S. current-account deficit continues and some knowledgeable people feel the need to improve the U.S. balance of payments on current account, pressures to change macroeconomic management and thus impove the balance of payments— pressures which would arise sooner or later in other countries—do not arise from within the U.S. Hence there is no chance for the IMF to make strong demands on the U.S. to tighten monetary and fiscal policy.

There is a remarkable asymmetry here. The U.S. has the largest quota in the IMF and thus has the largest voting power. When countries such as the U.K., France, and Italy in the past, and Brazil, Mexico, and Argentina more recently experience large current-account deficits, the IMF advises and/or requests that these countries tighten their fiscal and monetary policy and improve their balance of payments. When the IMF asks a country to take a stringent macroeconomic policy, there are usually strong dissatisfaction and adverse reactions within the country, but the deficit country has no choice but to more or less follow what the IMF dictates. For the U.S., however, especially now that gold convertibility has been abolished, because it possesses and issues the key currency, this sort of pressure does not operate. The IMF has no chance to intervene.

There are some people who assert that in the present float system, the mechanism to adjust current-account imbalances and recover balance of payments equilibria is lacking or that such equilibriating power is extremely weak. Such an assertion is, however, missing the mark since under both the old IMF system and the present float system, the basic mechanism for recovering the balance of payment equilibrium is such that the country which runs into a balance of payments disequilibrium tries to get out of it by undertaking an appropriate change in its own macroeconomic policy. In this way, the country that has developed a current-account imbalance has also been eliminating the imbalance.

When countries other than the U.S. wish to improve or eliminate their current-account deficits, improvement is achieved primarily through those countries own macroeconomic policies. Of all the countries that have had large current-account deficits, the U.S. is the only country that has severely criticized surplus countries and demanded through bilateral negotiations that surplus countries take macroeconomic measures which it is thought will contribute to reducing the U.S. deficit. Here, too, recent trends in the U.S. seem to be quite peculiar.

2. U.S. Congressional disregard of GATT. The second peculiar aspect of U.S. international economic relations is that, due to certain complicated circumstances at the time of the conclusion of GATT, the U.S. Congress did not ratify or in any way approve GATT as an international agreement, while the legislatures of most other member countries have approved GATT as an international agreement, giving it a status comparable to that of an international treaty. Since then the U.S. Congress has, in general, taken the position that GATT can be ignored. In the U.S. the legal status of GATT thus remains no more than an administrative agreement signed by the President on his responsibility as head of the executive branch.

For this reason, in the U.S. during periods of heightened protectionism since the 1960s, a large number of bills that clearly violate GATT have been introduced in the Congress, such as the Burke-Hartke Bill, the so-called Local Content Bills, the "Reciprocity" Trade Bill, and various protectionist articles of recent trade bills. The U.S. is the only member country of GATT whose legislature has behaved in such a manner.

This sort of thing is made possible by the character of the U.S. governmental system. In a parliamentary system like that of Britain or Japan, the Cabinet must be supported by the majority of the legislature (Diet or Parliament) in order to continue in office, whereas in the U.S. presidential system, major policy disagreements between the Administration and the legislature can exist and continue indefinitely.

In addition, treaties have a different status in the two systems. Under Japan's Constitution, international treaties ratified by the Diet take legal precedence over laws legislated by the Diet, so that the Diet cannot enact a domestic law that violates international treaties already ratified. In the U.S., on the other hand, treaties ratified by the Senate have the same legal status as domestic laws, so that the most recently ratified treaties or laws take legal precedence over prior treaties and laws. Thus, if a law is passed that conflicts with a previously ratified treaty, the more recent law takes precedence. In this way the U.S. Congress can unilaterally alter or even withdraw from international treaties without the consent of its foreign partners, insofar as the domestic legal status of the treaty is concerned. However, the U.S. Congress is usually cautious and prudent in legislating domestic laws that conflict with international treaties that have been previously ratified. In the case of GATT, the serious problem from a foreigner's point of view is that the U.S. Congress does not even treat GATT as constituting "existing law."

3. U.S. bargaining power. The third peculiarity that characterizes recent U.S. international economic relations is the fact that the U.S. has strong bargaining power in its bilateral negotiations, and does exercise it. The U.S. government can conduct bilateral negotiations to obtain concessions from other countries, citing the threat of protectionist sentiment in its Congress. In this way, the U.S. government has been successful in obtaining concessions—often unilaterally— through bilateral negotiations. Other countries, on the other hand, generally do not have much negotiating leverage vis-à-vis the U.S., and can do little even when the U.S. violates an important international agreement, as it did when the old IMF system collapsed. The following three cases exemplify the powerful bargaining power of the U.S.

1. It is debatable whether the Japan–U.S. semiconductor agreement, which was concluded in response to the strong demands of the U.S. government, included major violations of GATT. Few would disagree, however, that the retaliatory measures unilaterally taken by the U.S. government in response to an alleged violation of the agreement by Japan, in the form of a 100% tariff on goods which have no connection at all with semiconductors, was a clear violation of GATT. In view of the United States's strong negotiating position in this matter, the other country (in this case Japan) could not take effective countermeasures.

2. Recently the U.S. government, claiming that Brazilian computer software policy was unfair and hurt the interests of U.S. industry, demanded that the Brazilian government legislate to protect computer software copyrights. During the negotiation with Brazil, the U.S. government announced that it would institute an import embargo on 66 Brazilian products such as leather shoes and automobiles and raise import tariffs on Brazilian products, all unrelated to computer software, unless Brazil conceded on the software issue. At first Brazil resisted, but it finally gave in to the U.S. demands and enacted a new law on computer software copyrights. Had the U.S. actually implemented these types of import restrictions and raised tariff rates against Brazil based on the software copyright issue, its action would clearly be in violation of GATT. But because the Brazilian government did not want to risk losing the U.S. market for its industries, it decided to give in.

3. Korea's net indebtedness to foreign countries exceeded 50% of its GNP at its peak (1984–1985). It still probably exceeds 30% of Korean GNP. Between 1981 and 1983, after the second oil crisis, and especially in 1982, when Mexico's debt problem became acute, Korea experienced considerable difficulty in rolling over foreign borrowing. Consequently, the Korean government has understandably tried to reduce its foreign indebtedness at a fairly rapid pace, while its balance of payments on current account is favorable as it has been in the last two years or so—for the first time since the founding of the country. The U.S. government considers, however, that one of the "causes" of the U.S. current-account deficit is the undervalued currencies of Asian NIEs, including the Korean won. The U.S. government has been urging the Korean government to appreciate its currency.

As we saw in the previous section, while U.S. current-account balance deficits have been quite large in recent years, its net international investment position is probably positive, and even if it is negative the level of U.S. indebtedness to foreign countries is still at a very low level relative to GNP. U.S. indebtedness will continue to be much lower than the present Korean level, even if the present level of U.S. current-account deficits relative to GNP continues for another five or even ten years.

It is not advisable—I would even say it is unfair—to demand that such a small country as Korea (Korea's GNP is less than 1/45th that of the U.S.), which very recently experienced much difficulty in refinancing its debt, refrain from lowering the level of its foreign indebtedness simply in order to improve the United States's current-account imbalance. Because Korea is heavily dependent on the U.S. both militarily and economically, however, Korea seems to have no choice but to comply to some extent with the U.S. request that it appreciate its currency.

The strong bargaining position of the U.S. government in bilateral international economic relations, as we have seen in these examples, is based upon three factors, in my opinion: (1) On a purely economic level, the U.S. possesses a large domestic market for imports and well-developed financial markets. Foreign countries do not want to be even partially excluded from them. (2) In a number of cases the U.S. has undertaken economic sanctions against a country on economic, political, or military grounds. (3) The U.S. has overwhelming political and military superiority. These three conditions are not expected to change in near future.

Responsibility for the threat of a systemic crisis

The threat of a systemic crisis to the world trading system with GATT and the IMF at its center is not caused by the current-account imbalance between Japan and the U.S., the two largest economies in the system. Nor is it caused by the relative decline in importance or status of the U.S., which has been the leading member of the system, or by worsened economic conditions in the U.S. The main factor that threatens to lead to a systemic crisis is U.S. protectionism and politicization of trade issues, which are based on misperceptions and misunderstandings—or attempts to exploit misunderstandings—of U.S. current-account (or trade) deficits.

I want to stress, however, that the above should not be construed as asserting that the world trading system is in danger because the U.S. is behaving "badly" or that it is the U.S. that is "at fault." What I have offered thus far is essentially an objective analysis of facts and some proposals to improve the current situation. I have not discussed the situation in terms of "good guys" and "bad guys"; nor have I called anyone "responsible" for the difficulties the world trading system is now encountering.

"Good guys" and "bad guys" cannot be discussed without premises, which include strong value judgments. Even among economists, there are quite a few who condemn and acclaim bad guys and good guys, but there is not much to be gained from such discussions. Moreover, when people discuss who or which countries are "responsible" for certain things, what kind of "responsibility" are they talking about? Is it moral responsibility, political responsibility, or legal responsibility? Of these responsibilities—or "goods" or "bads"—the only one that can be discussed more or less objectively is legal responsibility. Thus, for the problems of international economic affairs such as those dealt with here, "responsibility" refers only to the objective criterion of responsibility under international law. Other kinds of responsibility or "goods" and "bads" cannot be discussed without clearly setting premises which belong to the domain of ethics or religion. Without defining the criteria according to which the judgement is made, the discussion will be unscientific and have no relation to economics as a science.

For what has already occurred, discussions of responsibility, or "goods" and "bads," are not very useful. We should talk about what kinds of actions are possible or desirable. In the next section, I would like to discuss from Japan's perspective what is possible and desirable in order to avoid a systemic crisis of the international trading system.

V. Concluding Remarks: The Future of the World Trading System and Japan's Role

As discussed in the previous sections, the threat of a systemic crisis in the world trading system now appears to be emerging. If this threat develops into a real crisis, it will bring about great losses for most countries participating in the world trading system, especially those that are heavily dependent on international trade.

Although GATT has been subject to some serious erosions in recent years, its fundamental rules are based upon a high degree of economic rationality. In the ongoing Uruguay Round, member countries, including the U.S., have proposed a number of important issues to be included in the agenda. Yet no proposal has been made which tries to modify the basic principles of GATT. Although no country is satisfied with all the aspects of current world trading arrangements, apparently the best choice for all nations is to cooperate in developing the system and working to improve it.

As discussed in the third section, it is unlikely that the current international monetary system can be changed greatly. The most advisable course for all countries that actively participate in the world trading and currency systems is to support and defend the current system and work together for its stable growth and gradual improvement and development.

The need for self-restraint by the U.S.

What is by far most necessary in order to alleviate the threat of a "systemic crisis" is self-restraint on the part of the U.S., particularly politicians and high-ranking officials in the Congress, the Administration, and the office of the U.S. Trade Representative (USTR).

The economic benefits that the U.S. receives from the world trading system are enormous. The political gains that accrue to the U.S. as the foremost leader of the world trading system are immeasurable. The idea that the U.S. is now suffering losses by participating in the world trading system and from international economic relations is entirely wrong. The U.S. is among the countries that gain the most from the present arrangements. Reducing the efficiency and ability of the system to work or disturbing and upsetting the system can only be detrimental to the national interest of the U.S. The United States will benefit most from faithfully observing its duties as a member of GATT and by assuming a leadership role in the stable development of the world trading system.

Some U.S. economists have told me that they fundamentally agree with my evaluation of the current U.S. economic condition and economic analyses of the causes of U.S. trade deficits and with the measures I propose for overcoming the present difficulties (cf. Section III of this paper). They say that U.S. politicians, however, will never agree with these economic arguments. If such is the case, then the threat of a "systemic crisis" comes from the failure of American economists to persuade and educate politicians and opinion leaders. Thus, the situation should be called an "education failure." Major industrialized countries should unite in requesting that the U.S. honor its obligations as a member country of GATT and the IMF. If the U.S. intends to reduce its current-account or trade deficit, then it ought itself to implement effective macroeconomic measures for that purpose.

Japan's international economic relations and political economy

Since the 1950s the rate of growth of industrial productivity in Japan has been extremely high, and Japan's relative importance in the international economic community has risen quickly. In a short period of time Japan moved from being a triflingly small country to being the second-ranked economic power in the world trading system. Japan is one of the countries that has gained the most from the world trading system, and it will continue to do so. Clearly, without current world trade arrangements, Japan's economic growth could not have occurred and would probably cease.

If the world trading system were to break down or disintegrate as a result of a systemic crisis, Japan, which is an island country and unaffiliated with any particular regional bloc, would suffer far more than the U.S. and the West European countries, which are either continental or have close relationships with their neighbors in the EC.

The Japanese economy has been developing very rapidly since the 1950s. As a result, Japan has not been able to keep pace in adjusting to the new situation. In terms of domestic economic configurations, institutional arrangements regarding international economic relations, people's perceptions, and social customs, Japan has not caught up with its changing status in the world economy. As far as international economic relations are concerned, Japan's ability to negotiate is not yet at a level commensurate with its new status in the world trading system. Neither is Japan's voice in the international economic community commensurate with its relative economic size, or with the percentage of funds it supplies for world economic development: for example, Japan's quotas in the IMF and IBRD are still smaller than those of Britain and France, not to speak of West Germany.

In the last 20 years or so, the Japanese government has made strenuous efforts to lower trade barriers, increase the openness of its domestic markets, and make domestic economic institutions harmonious with liberal and multilateral international economic relations. In the last decade these efforts have accelerated. However, the residues of numerous protectionist regulations of the past still remain, left over from older times when Japan was economically weak. It cannot be denied that these regulations tend to constitute barriers to the healthy development of Japan's international economic relations.

In Japan, an important problem in this regard is that marketplace rules and regulations are rather opaque. There are cases where the details of rules and regulations are not clear or easy to understand even for Japanese economists. It is important that, in addition to renovating rules and regulations so that they are harmonious with liberal and multilateral international economic relations, such rules and regulations be made as clear as possible to promote international understanding.

The problem of agricultural imports

One event that demonstrates how perceptions of the Japanese government and people are lagging behind the rapid economic progress that has taken place in Japan over the past 40 years is a ruling by a GATT panel in 1987 that Japan's restrictions on agricultural imports are in violation of the GATT Articles. Japan has enjoyed enormous benefits from the present world trading system and must now play a leadership role as the world's second largest economic power. Nevertheless, Japan has allowed itself to be found in violation of GATT rules.

Here I would like to present my view on the liberalization of agricultural trade in Japan. In 1956, 40% of Japan's population was engaged in agriculture. Today that percentage has fallen to a meager 6 to 7%, the majority of whom are people over 50 years of age. However, a great proportion of the voting public has some connection to agriculture. A majority of urban residents were either born in rural communities, are only one generation removed from farming families, or have relatives in rural communities. Thus, a great many people are strongly sympathetic to farmers. Furthermore, the policymakers who are responsible for Japan's current agricultural policies still have vivid memories of severe food shortages and the hunger during and after World War II.

Japanese agriculture and agricultural communities have undergone great economic and social changes over the past 30 years. In the process, both farming and non-farming populations have become much richer and more conservative. Now neither of these populations desire further changes in either agriculture or rural communities.

The strong political support for agricultural protectionism in Japan stems from both historical experience and current political conditions. It is not only the rural-based Liberal Democratic Party that opposes the liberalization of agricultural imports; the opposition parties, although they draw most of their support from urban areas, are even more strongly opposed to liberalization.

Trade in agricultural products is quite different from that in other goods or manufactures in that long-run price elasticity of supply is extremely high, whereas short-run elasticity is very low. At the time of short-run supply shortages and consequent supply and demand imbalances, the elasticity of export supply is nearly zero until the next harvest somewhere in the world. Importing countries are thus unable to obtain urgently needed supplies. In 1973, when the U.S. laid an embargo on the export of soybeans because of rising domestic feed grain prices, even soybeans that had been already contracted for and were waiting at American ports were not loaded onto ships. The Japanese were forced to learn about this peculiar aspect of agricultural trade through a rather rude and bitter awakening.

Japan is now by far the world's largest importer of foodstuffs, domestically producing only 30% of the grain it consumes. There are no other countries with a self-sufficiency ratio as low as Japan's, at least among countries with a fairly large population. Japan's attempt to maintain a minimum level of domestic supply in foodstuffs is similar to the United States's attempt in recent years to achieve self-sufficiency in energy. Even from a purely economic viewpoint, such a policy is not necessarily irrational. With the above points in mind, it is easy to understand why a complete and unconditional laissez-faire policy on Japan's agricultural imports is not advisable.

On the other hand, the desire to shield domestic producers from the impact of international competition which would result from liberalization of agricultural imports cannot be a valid reason to justify the continuation of import restrictions on a permanent basis. This is especially so in the case of agricultural products which have no value or only a limited value as essential foodstuffs. If other countries used similar arguments to justify quantitative import restrictions, the GATT system would collapse. One of the methods of maintaining security in the supply of foodstuffs would be to insure that domestic production remains above a certain level. This goal could be achieved, for example, by establishing a system such as a deficiency payment system for producers. Japan would thus be able to preserve at least a minimum domestic supply capacity without infringing upon the GATT rules. It would also be desirable to establish a stockpiling scheme, such as the one which has long been practiced by Switzerland or Sweden, to insure a supply of a number of essential foodstuffs.

A number of aspects of the current GATT regulations regarding agriculture are in need of revision. Examples are the lack of consideration given to countries with a high degree of import dependence and the toleration of agricultural export subsidies.[9] While the Japanese government should reform its food and agricultural policies to conform with GATT regulations, it is obvious that there is also a need to improve the agriculture-related articles.

The outlook for Japan–U.S. trade "friction"

Will the present threat of a "systemic crisis" in the world trading system develop into a full-blown crisis? Or will the threat of crisis gradually subside? On this point I prefer to be relatively optimistic.

There have been recent signs of a cooling off of protectionist sentiment in the U.S., perhaps as countervailing powers have worked to restrain more extreme protectionism. Japan's current-account surplus, which some (or perhaps most) Americans, and even some Japanese, have mistakenly regarded as the "root of all evil," has recently been declining quite remarkably, after showing strong J-curve effects stemming from the sharp appreciation of the yen since 1985. Japan's current-account surplus as a percentage of GNP, after peaking at 4.9% in the second quarter of 1987, fell rapidly to 3.3–3.6% in the latter half of 1987. This figure will likely fall below 3.0% in 1988. I consider the basic causes of the U.S. current-account deficit to be its excessive aggregate domestic demand, caused by large budget deficits and a low level of private savings. Policymakers, intellectuals, and opinion leaders in the U.S. are now gradually coming to recognize that in order to solve the trade problem it is definitely necessary to improve the macroeconomic performance of the U.S. economy.

While imbalances in international payments between major industrialized countries will not disappear in the near future, and friction in trade and other international economic affairs will continue, the probability that these imbalances and cases of friction will trigger a "systemic crisis" is gradually decreasing.

The future of the world trading system

As discussed in the preceding section, one of the background conditions that has given rise to the threat of a systemic crisis is Japan's challenge to the once-overwhelming predominance of the U.S. economy and its industries. The U.S.–Japan relationship cannot be understood, however, in terms of a relationship between a "hegemon" nation and a "challenger" nation. In this respect the U.S.–Japan relationship is entirely different from the relationship that once prevailed between the U.S. and Britain or, going further back in history, the relationship between the Netherlands, Spain, and Britain. Japan's challenge to U.S. predominance is limited to only certain "economic" areas, such as productivity and technology in a limited number of industries. In other areas Japan is in no position to challenge the U.S. Japan lags behind the U.S. not only in military and political power, but also in basic science and research, and in academic learning in general. In fact, in these fields Japan relies heavily upon the U.S.

Japan is an island trading nation, and, as was revealed at the time of the oil crises or the U.S. embargo on soybean exports, Japan is more vulnerable even in a purely economic sense than a continental country like the U.S., the Soviet Union, or China. Britain was able to achieve global hegemony as an island nation because it had a strong navy and control of the seas. Such power enabled Britain to maintain an empire with colonies all over the world. In the case of Japan, such an option is simply out of the question today.

There is a view that the current world trading system has up to now been supported by what is called the "Pax Americana," and that because the economic power of the U.S. has "declined," it is no longer able to support the Pax Americana system. It is feared that the system is nearing its end and that cases of friction and disruption will increase, leading eventually to a "systemic crisis." This view, however, is fundamentally mistaken on a number of points.

While the U.S. has maintained its overwhelmingly superior political and military position relative to other countries of the Western alliance, and the U.S. continues to exercise leadership in these areas, this has not always been the case in the economic realm, especially with regard to the world trading system centered around GATT and the IMF. GATT and the IMF are based upon multilateral economic agreements, and while the U.S. has had a great deal of influence and leadership in them, other major countries also have played important roles in the creation and development of these agreements. This can easily be seen in the history of protracted multilateral negotiations over the major revisions and improvements of the system—the Kennedy Round, the Tokyo Round, the introduction of the Generalized Scheme of Preferences in the case of GATT, and the creation of Special Drawing Rights and the Second Revision in the case of the IMF. The GATT and IMF systems were created and developed by a series of collective decisions and multilateral negotiations among major powers. Certainly the United States has not been the sole creator and support of the world trading system. It is also not accurate to say that the decline in U.S. economic power has made maintenance of the system more difficult. As discussed in Section III, the U.S. economy has not been weakened much in recent years, and it is unlikely that the U.S. dollar will lose its key currency position in the foreseeable future. The United States's strong bargaining power in bilateral economic relations has not been weakened, as we noted in Section IV.

The world trading system has developed through multilateral cooperation and collective decision-making among the major Western powers, although the influence of each of them has been changing over time. Japan did not participate in the creation of the system, and its influence was very small as recently as the 1970s, but Japan is now becoming the "Number Two" country in the system. It is clear that the U.S. will continue to be the leader of the system in the future.

In today's world one should not, of course, ignore the existence and influence of the Soviet Union and the Eastern European nations, as well as the influence of developing nations of the Third World.[10] In this environment, it is important to recognize that the common interests of the U.S., Europe, and Japan by far outweigh conflicts of economic interests among them, most of which are temporary and can be resolved if the parties concerned behave rationally and deliberately.

With this in mind, I believe that, in spite of the friction over various U.S.–Japan trade issues, and the rise of tension due to prolonged negotiation in order to resolve such problems, the differences are not as important as the fundamental common interests and the cooperative relationship that these two countries enjoy.

This chapter is a revised, English version of an article published in R. Komiya and MITI/RI (eds.), *Kokusaika-suru kigyo to sekai keizai* (Globalized business actitity and the world economy) (Tokyo: Toyo Keizai Shimposha), and R. Komiya, *Gendai Nihon keizai: Makuro-teki tenkai to kokusai keizai kankei* (The Contempory Japanese Economy: Its Macroeconomic Development). Tokyo: University of Tokyo Press, 1988.

Notes

1. The United States in the latter part of the 1940s and the first half of the 1950s strongly supported Japan's accession to GATT membership. Although the Western European nations were opposed, the U.S., wishing the stabilization and economic development of Japan and hoping to lessen its own burden of aid to Japan, conducted bilateral tariff negotiations with Japan, overcame Western European objections, and achieved its aim of Japanese membership in GATT. When one considers this early postwar history on the one hand and the Japan–U.S. trade confrontation today on the other, one is struck with a sense of irony. A number of Western European countries applied Article 35 of the GATT to Japan at the time of the latter's accession to membership, which meant excluding Japan from most-favored-nation (MFN) treatment within GATT. Many of the countries that joined GATT after Japan, especially newly independent British and French ex-colonies, also applied Article 35 to Japan. Therefore, although Japan was formally a member of GATT, its status was an anomaly, since it had formal GATT (MFN) relations with only a handful of major trading nations (notably the U.S.), until around 1970. Furthermore, even after a number of West European countries formally withdrew the application of Article 35 to Japan, many of them discriminated against Japan illegally. Some of these countries do so even today.

2. There might be undesirable effects on a country's trade and industrial structure resulting from wide fluctuations in exchange rates under the floating exchange rate system, or from large undervaluations or overvaluations of a country's currency over an extended period, such as the overvaluation of the U.S. dollar between 1980–1985. One method of avoiding these effects is the "import-export link system" proposed by the author. See Komiya, 1986.

3. See Section IV for further discussion on this point.

4. In this type of discussion, foreign investment and indebtedness usually include not only credit and debt, but also direct investment and portfolio equity investment, so that the terms "net creditor country" and "net debtor country" are not accurate; the net external investment position including direct investment and portfolio equity investment is a more appropriate basic indicator.

5. An example of a simple calculation on this point is as follows.
When it is assumed that
   (a) the U.S. net external investment position at present is zero; that
   (b) the price level is stable and the terms of trade are also constant; that
   (c) the ratio of the U.S. current-account deficit to the GNP of the U.S.
   continues to be zero for this period; and that
   (d) the growth rate of the U.S. GNP (real) is zero during this period, then
   the ratio of the U.S. net external debt to its GNP will be just 30% ten
   years later.
Assuming that (d') (real) GNP growth rate will continue to be 2% for a
decade, instead of 0% in (d), the ratio of net external debt ten years after
will be 27.5%, instead of 30%.
If the ratio of current-account deficit excluding returns from foreign investments and interest payments to the GNP of the U.S. is 3% every year,
instead of (c'), and if the real interest rate is 3%, under assumption (d'),
then the ratio of net external debt will be 31.4% ten years after. In this case
annual interest payment burden will be about 0.9% of the GNP. If the real
interest rate is 4% in this case, these figures will be 32.8% and 1.3%, respectively.
   6. This point is in principle similar to the one that some people in international institutions made a great fuss about at the time of the first oil crisis:
namely, that so-called "oil money" would not easily be recycled back to
international financial markets. As a matter of fact, "oil money" was automatically recycled back to the Eurodollar market. If the oil crisis had occurred
under the gold standard (or the gold exchange standard), the oil importing
nations as a whole would have had to hand over an enormous amount of
gold to the OPEC countries. However, under the floating exchange rate
system, the OPEC low absorber countries all had to purchase financial instruments (denominated mostly in dollars, and partly in British pounds at
the beginning) in international financial markets in an amount exactly equal
to their current-account surpluses.
   7. This argument is based on the "assignment" argument of economic
policy in an international economy. See Komiya, 1980.
   8. The percentage of imports to GNP in the U.S. was around 3% in 1960
but grew quite rapidly in the 1970s and has reached around 10% today.
Imports of highly visible items such as automobiles and consumer durables
have grown especially rapidly.
   9. For this reason, when Switzerland joined GATT it asked for and was
given a waiver of import restrictions on agricultural products.
   10. Japan can play an important role in North–South relations due to its
special position among the Western industrialized nations. In fact, Japan
has steadily expanded its role in North–South relations in recent years. Just
a short while ago Japan was a developing country: in the 1950s and 1960s
it went through the experience of borrowing from the World Bank. This
experience puts Japan in a special position to understand problems in the
South countries, and to make special contributions to North–South relations.

References

Komiya, Ryutaro (1980). "Is International Coordination of National Economic Policy Necessary?" in Peter Oppenheimer, ed., *Issues in International Economics*, Oxford Symposia, V. Stocksfield, England: Oriel Press.

Komiya, Ryutaro (1986). "Nichi-Bei Boeki Masatsu to Kokusai Kyoryoku" (U.S.–Japan Trade Friction and International Cooperation), Weekly *Toyo Keizai,* June 7 and 14 issues.

CHAPTER 3

JAPAN'S FOREIGN DIRECT INVESTMENT

The main purpose of this paper is to examine the phenomenon generally called foreign direct investment in a concrete case, that of present-day Japan, and to reconsider the theory of direct investment in the light of the findings. The paper begins by examining the concept of foreign direct investment and statistics compiled by national governments, in particular the Japanese government. It shows that the distinction between direct and indirect investment cannot be clear-cut, and that there exist wide grey areas of different shades in between (Section I). Then it sketches the history of Japan's foreign direct investment in post-war years (Section II), and surveys different types of investment included in the direct investment statistics (Section III).

A number of distinctive features of Japan's foreign direct investment as compared with other countries' are discussed (Section IV). Then theories of direct investment are reviewed and reconsidered in the light of Japan's experience, and the author's view on direct investment is developed (Section V). The last section summarizes the main conclusions (Section VI).

The paper does not go into the policy issues such as whether and in what ways a developing host country should restrict foreign direct investment, or a developed home country promote or restrict it. Such subjects require separate discussions. This paper is intended to facilitate better factual and theoretical understanding of foreign direct investment which must underlie any discussion of such policy issues.

I. The Concept of Direct Investment and Statistics

Foreign direct investment (FDI) is generally defined as a form of long-term international capital movement, made for the purpose of productive activity and accompanied by the intention of managerial control or participation in the management of a foreign firm. It is distinguished from indirect (portfolio, or securities) long-term investment where the investor is concerned only with the yields on securities or other claims acquired. It is not always easy, however, to ascertain whether or not such a productive or managerial intention accompanies the long-term capital movement. In fact, whether an investment is direct or indirect is not a black-and-white affair: there are wide "grey zones," as the examples below show.

Japan's official definition of direct investment

Within Japan's present legal framework the term "outward (overseas) direct investment" is defined to include (1) acquisition by residents of securities issued by non-resident corporations and (2) lending to foreign corporations, both for the purpose of establishing some long-term relationships with them, as well as (3) establishment of branch offices and factories. It includes shareholding with an equity share exceeding 10% in a foreign corporation, and long-term lending to—and holding of bonds issued by—such a corporation. It also includes equity ownership below 10%, if the resident corporation has some "close relationship" with the foreign corporation of which the equity share is acquired, such as the former's representative serving as a director of the latter, or a long-term purchase, licensing or agency contract between them. Moreover, some long-term credit not accompanied by equity ownership is included in outward direct investment, if a close relationship exists between the lender and the borrower.

The definition of inward direct investment by the Japanese government is not symmetric with that of outward direct investment. It includes, for example, acquisition by non-residents of any equity share of a corporation which is not listed in the stock exchange and acquisition, exceeding a certain amount, by non-residents of corporate bonds privately issued by a resident corporation.

Direct investment versus market mechanism

The fact that such legal definitions and treatments of FDI are complicated is quite revealing, since it substantiates the point that FDI is various forms of behavior through which a firm tries to organize productive activities in different locations, transfer resources, and collect and transmit information more efficiently—from the firm's point of view in the first place, but often also from a social point of view—than through the market mechanism. A branch office, a directly-owned factory or mine, and a wholly-owned subsidiary are "purest" or most "direct" forms of direct investment, whereas a minority-owned subsidiary with or without a management contract and a comprehensive long-term contract without involving equity ownership but covering wide areas of management and technology (e.g., the so-called "voluntary chain" stores in retail trade) or the *shitauke* (subcontracting) system in Japan are less direct, looser forms of the firm's organizational behavior, bypassing the use of open markets.

Thus it is intrinsically difficult to define what is FDI and what is not, whether from an academic or economic policy point of view. There are wide grey zones between "pure" direct investment and what is not direct investment.

Partly for this reason, statistics on FDI published by the governments of various countries are poor in quality as well as quantity— much poorer than, for example, international trade statistics.

Statistics on Japan's foreign direct investment

In Japan there are three major official statistical sources on outward FDI. The situation seems more or less similar in many other countries. First, there are statistics published by the Ministry of Finance (MOF) on the amount of outward FDI flows with industry- and country-breakdowns, approved by (until 1980) or notified to (after 1981) MOF (Table 1). These statistics, most commonly used in the literature on Japan's FDI, have three major defects: (1) firms sometimes do not actually undertake investment approved or notified, or do so only by a smaller amount, (2) the time of actual investment is generally later— sometimes much later—than the time of the approval or notification, and (3) the amount of investment includes certain types of loans and acquisition of bonds—which constitute a very large proportion of the total investment (Table 2)—whereas repayments of these loans or bonds are not covered by the statistics, nor are withdrawals of (or capital losses on) equity investment. Both (1) and (2) result in a substantial overstatement of the actual value of FDI.

Second, annual FDI flows are reported in the balance of payments statistics published by the Bank of Japan (BOJ). No country or industry breakdowns are given. Unlike the United States statistical practice, the retained earnings of Japanese-owned (totally or partially) corporations abroad are neither included in the annual flows of investment nor in the investment incomes in the current account. Hence the exact stock value of investment cannot be reached by cumulatively adding up annual flows. It is the same with the MOF's approval/notification statistics. Many authors do so, however, to derive the approximate stock value, since there is no other way.[1]

There are several other conceptual discrepancies between the MOF and BOJ series, and the discrepancy between the two series is substan-

Table 1
Annual Flows of Japan's Foreign (Outward) Direct Investment

(U.S. $ mil.)

Year	Total (Min. of Finance) [a]	Manufacturing industries (Min. of Finance) [a]	Total (Bank of Japan) [b]
1951–60 (av.)	28	13	14
1961–70 (av.)	329	81	181
1971	858	290	360
1972	2338	528	723
1973	3497	1499	1904
1974	2396	879	2012
1975	3280	924	1763
1976	3462	1025	1991
1977	2806	1074	1645
1978	4598	2038	2371
1979	4995	1693	2898
1980	4693	1706	2385
1981	8932	2305	4894
1982	7703	2076	4540
1983	8145	2588	3612
1984	10155	2505	5965
1985	12217	2352	6452
1986	22320	3806	14480

Source: See text and notes 1 through 4.

[a]The amounts approved or notified—Ministry of Finance, *Zaisei Kinyu Tokei Geppo* (Monthly Bulletin of Financial Statistics), various issues.

[b]Figures on the balance-of-payments basis—Bank of Japan, *Kokusai-Shushi Tokei Geppo* (Monthly Bulletin of Balance of Payments Statistics), various issues.

Table 2
Composition of Japan's Foreign Direct Investment Flows (by type of investment)

(U.S. $ mil.)

Period	Acquisition of securities	Credit	Others [a]
1951–60	122	94	67
1961–70	1198	1763	333
1971–80	16315	15105	1504
1981–86	33480	34419	1574

Source: MOF. See note 2 and Table 1.

[a]Investment in real assets including branch offices and, until 1980, real estate, on MOF basis.

tial. For example, BOJ's series includes *yushi baiko* loans for mineral resource development (see Section III) not in direct investment but in long-term loans. The timing of inclusion in the statistics is naturally different (see Table 1 for comparison of the two series).

Third, the Ministry of International Trade and Industry (MITI) conducts surveys of Japanese enterprises' activities abroad: a detailed survey once every three years since 1981, and a less detailed one in each year in which a detailed survey is not conducted.[2] MITI sends questionnaires to the head offices of Japanese parent corporations whose overseas FDI has been approved or notified in the past. The main defect of these statistics is that only about a half of the questionnaires are recovered. The recovery ratio is often lower for the detailed survey, for which the questionnaire is more cumbersome to fill out.

Pitfalls in direct investment statistics
There are many other sources of statistical and factual information on Japan's FDI, such as the "Yukashoken Hokokusho" (report on securities) filed with MOF by each "listed" corporation, publications of JETRO (Japan External Trade Organisation), Research Institute on Overseas Investment of the Japan Export and Import Bank, various industry associations, and so forth. Yet it is not possible to obtain accurate information on even a few key statistics. It is not an exaggeration to say that statistics on FDI are full of errors and pitfalls and that they generally lack international comparability.

Some of such pitfalls of direct investment statistics have already been mentioned. A few additional examples are now given:

(1) When a corporation (A) in country I invests in a "child" subsidiary (B) in country II—often a mere paper company in a tax-haven country—and then B invests in a "grandchild" subsidiary (C) in country III, the fact that A has a direct investment interest in C is rarely reflected in the statistics.

(2) A Japanese company participated in a British oil exploration project offshore of Abu Dhabi. In Japan's statistics, this was classified as investment in British mining.

(3) In the international comparison of the "ratio of overseas production" of manufacturing firms whose headquarters are located in major industrialized countries, the figures usually used for Japan have the following defects: the numerator is the total sales of all manufacturing corporations (hence excludes sales of independent proprietors) in Japan, while the denominator is the total sales of Japanese-owned overseas subsidiaries engaged in manufacturing, taken from the MITI

survey. On the one hand, as mentioned above, the recovery ratio of the questionnaires is only about half or less. On the other hand, the sales of all subsidiaries are included, whether wholly- or partially-owned, and even those of less-than-10-per-cent-owned ones, when there is a certain "close relationship" with the parent. The figures for other countries would have similar defects.

(4) If a Japanese construction company undertakes a construction project in a foreign country without establishing a subsidiary, or as a joint venture on a contract basis, its work is not counted as associated with FDI. But if the company undertakes the work by establishing a subsidiary in that country, wholly or partially owned, then the funds remitted to the construction work is included in FDI.

(5) The statistics on FDI generally record the amount of certain funds sent across the national border. A subsidiary in a foreign country often borrows funds and issues bonds or even new stocks there or in a third country, to expand its operation. But such financing is usually not recorded in direct investment statistics. Hence the statistics do not reflect exactly the changes in the scale of operation of overseas subsidiaries, even if they are substantial.

These examples amply demonstrate that there are many pitfalls and errors in statistics on FDI, and that the degree of their international comparability is low. Apparently different countries use different criteria, concepts, and procedures in compiling statistics on direct investment. Even just for the direct investment flows in the balance-of-payments statistics published in the International Monetary Fund (IMF) *International Financial Statistics*, different countries use different conceptual criteria.[3]

Thus, quite contrary to export and import trade statistics, whose degree of international comparability is fairly high relative to other economic statistics, generally statistics on FDI are deficient in international comparability, and their quality and quantity seem much poorer. This is partly due to the already mentioned fact that FDI is not a black-and-white affair, as in the case of export and import trade, but is a phenomenon taking place in wide grey zones.

In the following, however, I shall largely ignore these conceptual problems as well as defects and pitfalls in direct investment statistics. Hence the figures and statistics used below should be taken as indicating long-run trends and rough comparisons between countries.

II.   A Brief History

A minuscule beginning

With its defeat in the Second World War, Japan lost all its overseas territories, investments, and assets, so that when foreign investment resumed around 1950, accumulated overseas assets were nil.[4] Moreover, Japan had been a virtually closed country for several decades, and any expertise acquired by the Japanese business community accumulated in earlier years to run business abroad had been largely lost by then. This situation is in sharp contrast to that of Britain, the United States, and several other countries, which had large amounts of foreign direct investment (FDI) assets and managerial expertise carried over from the prewar years, and are now still leading direct investor countries in the world economy.

Although Japan's outward FDI was resumed in 1951, the amount invested and the scale of operation abroad remained minuscule in the 1950s and early 1960s (Table 1). This was partly due to the Japanese government's policy of severely restricting outward foreign investment, whether direct or indirect, primarily for balance-of-payments reasons. Outward investment involves an immediate loss of foreign exchange, similar to imports. It appears that the government tried to restrict both foreign investment and imports to the low level compatible with balance-of-payments constraints. This policy of severely limiting overseas investment had a counterpart on the side of capital import. Between 1956 and 1963 foreigners' direct investment in any industry in Japan was allowed, provided that earnings from investment and liquidation proceeds would not be converted into foreign exchange for repatriation. The restrictive policy pursued by MITI on inward direct investment commenced after 1963, when this "yen-basis investment" provision was abolished.[5] Wholesale capital flight appears to have been a nightmare for the Japanese foreign exchange authorities since the time of Japan's brief return to the gold standard from November 1930 to December 1931, when heavy capital outflows took place. Foreign investment, whether outward or inward, and whether short-term, portfolio or direct, was regulated, in principle, under the application-and-approval system until 1980, although as a matter of fact it was gradually liberalized throughout the 1970s.

In the early years after the resumption, Japan's outward FDI was concentrated mainly in two areas. First, Japanese trading companies, banks and later manufacturers established branch offices or subsidiaries in Japan's trade-partner countries, to assist and promote Japan's overseas trade. Secondly, from the last years of the 1950s a number of fairly large-scale investment projects were undertaken in natural-resource-related industries in foreign countries. In the 1950s and early 1960s four such "national"—in the sense that the government actively participated—projects, namely Alaskan pulp (started in 1953), Usiminus steel (Brazil, 1957), Arabian oil (1958), and North Sumatran oil (Indonesia, 1960), were dominant ones in the amount invested. In the 1960s and early 1970s development projects abroad for the supply of copper, lead, zinc, chromium, bauxite, iron ores, petroleum, coal, paper and pulp, mostly jointly with foreign governments and/or firms, were among Japan's most important overseas investment projects (Table 3).

In the 1950s and 1960s the Japanese government and business community were very concerned about the availability of these mineral and forestry resources. As the Japanese economy grew at an unprecedentedly high rate, it needed to expand rapidly the import of these natural resource products. It was thought that the supply of many of these natural resources was under the restrictive control of the exporting countries, international monopolies, or cartels, and that it was necessary for Japan to develop supply sources.

Until 1969 a firm undertaking FDI had to apply for the use of foreign exchange, and the application went through a strict screening process. Most projects approved, on the other hand, were given preferential treatment by the government such as overseas investment insurance, low interest-rate financing by the Japan Export and Import Bank and certain tax privileges. Also, two government enterprises were established specifically to undertake and promote overseas investment to develop new supply sources of minerals, one for oil and the other for other mineral resources.

Outward FDI was liberalized in several steps between 1969 and 1972, much faster than inward investment, which was also liberalized in several steps between 1967 and 1976. At present, on both outward and inward direct investment, only a few restrictions of minor importance remain.

Overseas investment "gannen"
The year 1972 was called the "gannen" of Japan's overseas (direct) investment. The *gannen* is the first year of the reign of an emperor in China or Japan. Japan's overseas FDI increased sharply in 1972 and 1973 (Table 1). In these two years many Japanese firms for the first time considered, planned, and undertook FDI as an important and integral part of their business activities. While Japan's outward

Table 3
Composition of Japan's Foreign Direct Investment Flows by Industry [a]

(U.S. $ mil.)

Period	Manufacturing	Agriculture & fisheries	Mining	Wholesale & retail trade	Finance & insurance	Transportation	Real estate business	Others
1951–60	127	7	86	32	11	0	0	20
1961–70	813	88	1046	351	308	0	0	688
1971–80	11,656	813	6273	5037	2119	0	354	6672
1981–86	15,633	380	5353	9129	15,673	7826	6531	8949

Sources: Same as Table 2.
[a]By industry in the host country in which investment is made.

FDI flows for the twenty-one years 1951 to 1971 add up only to 3.6 billion U.S. dollars, the total for just two years, 1972 and 1973, amounts to 5.8 billion.

Major factors behind this sharp increase were a large appreciation of the Japanese yen, the rise in real wages in Japan, and the large balance of payments surpluses. First, the yen went up from 360 yen to one U.S. dollar under the Bretton Woods regime to 308 yen in 1972 and then to around 265 yen to a dollar in 1973, raising all costs of production in Japan sharply relative to those prevailing in other countries, especially nearby Far Eastern countries. It also enabled Japanese firms to build factories and acquire equity shares in other countries much more cheaply than before. Secondly, in addition to the currency appreciation, real wages were rising sharply in Japan, changing its comparative advantage pattern: labor-intensive industries within Japan were losing competitiveness in international markets. A large number of manufacturing firms including many smaller ones, especially in labour-intensive industries, rushed to South Korea, Taiwan, Hong Kong and ASEAN countries for manufacturing activities there. Thirdly, Japan's balance of payments on current account recorded sizable surpluses for the first time after the Second World War, or, to go back further into the past, for the first time since the First World War. In view of the complaints from deficit countries, the Japanese government encouraged and promoted the use of foreign exchange, including outward FDI. The monetary authorities pursued extremely easy money policy in 1971 and 1972, and Japanese firms could easily finance FDI until the middle of 1973.

Stagnation after the first oil crisis

After the first oil crisis the level of annual direct investment outflows from Japan declined and remained largely stagnant until the beginning of the 1980s. Taking into account the high rate of inflation after 1973–74, one may say that the 1972–73 "gannen" peak level was not surpassed until 1981 (Table 1).

After the first oil crisis the Japanese economy—and the world economy at large—ran into the deepest depression or stagflation after the Second World War, and a large number of Japanese firms recorded losses: in the worst year, 1975, nearly one-third of the listed corporations recorded deficits on their operating accounts. This was perhaps the worst corporate performance among major industrialized countries in recent years. Many industries continued to have excess capacity and redundant personnel well into the last year of the 1970s. It is no wonder that FDI remained stagnant under such conditions.[6] Also, the yen exchange rate depreciated in 1974 and 1975 as a result of the first oil crisis and the ensuing large current-account deficits made FDI less attractive.

A large number of Japanese firms withdrew their investments from East and South-East Asian countries in this period, especially the period 1976–79.[7]

During this period, however, major changes in the conditions underlying Japan's FDI were taking place. At the beginning of this period Japan was still a medium-rank industrial power in the world economy. Its balance-of-payments position was jeopardized by the two oil crises, especially the first one. At the time of a sort of "seizing up" or a "clog" situation in the summer of 1974, Japan was considered—along with Italy—a country with the highest country risk among industrialized countries. Japanese banks then experienced considerable difficulties in rolling over short-term borrowing in the Euro-dollar market, and the phenomenon of the so-called "Japan rate"—Japanese banks having to pay several points higher rates than the London Inter Bank Offer Rate (LIBOR)—persisted for a number of weeks. When the wave of the second oil crisis subsided in the latter part of 1980, however, Japan emerged as one of the most active countries in world financial centers. By the early 1980s its country-risk rating was among the lowest three or four in the world.

In industrial technology, in the first half of the 1970s Japan was generally still behind the United States and Western Europe, and was exporting mainly manufacturing products using more or less labor-intensive, medium-level technologies such as textiles, iron and steel, ships and tankers, although higher value-added machinery and equipment were gradually replacing textiles and other labor-intensive products, steel, ships and tankers, as Japan's major exports. The value of motor vehicles exported exceeded that of ships and tankers for the first time in 1975. By the first half of the 1980s Japan's chief exports were automobiles, electronics products, communications equipment, semiconductors, electronically controlled machine tools and so on. Other industrialized countries, including the United States, were having difficulties in competing with Japan in many of these products even in their home markets, and the cases of what is called "trade friction" between Japan on the one hand and the United States and West European countries on the other were increasing sharply. Cases of trade friction on Japan's export side—there have been cases of "trade friction" on Japan's import side as well—arose first in textiles and other labour-intensive products in the 1950s and early 1960s, then moved to medium-level technology products such as ships, iron and steel, and colour TV sets in the late 1960s and 1970s, and by the middle of the 1980s were occurring most frequently in medium-to-high-level technology products such as automobiles, motorcycles, quartz watches, construction machinery, semiconductors, videotape recorders (VTRs), copying machines, computers, electronically controlled machine tools, telecommunications equipment, etc.[8]

The second upsurge of outward direct investment since 1981

Japan's outward FDI flows, which remained in the range between 2 and 4 billion U.S. dollars for the six years 1972–77 and in the range between 4 and 5 billion for the three years 1978–1980, sharply increased to nearly 9 billion in 1981, surpassed the 10 billion line in 1985, and then jumped up to over 22 billion in 1986 (MOF series). Thus the years since 1981 may be said to be the second upsurge, after the "gan-nen" years 1972 and 1973. Furthermore, the years 1985 and afterwards may prove to be another new era of activation of Japan's outward direct investment: in just two years, 1985 and 1986, it amounted to 34.5 billion U.S. dollars, which is nearly equal to the total investment of 36.5 billion over the 30 years from 1952 to 1981 (Table 1).

Sharp increase in tertiary sector investment. Besides the sharp increase in the total, two prominent tendencies in Japan's outward direct investment are observed since 1981, especially in recent years. First, there was a shift away from mining and natural-resource-related investment—and manufacturing—towards the tertiary industries (Table 3). In 1986, finance and insurance (32.3%) and real estate (17.9%) were the two leading sectors in Japan's outward direct investment, accounting for more than a half of the total between them. The shares of transportation (8.6%), commerce (8.3%) and services (7%, especially leasing business and hotels) were also prominent. On the other hand, the shares of manufacturing and mining in the 1986 outflow were only 17.1% and 3%, respectively: a substantial decline from their shares of 34.5% and 19.4% respectively in the total outflows between 1951 and 1980 (figures are those from the MOF series).

In mining there were a few large-scale, government-supported projects in the early part of this period (or the last years of the previous period), such as the Asahan Aluminium project in Indonesia, LNG (liquefied natural gas) in Brunei and Indonesia, and copper in Zambia. However, a generally declining tendency in the prices (or terms of trade) of minerals and natural-resource commodities and the excess supply conditions resulting from the worldwide depression after the second oil crisis diminished Japanese firms'—and the government's—interest in natural-resource investments. Although included in manu-

Table 4
Composition of Japan's Foreign Direct Investment Flows by Area of Destination

(U.S. $ mil.)

Period	North America	Latin America	Asia	Middle East	Europe	Africa	Oceania
1951–60	88	85	49	56	3	1	2
1961–70	824	482	703	278	636	92	279
1971–80	8886	5602	9082	1925	3832	1353	2244
1981–86	27,608	14,205	11,961	757	10,000	2233	2709

Source: Same as Table 2.

facturing (chemicals), large-scale petrochemical projects in Iran, Singapore and Saudi Arabia started in the early part of this period are also in a sense resource-related direct investment. But the enthusiasm for petrochemical projects rapidly subsided, partly because of the Iranian revolution and the Iran–Iraq war and partly because of the decline in oil prices and the worldwide glut of petrochemicals.

Direct investment in manufacturing has been generally increasing after 1980, but its growth was far outpaced by the growth of investment in the tertiary industries.

Shift away from LDCs toward developed countries. Secondly, in the area and country break-down, there was a remarkable shift from Asia, the Middle East, and Latin America towards North America, especially the United States, and Western Europe, that is, toward the developed countries and away from developing countries (Table 4). The United States has conspicuously risen as the host country not only of Japan's FDI but also of other countries' (Table 5).

In the area break-down North America accounted for about a quarter (26.8%) in Japan's total outward FDI flows between 1951 and 1980, but nearly half in 1985 and 1986 (45.0 and 46.8% respectively). The rise of North America in the share of manufacturing investment is more dramatic: it accounted for only 19.3% for the years 1951 to 1980, but more than half in 1985 and 1986 (52.0 and 57.8% respectively). The rise in the European share is less pronounced: from 12.3 per cent for 1951 to 1980, to 15.8 and 15.5% respectively for 1985 and 1986, but taking only manufacturing investment it rose from 6.7% for 1951 to 1980, to 13.7 and 9.7% respectively for 1985 and 1986.

In contrast the share of Asia in Japan's outward FDI declined sharply: from 16.9% for 1951 to 1980, to 11.7 and 10.4% in 1985 and 1986. In manufacturing investment the Asian share declined from more than one-third (36.4%) for the period 1951 to 1980, to only about one-fifth (19.6 and 21.2% respectively) for 1985 and 1986.

Table 5
The Values of Outward and Inward Direct Investment Outstanding and Ratios to GNP: Selected Countries, 1975–84ᵃ

(U.S. $ mil. and %)

		1975	1976	1977	1978	1979	1980
Japan	Outward D.I. (A)	8322	10,313	11,958	14,329	17,227	19,612
	Inward D.I. (B)	2084	2208	2229	2841	3422	3270
	GNP (C)	499,330	561,320	693,140	980,660	1,016,180	1,063,150
	(A)/(C) (%)	1.67	1.84	1.73	1.46	1.70	1.84
	(B)/(C) (%)	0.42	0.39	0.32	0.29	0.34	0.31
U.S.A.	Outward D.I. (A)	124,050	136,809	145,990	126,727	187,858	215,375
	Inward D.I. (B)	27,662	30,770	34,595	42,471	54,462	68,351
	GNP (C)	1,598,400	1,782,800	1,990,500	2,249,700	2,508,100	2,731,900
	(A)/(C) (%)	7.76	7.67	7.33	5.63	7.49	7.88
	(B)/(C) (%)	1.73	1.73	1.74	1.89	2.17	2.50
U.K.	Outward D.I. (A)	23,311	24,855	42,437	51,798	70,212	81,400
	Inward D.I. (B)	22,522	21,932	30,496	34,831	48,661	63,059
	GNP (C)	237,800	231,170	254,510	324,200	419,960	535,300
	(A)/(C) (%)	9.80	10.75	16.67	15.98	16.72	15.21
	(B)/(C) (%)	9.47	9.49	11.98	10.74	11.59	11.78
West Germany	Outward D.I. (A)	9,495	16,550	10,784	15,153	21,542	23,635
	Inward D.I. (B)	14,606	21,079	18,385	22,538	25,527	22,358
	GNP (C)	419,420	447,610	516,930	644,360	762,600	818,560
	(A)/(C) (%)	2.26	3.70	2.09	2.35	2.82	2.89
	(B)/(C) (%)	3.48	4.71	3.56	3.50	3.35	2.73

(Table 5, continued)

		1981	1982	1983	1984	1985
Japan	Outward D.I. (A)	24,506	28,969	32,178	37,921	43,974
	Inward D.I. (B)	3915	3998	4364	4458	4743
	GNP (C)	1,167,230	1,086,330	1,181,470	1,257,970	1,340,070
	(A)/(C) (%)	2.10	2.67	2.72	3.01	3.28
	(B)/(C) (%)	0.34	0.37	0.37	0.35	0.35
U.S.A.	Outward D.I. (A)	226,359	221,343	226,780	233,412	
	Inward D.I. (B)	90,421	101,844	137,061	159,571	
	GNP (C)	3,052,600	3,166,000	3,401,600	3,765,000	3,998,100
	(A)/(C) (%)	7.42	6.99	6.67	6.20	
	(B)/(C) (%)	2.96	3.22	4.03	4.24	
U.K.	Outward D.I. (A)	86,871	89,685	91,257	85,383	
	Inward D.I. (B)	56,324	50,437	51,308	42,607	
	GNP (C)	516,790	485,080	460,360	433,390	460,150
	(A)/(C) (%)	16.81	18.49	19.82	19.70	
	(B)/(C) (%)	10.90	10.40	11.15	9.83	
West Germany	Outward D.I. (A)	24,259	24,237	24,598	22,363	
	Inward D.I. (B)	18,849	17,926	16,227	14,485	
	GNP (C)	686420	658,960	659,250	621,630	632,600
	(A)/(C) (%)	3.53	3.68	3.73	3.60	
	(B)/(C) (%)	2.75	2.72	2.46	2.33	

Source: Bank of Japan, Gaikoku Keizai Tokei Nenpo (Yearbook of Foreign Economic Statistics), various issues.
The exchange rates at the end of the year were used for conversion.

Several factors may be pointed out as responsible for the major changes in the pattern of Japan's FDI just described:

1. *Financial deregulation and integration.* First, the development of the Euromarket (Euro-currency and Euro-bond markets) and financial deregulation first in the United States and then in the United Kingdom, Japan and other developed countries led to an acceleration of integration of the financial markets on a global scale, centered in developed countries but not confined to them. Since the basic change of Japan's law on foreign exchange controls in December 1980 toward deregulation, Japanese banks, securities companies and institutional investors, especially life insurance companies, were gradually freed from rigid regulations on their overseas activities, and their management horizons and business activities were expanded on a worldwide scale, resulting in a sharp increase in their FDI.

2. *Current-account imbalance.* Secondly, Japan began to run a large surplus in the balance of payments on current account after 1983. Japan's net international asset and liability position had already been much in excess of 1 or 2% on either side of GNP until 1981, but began to turn into a large net asset position after 1983. Japan has now become a large net investor country, and its foreign assets have been accumulating rapidly. In contrast, the United States's international asset and liability position has been deteriorating steadily.

A large capital outflow or capital export from Japan reflects the excess of saving over investment in Japan resulting from, among other factors, a substantial decline in the growth rate of the Japanese economy and scarcity of investment opportunities relative to the rate of saving at home. Portfolio investment has constituted a predominant part of Japan's capital export since the early 1980s, but it is no wonder that Japan's FDI outflows also increased sharply under such conditions.

A large part of Japan's FDI outflows is composed of loans, including—but not necessarily exclusively of—loans from the parents to subsidiaries (Table 2). Since in the first half of the 1980s the monetary conditions were predominantly easy in Japan where saving was in excess of domestic investment, while they were generally tight in the United States, subsidiaries of Japanese-based companies in the United States and elsewhere increased the proportion of loans from the parents in financing their operations, thus increasing FDI outflows from Japan.

3. *Trade barriers in the U.S.A. and Europe.* Thirdly, various types of tariff and nontariff barriers to trade were newly set up or substantially heightened by the United States, Canada and West European countries during this period, as Japanese exports of certain types of

manufactures to these countries increased sharply, and also as the bilateral trade imbalances between Japan and these countries grew rapidly. Not only actual increases of the trade barriers to restrict import from Japan, such as "voluntary" export restraints (VER), orderly marketing arrangements (OMA), the increases of tariff rates and cases of dumping charges, but also the possibility of some such import barriers being set up or heightened in the near future, promoted FDI by Japanese manufacturers into the United States and Western Europe. In the 1980s "to cope with trade friction" has become by far the leading reason for Japanese direct investment going to developed countries (Figure 1).

Along with the raising of such trade barriers a number of North American and West European central and/or local governments took various measures to encourage Japanese direct investment within their jurisdiction in the hope of increasing employment and industrialization.

An example of the earliest cases of direct investment by Japanese manufacturers to get over trade barriers newly set up by the United States is investment by manufacturers of color TV sets. An intergovernmental OMA was concluded between the Japanese and U.S. governments covering three years beginning from July 1977. Prior to this OMA Japanese export of color TV sets to the United States increased sharply and the Japanese manufacturers' share in the US market rose from 12.5% in 1974 to 30% in 1976. In response to the OMA most Japanese manufacturers of TV sets set up new factories or acquired existing ones in the United States, and local production in the United States partially but increasingly replaced export from Japan. Some manufacturers set up factories in East or South-East Asian countries which were not covered by the OMA agreement and exported from there to the United States. Export from such countries even enjoyed a lower tariff rate under the Generalized System of Preference (GSP) of GATT for developing countries. Japanese manufacturers were not necessarily forced to cut their domestic employment much, since major parts and assemblies often continued to be manufactured in Japan and exported to their subsidiaries in the United States or elsewhere, and since Japanese manufacturers were able to expand their sales in the United States (Figure 2A).

Since then more or less similar types of direct investments in the United States and Western Europe were made by Japanese manufacturers of automobiles, motorcycles, TV sets, VTRs (Figure 2B), other electronics products, semiconductors, copying machines, machine tools and some other products. In later years, some of the channels of exporting through subsidiaries in East and South-East Asian countries

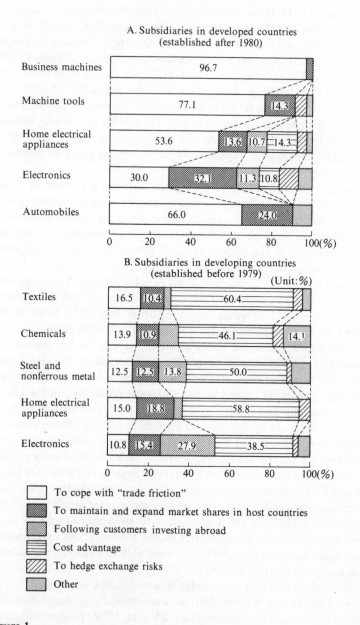

A. Subsidiaries in developed countries
(established after 1980)

Business machines — 96.7

Machine tools — 77.1 | 14.3

Home electrical appliances — 53.6 | 13.6 | 10.7 | 14.3

Electronics — 30.0 | 32.1 | 11.3 | 10.8

Automobiles — 66.0 | 24.0

0   20   40   60   80   100(%)

B. Subsidiaries in developing countries
(established before 1979)
(Unit: %)

Textiles — 16.5 | 10.4 | 60.4

Chemicals — 13.9 | 10.9 | 46.1 | 14.1

Steel and nonferrous metal — 12.5 | 12.5 | 13.8 | 50.0

Home electrical appliances — 15.0 | 18.8 | 58.8

Electronics — 10.8 | 15.4 | 27.9 | 38.5

0   20   40   60   80   100(%)

☐ To cope with "trade friction"
▨ To maintain and expand market shares in host countries
☐ Following customers investing abroad
▤ Cost advantage
▨ To hedge exchange risks
▨ Other

Figure 1
Comparison of the motives for overseas direct investment.
Source: MITI, *Tsusho Hakusho* (International Trade White Paper), 1986,
p. 182; based upon a special questionnaire survey.

were closed or narrowed, as the United States or European countries took measures to restrict imports from such countries, or at least decided not to apply the GSP tariff rates.

4. *Large appreciation of the yen.* Fourthly, the Japanese yen exchange rate began to appreciate sharply beginning from the G-5 meeting at the end of September 1985, and went up from the range of

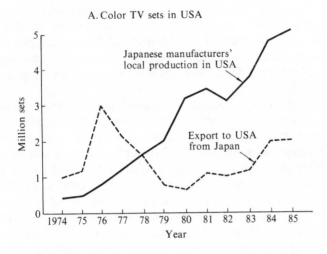

A. Color TV sets in USA

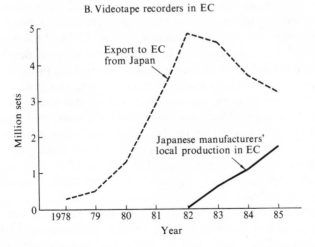

B. Videotape recorders in EC

Figure 2
Replacement of export by local production.
Source: MITI, *Tsusho Hakusho* (International Trade White Paper), 1986, p. 193.

240–250 yen to a US dollar in the spring and summer of 1985, to the range of 140–150 yen in the middle of 1987. This is indeed a rise of about 70%. The appreciation of the yen on an effective rate basis was somewhat smaller, but still amounted to nearly 50%. East and South-East Asian currencies were more or less tied to—or appreciated only a little vis-à-vis—the dollar, so that the Japanese yen rose sharply vis-à-vis the currencies of Japan's neighbor countries.

Such a large yen appreciation must have contributed substantially to a sharp increase in Japan's direct investment outflows in 1986 and 1987.[9] It meant that the costs of FDI declined sharply, and that wages and other costs of production in Japan rose as sharply, relatively to those in the United States and neighbor Asian countries, in a very short period.

The full effect of the recent yen appreciation on Japan's outward FDI is still unknown. It is bound to be accompanied by prolonged lags. Obviously it takes much time for a firm to plan and execute a change in the location of production activities, or to decide the direction for a major expansion of its operations. At present many Japanese firms are considering shifting some parts of their operations to the United States, Western Europe and/or East and South-East Asian countries. It is likely that there will be a continued upsurge of Japan's overseas direct investment. On the other hand, it should also be noted that the large yen appreciation has been bringing great hardship to many Japanese-owned subsidiaries abroad, as they depend much on materials, parts and assemblies imported from their parents in Japan.

5. *Worsening of investment environment in LDCs.* An important factor which has contributed to a decline in the share of developing countries including those in East and South-East Asia, in the country break-down of Japan's outward direct investment, is a general tendency to a worsening of the investment environment in these countries. In addition to the problem of accumulated debt, wars, civil wars and political instability repelling foreign investment from a number of developing countries, economic conditions in most developing countries generally deteriorated in the first half of the 1980s as a result of worldwide depression and stagnation in world trade, especially in primary commodities.

Moreover, the government policy and public attitude in some developing countries toward incoming foreign direct investment vacillated much within a short period. The list of measures adopted by developing countries toward foreign direct investment is a really long one, including all sorts of prohibitions and restrictions on the one hand, and a number of measures intended to promote investment.

They are changed often and substantially. By and large changes in recent years in governmental policies of those developing countries which had been the major host countries to Japan's direct investment were making them less attractive as places in which foreigners invest.

III. Varied Types of Direct Investment

When people speak of FDI they tend to think of a large "multinational" corporation engaged in large-scale mining, plantation agriculture or manufacturing at establishments located in many countries, all of which are controlled and directed by a headquarters in the investor's home country. But such an image is obviously little more than a stereotyped picture of FDI, applicable to only a small part of it. As a matter of fact there are a wide variety of types of investment, perhaps in any country's FDI. I have been struck by the wide variety of different types of investment,[10] some of which are now described:

1. *Mining and other natural-resource development projects.* As already mentioned, their relative weight in Japan's FDI was quite large in earlier years. In recent years, as a result of the strengthening of the assertion of "permanent sovereignty over natural resources" by developing countries, FDI of this type often takes the form of a "long-term credit with a product sharing" arrangement (called *"yushi baiko"* in Japan) without equity participation, in which the repayment is made through export of minerals or other products over an extended period after the development project succeeds. Such an investment project involves no equity ownership, but is obviously quite risky and treated as direct investment by the Japanese government.

2. *Manufacturing over the fence of protective tariff and nontariff barriers.* This is one of the traditional types of FDI, quite common in many countries. A large number of developing countries and Australia have long been pursuing a policy of raising the tariff rates or setting up formal or informal quantitative import restrictions on the one hand, and inviting FDI in manufacturing, often providing some preferential treatments such as tax holidays, low-cost financing, and offers of land for factories at favorable terms, on the other hand. It is needless to say that the proclaimed aims of such a policy are generally, first, to gain in employment, and, secondly, to obtain technological and managerial expertise. But the domestic users of the products have to pay higher prices, at least in the short run, and the cases of successful development of viable—in the sense of becoming competitive without protection—industries in the long run are not many. A large part of

Japanese investment in manufacturing industries in these countries has been of this type.

The United States and West European countries had generally been critical of such a policy, but recently a number of them began to pursue similar policies themselves. A large part of the recent rush of FDI by Japanese manufacturing firms there can be classified in this category (Figures 1A, 1B, 2A, and 2B), although perhaps the changes in cost conditions resulting from the rise in real wages in Japan and the yen appreciation are also important as factors behind it.

The scale of operation under this type of manufacturing investment is generally small, and the cost of production tends to be much higher than the cost at the "base factories" in the home country, where the scale of operation is by far greater. This type of investment is not altogether import-substituting or trade-replacing, since the subsidiaries behind the protective barriers usually import parts and assemblies from the parent firms in the home country or affiliates in third countries, and trade in them often expands over time. The host country is often keen, however, to raise what is called the "local content."

It is ironic that in the United States, which was the country strongly opposed to the local-contents requirements for FDI set up by development countries in the past, not only have many "local-contents bills" been introduced in Congress, but also in the actual planning of investment projects its local governments and communities often request higher local contents than the investors have planned. In EC only those products in certain categories manufactured in an EC country which have local contents higher than 45–60% are considered as made in EC and will not be subject to EC's common external tariff rates when traded within EC. This amounts to a policy of requesting subsidiaries of non-EC manufacturers in EC to raise the local contents above that ratio.

3. *Manufacturing investment in low-wage countries serving as the bases for export.* Some of the Japanese-owned manufacturing subsidiaries in Asian industrializing countries—that is, South Korea, Taiwan, Hong Kong and Singapore, and other ASEAN countries—are established to take advantage of lower labor cost in these countries,[11] and to export their products back to Japan and/or third countries, especially the United States and Western Europe.

The mainland Chinese government generally requests the direct investor to achieve at least a balance between its foreign exchange payments and receipts and preferably an excess of the receipts over payments, so that the investor must export a substantial part of his products.

Such investment is sometimes induced by the fact that export from these countries to the United States or Western Europe is not subject to VER, OMA or other quantitative restrictions which cover export of certain products from Japan, and sometimes even enjoy the GSP tariff rates (see Section II above).

Certain types of Japanese direct investment in the food-processing industry in Asian countries are made to take advantage of the facts that not only wages but also raw materials—agricultural products—are cheaper in the host country, and that certain parts of food processing are highly labor-intensive. For example, a number of Japanese trading and food-processing companies have been involved in Thailand, mostly with minority equity shares, in business producing corn (maize) and other feedstuff for chicken, raising chicken and then preparing chicken meat for *yakitori* and other chicken dishes. The products are frozen and shipped to Japanese restaurant chains and food processing firms.[12]

Recently, however, not only are real wages rising rapidly in Hong Kong, Singapore, Taiwan, and South Korea, but these countries now do not welcome FDI for the purpose of taking advantage of lower wages. Their policy is shifting toward attracting foreign investment in higher-technology industries.

4. *Wholesale and retail trade.* In terms of the sales of subsidiaries in host countries classified by industry, wholesale and retail trade is by far the leading sector in which Japanese firms invest, with a share of 83% in 1983, followed by manufacturing in second place with a meagre share of only 14.5%, according to a survey by MITI.[13]

Japan's large trading companies (*sogo shosha*) have always been leading figures in foreign direct investment. When Japanese corporations are listed in the order of the amount of overseas direct investment, all the leading trading companies are among the top ten or fifteen. Trading companies have invested heavily, not only in their overseas networks for exporting and importing business, but also in mining and other natural-resource projects, as well as in manufacturing industries. In the mining, forestry, fishery and manufacturing investments they participate mostly with minority shares, jointly with local and/or Japanese mining, manufacturing or other firms, or with the governments of the host countries. Besides assuming investment risks, trading companies engage in the trading aspects of the projects (marketing of outputs, procurement of plant and machinery, etc.).

On the other hand, not only trading companies, but also Japanese manufacturers, invest heavily in wholesale and retail trade abroad. Japan has a strong comparative advantage in fabricating and assembling type manufacturing industries using mass-production technologies. Typical examples of such industries are automobiles, electronics products, cameras, watches, semiconductors, electronically controlled machine tools, and stereo equipment. These industries are characterized by "product differentiation," and the products are sold to a large number of customers, as they are mass-produced. It is essential for the success of the manufacturer in these fields to establish and maintain an efficient marketing and servicing network on a global basis.

Such a network, or a part of it, can be set up and maintained by the manufacturing firm itself, by a cooperating Japanese trading company or by a local importer acting as a general agent. But the manufacturing firm often finds it advantageous to set up its global network itself. It requires a substantial amount of investment in wholesale and retail trade.

5. *Finance and insurance.* As mentioned earlier, since the beginning of the 1980s, and especially since 1985, Japanese banks, securities companies, and insurance companies have been actively establishing subsidiaries abroad and acquiring or merging with foreign firms. Also, Japanese non-bank (insurance, trading and manufacturing) firms are establishing wholly-owned "finance companies" in the United States, Britain, and such tax-haven countries as the Bahamas, Cayman Islands, Hong Kong, Luxembourg, and Panama.

A remarkable phenomenon in recent years is that many Japanese firms have come up on the list of the world's 10, 20 or 100 leading banks or securities underwriters. Some of them are expanding their business even in purely domestic markets in foreign countries such as retail banking in California or Britain.

6. *Investment in real estate.* One of the new developments in Japan's FDI in the last few years is a sharp increase in investment in real estate business abroad, especially in the United States.[14] There are various types of investment in this category, such as investment by real estate firms engaged in the planning and development of community and shopping centers, or investment to acquire buildings for rental offices and apartments. The amount of real estate properties acquired by borrowed funds is not covered by FDI statistics, which include only the amounts remitted from parents to subsidiaries.

A not insignificant part of Japan's FDI in real estate in the United States since 1984 has been made by life insurance companies, as a way of diversifying their "portfolio" of investments. They are accumulating an enormous amount of funds annually, and investing a part of them in bonds denominated in foreign currencies, especially U.S. treasury bonds, and equity stocks of foreign corporations. Since around 1984 they are investing also in real estate in the United States through local subsidiaries.

7. *Flag-of-convenience ships.* Many Japanese-owned ocean-going ships are today operated under a flag of convenience, namely as ships registered in countries with low taxes on ships such as Panama, Liberia or Hong Kong. In the country break-down list of Japan's outward direct investment, surprisingly Panama is in second place—in terms of the amount invested, accumulated over 1951–86—next to the United States at the top, and Liberia eighth. The amount of Japan's FDI in even the latter country is more than the amount invested in Korea, Taiwan or Singapore, or in any European country except Britain. A predominant part of Japan's FDI in Panama and Liberia is in subsidiaries for the purpose of owning, operating and/or leasing flag-of-convenience ships, although Panama has recently also hosted financial subsidiaries.

8. *Research laboratories.* Recently a number of Japanese manufacturing firms in such industries as electronics, chemicals, pharmaceuticals, and rubber have established or expanded research laboratories— primarily for basic research but sometimes also for development research—in the United States, Britain and West Germany, and employed scientists and engineers of these countries.[15] Similar moves by some U.S. and European firms to establish research laboratories in Japan and hire Japanese scientists have been taking place from much earlier times. Some of these Japanese and foreign firms made direct investment only in research laboratories in the country in question, having no production facility at all there.

IV. Characteristics of Japan's Direct Investment

In this section a few characteristics of Japan's outward foreign direct investment (FDI) will be discussed, in comparison with other major investor countries'. To discuss such characteristics fully it is necessary to have comparable statistics for the countries concerned. As noted in Section I, however, statistics on FDI are not readily available, and the degree of their international comparability seems rather low. The following discussion is mostly based upon generally available information.

Still in the early stage of development

In terms of the overall size of the amount of outward FDI outstanding, Japan now occupies somewhere between the third and seventh place among the top direct-investor countries, after the United States and Britain, and possibly West Germany, the Netherlands, Canada, and Switzerland. Thus Japan is among the world's largest investor countries, but it is not an investor country as "mature" as other leading investor countries. Japan is the latest-comer in this field, and is still in its very early stage of development as a direct investor country.

The fact that Japan is far from a state of full growth or maturity as a direct investor country is reflected in a number of statistics. In an international comparison of the ratio of the outstanding value (stock) of outward—and also inward—FDI to GNP, the ratio of the annual FDI to gross national saving, or the ratio of Japanese manufacturing enterprises' overseas production to their total (domestic plus overseas) sales, Japan's ratios are the lowest among the major investor countries (Tables 5 and 6). Thus the relative weight of FDI—both outward and inward—in the national economy is still small in Japan.

Also, the share of FDI in the total capital outflow is still small in Japan. Especially in recent years, indirect (portfolio) investment is dominant in the total capital outflow from Japan. Some of the other major direct investor countries, such as the United States, West Germany and Sweden, have been even net capital importers on direct investment accounts.

In an international comparison Britain stands out as the most advanced in FDI, in terms of the ratio of the value of investment outstanding to GNP, among the major industrialized countries compared (Table 5). If comparable statistics were available, however, perhaps three "great" direct-investor countries among smaller European countries, namely the Netherlands, Switzerland, and Sweden,

Table 6
Overseas Production of Manufacturing Firms: Selected Countries[a] (%)

Year	Japan	USA	West Germany	Total Outside of EC
1978	1.8	17.9 (1976)	13.4	9.0
1979	1.6	n.a.	13.7	9.2
1980	2.9	n.a.	14.7	10.1
1981	3.4	n.a.	16.8	12.0
1982	3.2	18.8	17.0	12.1
1983	3.9	17.3	17.4	12.5
1984	4.3	16.2	19.3	14.2

Sources: For Japan, MITI's survey: *Wagakuni Kigyo-no Kaigai Jigyo Katsudo* (Overseas Activities of Japanese Enterprises), 1987 (see text). The figures for the U.S.A. and West Germany are based upon respective countries' official statistics.

[a]The value of production by overseas subsidiaries of manufacturing firms divided by the value of total manufacturing production of each country.

would be seen to be more advanced than Britain as a direct investor country.

Major direct-investor countries other than Japan, namely the United States, Britain, West Germany, other EC countries, and Canada are also important as host countries to FDI, but Japan's share in the world as the host country of FDI is still small.[16]

A small share of manufacturing and large shares of investment in developing countries

The share of manufacturing industries in overseas FDI is relatively small in the case of Japan, probably substantially smaller than in the case of the United States, Britain or West Germany, especially when petroleum refining is included in manufacturing.[17] The share of manufacturing would be perhaps much higher in the case of Sweden, Switzerland, and the Netherlands. In Japan's FDI the shares of (i) sectors supporting export and import trade such as retail and wholesale trade and finance, (ii) a sort of substitute for indirect (portfolio) investment such as acquisition of real estate, and (iii) investment for the purpose of maintaining flag-of-convenience ships, are quite large relative to the share of manufacturing.

In the regional breakdown of Japan's FDI, the shares of developing countries used to be relatively large, as compared with FDI by the United States and West Germany. Much larger shares of FDI of the latter and other major investor countries have gone to the United States, EC, Canada and other developed countries.

Such a tendency for Japan's FDI to concentrate in developing countries seems to have been more pronounced in the case of FDI in the manufacturing sector, although this tendency is recently being corrected (Sections II and III).

These characteristics indicate that Japan is still a newcomer as a direct-investor country. The share of investment in manufacturing as well as that of developed countries in destination will rise, as Japan becomes more mature as a direct investor country in coming years.

Low profitability

Although reliable data on profits earned by Japan's overseas FDI are scarce, they indicate that its profitability is often lower than that of capital at home.

According to MITI's survey (see Section I), when the ratio of net profit to sales is compared between overseas subsidiaries of Japanese corporations on the one hand and their parent corporations and all the domestic corporations in Japan on the other, in recent years

Table 7
The Rate of Profit of Foreign Direct Investors in U.S. Manufacturing
Industries[a]

	1980	1981	1982	1983	(%) 1984
Japan	5.2	3.3	..4.6	..4.3	0.2
All countries	10.3	3.4	0.0	1.8	5.4

Source: From a table in: Japan Export-Import Bank, Kaigai Toshi Kenkyusho-Ho (Bulletin of the Research Institute on Overseas Investment), vol. 12, no. 10 (October 1986) (based upon US Department of Commerce, Survey of Current Business, various issues).
[a]Profits divided by the average of the amounts of investment at the beginning and end of each year.

the average profit rate tends to be lower for the former. This is true especially for subsidiaries engaged in manufacturing set up recently in North America and Europe. On the other hand, for subsidiaries engaged in mining in the Middle East and Oceania, those engaged in manufacturing in Asia, and in wholesale and retail trade in North America, the profit rate seems to be relatively high.

Also, according to U.S. Department of Commerce data on foreign-owned subsidiaries in the United States, the rate of profit on investment earned by Japanese-owned subsidiaries in the U.S. manufacturing sector is much lower than the average rate earned by all foreign-owned subsidiaries in the same sector (Table 7). Especially in 1982 and 1983 the profit rate turned negative for Japanese-owned subsidiaries.

One of the reasons for the low profitability of Japanese FDI may be that the length of the period in operation of Japanese overseas sub-

Table 8
The Proportion of Japanese-owned Subsidiaries Earning Positive Profits in 1984 (by year of establishment) [a]

	Up to 1972	1973–75	1976–78	1978–81	(%) 1982–84
Total	83.2	78.8	79.2	75.8	68.4
of total:					
Asia	82.6	79.2	79.3	78.5	72.6
North America	84.3	80.8	79.3	67.5	61.4
of total:					
Manufacturing	84.2	79.4	80.3	77.8	69.5
Wholesale &					
retail trade	83.4	81.6	80.7	76.5	67.9

Source: MITI's survey (Wagakuni Kigyo-no Kaigai Jigyo Katsudo [Overseas Activities of Japanese Enterprises], 1987) (see text).
[a] The dates at the head of the columns indicate the years in which Japanese-owned subsidiaries were established.

sidiaries is still generally short, especially for the case of manufacturing investment in the United States and Western Europe (see Table 8).[18] Several other reasons for low profitability in the case of the manufacturing sector will be considered below.

On the other hand, the rate of profit earned by Japanese FDI in retail and wholesale trade is relatively high, perhaps because many of the Japanese-owned subsidiaries in this area have long been in existence. Also, when the import of certain products dealt with by an overseas subsidiary engaged in retail and wholesale trade comes to be subject to some not-too-restrictive quantitative restrictions such as an import quota system, VER or OMA, a part of the premium between the supply cost and demand price often accrues to the subsidiary.

Active participation by smaller businesses

Smaller businesses—in Japanese terminology "small- and medium-size businesses"—are legally defined in Japan as firms employing 300 (100 in wholesale and 50 in retail trade) employees or less, or corporations with paid-in capital of 100 (30 in wholesale and 10 in retail trade) million yen or less. If either of these two criteria is met, the firm is classified as a small- or medium-size business and eligible for various privileges including low-interest financing under a special government programme, protection under certain provisions of the anti-monopoly law, and certain special tax treatments. In terms of the number of employees, smaller businesses cover between 70 and 75% of Japan's manufacturing sector and between 80 and 85% of all sectors excluding agriculture and finance (but including manufacturing).

The coexistence of a large number of smaller businesses along with large-scale, modernized enterprises was once called the "dual structure" of the Japanese economy, and was considered one of its weaknesses in the 1950s and 1960s. But the relative weight of smaller business in terms of employment has not diminished in recent years. As a matter of fact, it has risen slightly since the early 1970s. Nowadays a majority view is that the existence of thick layers of a wide variety of smaller businesses with their flexibility and innovativeness is one of the sources of strength of the Japanese economy.

Smaller businesses play important roles in the Japanese economy, and their roles both in export and in FDI are no exception.[19] Smaller businesses have a considerable share in Japan's FDI (Table 9). This situation is in sharp contrast to the situation of some other countries where large firms are dominant both in export and in FDI. Smaller businesses' share is especially high in manufacturing investment going to Asian countries.

Some of the cases of FDI by Japanese smaller businesses in the manufacturing sector are those in which smaller-business subcontractors are following their parents to the United States, Asian industrializing countries, and elsewhere. But a majority of the cases seems to be direct investment by "independent" (as opposed to subcontracting) small-business manufacturers. There are a number of cases in which Korean small businessmen working in Japan invest back in South Korea. In such cases linguistic and cultural barriers to "foreign" direct investment should be very low.

Characteristics of Japanese-owned subsidiaries engaged in manufacturing abroad

As stated above, Japan's FDI is still in the early stages of development, especially in manufacturing. Not only is the ratio of overseas production by Japanese manufacturing firms to their domestic production low relatively to their U.S. or West German counterparts (Table 6), but they also have few well-established, large subsidiaries in foreign countries comparable to subsidiaries of General Motors and Ford in West Germany, IBM in Japan and many other countries, GE and Ericsson in Latin America, or Unilever, Nestlé, Ciba-Geigy, Philips and major petroleum companies all over the world.

These U.S.- and European-based manufacturing firms and many

Table 9
The Proportion of Small- and Medium-Sized Firms in Japan's Overseas Direct Investment[a]

(no. of cases, %)

Year	Total (A)	Small & medium-sized (B)	(B)/(A) 100
1974	1271	482	37.9
1975	1346	488	36.3
1976	1026	374	36.5
1977	1223	369	30.2
1978	1253	422	33.7
1979	1453	485	33.4
1980	1328	408	30.7
1981	1281	394	30.8
1982	1367	371	27.1
1983	1161	487	22.1
1984	1488	341	22.9
1985	n.a.	n.a.	n.a.

Source: Same as for Table 7.
[a]The number of cases of overseas direct investment approved or notified.

others have large, well-established subsidiaries abroad, and are among the leading firms in the respective industries in the host countries, and engage in full operation including production, marketing, exporting, and, not infrequently, research and development. They are appropriately called multinational corporations in the sense that they engage themselves in full operation on a substantial scale in a number of countries.

It is no exaggeration, however, to say that there are no overseas subsidiaries of Japanese manufacturing firms which have their roots as deep in the soil of the host countries as such subsidiaries of U.S. and European multinationals.[20] Although many Japanese manufacturing firms have come up in the list of world's largest firms, their main overseas operation has so far been export sales and related activities.

FDI for the purpose of "production," as distinguished from marketing and assembling by Japanese manufacturing firms, at present consists mainly of the following two types. The first type is FDI behind protective tariff and nontariff barriers. The factories built for this purpose are generally small and their "local contents" are low. Leading Japanese automobile manufacturers have five to ten overseas plants each, but almost all of these plants are very small compared with their home factories in Japan, of the order of one twentieth or even less, and depend heavily on parts and assemblies supplied from Japan. The situation is more or less similar in electronics products, electrical appliances, copying machines, and machine tools.

The second type is direct investment in newly industrializing economies (NIEs) and other countries in Asia to take advantage of low labor costs. In this type of investment those processes of production which are labor-intensive and technologically less sophisticated are transferred abroad from Japan. The scale of operation is not necessarily smaller than at home, but normally technologically sophisticated processes as well as product planning and designing, research and development, and other head-office functions all remain in Japan. Moreover, since these Asian countries adopt more or less restrictive policies, such as phased localization, or not allowing majority ownership, and their policies and political attitudes toward foreign investment tend to vacillate, most Japanese firms feel that they cannot depend entirely on just single overseas plants for any process, nor invest heavily in these countries for essential parts of their production.

Thus both types of overseas factories of Japanese manufacturing firms tend to take the form of small—sometimes miniature—branches or offshoots of the plants at home. Generally speaking they are relatively new, immature, small in scale, and technologically inefficient. This may well be the reason for their low profitability.

Will some of these overseas subsidiaries of Japanese manufacturing firms grow up in the future to become fully-fledged, deep-rooted and more autonomous than their U.S.- or European-owned counterparts?

As far as subsidiaries in developing countries are concerned, a majority view may be that the future outlook does not seem too bright. Even setting aside the international debt problems and political difficulties some developing countries have run into, the policies of most developing countries toward FDI do not seem to be liberal and stable enough to allow one to be optimistic.

What is the perspective for Japanese-owned manufacturing subsidiaries in developed countries, especially in the United States and Western Europe? It is definitely brighter there than in developing countries. Yet there are a number of difficulties for Japanese firms in expanding their production—as opposed to marketing—activities there.

Even if the language barriers, which are still a serious problem at present,[21] are somehow overcome, some of the Japanese management, production and employment practices which form the basis of the strength of Japanese manufacturing industries, especially in the fabricating and assembling type of manufacturing using mass-production technologies, do not seem to be easily transplanted to North America or Europe. It would be difficult to transfer Japanese-type labor management and subcontractor–parent relationships to a foreign land with basically European cultural traditions. There are a number of studies on how Japanese-type management practices have been introduced in subsidiaries abroad,[22] and some of them report that Japanese practices are bringing successes. But so far only a small part or limited aspects of Japanese practices have been transplanted or experimented with in subsidiaries abroad.

Some of the difficulties encountered in bringing Japanese ways of management and industrial relations into countries with European cultural traditions are as follows:

(1) In Japanese industries the labor union is organized on a company-by-company basis, and a union is usually composed of all the "regular" employees of the company, including both blue-collar and white-collar workers. The management and the labor union of a company cooperate closely, share the benefits of its successful operation, and have a feeling of solidarity. Such union structure cannot be brought into subsidiaries in North America and Europe. There the labor unions or some other

bodies representing employees, especially blue-collar employees, tend to be antagonistic, or at best neutral, to the management, and are rarely cooperative with management. Japanese managers are often dismayed at dealing with union representatives in foreign countries.

(2) One of the major sources of Japanese firms' strength is that an employee serves in the same firm for a long time—the so-called life-time employment practice—is promoted regularly in terms of salary and post, and experiences a number of different kinds of post in different divisions—that is, he (or she) is promoted in a "spiral," not "linear," way. In this way the employees get extensive training on the job and come to know much about the firm and colleagues working together within the firm.[23] But this gives rise to a number of difficulties for firms engaged in extensive overseas operation. One of them is what is called *tanshin-funin*: a large number of Japanese businessmen and engineers are serving in foreign countries alone away from their families, who tend to remain in Japan, especially when they have school-age children and/or aging parents to take care of.

(3) The Japanese practices of long-term (or life-time) employment, extensive on-the-job training, and regular promotion in a "spiral" way give rise to certain difficulties in absorbing and assimilating foreign white-collar workers, engineers, and managers, very few, if any, of whom speak the Japanese language, into the body of the Japanese firm's permanent employees. The operating language in the top and middle management is Japanese for most Japanese firms.

(4) Japanese firms are more egalitarian than U.S. or European firms with respect to income distribution between blue-collar and white-collar employees and between highest paid (that is, the president and other top managers) and the rank and file, and with respect to such matters as the use of common canteens and entrances by blue-collar and white-collar employees. This is welcomed by foreign blue-collar workers, but not by white-collar employees, engineers, and managers. Together with the difficulties explained in (3), generally speaking Japanese-owned subsidiaries in North America and Western Europe are not popular as employers of white-collar workers, and have difficulties in attracting and keeping capable non-Japanese managers and engineers.

(5) Japanese large firms, especially in industries such as automobiles, electronics, electrical appliances, machinery in general, and iron and steel depend heavily on the system of subcontracting. The relationship between a parent firm and its subcontractors is a long-term one based upon mutual trust, in which the parent firm often provides financial and technological assistance to its subcontractors, and the latter

seriously endeavour to meet the needs of the former. That such a relationship is difficult to establish outside of Japan is one of the causes of technological inefficiency and high costs at overseas subsidiaries as compared with production at home.[24] To overcome this difficulty, when a Japanese automobile manufacturer builds a plant in the United States or Europe, a number of its major subcontractor firms follow it and build plants nearby. But such a move tends to give rise to new cases of "economic friction" accompanying FDI, since the producers of automobile parts in the host country protest that they will lose their market shares.

In spite of these difficulties, however, since Japanese firms are steadily accumulating "managerial resources," including expertise to run subsidiaries in foreign countries efficiently, FDI by Japanese manufacturing firms is likely to increase steadily and perhaps fairly rapidly.

V. Theory of Foreign Direct Investment

I first became interested in the economics of foreign direct investment (FDI) around 1966 at the time of the public discussion in Japan on the government policy to liberalize inward direct investment into Japan. My view on FDI then (Komiya, 1967, 1969; Sumita, Komiya and Watanabe, 1972) was based upon—and extended—Penrose's (1956, 1959) view of the growth of the firm and foreign investment. Its main points are:

1. FDI takes place when the firm grows and accumulates "managerial resources" within it, and tries to make use of them in most profitable—and efficient—ways. The firm often finds it more profitable (over the long run) to use them abroad than within the country where its head office is located.

2. The existing economic theories of FDI tend to treat FDI as international movement of "capital" in the sense of funds or general purchasing power. This misses the essence of FDI, which is not so much international movement of "capital" as of "managerial resources"—that is, managerial, technological, marketing, and organizational know-how and expertise—necessary to run a firm efficiently.[25] Some managerial resources have a public-goods character, or a partially public-goods character, within the firm.

3. FDI originates from those countries and industries which have accumulated or are accumulating "managerial resources," and goes to countries where managerial returns are high. The firm undertaking

FDI is often a Schumpeterian innovator, and is making a new entry in an industry in the host country.

4. Conditions determining the flows of FDI are not too different from those determining the flows of "internal" direct investment, that is, direct investment between regions within a country. But political and cultural barriers for direct investment are generally much higher between countries than between regions within a country.

5. On the other hand, tariff and nontariff barriers to import often induce FDI, and are intentionally employed by national governments to promote inward FDI. This is an aspect absent in the case of "internal" direct investment.

The dominant theory of FDI in the late 1960s and early 1970s was the oligopoly theory or the monopolistic MNE (multinational enterprise) theory of FDI advocated by Hymer (1960), Kindleberger (1968, 1969 and elsewhere), Caves (1971) and Caves and Jones (1981) among others. The Hymer–Kindleberger theory asserts that monopolistic or oligopolistic elements are essential for FDI, and that the success of FDI is based upon some monopolistic advantages.

There were a few other theories in the late 1960s and early 1970s such as the product life cycle theory (Vernon, 1966), and an argument emphasizing the investor's risk diversification to cope with exchange rate fluctuations (Aliber, 1970). From the early 1970s Kojima argued in a number of his writings (for example, Kojima, 1977, 1985) that while the U.S. or "multinational" type FDI is generally trade-reducing, the Japanese type FDI is, in contrast, generally trade-increasing (or should be trade-increasing). But I found none of these theories or arguments convincing.

After participating in a United Nations study group on multinational corporations in 1973 and 1974 (United Nations, 1974), my interest shifted away from FDI and multinational enterprises. Looking through statistical and other data on Japan's FDI and recent literature on FDI recently, however, I felt that what I wrote on FDI in the 1960s and early 1970s, in particular the growth-of-the firm theory or the managerial-resources theory of FDI, was basically correct. I have been surprised to find that in the literature on FDI written in Japanese recently, the concept of "managerial resources" which I first proposed in 1967 (Komiya, 1967) is now widely and frequently used.

The oligopoly or monopolistic advantage theory of FDI seems to be on the decline. On the other hand, the views which emphasize the economies associated with internalization within the firm organisation (Williamson, 1975; Imai, Itami and Koike, 1982) seem to be on the rise.[26]

6. When transferring goods, services, and other resources, and exchanging information and knowledge between different locations, it is often more efficient to use some intrafirm or semi-intrafirm organization than to use the market. The market here means selling and buying between independent firms, especially in the form of an arm's length, spot transaction each time. FDI is such an intrafirm or semi-intrafirm organizational form of transferring resources and information between different locations and organizing productive activities at different locations.

Thus when some organizational way of transferring resources and information is more efficient than the transfer through the market mechanism, a firm undertakes direct investment whether internationally or within a country. This is the "demand side" of FDI. It must be emphasized, however, that to be able to use an intrafirm, non-market way of transferring resources and information, the firm must have accumulated within it "managerial resources" to be applied to FDI. If such managerial resources can readily be procured through the market, other firms—or rather, the particular firm in question—will be able to undertake the transfer or the productive activities at different locations. Hence the growth of the firm and accumulation or availability of "managerial resources" within it are essential on the "supply side" of FDI, as stated above.

When FDI is viewed in this way, as a non-market way of transferring resources and information, it is perhaps easy to understand the following point.

7. There are many forms of FDI of different shades, from the use of a straightforward intrafirm organization such as a branch office, or a wholly-owned subsidiary, to weaker and shorter-lived forms having an element of the market, such as the combination of a loan and a long-term purchase contract, the so-called "fade-away" or "turn-key" arrangement, technology licensing combined with minority shareholding, and so on.

Thus whether or not a certain pattern of behavior or activity of a firm is direct investment is not a black-and-white affair: there are wide grey areas of all shades between the purely organizational forms and the pure market mechanisms.

Below I make some comments on points (1) to (7) which summarize my theory of direct investment, and give a few examples to illustrate it.

(i) Points (1) and (2) mean that FDI is generally beneficial to both the host and home countries. In the host country the productivity of other factors of production are raised by incoming managerial resources, outputs increase more than the profits earned by the foreign direct investor, and the home country also gains since managerial resources earn higher returns abroad than they can earn at home, except in pathological situations.

(ii) The oligopoly theory of FDI, the product-life-cycle theory of FDI, and Kojima's argument contrasting U.S. or multinationals' "anti-trade" FDI with Japanese "pro-trade" FDI all seem to emphasize, respectively, particular aspects of particular countries' FDI in particular periods, neglecting other aspects and situations in other countries and other periods. Since counterexamples to their assertions abound, they cannot be claimed to be *the* general theory of direct investment, or a statement of general validity.

(iii) Investment including FDI in the flow sense takes place only in a changing world, not in a stationary one. There must be some new factors or changing conditions shifting the status quo for FDI in the flow sense to take place. Such industrial organization concepts as oligopoly, imperfect competition, product differentiation, and economies of scale or scope are all concepts of basically static economic theory. It is intrinsically contradictory to explain FDI in the flow sense, which is taking place in a changing, dynamic world, by the use of basically static concepts formed to describe a stationary state.

FDI in the flow sense often constitutes a new entry into an industry in the host country, and is undertaken by a Schumpeterian, innovative firm which has some special managerial resources lacking in the firms of the host countries. I belong to the school which considers, for example, the A & P company in the 1930s, which was accused—erroneously—of predatory dumping and other monopolistic practices, not as a monopolist or oligopolist, but as a Schumpeterian innovator in a rapidly changing and increasingly competitive market.[27]

(iv) The fact that in Japan small- and medium-sized businesses are quite active as direct investors itself almost invalidates the oligopoly theory of FDI. An example of a small business which is a really innovative direct investor is a manufacturer of *jika-tabi*, a traditional-style footware made of rubber and cloth used by Japanese farmers and construction workers. It was established in 1948 and now employs only 27 employees in Japan, and its paid-up capital is merely 96 million yen. It is so small that most Japanese have never heard its name. The production process is highly labor-intensive, so the costs went up sharply in the 1960s with the rise in the general wage level. When the firm decided to build a factory in Taiwan in 1968, its share the *jika-tabi* market was about 20%. The factory was successfully operated for some time, but wages in Taiwan rose rapidly, and it was shut down in 1982. In the meantime the firm opened a factory in Korea in 1973 and ran it until 1984. Here again wages rose rapidly, and investment there proved to be unprofitable. Now the firm has one factory in the Philippines operated since 1979 and one in China (mainland) operated since 1983. In all of these cases all the output is exported to Japan since there is no demand for this kind of footwear outside Japan. It has no factory in Japan now. The firm's market share had risen to 65% in 1986. Looking at the figure for market share, one might call this firm an oligopolist or monopolist, but the amount of funds used by this firm is very small and the technologies used are labor-intensive, light-industry ones, with no sophisticated "high technologies" involved. The firm is a Schumpeterian innovator which others have found difficult to imitate. There must be some special managerial, technological and organizational expertise involved in running the *jika-tabi* business efficiently and successfully. Otherwise other businessmen in Taiwan, Japan, the Philippines or China would have been able to imitate it.

(v) Japanese manufacturing firms have had great success in the fabricating and assembling type of manufacturing using mass-production technologies, but so far have undertaken FDI only to a limited extent. As already mentioned, the ratio of the value of production in foreign countries to that of domestic production is much lower for representative Japanese manufacturing firms than for similar firms in Western Europe or the United States. Moreover, a large part of the FDI they have so far undertaken appears to be induced by tariff and nontariff barriers to import or threats or possibilities of establishing such.

Although Japanese firms in such industries as automobiles, machinery, electrical machinery, and electronics have developed highly efficient production technologies, and accumulated managerial resources to run factories and firms in Japan, it is not easy to transfer their technologies to foreign countries because of the differences in employment practices, the labor union structure and parent–subcontractor relationships. They have not yet accumulated the managerial resources necessary to run factories abroad as efficiently as those at home.

(vi) Most large firms in the industries mentioned in (v) might be described as oligopolists in markets characterized by product differentiation, but they are severe competitors with each other, especially in developing new products, improving the quality, and lowering the costs of existing ones. They allocate a large amount of expenditure to research and development, product planning, market research and investment, not only in plant and equipment but also in laboratories and marketing networks. They are better viewed as mutually competing Schumpeterian innovators and followers in rapidly changing, dynamic environments, than as oligopolists or monopolists in a stationary market.

(vii) There are no theoretical reasons to associate oligopoly with FDI. Suppose that an industry is dominated by a few oligopoly firms on a worldwide scale, say two or three firms each in country A and country B. There appear to exist no incentives for these oligopolists to make FDI in their rivals' country or in a third country, simply because they are oligopolists. If economies of scale are substantial, it would be better for each of them to produce at only one factory in their respective home countries, and export from there to all over the world. There is no reason for FDI for the purpose of marketing either, unless there are some advantages in intrafirm organization of having subsidiaries for marketing over a more market-oriented approach such as securing a general agent in each importing country.

Another alternative to FDI available to "oligopolists" in the market characterized by product differentiation is what is called the OEM (original equipment manufacturing or manufacturers) arrangement. This is an alternative to FDI for the purpose of manufacturing in a low-cost country. Under this strangely named arrangement a firm, A, in country I asks another firm, B, in country II (I and II can, of course, be the same) to manufacture and supply a product to be sold by A with A's brand name in country I or elsewhere. Not infrequently A and B are, by and large, competitors in the same industry. The OEM contract is nowadays a quite common practice in automobiles, construction machinery, electronics products, electrical appliances, computer terminals, office machines, machine tools and so on. Thus an "oligopolist" firm has a choice whether to make FDI for the purpose of production by itself in a low-cost country, or make an OEM arrangement with a manufacturer in a low-cost country.

The OEM arrangement, sometimes accompanied by minority shareholding, is a practice belonging to a grey zone between a pure market relationship and a pure intrafirm organization, and illustrates point (7) above.[28]

VI. Conclusions

This paper examines Japan's foreign direct investment (FDI) in recent years and reconsiders the theory of FDI in the light of Japan's experience. Direct investment, whether international or within a country, takes place when a firm considers that some intrafirm or partially intrafirm way of transferring resources and information between different locations is more advantageous—and more efficient—than transfer through the market mechanism. There are many such intrafirm or partially intrafirm ways of transfer, so that direct investment is not a black-and-white affair, but a phenomenon taking place in a wide range of grey zones.

A necessary condition for FDI to take place is that the firm has specific managerial resources accumulated within it, or is accumulating them. FDI in the flow sense is taking place in a changing, dynamic situation, and is generally undertaken by a Schumpeterian, innovative firm attempting a new entry into an industry in the host country. National borders are naturally a high barrier to FDI just as they are to foreign trade, but at the same time tariff and nontariff barriers to import trade promote FDI, and are intentionally used for such a purpose.

Japan's outward FDI includes a wide variety of different types such as natural-resources development projects by mining/petroleum and paper and pulp companies, ownership of flag-of-convenience ships by shipping companies, investment in real estate by institutional investors and acquisition of laboratories for research and development by manufacturing firms. In terms of the total value of FDI outstanding, Japan ranks somewhere between the third and seventh largest investor countries of the world. Annual FDI flows from Japan have recently been increasing by leaps and bounds, especially when the yen exchange rate appreciated sharply. Yet as a whole Japan is still in a very early stage of development as a direct investor country.

The relative importance of FDI in the Japanese economy is still small. While the share of trade-related investment in FDI is high, the share of manufacturing in FDI is still small. In the destination of FDI the share of developing countries has been relatively high. The profitability of Japan's FDI seems relatively low, reflecting its immature state. There are few large, really multinational, enterprises based in Japan, comparable to U.S. or European-based ones.

Recently a big shift in Japan's FDI flows is taking place away from developing countries, including those in East and South-East Asia to developed countries in North America and Western Europe, especially the United States. The shift has been caused by several factors including the worsening of investment environments in most developing countries on the one hand, and the heightening of barriers to imports from Japan in the United States and some European countries on the other. Thus the pattern of Japan's FDI has been much affected by the trade and investment policies of the host countries, as well as by changes in the yen exchange rate.

There are several difficulties in transferring to overseas subsidiaries Japanese managerial, personnel and subcontracting practices, which constitute the basis of the strength of Japanese firms, especially those in fabricating and assembly type manufacturing using mass-production technologies. However, since Japanese firms are rapidly accumulating "managerial resources" including the expertise to run subsidiaries in foreign countries, and since Japan's balance of payments on the current account is expected to run large surpluses for some time, annual FDI flows of Japanese manufacturing firms are likely to continue to increase in the coming years.

This chapter first appeared in *International Finance and Trade in a Polycentric World*, Vol. 92 in the International Economic Association conference series, edited by Silvio Borner (London: Macmillan, 1988).

Notes

1. Such a procedure involves another serious valuation problem, since it amounts to adding up values at different time points without adjusting for changes in prices or exchange rates over time.

2. The results of these surveys are published, respectively, as MITI, *Kaigai Toshi Tokei Soran* (Statistical Survey of Overseas Investment), and MITI, *Wagakuni Kigyo no Kaigai Jigyo Katsudo* (Overseas Business Activities of Japanese Firms).

3. In particular, the threshold line of the effective management control given in IMF's *The Balance of Payments Manual* is 50 per cent by an individual resident and 25 per cent by a single or organised group, but actually different countries use different percentages. Accumulation of retained earnings is to be included in both the annual flow of direct investment (in capital account) and that of investment income (in invisible trade), but few countries other than the United States observe this accounting principle.

4. For more of the post-war history of Japan's FDI see Hamada (1972), Kojima (1977, 1985), Sekiguchi (1979a, b), Sekiguchi and Japan Economic Research Centre (1982), and Sekiguchi and Matsuba (1974).

5. See Komiya (1972), pp. 150–52.

6. On the other hand, the Japanese government supported several large-scale foreign investment projects to secure and diversify energy supply sources during this period.

7. See Zaigai Kigyo Kyokai (1986) and Horaguchi (1986).

8. For a historical review of the cases of "trade friction" situations Japan has been confronted with—or has given rise to—see Chapter 1.

9. It may be noted that, somewhat paradoxically, the recent large yen appreciation has also caused an increase in foreign—especially West Euro-

pean—firms' direct investments in Japan for assembling, manufacturing, marketing and servicing their products.

10. JETRO (1987) and other publications of JETRO (Nihon Boeki Shinko kai, Japan External Trade Organisation), MITI's annually published *Tsusho Hakusho* (International Trade White Papers), articles published in Japan's Export-Import Bank's *Kaigai Toshi Kenkyusho-Ho* (Bulletin of the Research Institute on Overseas Investment), publications of other Japanese banks' research departments, and reports and articles in daily newspapers (especially *Nihon Keizai Shinbun*) and other periodicals.

11. It is perhaps needless to say that a typical Marxist indictment that the monopoly-capitalists as direct investors "exploit" workers in lower-wage countries through such direct investment is basically mistaken. First, the workers in the host countries usually benefit from greater employment opportunities and higher wages. Secondly, the use of lower-cost labor usually results not in higher profits but in lower prices of products over the long run when the markets of products are competitive—which is true in almost all cases, over the long run—and benefits accrue mostly to the users of the products.

12. Some Japanese investors have been induced to engage in food processing abroad at least partly because Japan's effective rate of tariff protection for some food processing industries is negative. The import of rice, wheat, barley, sugar (molasses) and a number of other agricultural products is either totally prohibited or under highly restrictive quotas, or the tariff rates on them are very high. As a result, Japan's domestic prices of such products are very high relative to prices in exporting countries. On the other hand, import of certain processed agricultural products such as *sake* (rice wine), *senbei* (rice cake), or glutamic soda are not subject to quantitative import restrictions, and the tariff rate is moderate to high, but not prohibitive. Thus the effective rates of protection for a number of food manufacturing processes are negative, inducing Japanese firms to engage in overseas production of such processed foods. Recently many Japanese foods such as *yakitori* (frozen), *sake, miso* (bean paste), *umeboshi*, never produced in countries other than Japan before, or those never imported into Japan earlier (e.g., eels), are now produced in Asian countries—and even in the United States—often with the participation of Japanese investors, and imported into Japan.

On the other hand some food processing firms, often small ones, have gone to invest in the United States and Britain to produce traditional Japanese foods such as *tofu, yakitori* and *kamaboko* for local consumption, as they become increasingly popular there.

13. MITI, *Kaigai Toshi Tokei Soran* (Yearbook of Overseas Investment Statistics), 1983 edition.

14. When a Japanese resident, whether an individual or a corporation, purchased real estate in a foreign country directly, it was included in Japan's outward FDI until December 1980, when such a purchase was completely liberalized. Since then it has not been included in the amount of FDI. Hence the statistics on FDI before and after 1980 are not comparable in this regard. When a Japanese resident establishes a subsidiary abroad engaged in real estate business, however, the remittance to the subsidiary is included in FDI. Japanese life insurance companies almost always own real estate in the United States in the latter way.

15. According to a report in *Nihon Keizai Shinbun* (Japan Economic Daily), 24 May 1987.

16. The fact that the level of inward FDI into Japan is still low does not necessarily reflect the alleged 'closedness' of the Japanese economy. According to a well-known index of business environment for foreign investors prepared by an American business research firm, Japan is now rated at the top, second only to Switzerland and higher than the United States and any EC countries. The index takes into account numerous factors including attitude to foreign investors, availability of local managers and partners, nationalism, bureaucratic delays, and enforceability of contract.

17. Nihon Keizai Kyoiku Center (1987) estimates the share of developed countries in the regional breakdown of overseas direct investment (the value outstanding) made by Japan, the United States and West Germany at the end of 1980 (1979 for West Germany) as follows (figures in parentheses are for the manufacturing sector):

	%	%
Japan	44.8	(31.9)
United States	73.5	(80.2)
West Germany	78.6	(77.2)

18. One might ask whether the difference in the profit rate results from Japanese direct investors' practice of transfer-pricing, whereby they try to transfer overseas profits to Japan. My impression is that they do not do so much. The tax rate on corporate profits is now higher in Japan than in the United States and most other countries, and nowadays the tax authorities in most countries are intensely watchful of wholly-owned (or even majority-owned) subsidiaries of foreign corporations with respect to the possibility of transfer-pricing. There exists a strong incentive for transfer-pricing, however, in countries where remittance of profits and repayment of loans is subject to restrictive exchange controls or where there is a possibility of such controls.

19. It is perhaps well known that Japanese small businesses are quite active in export trade. It is less well known that they account for a substantial proportion in the export and import of technologies (see Koshiba, 1987).

20. It is not easy to predict which Japanese companies will become multinationals in the sense given in the text. Perhaps Honda, Sony and Matsushita may be among the leading candidates.

21. For example, which language is to be used in conducting the top and middle management meetings, or in correspondence between subsidiaries and the head office, is a difficult problem for Japanese emerging 'multinationals'.

22. Recently a large number of case studies and surveys of management practices and/or industrial relations at Japanese-owned subsidiaries in foreign countries have been published. Two examples available in English are Takamiya and Thurley (1985) and Dunning (1986).

23. On these and other structural and behavioral characteristics of the Japanese firm, see Komiya (1986).

24. See, however, Dunning (1986) for the favorable effects of Japanese-owned subsidiaries on the subcontractors in Britain.

25. Foreign-owned firms often raise funds from the financial markets in the host countries and sometimes borrow heavily there, especially in developed countries.

26. See, for example, Teece (1985).

27. See Adelman (1959) and Komiya (1972, p. 162).

28. I will not deal with two theoretical problems related to FDI: (1) the effect of FDI on the balance of payments of the host and home countries, and (2) the effect of FDI on the employment of the home country, and the possibility of deindustrialization of the home country as a result of large direct investment outflows. These are difficult problems and cannot be dealt with within this limited space. I wish to note, however, that most discussions on these two problems are unsatisfactory to me because they try to deal with these essentially macroeconomic problems by a partial equilibrium approach. To answer the first problem adequately, the impact of FDI on the total savings and domestic investment and the likely change in the income levels of countries concerned must be analysed. Also, it is necessary to have a satisfactory macroeconomic theory on the mechanism and factors determining the level of unemployment in a national economy, in order to discuss the effect of FDI on unemployment. By and large I believe both effects (1) and (2) would not constitute a serious economic problem for the national economy, whether of a home or host country, so long as (i) it is basically healthy and possesses a proper degree of flexibility, and (ii) the government pursues appropriate macroeconomic policies and policies to assist adjustment for resource reallocation.

References

Adelman, M.A. (1959). *A & P: A Case Study in Price-Cost Behavior and Public Policy*. Cambridge, Mass.: Harvard University Press.

Aliber, R.Z. (1970). "A Theory of Direct Foreign Investment," in Kindleberger, C.P. (ed.) *International Corporation, A Symposium*. Cambridge, Mass.: MIT Press.

Caves, R.E. (1971). "International Corporation: The Industrial Economics of Foreign Investment," *Economica* (new series), vol. 38, no. 149.

Caves, R.E. and R.W. Jones (1981). *World Trade and Payments*, 3rd ed. Boston: Little-Brown.

Drysdale, P., ed. (1972). *Direct Foreign Investment in Asia and the Pacific*. Canberra: Australian National University Press.

Dunning, J.H. (1986). *Japanese Particjpation in British Industry*. London: Croom Helm.

Hamada, K. (1972). "Japanese Investment Abroad," in Drysdale (1972).

Horaguchi, H. (1986). "Ajia ni okeru Nikkei Shinshutsu Kigyo no Tettai: 1971–84" (Withdrawals of Japanese Overseas Investments in Asia), *Ajia Keizai* (The Asian Economy), vol. 27, no. 3 (March).

Hymer, S. (1960). *The International Operations of National Firms: A Study of Direct Foreign Investment*. Cambridge, Mass.: MIT Press.

Imai, K., H. Itami, and K. Koike (1982). *Naibu Soshiki no Keizaigaku* (Economics of Internal Organisation). Tokyo: Toyo Keizai Shinposha.

JETRO (Nihon Boeki Shinko-kai—Japan External Trade Organisation) (1987). *Sekai to Nihon no Kaigai Chokusetsu Toshi:* 1987 (World's and Japan's Overseas Direct Investment). Tokyo: JETRO.

Kindleberger, C.P. (1968). *International Economics, 4th ed.* Homewood, Ill.: Irwin.

Kindleberger, C.P. (1969). *American Business Abroad.* New Haven: Yale University Press.

Kojima, K. (1977). *Kaigai Chokusetsu Toshi Ron* (On Overseas Direct Investment). Tokyo:Daiyamondo-sha.

Kojima, K. (1985). *Nihon no Kaigai Chokusetsu Toshi* (Japan's Overseas Direct Investment). Tokyo: Bunshinsha.

Komiya, R. (1967). "Shihon-Jiyuka no Keizaigaku" (Economics of Liberalization of Direct Investment), *Ekonomisto,* 25 July 1967. A revised version is included in R. Komiya, *Gendai Nihon Keizai Kenkyu* (Studies on the Contemporary Japanese Economy). Tokyo: University of Tokyo Press, 1975.

Komiya, R. (1969). "Chokusetsu Toshi to Sangyo Seisaku" (Direct Investment and Industrial Policy), in Niida, H. and Ono, A. (eds) *Nihon no Sangyo Soshiki* (Japan's Industrial Organisation). Tokyo: Iwanami Shoten.

Komiya, R. (1972). "Direct Foreign Investment in Postwar Japan," in Drysdale (1972).

Komiya, R. (1986). "Nihon Kigyo no Kozoteki Kodoteki Tokucho," Discussion Paper 86-J-4, Faculty of Economics, University of Tokyo. An English version is: "Structural Behavioral Characteristics of Japanese Firms," a paper presented to the Hitotsubashi/Stanford GSB Conference on the Perspectives and Nature of the Corporation, 29 March–1 April 1987, Ito, Japan.

Koshiba, T. (1987). "Wagakuni Chusho-Kigyo no Kaigai Chokusetsu Toshi to Gijutsu Boeki" (Small- and Medium-size Businesses in Japan's Overseas Direct Investment and Trade in Technologies), *Tohoku-Gakuin Daigaku Ronshu,* no. 104.

Nihon Keizai Kyoiku Center (Japan Center for Economics Education) ed. (1987). *Kaigai Chokusetsu Toshi no Hanashi* (On Overseas Direct Investment). Tokyo: NKKC.

Penrose, E.F. (1956). "Foreign Investment and the Growth of the Firm," *Economic Journal,* vol. 66.

Penrose, E.F. (1959). *The Theory of the Growth of the Firm.* Oxford: Blackwell.

Sekiguchi, S. (1979a). *Kaigai Toshi no Shintenkai* (New Developments in Overseas Investment). Tokyo: Nihon-Keizai Shimbunsha.

Sekiguchi, S. (1979b). *Japanese Direct Foreign Investment.* London: Macmillan.

Sekiguchi, S. and Japan Economic Research Center, ed. (1982). *Kan-Taiheiyoken to Nihon no Chokusetsu Toshi* (Pan-Pacific Area and Japan's Direct Investment). Tokyo: Nihon-Keizai Shimbunsha.

Sekiguchi, S. and K. Matsuba, (1974). *Nihon no Chokusetsu Toshi* (Japan's Direct Investment). Tokyo: Nihon-Keizai Shimbunsha.

Sumita, S., R. Komiya, and Y. Watanabe (ed.) (1972). *Takokuseki Kigyo no Jittai* (The Realities of Multinational Firms). Tokyo: Nihon-Keizai Shimbunsha.

Takamiya, S. and K. Thurley, eds. (1985). *Japan's Emerging Multinationals*. Tokyo: University of Tokyo Press.

Teece, D.J. (1985). "Multinational Enterprise, Internal Governance and Industrial Organization," *American Economic Association (Papers and Proceedings)*, pp. 233–38.

United Nations (1974). *The Impact of Multinational Corporations on Development and on International Relations*. New York: United Nations.

Vernon, R. (1966). "International Investment and International Trade in the Product Cycle," *Quarterly Journal of Economics*, vol. 80.

Williamson, O.E. (1975). *Markets and Hierarchies*. New York: Free Press.

Zaigai Kigyo Kyokai (Association of Overseas Enterprises) (1986). *Kaigai Chokusetsu Toshi to Tettai* (Overseas Direct Investment and Withdrawals).

Japanese Enterprises

CHAPTER 4

THE STRUCTURAL AND BEHAVIORAL CHARACTERISTICS OF JAPANESE FIRMS

This chapter discusses the structural and behavioral characteristics of typical large Japanese firms, which, I believe, are considerably different from those of typical large American or European firms. First, certain distinct features in the structure of Japanese firms are described (Sections I and II), and then their behavioral characteristics discussed, as resulting from their structural characteristics. "Structure" here refers to more or less persistent "anatomical" characteristics, and "behavior" refers to the decisions and patterns of action of firms in response to changes in environment; these terms are analogous to "market structure" and "market behavior" (or conduct) in the theory of industrial organization. The analysis of the behavioral characteristics of Japanese firms is divided into two parts: a static theory dealing with stationary states (Section III) and a dynamic discussion explicitly taking into consideration the growth of firms (Section IV). Finally, a few characteristics of Japanese firms which are not taken up in earlier sections but worth emphasizing in my view are discussed in some detail (Section V).

Although I confine the following discussion to large firms, the importance of medium and small firms can hardly be overlooked in any discussion of "Japanese firms." According to the Medium- and Small-Size Enterprises Law, medium- and small-sized enterprises are defined as those with (i) 300 employees or less (for wholesale businesses, 100; for retail and service businesses, 50) and (ii) capital of 100 million yen or less (wholesale businesses, 30 million yen; retail and service businesses, 10 million yen). In terms of the number of employees, the proportion of medium- and small-sized enterprises in all sectors of the Japanese economy has not shrunk in recent years, but is on the rise.[1] Medium- and small-sized firms have, by virtue of the aforementioned law and others, received certain favors from the government. These favors notwithstanding, the basic strength of these smaller firms stems primarily from their own management strengths.

It is essential, therefore, to understand the structure and behavior of smaller firms in order to understand Japanese firms and the Japanese economy. But the limited space of this paper does not allow such elaborations. The following discussion is limited to large firms.

I. Structural Characteristics of Japanese Firms

Compared with their counterparts in Western Europe and North America, and also with those in China, Japanese large firms are marked by the following structural characteristics:

Legal forms
Large firms in Japan are, by and large, joint-stock companies listed on the stock exchanges. The total number of listed companies is about 2,000. Although in number they represent less than 0.1% of all corporations, in sales they account for about 40% of the total. Among them, about 1,100 are joint-stock companies listed in the First Sections of the Tokyo and/or Osaka Stock Exchanges. They thus can be looked upon as the population of typical large Japanese firms. The scale of these 1,100 companies varies a great deal, from the very recently privatized mammoth NTT (Nippon Telegraph and Telephone Company) with 290,000 employees[2] to those with less than 100 employees (which hence fit into the definition of "medium- and small-size enterprises").

Among the large joint-stock companies that are not listed, some are sought after by college graduates as favorable places of employment. They include, for example, (i) companies owned by a family or families such as Idemitsu, Seibu Department Stores, Suntory, Takenaka Engineering, Yamazaki Works, and YKK; (ii) majority-owned subsidiaries of other listed companies or foreign enterprises such as Epson, Fuji-Xerox, IBM Japan, Japan Oil Development, Mitsubishi Motor, and Yokokawa-Hewlett Packard; (iii) communications media companies such as the large newspapers, television and radio broadcasting companies, publishing houses, and advertising agencies; (iv) fast-growing new companies such as Shinkawa (semiconductor bonding machines), World (apparel), Japan Life (apparel), the Mori Buildings (real estate), consumer credit companies, and so on.

The typical firm that represents Japanese "big business" is, however, one listed in the First Sections of the stock exchanges whose stocks are widely traded. Large enterprises that are not listed are few in number, and cannot be considered typical Japanese big businesses.

Separation of ownership and management

Stock ownership of the companies listed in the First Sections of the stock exchanges is widely dispersed except for that in the subsidiaries of large corporations, such as Hitachi Metals, Matsushita Electric Works, Yamatake-Honeywell, Fujitsu, Fanuc, etc. The top shareholder of the largest corporations holds usually less than 5% of the shares; that of second-rank (in size) companies, less than 10%. Companies in which the largest shareholders own more than 10% of the total shares are rare. The large shareholders are usually city banks, long-term credit banks, life insurance companies, or trust banks, except for subsidiaries of other listed companies such as those mentioned above. In addition, trading companies, other companies which are major clients, foreign institutional investors, employees' stock-holding funds, owners and their family members, and family-owned trading and/or real estate companies also appear in the large shareholders' lists from time to time. So do scholarship funds and educational and research foundations set up by the founders, their families, or the corporations themselves. Some individuals have managed to remain on the top-ten shareholder lists of medium and small companies, but for large companies such examples are rare.

The shareholding percentage of a bank or other financial institution in any joint-stock company is limited to 5% by the Anti-Monopoly Law as amended in 1977 (it was 10% before the amendment). At the time of the amendment, life insurance companies made a special appeal for the right to hold 10%, and won their case. Since then, they have called themselves "silent partners," and tend to adopt a policy of not interfering with the management of the companies of which they are large shareholders.

The percentage of shareholding by individuals among the listed companies was 53.1% in 1955. By 1985 it had dwindled to a meager 25.2%. The reasons behind this are several: (i) the decreasing number of owner-managers, due to heavy inheritance and income taxes and the rapid growth of companies creating a demand for equity capital that the owner-managers alone cannot meet; (ii) what is called by the management a "shareholding stabilization policy;" (iii) individual investors' preference for the safer deposits and loan trusts over shareholding; (iv) increasing parent-subsidiary relationships between companies and shareholding tied up with business relations.

Many large Japanese companies have the family name of the founder incorporated into the company name. In most of these companies, the founder and his relatives were active managers and large shareholders at the beginning, often serving as chairman or president; today, the name remains, but family members or relatives have often disappeared altogether from the managing board and/or from the list of shareholders of these companies. Examples that come to mind are C. Itoh, Furukawa Electric, Hazama-gumi, Iino Shipping, Ikegai Corporation, Kawasaki Steel, Nishimatsu Construction, Nomura Securities, Nozaki, Tanabe Pharmaceuticals, and Yamanouchi Pharmaceuticals. The list will be much longer if we include those companies that were not named after their founders in the beginning. More than half of the companies listed today were established by individual "capitalists" who played the double role of large shareholder and chief manager. The subsequent decline of their families has left these companies controlled by salaried managers, not by capitalists.[3]

In the separation of ownership and management in large firms, I believe Japan is the most advanced among the industrialized countries including the United States.

Employees

The core employees of a large Japanese firm are protected by the umbrella of the lifetime employment and seniority promotion systems. The definitions and actual practices of these two systems do not lend themselves to easy explanation. Briefly speaking, however, the lifetime employment system is one in which, first, companies employ graduates at the time they graduate from high schools, universities, or graduate schools. From the point of view of the employee, this process is called *shushoku*, or securing a vocation, a Japanese concept that does not have an exact English equivalent. Second, even when the company falls into dire straits or for whatever reasons, these employees will not be dismissed or laid off. Continued employment may mean being transferred to another, closely related company for a certain time (*shukko*, on-loan service), usually with no loss in salary, other compensations, or fringe benefits. Third, the employee, for his or her part is free to resign after giving appropriate notice. In fact, voluntary resignations and mid-career mobility have increased in recent years.

The seniority promotion system is one in which a regular, full-time employee receives pay raises at definite intervals (usually 1–2 years) and is promoted to new positions regularly (every 2 to 5 years) on the basis of age and seniority.

A distinguishing characteristic of the Japanese seniority promotion system is that an employee's successive promotions are made in a spiral, rather than a linear, way. Instead of linear promotions from a position low in the chain of command to progressively higher posts in the hierarchy, Japanese firms (and government ministries and agencies) generally promote an employee from a section of one department to a somewhat higher post in a section in some other department, or from a post in the home office to a somewhat higher post in a factory or a branch office unrelated to the former post.

Usually, the lifetime employment and seniority promotion system encompass only the employees known as *sha-in*, which literally means "company members": again, no English equivalent exists. The *sha-in* employees comprise only "permanent" or long-term employees who "entered the firm" (*nyusha* or *shushoku*) upon graduation from school, although a few hired later could also be included. Part-timers, temporary employees, and "outside" workers (those dispatched by a subcontractor company which hires them) are not "company members." Before World War II, white-collar "permanent" employees were classified into a number of strata, such as company members, quasi-members, hirees, apprentices, etc. Also, white-collar employees were clearly distinguished from blue-collar employees, as they are in Britain, the United States, most European countries, or China today. "Company members" then constituted a small elite group of long-term employees.

With the rise of labor unionism after the war, much of the prewar differentiation (or discrimination) among employees was abolished. All long-term employees became "company members" in the early 1950s, and are now treated on a much more egalitarian basis than in the prewar period. Of course, the salary and other factors in employment by the firm do vary substantially today depending on schooling, number of years of service, position, and whether the employee is white-collar or blue-collar, but the disparity within a firm is smaller in the case of large Japanese companies than anywhere else in the world.

This sort of egalitarianism, however, does not extend to temporary employees, part-timers, and *shokutaku* (non-regular staff members). Most such employees are not members of the labor union, and they are not eligible for some of the fringe benefits, such as company housing. Government and other statistics on employment frequently count most such non-regular employees among the firm's employees. But the figure for number of employees given by the firm in its annual financial reports, for example, counts only "company members" (*sha-in*). It would thus be a mistake to conclude from some government statistics that the mobility of Japanese labor is rising and that hence the lifetime employment system is breaking down.

Most female regular employees join the company upon finishing high school or junior college, although lately Japanese firms are employing more graduates of four-year colleges. They work as "company members" often just for two to four years and at most six to eight years, until marriage or the birth of their first child. Thus even *sha-in* women employees constitute a "transient" labor force in the firm: they fall into a grey area between the core, male, white-collar employees, covered by the aegis of lifetime employment and seniority promotion, and the part-time and temporary workers who do not enjoy these protections.

Accurate estimates are difficult to come by, but I would say that approximately one-third of the total labor force may be under the lifetime employment and seniority promotion systems.[4]

Managers

One of the most remarkable features of large Japanese firms is that a very high proportion of the top management (chairmen, presidents, vice-presidents, managing directors, directors) and the middle management (heads of divisions and departments, section managers, etc.) are selected from among employees who joined the company at graduation and have risen up the ladder step by step through the process of seniority promotion.

Wage disparities among staff members of large corporations tend to be relatively small. In the typical large firm, the total annual income, inclusive of salaries and bonuses, of the lowest employee may be between one-tenth and one-fifteenth that of the highest-paid (that is, the company president) before taxes, and perhaps more than one-tenth after taxes. In international comparative terms, Japan posts lower wage differentials between white-collar and blue-collar and between managers and regular employees (excluding part-time labor) than any other Western developed country, or such countries as Singapore and Korea, as far as I know.

In Japanese firms, "management" thus emerges as the representatives of the employee group.

The economic rationale for the lifetime employment and seniority promotion systems

Behind the Japanese seniority promotion system perhaps lies the Confucian notion that there should be "an order between the young and the elder," as well as the traditional Japanese view of the life cycle as a process of cultivating oneself and accumulating knowledge, skills, and experience, eventually to become the head of the group, to be taken as a model by others. The historical and cultural background of the lifetime employment and seniority promotion practices of contemporary Japanese firms undoubtedly reflects the organizational principles of Japanese traditional organizations: the extended farming family of old times, the merchant house of the medieval age, the *han* (feudal domain) government of the Tokugawa era.

It must be noted, however, that the lifetime employment and seniority promotion systems became firmly rooted in Japanese industry and business, covering both white- and blue-collar workers, only in the mid-1950s, when the labor union activism of the early postwar years began to fade. It was not until the 1960s, in fact, that these practices spread to medium-sized firms.

What are the reasons why these practices spread from the late 1950s on to cover a major part of the Japanese labor force? The decisive factor was, I believe, simply that the lifetime employment and seniority promotion systems proved to be more economically rational and efficient than other models of corporate organization and employment practices, given the social environment and cultural traditions of contemporary Japan.

With these systems, the typical Japanese firm constitutes an elaborately built organization in which what I call "managerial resources" are abundantly accumulated. "Managerial resources" are know-how and capabilities in a particular business area, including engineering technologies, organization of production, quality control, marketing, research and development, and information gathering and analysis, as well as general administrative and organizational capabilities and ability to efficiently procure raw materials, other resources, and capital funds. Like good universities or research institutes, such organizations are really conglomerate assemblies of human capital. They cannot be built in a short time. Enduring attention to training and skill development for each member of the firm, moreover, is necessary to maintain and extend the capabilities of individual employees of which the firm is composed. On-the-job training is particularly important. The lifetime employment and seniority promotion systems produce excellent results for both the firm and its employees, given these goals. High inter-firm labor mobility, over-emphasis on specialized abilities and immediate results at the expense of the seniority principle, or personnel policies that do not involve regular raises, promotions, and job rotation would lead to lower efficiency, at least in the contemporary Japanese environment.

Labor unions

It is well known that most Japanese labor unions are organized on a company-by-company basis. All regular employees of a firm, whether blue- or white-collar, are enrolled in the union upon entering the company, and the union does not have any members working in other firms.[5] Typical Japanese unions are "company-based unions" on the "union shop" model. However, as noted above, part-timers and other non-regular employees are not usually included, and it goes without saying that managers above a certain level and employees in sections responsible for employment and personnel affairs do not belong to the union.

As a result, there are far more labor unions in Japan than in other major industrialized countries (see Table 1). As Table 1 indicates, the unionization rate in Japan is relatively low, as in the United States. This is particularly true of employees of medium- and small-sized enterprises. Widespread union organization covers only large corporations and the public sector; the majority of workers in smaller firms are not unionized.

Why did Japan develop company-based unions, a model of union organization not found in other industrialized countries? The answer is simple: employees who work long years together in a firm under the lifetime employment and seniority promotion systems tend to hold their interests in common. Their identification with the employees of other firms tends to be much weaker. Thus the labor union based in a firm and the firm's management naturally develop common interest over a broad range of areas. Over the long term, then, and considered rationally, the management and the union have few conflicts of interest

Table 1
Number of Labor Unions and Unionization Rate

	Number of Unions	Unionization Rate (%)
Japan	34,216 (1986) (an increasing trend seems to have stopped)	28.2 (declining)
U.S.A.	176 (1984) (declining)	23.9 (1980) (declining)
Britain	373 (1985) (fairly rapidly decreasing)	49.8 (1985)
West Germany	about 20	41.5 (1986)
France	n.a.	about 20 (1983)
Sweden	about 75	about 80 (1983)

Sources: Labor statistics of individual countries.

when the firm exhibits steady growth. This point will be further discussed below.

II. Ownership and Control of Big Business

The largest shareholders in Japanese firms are banks (including long-term credit banks and trust banks), insurance companies, trading companies, and affiliated companies. Similarly, the largest shareholders in the last two are banks and insurance companies. Shares in a bank are held by other banks, insurance companies, and the bank's leading customers. Who, then, really owns these large companies?

Who owns the large firm?

When one nets out these interlocking shareholdings, insurance companies emerge as the leading holders of large companies' stocks. Disregarding the insurance companies established by foreign companies or with foreign participation, which were all recently established and are relatively small, only four of the twenty insurance companies in Japan are stock companies, and they are relatively small. The other sixteen, including the very large Nippon, Dai-ichi (First), Sumitomo, and Asahi, are all mutual companies, which legally are owned by their *sha-in* or "company members." In the case of the life insurance mutual company, the term *sha-in*, "company members", has a special usage: it signifies those who subscribe to life insurance plans offered by the company (see Chapter 5). To put things in order, then, after all the interlocking shareholdings are cancelled out, and assuming that those left are the true owners, we find that the core of big business in Japan is owned, at least legally, by perhaps the forty or fifty million subscribers to private life insurance plans.

In view of these facts, it is obvious that the old proposition of Marxian economics that "the basic class opposition in the capitalist society is the opposition between the working class and the capitalist class" does not hold in a "capitalist" society like Japan today.

"The capitalist is the common foe of labor and management"

An interesting example of an unsuccessful buy-out takeover took place early in 1981, when Daiei, Inc., attempted to acquire a substantial amount of stock in Takashimaya Co., Ltd. Daiei (capitalized in 1981 at about 8 billion yen) is a relatively new company that operates a chain of large supermarkets. Daiei's founder and president, Tsutomu Nakauchi, is a vigorous and versatile entrepreneur, a real capitalist in name and in fact. With a 20% interest, he was Daiei's largest share-holder. By contrast, Takashimaya is one of Japan's oldest and most prestigious department store chains. With members of the Iida family as chairman, president, vice-president, and managers in other important positions, Takashimaya was known for its strong family flavor. In 1981, however, no member of the Iida family was among the company's top twenty shareholders (the 20th held 0.66%), and the entire family together held no more than a 1% share in the company. Daiei bought a large number of Takashimaya shares from Juzenkai, a medical foundation notorious for its stock-cornering activities, and at one time held 10.5% of Takashimaya's shares. Fearing that Daiei might exercise its right as a major shareholder (more than 10%) to review the department stores' account books, which would reveal to Daiei, a competitor, Takashimaya's procurement routes, the prices it paid for goods, and other secret information, Takashimaya's management fought back. In the end, Daiei was not able to gain access to the account books or to put its managers on the Takashimaya board. At the present time, Daiei remains only the second largest shareholder (5.7%).

Daiei's intrusion failed because Takashimaya's management, employees, and banks worked together to fend off the invader. Professor Tadanori Nishiyama has noted in this connection that "Japanese management is extremely averse to capitalism—the capitalists are, so to speak, the common foe of labor and management."[6] This amusing observation, if somewhat overly sensational, seems not too far off the mark.

What does it mean to "own" and to "control"?
I have used terms like "own" and "control" without clearly defining them. In part, this is because their meanings are hard to pin down. In certain cases, such as a child "owning" a bicycle, or an urban resident "owning" consumer durables or a house, or a farmer "owning" the land he tills, the sense of the term is relatively clear. But in a society such as Japan, the ownership of certain types of assets (especially once their values exceed a certain magnitude), shares in corporations, and possession of famous historical or cultural objects are all subject to a variety of complicated legal, social, and cultural restrictions, including taxes.

An organization as complex as a large contemporary firm involves complex mechanisms for distributing the surplus it generates. Irrespective of legal definitions of rights and responsibilities, ownership of the firm, in an economic sense, is not easily defined. "Ownership" is not a black-and-white affair, but a "grey" matter to varying degrees: who gets what share in the firm's profits, who is responsible for the losses, and who participates to what extent in its managerial decision-making process.

"Control" or "manage" (Japanese, *shihai*) is even more difficult. The Japanese word *shihai* expresses a number of nuances, and depending on context can be rendered into English as control, manage, govern, direct, rule, dominate, or sway. Unless one's purpose is propaganda, it is best to avoid using the term at all in social-science discourse unless its meaning is clearly defined at the outset.

III. Behavioral Principles of Japanese Firms: A Static Theory

Standard microeconomic theory of the firm assumes that in a private market economy firms act in such a way as to maximize profits. Numerous scholars have challenged this "profit-maximization" hypothesis and proposed alternative explanations of corporate behavior.

What is the value of these alternative hypotheses of corporate behavior? They contain much that is worth noting and are convincing in some respects. However, their clarity and fit with observed experience are not enough to lend them sufficient weight to replace the neoclassical profit maximization theory or its dynamic version, "maximization of corporate net worth" (total stock value).

For quite some time, though, I have felt that the simple theory of profit maximization does not offer a compelling explanation of the behavior of large Japanese firms, and the theory, I believe, stands in need of revision, especially in the following areas.

The notion of "our company"

As mentioned above, managers in Japanese firms tend to act as representatives of the employee group (that is, of the regular "company members") rather than as agents serving the interests of the shareholders. As a result, shareholders have little say in the operation of the firm.

The core of a typical large Japanese firm is the group of its "company members." When reporting to shareholders at annual meetings, the managers of American firms frequently use such phrases as "Your company has . . .", whereas Japanese managers speak of "Our company . . ." instead. Moreover, even non-managerial employees regularly use "our company" or "we (the company) do such and such" in everyday conversation. Such a difference in terminology amply demonstrates the fact that, more than anything else, large Japanese corporations exist for the benefit of their employees.

The employees (*sha-in*) of large Japanese firms have a share in the profits of the firm, broadly defined, through the salaries and bonuses which differ from those of other firms according to the results achieved by the firm. The profits accruing to the employees take many forms such as company housing, hospitals, other welfare facilities, and lump-sum retirement allowances and annuities after retirement. All of these depend very much on the performance of the company. Thus, I believe that Japanese firms, whether they are legally joint-stock companies or mutual companies, all closely resemble what is called the "labor-managed firm" in economic theory.

Of course, the typical large Japanese firm is organized as a joint-stock company, and a portion of the profit, whether broadly or narrowly defined, is indeed distributed to the shareholders. Any argument or theoretical model that disregards this fact is not appropriate when discussing typical large Japanese firms.

A simple static model
In order to approach a theory describing the behavioral principles of the typical large Japanese firm, as a first approximation a simple static model now is presented. It is assumed that the management distributes a certain proportion of the profit to the shareholders and the rest (plus, of course, wages and salaries) to the "company members." It is assumed that the levels of output and capital and labor inputs are set in such a way as to maximize the per capita income of the "company members."

The model may be formulated in a very simple way as follows. A firm's production function is expressed as

$$X = F (L, K)$$

X represents the firm's level of output. L and K represent, respectively, the amounts of labor and capital inputs. The function F must be considered as different from firm to firm and is not linear-homogeneous. Otherwise the model will lose its validity as a theory applicable to large Japanese firms (and most likely to firms in other countries as well). Next, let p represent the price of the product, w the wage rate as determined on the labor market, and r the rental price of capital (the interest rate or the rate of return on stocks), again as determined by the capital market. Any profits available after all the costs are subtracted will be shared between workers (employees) and capitalists (shareholders) in the ratio $\beta: (1 - \beta)$. Therefore, if W stands for the total income received by the firm's workers and R the total income accruing to the firm's investors, we arrive at the following equations:

$$
\left.
\begin{aligned}
W &= (pX - wL - rK) + wL \\
R &= (1 - \beta)\,(pX - wL - rK) + rK
\end{aligned}
\right\} \qquad (1)
$$

Thus, the hypothesis here about the behavior of large Japanese firms is: the firm acts in such a way as to maximize the per capita income of workers, under a profit-sharing scheme in which the firm's profits in excess of costs (including wages) are distributed in a fixed proportion between employees and shareholders.

The income of an individual worker can be expressed, then, as

$$
i = \frac{\beta(pX - rK)}{L} + w(1 - \beta)
$$

If F possesses the differentiability and second-order properties usually assumed in this sort of exercise, then the firm will determine the level of labor input (employment) so as to satisfy the equation

$$
\frac{\partial i}{\partial L} = \beta\,\frac{pF_L \cdot L - (pX - rK)}{L^2} = 0
$$

where F_L and F_K are the first partial derivatives of the production function F, and represent, respectively, the marginal (physical) productivity of labor and capital. As a result, the firm will employ the amount of labor that makes its marginal (value) productivity equal to its average net productivity, i.e.,

$$
pF_L = \frac{pX - rK}{L} \qquad (2)
$$

By "net" is meant the amount after the costs of capital and all other factors of production have been deducted. This behavioral pattern resembles that deduced from the theory of labor-managed firms.

On the other hand, the amount of capital used will be determined to fulfill the following equation:

$$
\frac{\partial i}{\partial K} = \beta\,\frac{1}{L}\,(pF_K - r) = 0
$$

or,

$$
pF_K = r \qquad (3)
$$

The amount of capital used, in other words, will be such as to make the marginal productivity of capital equal to the cost of capital at which capital funds are procured from the capital market. This is nothing other than the ordinary optimization condition pertaining to the various inputs.

Now, if the firm is dominated not by its workers but by a capitalist who maximizes the return on capital, then the maximization conditions will be different from those given in equations (2) and (3), in a symmetrical way:

$$pF_L = w \tag{4}$$

$$pF_K = (pX - wL)/K \tag{5}$$

In both equations (2) and (4), it should be noted, the per capita income each worker receives from the firm is equal to the marginal productivity of his labor.

The above argument must be revised somewhat if the firm is a monopolist whose product price is not fixed. In place of price p in the right-hand side of equations (2) and (3), marginal revenue $p(1 - 1/e)$, must be inserted where e is the price elasticity of demand for the firm's product. In all other aspects the argument would stand as above.

A graphic representation of the theory of the labor-managed firm

The pattern of behavior described by the simple static model of the

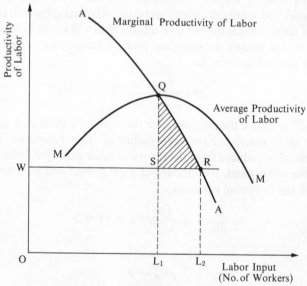

Figure 1: Equilibrium for the Labor-Managed Firm

labor-managed firm may easily be understood through the graphic representation in Figure 1.

The horizontal axis in Figure 1 marks the amount of labor input, i.e., the number of workers constituting the labor-managed firm. Curve AA represents the average productivity of labor when the inputs of other productive factors are given. Curve MM represents the marginal productivity of labor under the same conditions. To workers already employed by the firm, the most advantageous number of workers is L_1, which corresponds to Q, the point at which lines AA and MM intersect. This is because the per capita income (which is equivalent to the average (net) productivity of labor) earned by each worker reaches a maximum at that point. Any reduction or increase in the number of workers will result in a loss in the per capita income and prove less advantageous to the workers.

Equation (2) above can easily be understood by applying the same principle.

A firm that maximizes the return to the owners of capital would, under the same constraints, employ an amount of labor, L_2, corresponding to R, the point at which the wage rate, w, prevailing in the outside labor market equals the marginal productivity of labor. This is the situation described by equation (4).

If, moreover, the labor-managed firm is able to hire at the market wage rate w non-member workers who can be as productive as members in certain kinds of job but can be excluded from sharing the profits of the firm, it will be advantageous for the member workers to employ them in the amount represented by the segment L_1L_2. By so doing, the total income available for distribution to member workers will be increased by the amount represented by the shaded area QRS.[7] In other words, member workers "exploit" non-member workers. This would explain the behavior of Japanese firms when they hire temporary workers, part-timers, and others who are not treated as "company members."[8]

What does the static theory tell us?

I believe that the static theory outlined in equations (1)–(3) is very simple, yet highly relevant as a first approximation of the behavior of typical large Japanese firms. It seems particularly useful in explaining the following three widespread phenomena or tendencies.

1. *Inter-firm wage differentials*. The wage differentials between large, medium-to-small, and very small firms in Japan are quite large, compared with those in other developed countries. Significant differences

in wages and salaries also occur among large firms listed in the first section of the stock exchange. By wage differentials is meant differences or disparities among firms in the total benefits awarded workers, including not only wages, salaries, and bonuses but also all kinds of fringe benefits. The nature of these wage differentials is readily understood when we visualize each firm as possessing different technologies, a different accumulation of managerial resources and hence a different production function, and workers of a firm as having a share in the firm's profits, as described by the simple static theory just presented. Such managerial resources cannot be represented by the amounts of labor and capital, or of other factors of production.[9]

In the past, the wage differentials in Japan between large firms and the medium-to-small firms (of which the wage disparity is most obvious) and the economic structure that was regarded as the cause of the wage differentials were called the "dualistic structure" of the Japanese economy. Once we realize that large Japanese firms resemble labor-managed firms, however, we can see that wage differentials will occur normally and permanently between firms even when each firm acts rationally and each worker receives an income equal to his marginal productivity.

2. *Large Japanese firms are kept "slim."* A comparison of large Japanese firms and their American counterparts reveals that the Japanese firms have far fewer employees in relation to sales. Table 2 gives some examples. Toyota's annual sales amount to some one-third those of General Motors, but it employs less than one-twelfth the number of workers of GM, and similarly for Hitachi vs. General Electric.

As these examples illustrate, the large Japanese firm is kept "slim"— that is, its main body (the parent company) hires a relatively small number of employees. Particularly since the first oil crisis in 1973–1974, firms have pursued what is called "weight-reducing" strategies. One of the primary reasons for their making active use of subsidiaries, affiliated companies, subcontracting, temporary workers, and part-timers is the realization that it is more rational to share the common

Table 2
A Comparison of Size: Hitachi and GE, Toyota and GM

Company	Sales (trillion yen)	No. of Workers (thousands)	No. of Shareholders (thousands)
Hitachi	2.9	98	210
GE	6.1	359	483
Toyota	6.0	65	62
GM	17.2	876	854

Sources: Financial statements of the respective companies for 1986. Sales for GE and GM were converted at 167 yen per dollar.

profit under the umbrella of a firm among as few workers as possible, both in terms of work-incentives and from the standpoint of equity of income distribution.

3. *Strict selection of employees.* Japanese firms in general are quite cautious about selecting applicants when hiring them as "company members." The large expenditures for the rigourous screening of applicants, the various types of internal schooling and on-the-job training after employment may follow naturally from lifetime employment, but they make even more sense when we realize that Japanese firms resemble labor-managed firms.

In Japanese firms (and faculties of universities as well), the existing employees (or professors) seek to hire only those people whose abilities would match or surpass their own and who they feel will be capable of contributing even more to the company (faculty) than they themselves do. They are also quite enthusiastic about educating and training new and junior "company members." The reason for their concern is that if the newcomers perform (or can perform) at a level that is worth only the common wage rate prevailing in the external labor market, then the existing employees, too, will suffer a loss of income. In firms that behave in the manner described by the standard theory of firms, this sort of issue would not arise, since the employees are assumed to receive wages and other benefits equal to the rate prevailing in the market for each job classification, and contribute to the firm in accordance with the remuneration they receive.

Differences from the labor-managed firm

The formal structure of the labor-managed firm is similar to that found in Japan's agricultural, fishery, and consumers' cooperatives, credit unions, credit associations, and other mutual and cooperative organizations. These organizations are basically egalitarian in structure; at least in theory all members share equally in rights and responsibilities. Typical Japanese firms, by contrast, are not egalitarian, but hierarchical, organizations. Posts, rights, power, and rewards are apportioned to each employee hierarchically on the basis of schooling, the length of service within the firm, abilities, and contribution to the firm.

This combination of hierarchical organization and a graduated distribution of income cannot be explained by the simple theory of the labor-managed firm outlined above, nor, it seems, by most other theories.

Moreover, according to the theory presented above, a portion of the profits left after expenses is distributed to the workers while the remainder goes to the owners of the capital, but why does the distribution take this form? And what factors determine the distribution ratio between workers and capitalists? The static theory presented here does not provide answers to these questions.

IV. Growth of the Firm and Income Distribution

The demand for continuity of the firm

As mentioned in Section I, the Japanese firm is conceived of as an elaborately organized body consisting of managers, engineers, skilled workers, and clerical and sales staff who together represent an accumulation of managerial resources in a certain area of business. Year after year this organization has to hire new "company members" under the system of lifetime employment, and trains them within it in order to develop human resources. Hence, the continued existence of the firm is vital. An emphasis on continuity is one of the most remarkable features of the behavior of Japanese firms, which derives from the constraints imposed by the lifetime employment and seniority systems. In Japan, firms that have become larger than a certain size are rarely liquidated, go bankrupt, or are absorbed by other firms. At least they do so at a much lower rate than firms in other developed countries.

Should a large corporation in Japan fall into financial difficulties and go bankrupt or be absorbed by another firm, the firm's "company members" face severely straitened circumstances. Their situation is rather like that of the "masterless samurai" (*ronin*) of the Tokugawa era, who had to wander about the country because their *han* (domain) had ceased to exist as a result of some misbehavior on the part of the family head. When the possibility of such a decline is foreseen, the firm will not be able to bring in promising new employees, and capable existing employees will move to other firms. The firm may also have trouble procuring capital. The task confronting managers, then, is to maintain performance at least at a level that removes all doubts about the firm's continued viability.

Internal pressure for growth of the firm

The firm, however, cannot continue to exist merely by repeating the same operations year in and year out. Almost all products possess a life cycle. Older products eventually face falling demand as they saturate the market or are replaced by newer products. Even when there is steadily growing demand for the firm's products, strong domestic or foreign competitors may drive out the firm. Therefore, the firm must incessantly try to develop new products and open new markets, just for its survival.

Hence, even if the firm's goal is simply to maintain its current size in terms of sales or numbers of employees, it cannot afford to pay out to its shareholders and employees all the profits that remain each year after expenses are deducted.[10] In order to remain at the same level of productive activity the firm must invest a portion of its profits (broadly defined) in research and development, in the commercialization of new products, in opening up promising new markets, and in investment in plant and equipment.

Japanese firms, moreover, face intense internal pressure for growth. First of all, "company members" want the income they receive from the firm to grow steadily every year at a rate commensurate with or possibly higher than that of other large firms. Faster growth of the firm also benefits "company members" in several other ways:

(a) Under the Japanese seniority promotion system, faster growth of the firms leads to surer opportunities for faster promotion in posts, and hence faster raises in salaries.

(b) Long-term employees, whether white- or blue-collar, when they reach the retirement age of 55 or 60, will find their chances of advantageous reemployment considerably improved if the firm is expanding steadily.

(c) An employee of a rapidly growing firm will have many employees in the same firm younger than himself, which means the strengthening of the financing of firm's pension scheme and the like.

For these reasons, large Japanese firms which possess the structural characteristics outlined in Section I also exhibit a strong disposition toward continuity and strong internal pressure for growth of the firm, as their behavioral characteristics.

Theory of maximization of the firm's present value

The standard microeconomic theory of the firm states that over the longer run, the firm's management will act to maximize the firm's present value. According to this theory, the firm has to allocate "growth expenses," including research and development, market development, and other expenditures, in order to realize the growth of profits through broadening of the scale of its business activities. It is assumed that a relationship exists between these "growth expenses" and the rate of growth of the firm's sales. The owners (shareholders) and their agent, the management, deduct these growth expenses from the firm's gross profit to arrive at the firm's net profit (net income). The present value of the firm is computed by discounting the flow of net incomes at an appropriate rate and then summing them up. It is equal to the total value of its stock at the current market price. It is this value, according to the theory, which the owners and managers seek to maximize.

This theory can be expressed in the following equations. First, let $R(t)$ represent the firm's gross profit for period t. The firm will spend a fixed portion of the gross profit as "growth expenses" $M(t)$. Therefore,

$$M(t) = mR(t),$$

in which m is a constant. The rate of growth of the firm's profit, g, depends on m.

$$g = g(m)$$

The flow of net incomes of the firm can be expressed as

$$(1 - m)R(0), (1 - m)R(1), \ldots, (1 - m)R(t), \ldots$$

Discounted at rate ρ, the net flow of incomes is expressed as

$$(1 - m)R(0), (1 - m)R(0) (1 + g)/(1 + \rho), \ldots,$$
$$(1 - m)R(0) (1 + g)^t/(1 + \rho)^t, \ldots.$$

The present value of the firm V is equal to the sum of these terms. In other words,

$$V = R(0) (1 - m) \sum_{t=0}^{\infty} \frac{(1 + g)^t}{(1 + \rho)^t}$$

Assuming that the series is convergent,

$$V = R(0) (1 - m) (1 + \rho)/[\rho - g(m)]$$

The firm will set m so as to maximize its value, V. V will reach a maximum when

$$\frac{\partial V}{\partial m} = R(0)(1 + \rho) \frac{-[\rho - g(m)] + (1 - m)g'(m)}{[\rho - g(m)]^2} = 0$$

In short, m is set to satisfy

$$(1 - m)g'(m) = \rho - g(m) \tag{7}$$

Thus the firm's management, as the representative of the shareholders, will set M, the proportion of the gross profit spent for growth expenses, at a level that will satisfy equation (7). This theory is based on internal financing, which assumes that all the funds necessary to meet investment and research and development expenses will be derived from the firm's gross profit. Although it makes no provision for the possibility of raising funds through external financing such as new stock issues or borrowing, its conclusions are not affected significantly by the introduction of the possibility of external financing.

Revisions necessitated by our hypothesis about Japanese firms' behavior
The traditional theory just outlined needs to be revised according to the hypothesis about Japanese firms' behavior presented in Section III. It was assumed there, as a first approximation in equation (1) above, that the firm's managers distribute a portion of the profit to the shareholders and the remainder to the employees. Under this condition, the firm's management, as the representative of its employees, will set its growth rate so as to maximize the present value of the net flow of incomes (including a portion of the profit) for each of its present employees.

But employees, unlike capital, are not immortal. If an employee knows how many more years he or she can work for the firm, and has good expectations of being able to work for the full term, then a growth policy that maximizes the total value of his or her earnings during that period, after allowing for an appropriate discount rate, will prove most advantageous.

As noted above, the employee group, including managers, is not a homogeneous body. Wages and salaries, fringe benefits, and the right to participate in the firm's decision-making are arranged hierarchically. Individual interests vary considerably depending on age, position, and expected length of employment. The length of employment, for example, is generally very short in the case of female employees, as noted earlier. The most beneficial discount rate also varies widely from one individual to another.

We should also remember that employees enjoy the additional benefits (a), (b), and (c) noted above from the growth of the firm.

"The distribution revolution"
In Section III it was assumed that the firm's profit would be distributed between its employees and shareholders at a given ratio $\beta: (1 - \beta)$. It is, however, an *ad hoc* simplification to assume that this distribution ratio is arbitrarily fixed. Rather, this ratio would vary depending on the economic conditions surrounding the individual firm, its employees, and the shareholders.

The first area of inquiry for empirical research on Japanese firms would be to investigate the magnitude of their profits and to analyze how they are distributed. In a broad sense relevant to the theory presented in Sections III and IV, the profits of a firm should include that portion of wages, salaries, bonuses, and fringe benefits which exceeds those prevalent in the outside labor market. Also, a portion of business expenses (expense account outlays) which can be considered supplementary incomes for executives, as well as a large part of expenditures for research and development, and the amounts transferred to certain types of reserves beyond the appropriate levels should be added to what is given as "net profit" in the usual corporate financial statements. How large is the profit in this sense in each firm and in Japan as a whole and how it is shared among workers, managers, and shareholders are most interesting questions.

Although it is unscientific to argue without statistical evidence, I feel that a large proportion of the broadly defined profit of Japanese firms falls to the employees and managers. Take, for example, simple business expenses (expense account outlays) of Japanese corporations. Their total amount now exceeds the total dividend payments. This was not the case until the 1960s.[11]

Nonetheless, facts on these matters are not readily available, and we must wait for a detailed statistical analysis of income distribution within and among Japanese corporations. It would be helpful, for example, to have a clear picture of the relationship between a company's profits and its salary and bonus levels based on corporate financial statistics.

A second area of inquiry with regard to the tendency of employees of large Japanese firms to share the firms' profits to a significant extent would concern how it has become possible for them to take part in profit-sharing. In joint-stock companies, the shareholders are supposedly the owners, and the profit should return to them. A large part of this profit (perhaps the larger part) now seems, however, to be going to employees and managers. Why have the shareowners stood idly by? Why have they not resisted this "distribution revolution?" And why are they not now rebelling and attempting to reclaim a larger part of the profits?

My tentative answers to these questions are the following. The supply and demand relationships for capital funds and for persons with managerial skills changed greatly between the prewar and postwar years, and so did the profit-earning power of a firm as a team which has accumulated managerial resources. Such changes altered the economic power relationships among capitalists, managers, and employees. This is the background for the "distribution revolution" in Japan which has taken place in recent years.

On the one hand, the savings rate of the economy as a whole rose substantially, bringing forth abundant supplies of capital funds. Capital markets were also modernized, making available the supply of equity capital as well as loans. Thus firms possessing superior managerial capabilities or management that displayed strong possibilities of future growth were able to procure the funds they needed from capital markets or from financial institutions without much difficulty.

On the other hand, it was necessary to create a large, efficient organization to ensure continuity and steady growth, and to assemble and accumulate the managerial resources necessary for efficient business activities. Such organizations cannot be run by a single capitalist or a small group of capitalists who are owner-managers. In addition, steeply progressive income and inheritance taxes hastened the demise of the individualistic capitalists.

Factors determining the distribution of profits

A third area of inquiry would concern the factors that are thought to determine the pattern of profit-sharing. I have not yet reached a theoretical understanding of this point that is both logically consistent and factually convincing; nevertheless, some factors which appear to me to exert important influences on the pattern of profit-sharing can be identified.

(a) *Comparison with other firms in the same industry.* The levels of salaries, bonuses, and fringe benefits given to employees of a firm, from the president and other full-time directors to the rank and file, as well as the proportion of the profit shared by employees (including, again, full-time directors)—that is, β in equation (1)—seem to be much affected by the levels of salaries, benefits, and profit-sharing ratios of similar-sized firms in the same industry. Labor mobility among large firms in the same industry is very low in Japan; nonetheless, profit-sharing within each firm is strongly influenced by what the firm's rivals—or "brothers"—in the same industry are doing.

One reason for this state of affairs is that maintaining a respectable salary schedule and benefits is vital for the firm if it is to retain its prestige and credibility within the industry, to preserve and bolster employee morale and to recruit promising young employees.

(b) *The firm's growth rate.* Even if it seeks only to preserve a certain scale of operation, the firm needs to recruit and hire new employees to replace those retiring. And in order to secure promising young people in the labor market, the firm must be able to convince prospective employees that it can offer them advantageous treatment throughout their professional or vocational careers.

If the firm is very small, and its rate of growth of employment is zero, it will need only to replace departing employees by recruiting a few new employees each year or once every few years. The firm should be able to meet its labor requirements even if the benefits paid to existing workers are not too high. High-profit enterprises which have almost no possibility for expanding employment, such as luxury restaurants and hotels (the situation is quite different if they decide to expand as a chain) or specialty publishing houses that are famous in a particular narrow field but are otherwise tiny operations, would exhibit a behavior pattern considerably different from that of the large firm. Their behavior would be closer to that of the West European, especially Continental European, owner-operated firm. Employee benefit levels, in other words, would be held at a point only slightly above the level employees could earn on the open labor market, and the ratio of profit-sharing with employees, β, would be low. Moreover, the profit-sharing ratio would fluctuate widely depending on the size of the total profit. The greater portion of the profit, in other words, would redound to the capitalists.

The high-growth, large firm exhibits a different pattern. It must recruit new employees each year from among new high school and college graduates. In order to gain ground in this market, the firm must offer a high level of monetary and non-monetary rewards to its employees and promise them attractive working careers.

Since a high rate of growth of the firm's sales (or a high probability of such growth) commonly indicates that profits (or expected profits) will be high, we can see that high growth will normally make possible high salary and benefit levels.

Compared with countries in which inter-firm mobility of workers and managers is high and profit-sharing elements play only a small part in non-executive employee earnings, however, we can see that the above situation can act as a check on the growth of high-profit businesses: it will reduce the share of profits that accrues to the capitalists, and can be reserved or reinvested within the firm.

(c) *Growth of the firm and capital procurement.* A situation similar to that just outlined exists with respect to capital procurement. If management of the firm is indeed completely dominated by the employees, headed by the top management, one may wonder why they do not keep all the profits for themselves. Why do they distribute some part of the profits to shareholders and reserve some of them within the firm?

A joint-stock company will need additional equity capital in order to grow. Moreover, at least a part of equity capital will have to be raised by issuing new shares: the rest may be met by retained earnings.

Many firms, furthermore, need to borrow money or issue bonds just to continue to exist. To maintain a foothold or to improve, if possible, one's position in the capital and short-term financial markets, the firm must earn and distribute sufficiently high profits for the owner of equity capital and ensure that it can readily increase its equity capital and debt, whenever necessary.

What if the employee-dominated firm decided to switch from the joint-stock company to some cooperative form, in order to avoid the trouble of having to make annual payments of dividends to shareholders and of having occasionally to ask them to provide additional equity capital? What would happen if the employees as a whole bought the 51 % of the stock necessary to assure majority control, dissolved the company, and reconstituted it as a cooperative firm entirely owned and controlled by employees?

I do not know whether such a scenario is legally feasible in Japan, but even assuming that it is, it is hard to see how such a move could work to the employees' benefit. It would likely result in a number of inconveniences. From the standpoint of economic advantage, it seems that by investing heavily and becoming the owners of their workplace, the employees would be assuming too great a risk compared with the benefits derived. For the employees, instead of investing such large amounts of funds in the company in which they work, it would be far more advantageous to diversify their portfolios and invest the funds in several companies' stocks. Since the employees who share in the profits of the firm already hold a significant stake in the firm, it would not be advisable to increase their holdings. Also, this scenario would involve an inconvenience in transferring the equity rights held by retiring members (or members who die after retirement) to new members.

In the light of these considerations, we can see that the present form of joint-stock company with outside shareholders offers a high degree of economic rationality.[12]

V.   Additional Remarks on Behavioral Characteristics

I have described some of the structural characteristics (i.e., long-term organizational characteristics) of typical Japanese firms, large firms in particular, which I believe are in contrast to typical firms in Western Europe and North America, and discussed the behavioral characteristics of Japanese firms that result from their structural characteristics. Because of the nature of the issue and the need to consider a wide range of points, the discussion cannot be contained in a limited space. I have not been able to touch sufficiently upon many characteristics of Japanese firms. What follows, then, are brief statements of my views on points I would like to emphasize.

The interests of labor and management

In a large Japanese corporation, the employer—that is, the management team representing the firm—and the labor union, which is organized separately company by company and contains only regular, full-time employees (whether white-collar or blue-collar), experience conflicting interests to only a limited extent. To the labor union, the firm is the goose that lays golden eggs, and it would not do to harm the goose, lest it cease to lay eggs. Seen from the management side, some of the employees who constitute the labor unions will one day be their successors.[13] The managers' incomes, moreover, are sustained by the entire employee group, and they have to cooperate to promote the growth of the firm and share the fruits of that cooperation.

Of course, the interests of labor and the management differ in a number of areas. It is a mistake to believe that Japanese labor unions do not adequately protect the interests of workers. Indeed, the British sociologist Ronald P. Dore states that Japanese unions play a more active role in improving working conditions and handling workplace complaints than do their British counterparts.[14]

Conflicts of interest arise when the firm runs into severe financial difficulties and has to discharge even some of the regular, "lifetime" employees. Conflicts also exist within the employee group, in relation to the hierarchical structure. For example, it would not be far off the mark to argue that women employees, who have been treated more or less as "transient" or "peripheral" members of the firm, are "exploited" by the other employees. Temporary employees, part-timers, and outside workers, as well, are at a substantial disadvantage compared with regular employees in terms of income and working conditions.

Just as unfavorable treatment of employees can prove disadvantageous from the management point of view, especially in relation to recruiting new employees, an overly strong bias in favor of the employee group in profit-sharing can cause the rate of profits and dividends to fall below the level acceptable in the capital market. The firm will then find its position in capital and financial markets considerably weakened and its ability to procure the funds necessary for growth impeded. Not only managers but also the leaders of the company-based labor union therefore pay attention to the firm's rates of profit and dividends, and as a consequence they may appear to act in the interest of shareholders.

Corporate groups

The fact that Japanese firms endeavor to keep themselves "slim" and the strong tendency toward specialization give rise to the phenomenon of groups of associated or interrelated firms. This is one of the peculiarities of the industrial structure in Japan. The production and other business activities that in the West take place within a single firm are in Japan often spread across a number of firms, which carry them out under close cooperation.

These groups are commonly known *keiretsu* or "firm groups," but I think one should distinguish three different usages of the term corresponding to three different types of groups:

(a) The descendants of the three old *zaibatsu* groups, that is, Mitsui, Mitsubishi, and Sumitomo.

(b) The "business groups" formed around the Dai-Ichi Kangyo Bank, the Fuji Bank (the Fuyo Group), and the Sanwa Bank. These three groups plus the three former *zaibatsu* groups constitute what are frequently referred to as the "six largest *keiretsu*."

(c) The industrial groups formed around giant corporations. These are composed of subsidiaries, allied firms, important customers, subcontractors (primary, secondary, and tertiary), wholesalers, and retailers. Examples include the Matsushita Group, the Toyota Group, the Hitachi *keiretsu*, and the Shin-Nittetsu *keiretsu*.

Of these three types of groups, the third—that is, the groups formed around a giant corporation—are not much different in nature from the industrial groups found in other developed countries. Several special characteristics should be mentioned, however: (1) As we noted in Section I, large Japanese firms try hard to remain "slim," so a group will contain quite a few firms in addition to the central firm. (2) Business relations within a group are based on the mutual (long-term) advantages for the parties involved. When a transaction takes place within a group, it is most unlikely that a firm will purchase materials or parts at a higher price than it would from firms outside the group or that it will purchase goods of inferior quality. If firms in a group engaged in such practices, they would soon fall behind the competition in their own fields. In other words, over the long term transactions within the group must conform to the same or even better standards of quality and prices as would prevail in transactions with firms outside of the group. Only when the conditions are advantageous to the parties concerned will the transaction take place within the group. (3) Relations between the firms in an industrial group are not based on short-term interests, nor do they always rely on contracts. Instead they are based upon mutual trust cultivated over the years between the members of the firms' top managements. Except for majority- or minority-owned subsidiaries and their parent, the trade relations within the group are not rigidly fixed but subject to change; and viewed from a long perspective, competitive forces have more than enough room to operate.

The old *zaibatsu* groups were formerly centered around *zaibatsu* holding companies, but after the dissolution of the *zaibatsu* immediately after World War II these groups became loose coalitions of former subsidiaries of the prewar holding companies. Each group includes a bank, a trust bank, a trading company, a life insurance company, and a casualty insurance company. The *zaibatsu* group features close trading relations based on established business relations and mutual trust over many decades. However, point (2) above is fully applicable to this group as well. Merely because a transaction takes place within the group does not mean that the firms will accept inferior products at inflated prices. Moreover, in recent years the relative weight of intra-group transactions seems to be declining in each of the three groups. The central organs of these groups—be they monthly meetings of the presidents of member companies or the group's central bank or trading company—can exert only limited leadership. They can still behave in unison, however, on such occasions as business ventures in new industries (petrochemicals, aluminum refining, atomic energy, leasing), large-scale overseas projects, intra-group labor transfer from declining industries to rapidly growing ones, and sponsoring socio-cultural activities.

The three largest *keiretsu* not descended from the *zaibatsu*—that is, the Dai-ichi, Fuji, and Sanwa groups—have little more than their monthly "company-president meetings," which are primarily of a social nature, with little functional significance. These industrial groups are, therefore, more imaginary than real.

Mark-up pricing

According to the "mark-up pricing hypothesis" or the "full-cost pricing principle," the market price of manufactured products is determined by adding a certain "mark-up rate" to production cost. Among British economists and some Japanese scholars who are influenced by the former, this seems to still be an influential hypothesis.[15]

The hypothesis was derived from fieldwork results of R.L. Hall and

C. J. Hitch in 1938, and has been used without being much questioned until today. It is, however, inadequate in explaining price formation in Japan, and perhaps in Western Europe and the United States as well.

Manufacturers determine the price of their products not only according to production cost, but also according to the state of competition in the market, price elasticity of demand, the pricing policy of competitors, and their own level of capacity utilization. Much evidence suggests that it is unlikely that they would simply apply a mark-up rate to determine the price:

(i) Even for a high-technology product such as integrated circuits, when overproduction occurred in 1985, the price of 64 DRAM plummeted to 120–140 yen, one-fifth of the 1984 level; 256 DRAM were selling at 330–440 yen in 1985, about one-tenth of the 1984 level.

(ii) There have been a large number of complaints against Japanese firms about dumping of their products when exporting to the United States.

(iii) When reporting the performance of companies, newspapers, magazines, and the *Quarterly Handbook of Listed Companies* often contain descriptions such as "the sales figures of the departments that are not doing so well have been withheld"; "sales this period include unprofitable orders accepted in earlier slack periods which barely covered costs, so that the recovery of profits will have to wait until the next period" (for shipbuilding, construction, and plant engineering firms); "profits soared because of a large increase in the sales of a certain department which has a number of products that no other company can compete with"; and so on.

(iv) The price of ships and unit prices of construction projects fluctuate widely according to the state of the shipbuilding or construction business. In times of depression prices can fall by half in a year or two, and when business is brisk they can double or triple in a short time.

(v) In Japan, in times of depressed domestic demand, often the so-called "export-drive effect" works to increase export sales.

As mentioned in Section IV, Japanese firms are always searching for new directions for development. One area in which much R&D effort is now concentrated is biotechnology, which involves close to 100 companies in diverse industries ranging from chemicals and chemical fertilizers to pharmaceuticals, food, beer, and fermentation. Companies now undertaking research in biotechnology include such outsiders as Hitachi and Toray. Another example is office automation: over 50 companies from the fields of electric engineering, home appliances, computers, office machines, cameras, precision instruments, audio equipment, and computer software are already selling products in this area.

In short, in an economy as dynamic as Japan's, where, on the one hand, R&D on new products and advances into promising potential markets are brisk, and, on the other hand, old industries are rapidly declining due to reduced demand and competition from imports, old-fashioned practices such as "mark-up pricing" cannot be widely maintained.

VI. Concluding Remarks

This paper adopts a positivist approach to assembling and analyzing facts related to the structural and behavioral characteristics of large Japanese firms as distinct from their American and European counterparts.

The basic assumptions in this paper have been the following. First, in Japan the separation of management and ownership in large firms has advanced much in the postwar years, perhaps more than in any other major industrialized countries of the "West." Generally a firm's shareholders can now exercise little influence over its management, so long as it does not run into financial difficulties.

Second, in Japan since the 1950s as a result of the separation of management and ownership, the spread of the lifetime-employment and seniority promotion systems and unprecedented economic growth, a well-managed major firm in each field has developed as a carefully built organization consisting of managers at various levels, engineers, skilled workers, and other personnel, and having managerial and technological expertise in its specialized field.

Most of the members of the top management of a large Japanese firm are selected from among those who have served for a long time as regular, core employees of the firm.

The management of typical large Japanese firms may be conceived of as the representative of the regular core employees of the firm, rather than of the shareholders. Thus large Japanese firms come to possess certain characteristics similar to those of the "labor-managed firm." I hypothesized that a typical large Japanese firm behaves in such a way as to maximize, under a number of constraints and over the long run, the benefits accruing to its regular, core employees, and that the latter generally actively cooperate with the management in working toward such an objective.

Third, with the lifetime employment and seniority promotion systems it is advantageous for the regular, core members of a firm that the firm continue at least to exist and to grow at a fairly rapid rate if possible. Some of the aspects of Japanese firms' behavior are best understood in this context of pressure from the inside towards continued existence and a high rate of growth.

With these basic assumptions I have attempted to discuss a number of problems and issues related to the structural and behavioral characteristics of Japanese firms. I have not entered, however, into any normative evaluation of these characteristics.

This chapter is a somewhat shortened translation of a paper written in Japanese and published in *Keizaigaku Ronshu* (*Journal of Economics*), The University of Tokyo, Vol. 54, Nos. 2 and 3 (July and October 1988).

Notes

1. The proportion of the total labor force employed by firms with less than 300 employees for 1957 and 1969, and by medium- and small-size enterprises as defined in the text for other years, is as follows:

	Manufacturing	Non-Primary Industries (Including Manufacturing)
1957	73.5%	82.8%
1969	69.0	78.3
1978	73.4	81.1
1981	71.9	81.4
1986	72.2	80.6
1988	72.9	n.a.

Sources: MITI, *Kogyo Tokei-Hyo* (The Census of Manufactures), and Prime Minister's Office Bureau of Statistics, *Jigyosho Tokei* (Statistics on Establishments).

2. If unlisted companies are included, the largest (in terms of employees) private companies in Japan, excluding those which were formerly government-owned, is Nihon Life Insurance Company (90,000). It is not a joint-stock company, but a mutual company. The largest Japanese companies are much smaller than the largest American companies in terms of the number of employees: compare General Motors (876,000 employees in the United States), Sears and Roebuck (485,000), and IBM (403,000).

3. Nishiyama, 1983. I find Nishiyama's analysis of facts fascinating, but cannot agree with some of his assertions.

4. Nearly 30% of the Japanese labor force consists of independent proprietors and their family members. The remaining 35–40% comprises highly mobile labor not covered by lifetime employment practices.

5. There are many exceptions to this general rule, which I will not go into here.

6. Nishiyama, 1981.

7. It may be argued that if non-member workers can perform any kind of work as productively as member workers, members would do better not only by employing the outside, non-member workers represented by L_1L_2, but also replacing the member workers, perhaps as they reach the retirement age, by non-member workers and sharing the surplus (profits) among the reduced number of members. It would be best for a very small number of workers to restrict membership as much as possible and to hire the outsiders at the going wage rate and exploit them.

But this is obviously an absurd picture of a labor-managed firm. It is better to presume that certain essential functions within the firm cannot be assigned to the non-member workers or that workers do not or cannot perform as productively as member-workers unless they are allowed membership and are entitled to profit-sharing. It would be more realistic to assume that there are certain kinds of jobs which can be done well by either members or non-members, and some others which can be done efficiently only by members who have an interest in the firm's profitability. Apparently Japanese firms are assigning the former kinds of jobs as much as possible to outside, non-member workers.

8. A similar relationship pertains with regard to capital as well. The distinction between loans from financial institutions or corporate bonds, on which only interest at the market rate is due, and stocks (equity capital), which receive a share of the profit, somewhat resembles that between the income received by non-member and member workers of the labor-managed firm.

9. From a number of simplified hypotheses, J.H. Drèze has shown that the equilibrium established in a capitalist economy, in which all firms simply attempt to maximize profits, is exactly the same as the equilibrium established in a "labor-managed" economy, in which all firms seek to maximize workers' per-capita income. (See Drèze, 1976.) However, his proof rests on the hypothesis that any firm can imitate another firm's production function and commence production in the same manner as the other firm. In other words, any firm could start right away doing what IBM or Sony does simply by assembling the same number of workers (L) and the same amount of capital (K). This sort of proof demonstrates how meaningless are the assertions of some abstract theories.

10. In the current Japanese environment, the firm must raise its wage and salary levels by several percentage points annually. In order to maintain a certain level of employment, therefore, the firm must expand its sales by a comparable percentage each year.

11. Of course, not all business expenses should be thought of as the distribution of profits. And it goes without saying that the distribution of this benefit is highly hierarchical.

12. Since in a joint-stock company the financial risks accompanying the firm's management are assumed by possessors of capital—that is, by the shareholders, who provide the firm with owned capital (although, as argued here, a part of the risks in Japanese firms is borne by the employees)—and since some of the owners of capital earn large incomes, the claim that the Japanese economy is "not capitalistic" is not convincing. On the other hand, the assertion that "Japan is a capitalist country" is no more convincing. In

either case a clearer definition of capitalism is needed. Until such a definition is given, the question of whether or not Japan is a capitalist country falls back readily on semantics. In my view, the Japanese economy is based upon private firms and a competitive price mechanism, with which the government interferes directly and indirectly through its economic policies. Owners of capital funds play a limited role within this framework.

13. According to a recent survey, 96% of Japanese executives were formerly members of their firm's labor union, and some 30% had at one time been union officials (members of the central executive committee, the central committee, etc.).

14. See Dore, 1973. This famous work details a number of differences between Japanese and British firms, and offers a number of interesting insights.

15. For example, M. Kalecki, Joan Robinson, J.R. Hicks (the notions of fix-price and flex-price), and Morishima, 1984. Recent papers on macroeconomics by British economists that are based on this hypothesis are too numerous to cite.

References

Dore, Ronald P. (1973). *British Factory, Japanese Factory: The Origin of Diversity in Industrial Relations*. Berkeley: University of California Press.

Drèze, J.H. (1976). "Some Theories of Labor Management and Participation, *Econometrica*, November issue.

Morishima, Michio (1984). *Mushigen-Koku no Keizaigaku* (The Economics of a Country with no Resources). Tokyo: Iwanami Shoten.

Nishiyama, Tadanori (1981). *Nihon wa Shihonshugi no Kuni de wa Nai* (Japan Is Not a Capitalist Society). Tokyo: Mikasa Shobo.

Nishiyama, Tadanori (1983). *Datsu Shihonshugi Bunseki* (Away from Capitalism). Tokyo: Bunshindo.

CHAPTER 5

JAPANESE FIRMS, CHINESE FIRMS: A COMPARISON

The Japanese Firm (I): Its Functions

Obviously, there is great diversity among Japanese firms: for example, they can be classified according to size; type of ownership, as discussed later; and industry. Without touching upon such taxonomy, the discussion here will be concerned mainly with typical Japanese firms, which are relatively large scale (in terms of sales, employment, etc.), are listed on the stock exchange, and are engaged mainly in manufacturing.

The central agents of the spectacular economic growth of postwar Japan, based on rapid development of industry, manufacturing industry in particular, were private firms,[1] both large firms and medium- and small-scale firms which complemented and competed with them. Japanese medium- and small-scale firms show wide variety, and many of these along with large-scale firms, have made important contributions to the industrial development of Japan. A number of firms, starting as small companies in the postwar period, grew rapidly and were transformed into giant corporations (like Sony, Sanyo Electric (Sanyo Denki), Pioneer Electronic Corp., Kyocera Corp., and Honda Motor Co. (Honda Giken)). However, the constraints of space do not allow us to discuss medium- and small-scale firms here.[2]

What kind of entity is a typical Japanese firm, for example, a giant corporation like Hitachi Ltd. (Hitachi Seisakusho), Matsushita, NEC (Nihon Denki), Toyota Motor Corp. (Toyota Jidosha), Mitsubishi Heavy Industries (Mitsubishi Jukogyo), Toray Industries, Asahi Chemical Industry (Asahi Kasei), Nippon Oil (Nihon Sekiyu), or a somewhat smaller but internationally known firm which is listed on the stock exchange and is larger than a certain size? What role does it play in the national economy? How is it run as a business organization? It is difficult to answer these questions in general terms. In what

193

follows, I adopt the viewpoint of a comparative analysis of Japanese and Chinese firms, and discuss points that I consider important from the specific standpoint of China's economic development strategy. These include the (I) functions, especially the functions of the head office, (II) behavioral principle and distributive structure, and (III) patterns of ownership (including the relationship between ownership patterns and firm behavior) of a typical large Japanese firm.

1. The role of the firm

In an economy like Japan's, based upon a competitive market mechanism and private firms, the firm is the nucleus of production activity and its main role is to produce goods and services. In the manufacturing sector particularly, barring a few exceptions like the Japan Tobacco and Salt Public Corporation before its recent privatization, the production activity is mostly undertaken by purely private (privately owned) firms. In an industrialized society like Japan, however, a firm does not repeat production of exactly the same goods and services every year. The first characteristic function of a Japanese firm, especially one above a certain minimum scale, that we would like to emphasize, is that it does not operate in a stationary state in which the same conditions are repeated. Such firms forecast and react to the continually changing national and international economic environment, which is in a state of continuous flux and evolution, and actively pursue technological changes and develop new markets, thereby inducing economic changes and development. Therefore, the functions related to formulation of a response to changing environment and of creative development of themselves account for a high proportion of a firm's functions.

In modern industrialized societies, the size of a national economy expands year by year, and new technologies and products continuously replace obsolete ones. Under such conditions firms that simply regenerate their production activity with unchanging scale and technologies are bound to fail in competition with other firms and thus go out of existence. Therefore, for their own development, or even simply for their own existence, firms must develop new technologies and new products, open new markets, and expand and improve their production facilities, and hence enlarge the scale of their business operations.

2. Profits and resource allocation

Profits are a very important barometer of the health of firms. The destiny of a firm and the speed of its growth depend crucially upon whether or not it can earn profits, and if it can, upon the size of the profits. Profits serve two important functions in the process of resource allocation within a competitive market mechanism.

First, in a market mechanism firms concentrate their efforts on earning profits, but only those firms which succeed in developing superior new technologies and/or products, engage in continuous rationalization of production processes, improve quality control, and break into new industrial fields and new markets can earn profits. According to the labor theory of value, production activity using hired labor is thought of as generating "surplus value" through the exploitation of labor, and "capital" is considered to be self-propagating. To some extent such a view of a firm might have been appropriate to 18th- or 19th-century firms, but it is inapplicable to a modern firm. Earning profits over and above "the cost of capital" incurred by a modern firm when raising necessary funds in the capital market depends upon the ability of the firm to bring about and implement some "new combinations" or "innovations" which cannot be imitated easily by other firms.[3]

Second, sufficient profits are a necessary condition for the development of a firm (or, simply for its survival). This is necessitated by the fact that though a part of the funds needed for research and development of new technologies and products, construction of new factories, expansion and renovation of plant and equipment, etc., can be raised by incurring debts, such as borrowings from financial institutions, or by increasing equity participation (i.e., a new issue of stocks), a part of it must be covered by retained profits. Furthermore, sufficient profits or assured future profitability is indispensable for incurring debt or issuing new stocks. Thus, only a firm that shows sufficient profitability can develop.

From the above discussion, it is clear that the competitive market mechanism allocates additional funds (borrowings, new stock issues, retention of profits) to more profitable sectors (or the sectors where profitability is expected to be high) and thereby determines the course of the development of the economy as a whole.

3. The essential functions of the head office
In an industrialized society, how does a large firm which ceaselessly pursues innovations for the purpose of enhancing profits operate? Let us look at the behavior of such a firm by observing the functions performed by its head office.[4]

The head office of a typical large-scale Japanese firm is the nucleus of its organization, and its main functions are:

(a) Supervision of current production activity of all the constituent parts of the firm (divisions, subdivisions, factories, establishments, branch offices, sales offices, subsidiaries, and affiliates);

(b) Research and development and product planning for developing new technologies and products;

(c) Investment planning for diversifying into new business fields, construction of new factories, and expansion, improvement, and renovation of existing productive facilities;

(d) Marketing activities related to new products, new fields, new markets (export markets, etc.), and new customers;

(e) Corporate finance to procure funds necessary for continuing and expanding business at the lowest possible cost;

(f) Personnel affairs related to the composition of its employees (including executives), development of their capabilities, and their treatment: namely, planning and implementing policies related to hiring, promotion, transfers, retirement, training, remuneration, rewards, and punishments.

Let me append a few comments to our discussion above. First, all of the large Japanese firms are multiproduct firms. For example, in prewar years Hitachi Ltd. started as a manufacturer of small-sized electric motors and diversified into heavy electric machinery, telecommunications equipment, and rolling stock. In the postwar period it spun off its metal, transmission wire, and chemical divisions as independent subsidiaries and further diversified into household electric appliances and electronics, and later mainframe computers as well. Toray Industries, beginning as a rayon manufacturer, diversified into nylon and other synthetic fibers in the postwar era and, recently, began shifting over to specialty chemicals and plastics in an attempt to reduce its textile business, within a few years, to under 40% of sales as a strategy to move gradually out of textiles. Asahi Chemical Industry, another producer of synthetic fibers, is increasing its share of housing and pharmaceuticals and is further diversifying into food products and office equipment. Even automobile manufacturers, which generally have a strong tendency to specialize in automobiles, are, besides producing passenger cars, trucks, commercial vehicles, and buses, producing textile machinery (Nissan Motor Co.), aircraft parts (Nissan, Fuji Heavy Industries), housing (Toyota Motor Corp.), motorcycles (Honda Motor Co.), and so on.

As is clear from the examples above, firms try to utilize more fully their technological, marketing, and other business-related capabilities, that is, "managerial resources" they have accumulated in the past, and move away from stagnating sectors to new growth areas where these capabilities or resources can be applied profitably. To a certain extent the diversification of business activities also helps to lower the risks accompanying growth into new fields. For these reasons, the business activities of a firm, of necessity, divide into a number of business areas and, hence, centralized supervision and coordination become an important task for the head office.

Second, since the business activities of a firm extend over a number of areas, and since marketing, an important aspect of business activities under the competitive market mechanism, is inevitably dispersed geographically, a firm's establishments (factories, mines, sales offices) are located nationwide and even abroad. Furthermore, if, concomitant with growth into a new field or a major expansion of existing facilities, a new factory is built at the best possible location, geographical dispersion of a firm's establishments is inevitable. The head office is responsible for the control and coordination of branch establishments.

Third, I may have given the impression in the above discussion that the activities listed under (a) were the firm's current activities while those under (b) to (f) were related to the development of the firm. In fact, however, there is no easy way to distinguish between the two types of activities; in particular, to a considerable extent (d), (e), and (f) have elements involving current, day-to-day operations. Furthermore, the head office (plus the central research institute controlled by the head office) is not the only place for the conduct of activities listed under (b) to (f). A large number of firms actively carry out research and development, investment planning, and marketing at the plant or sales-office levels as well. All that I intend to emphasize here is that a large fraction of the activities listed under (b) to (f) and carried out mainly by the head office arise because of the dynamic nature of the firm, which strives for growth and development in a changing world full of uncertainty, and that many such activities are not necessary if the firm operates in a stationary state where the same production activities are simply repeated. To find new business activities which are not of current, routine, or day-to-day type, but involve active identification of new business opportunities in the face of an unknown and highly uncertain world, and to implement and execute them are the essential functions of a modern firm.[5]

The Japanese Firm (II): Behavioral Principles and the Pattern of Income Distribution

In the introductory microeconomic theory of firms, a simplified theoretical model is constructed in which firms are portrayed as making decisions regarding the scale of production (sales) and the quantities of factors of production to be purchased (including labor employed) in order to maximize their profits. Also, the orthodox theory with respect to financing investments is based upon the hypothesis that management as a representative of the stockholders tries to maximize the stock price (thereby maximizing the value of the firm, which is equal to the product of the total number of outstanding stocks and the stock price).

1. Profit maximization and competing hypotheses

The orthodox profit-maximizing hypothesis has been confronted with a number of competing hypotheses. For example, the sales maximization hypothesis by William J. Baumol postulates that a firm maximizes sales (or growth rate of sales) under a given rate of profit. The "satisficing hypothesis" (or the hypothesis of a "satisficing" level of profits) of Herbert Simon states that, in view of the intricate nature of internal organization of a modern firm, although firms do try to achieve a certain minimum level of profits, they do not necessarily maximize profits, as they feel satisfied once the minimum is achieved. Still another hypothesis, by Masahiko Aoki,[6] takes a game-theoretic approach and visualizes the firm as a three-person, cooperative game among the group of stockholders; the employees' group (or the labor union representing their interests); and the management, which acts as a referee mediating between the other two groups.

Though these alternative hypotheses are noteworthy, and convincing to a certain extent, they do not, in my opinion, carry enough weight to replace the profit maximization hypothesis in terms of either empirical validity or theoretical simplicity. As a first approximation, the hypothesis that a typical large-scale Japanese firm maximizes its profits from a long-term perspective seems to hold sufficient empirical validity in my view. I think, however, that motivation for a firm to maximize its profits and the mechanism through which this maximization is achieved are quite different from those implicitly assumed by orthodox theory. I am not naive enough to think that I can easily persuade others on this controversial problem, which has long been the subject of intense discussion and debate. Even so, in what follows, I would like to put forth my views on this problem by considering a typical large-scale Japanese firm as the basis of discussion.

2. The managers

A large Japanese firm shows certain distinct characteristics with respect to the selection of managers that are rarely observed elsewhere.

(a) Almost all the members of the top management of a large Japanese firm come from the ranks of employees who have worked within the same company for 30 to 40 years, since graduating from school.

(b) The employees (especially white-collar workers, though it holds to a certain extent for blue-collar workers as well) are promoted gradually and steadily, with a regular periodicity of once a year to once in 3–4 years, in terms of their salaries and posting. It is from within these cadres that candidates for the top management emerge. The newly hired white-collar workers (university graduates) enter a firm with the ambition of becoming the president of the company after a few decades or, failing that, a director or at least an executive at the level of the head of a department.

(c) Above all, the management is to be characterized as the representative of the employee group. This is something unique to Japanese firms with practically no parallels in other countries.[7] A manager who makes light of employees' interests cannot retain his position, or, rather, cannot achieve such a status. If, by chance, such a person becomes an executive, the firm cannot flourish.

(d) The employee group, referred to above, is by no means a group composed of more or less homogeneous members like a labor union or an agricultural cooperative association. It is a group with strong hierarchical structure within which one's status, remuneration, authority, and reputation are determined by one's educational background, length of service, ability, and performance.

The management, especially the president or a small number of top executives around the president, has effective control over a large Japanese firm. That is, they wield, in effect, the main decision-making power in matters of importance to the company.

3. Powers of the stockholders

The stockholders are the legal owners of the firm and have legal rights to make major decisions with respect to its management, such as appointing the president and other directors, changing articles of incorporation, and approving financial statements. In large Japanese firms, however, the owner-manager type of stockholder with an effective voice in business matters is exceptionally rare.[8] In a typical large-scale Japanese firm, even the largest stockholders either refrain from intervening, or cannot intervene, in managerial affairs as long as the company is showing more than a certain minimum rate of profit.[9] The stockholders, or more precisely, large stockholders—which are mostly financial institutions or financially related companies—have a say in managerial affairs only when the company encounters financial difficulties or when, because of financial difficulties, merger or collaboration with other firms is contemplated, that is, when the very existence of the firm becomes the subject of discussion.

On problems involving a major financial and managerial decision such as changes in articles of incorporation, large investment projects, advancing into new business fields, capital increases, issuance of new stocks or bonds, and dividend policies the management often informs the large stockholders in advance and obtains their prior consent. It is normal practice for large stockholders to accept the management's proposals as long as the firm is being run more or less satisfactorily. It is also true that any interference exceeding established norms by the large stockholders, normally the financial institutions and banks of which the firm is a customer, is disliked by the management and can induce the firm to approach other banks or life insurance companies, and could result in the loss of a customer for them.

Though the stockholders are legally entitled to nominate the executives of the firm, this is merely a formality. In practice, the management chooses its own successors—except at the time of establishment or when the firm has encountered financial difficulties.

Takeovers (replacement of the management control) by acquisition of over half (or nearly half) of the total stocks through the stock market or by takeover bids (proposals to acquire management control), not uncommon in the United States and Europe, are practically nonexistent in Japan. Japanese managers are virtually free of takeover threats.[10]

The striking weakness of Japanese stockholders' control over the management of the firm, however, does not imply that their interests are neglected. We will come back to this point later.

4. Profits and distribution thereof

When I say that as a first approximation large Japanese firms can be thought of as maximizing profits, the term "profits" is to be interpreted more widely than the usual financial profits of the firm, that is, net profits on the profit and loss account. The profits in this context should include a part of the wages, salaries, and bonuses to the employees (wages, salaries, and bonuses over and above the levels in the external labor markets), a large part of the R&D and other expenditures related to subsequent development of the firm, and a part of the depreciation allowances. In my opinion, the firm endeavors to earn a positive "profit" or "surplus," in excess of the costs incurred on current activities (including the cost of capital), and to maximize it over the long run.

How are these profits, defined broadly, distributed?

(a) *The employees' share.* A substantial proportion of the "broadly defined profits" in the above sense goes to the employees (and executives) in Japan. The employees of a large Japanese firm receive a portion of the profits in accordance with their positions within the company. Successful, highly profitable, and growing firms pay large bonuses (equivalent to 3–4 months' and, sometimes, even 6–8 months' salaries a year), higher salaries, and abundant fringe benefits. Part-timers and temporary workers, however, are not considered members of the "firm household" and are virtually left out of the distribution of profits. On the other hand, the wage differential (including distribution of profits in the above sense) between regular blue-collar and white-collar workers is negligible at the time of initial appointment on graduation from school, and is much smaller afterward when compared with that in other countries. As far as regular employees are concerned, intrafirm salary (plus bonus) differentials are relatively small, and the difference between the lowest and the highest (the president) salaries is somewhere between 1:10 or 1:15, and is much smaller than that in countries such as the United States (perhaps 1 to 50 or even 100).[11] The maximum bonus per capita of employees who are not directors is practically the same as the minimum for a full-time director, and changes in compensation between employees and members of the top management are continuous and do not show a large gap.

(b) *R&D and investment.* A large part of the profits is used for research and development, opening new markets, expanding production facilities, and investment in affiliated companies. Of these, a large proportion of the expenditures on research and development (R&D) and opening new markets is treated as expenses for accounting purposes while investment in plant and equipment and investment in affiliated companies are undertaken out of retained profits,[12] but seen in a broader perspective, all these expenditures are a part of the "surplus" as discussed above.

(c) *Dividends.* A part of the net profits, after payment of corporate taxes, is paid out as dividends to the stockholders. A comparison of Japanese and American corporations in terms of distribution of profits reveals the dividend propensity (the ratio of dividends paid out to net profits) to be substantially lower for Japanese corporations. The dividends paid out to the household sector from the corporate sector have accounted for 15–20% of profits in recent years, and the remainder has been retained within the corporate sector. Since this ratio pertains to the narrower concept of accounting profits (net profits after tax), if the profits are defined broadly to include R&D expenditures and a part of the salaries and bonuses, it would be obvious that only a very small proportion is disbursed to the stockholders as dividends.

5. Valuation of profits and distributional conflicts

The time for profits to emerge and the time for making expenditures needed to generate these profits differ, giving rise to the problem of valuation of expenditures and incomes at different points of time in "maximizing" profits. The standard discount rate used for computing the present value of the future profits would be the cost of capital incurred by the firm for raising funds in the capital market, but this cost may not be the same for different types of investment or R&D projects. Moreover, the subjective discount rate (time preference) of individual stockholders and employees cannot be completely neglected.

As profits rise with the growth of the firm, the dividends, paid out of the profits, and capital gains on the outstanding stock accrue to the present stockholders. On the side of executives and employees, an increase in the number of employees with the growth of the firm results in a fall in the share going to the present employees.[13] To simplify matters, however, let us ignore the details of such differences and assume that the management and the employee group as well as the stockholders evaluate profits using the same discount rate[14] and that the benefit each employee receives from the growth of the firm's profits is proportional to the growth rate of the firm.[15] Further, let us also assume that the relative share of dividends and disbursements to employees in the profits, broadly defined, is constant because of conditions prevailing in the external markets.

Under these simplifying assumptions the employees' and the stockholders' interests in the growth of the firm through expenditures on R&D, opening of new markets, and investment in plant and equipment as well as retentions from net profits—that is, the investment-dividend policies—are basically in agreement. In these circumstances, the management will aim at maximizing the discounted present value of the income stream consisting of net profits after deducting expenditures for the growth of the firm from the broadly defined profits. Such a policy maximizes the benefits to both the stockholders and the employees.

The above statement, however, begs the following two questions. The first question is concerned with the reasons why the stockholders, the firm's formal owners, to whom the profit legally belongs and who have full rights to its disbursement, allow the management and employees to acquire a large proportion of the firm's profits. Why do they feel satisfied with the meager amount of dividends received? This question can be answered as follows. First, in a country like Japan today, where in effect the employee group, led by management, controls the firm, there is no other way to run a large firm. Second, the firm that fails to approve a distributive pattern similar to that prevailing in other large firms (especially those in the same industry) despite sufficient profits earned, finds itself at a disadvantage in recruitment of new employees and fails to attract superior talent.[16] Third, allocation of profits to the workers affects worker morale and, hence, productivity. Fourth, low dividend propensity (ratio of dividends to net profits) does not necessarily run counter to stockholders' interests. Substantial retentions and high R&D expenditures raise stock prices, giving rise to capital gains, and, partly for tax reasons, this may well be preferred by most of the stockholders.[17]

The second question is, "If the management representing the employee group is in effective control of the firm, why does it not appropriate all, or a major proportion of, the profits (defined broadly) for itself?" The answer to this question lies in the fact that rapid growth of the firm is in the interest of the employees and, in a competitive market setup like Japan's, a large part of the R&D and market development expenditures as well as a part of investment in plant and equipment necessary for the development of the firm must be financed out of profits.

Given the employment practices followed by large Japanese firms, the growth of the firm is beneficial to the workers in two ways. First, steady growth of the firm, with rising profits, gives workers a share of the increased profits. Second, steady growth of the firm implies stable employment and faster promotion opportunities. Furthermore, a rapidly growing firm provides favorable reemployment opportunities in its subsidiaries or affiliated firms for its employees, who all have to retire at the age of 55 (or, more precisely, somewhere between 55 and 65 depending on the firm or on whether the worker is an ordinary employee, a director, a managing director, and so on).[18]

Following the above reasoning, one can see that the intrafirm income distribution of a Japanese firm (especially large amounts of profits paid out to employees and low dividend rates) is in a broad sense constrained by external market conditions despite special features quite different from those of large firms in other countries, such as the management as the representative of the employees, lifetime employment practices, and the seniority wage systems. That is, a firm that is penurious in making distributions to its own employees finds itself at a disadvantage in recruiting new employees and cannot avoid a loss in worker morale. On the other hand, if the net profits and dividends are exceedingly low because of excessive payments to employees, the firm is at a disadvantage in the capital market when raising funds through borrowings from banks and other financial institutions or through issuance of new stocks or corporate bonds. Thus, the "standards" set by the external labor and capital markets are thought to have significant influence upon distributional relationships within the firm.[19]

6. Pricing policies

Looking at the behavior of Japanese firms from a Schumpeterian perspective, which visualizes firms as pursuing development and growth in an environment characterized by uncertain and rapid changes, we can easily see that the "sales maximization hypothesis," which considers the firm as maximizing sales rather than profits in a static setup, is unrealistic. That is, most manufacturing firms possess at least one product, or "profitable item," that generates high profits, as a result of a successful, or more than successful, stage of "product planning" over a number of years. A firm that has generated sufficient profits through such a product or area endeavors to grow by ploughing these profits back into R&D of the next-generation products or product areas, investment in plant and equipment, and development of a sales network, etc. Normally, the firm does not reduce the prices of such "profitable products." The policy of increasing sales volume through price reductions of such products is rarely adopted. Unless the firm earns sufficiently large profits on such successful products or fortunate developments allow the firm to earn large profits, it would become impossible to carry out the R&D and investment programs necessary for future development.

For example, when Fujitsu, Hitachi, or NEC made the decision to enter into manufacturing of mainframe computers, or Mitsubishi Heavy Industries into manufacturing of passenger cars, they must have been prepared to incur losses for the first 5 to 10 years. It was possible for these firms to enter these areas, which require very large amounts of funds, despite immediate losses foreseen, because the firms were earning large profits in their respective former areas, i.e., telecommunications equipment, heavy electrical machinery, industrial machinery, and shipbuilding.

From financial reports on the business performance of the firms, it is easy to see that the so-called "full-cost principle" of pricing has no validity in contemporary Japanese industries. It postulates that a firm sets the price by marking up costs by a fixed profit margin, but statements which invalidate such a postulate abound in these reports. It is said, for example, about firms with several product areas or divisions, that "profits have been low due to severe competition in obtaining orders in a certain division," "business did exceptionally well as sales of a certain profitable product increased greatly," "a certain division of the firm is now being rationalized because of losses but it is expected to generate a profit only from the next term," "profits have been high because of the popularity of some new product where other firms have failed to follow and the firm is the sole runner," and so on. It is clear that, in setting prices for their products, firms carefully consider the competitive conditions (price elasticity of demand) prevailing in their respective markets and do not simply apply a uniform fixed markup ratio to all the products.

The Japanese Firm (III): Forms of Ownership and Behavior Patterns

Japanese firms show diversified forms of ownership. I shall restrict my discussion primarily to privately owned firms, leaving out, for the time being, government enterprises[20] fully or partially owned by central or local governments.

1. Joint-stock companies

Most of the large Japanese firms are joint-stock companies whose shares are listed on the stock exchange,[21] and the separation between their ownership and management is well advanced. For large firms, Japan shows the highest degree of separation of ownership and management among the major industrialized countries.[22]

As compared to this, owner-managers (the owner of the firm running it as a manager) play an important role in medium- and small-scale firms, though a large number of such firms above a certain size are organized as joint-stock companies, limited-liability companies (yugen-gaisha), or partnership companies (gomei-gaisha). If a semblance of the 19th century "capitalist" exists in Japan, it is the owner-managers of the medium- and small-scale firms.

2. Collective firms

Besides the "capitalist" firms, in which the owners have an ownership share in the firm and are vested with the legal rights of stockholders (owners) in proportion to their capital participation, a number of collective firms (cooperative firms), according to Chinese terminology, also exist in contemporary Japan. Life insurance companies, agricultural cooperatives, fisherman's cooperatives, consumers' cooperatives, and credit associations fall into this category. Furthermore, incorporated bodies like the Japan Management Association, or institutions like the Central Cooperative Bank for Agriculture and Forestry (The Norin Chukin Bank) and the Central Cooperative Bank for Commercial and Industrial Cooperatives (The Shoko Chukin Bank), established under special legislative provisions, may also be regarded as collective firms. With respect to their economic functions, these cooperative firms do not differ significantly from private enterprises organized as joint-stock companies.

Except for three smaller companies and recently established foreign-owned ones, Japanese life insurance companies are all mutual companies organized to share the risk burden by treating, pro forma, all holders of life insurance policies as owners of the company. In Japan the major stockholders of large firms are mainly banks, trust banks, life insurance companies, trading companies, and some other related companies, while the major stockholders of the large trading companies and others are banks and insurance companies. Moreover, large stockholders of large banks are either other banks or insurance companies, and there is a strong tendency toward mutual stockholdings. Thus, insurance companies own a conspicuously large proportion of stocks in this system of mutual stockholdings among large firms and banks, but, because they are not joint-stock companies themselves, they cannot be owned by other large firms. In this sense, one can say that the life insurance companies stand out as the apex of the ownership structure of large Japanese corporations. It is notable that life insurance companies thus occupying the position at the apex are collective firms (see Chapter 6).

In the case of a cooperative society, the members of which must meet certain qualifications, the funds collected from the members form its capital and the society is run for the purpose of increasing the welfare or benefits of its members. Unlike members of other private firms, each member of the cooperative society has one vote in the decision-making process, regardless of the amount each has contributed.

Who, then, controls these cooperative firms that are neither joint-stock firms nor individually owned or family-owned firms, or institutions like the Central Cooperative Bank for Agriculture and Forestry or other special types of corporations (incorporated bodies called "shadan hojin," medical corporations etc.) in which the ownership is not clearly defined? How are decisions made in these private firms and what are their behavioral principles? This is an interesting problem from the point of view of comparative economic systems. An empirical and theoretical investigation into this problem would be quite worthwhile.

3. Behavior patterns of collectively owned firms

Although I am not thoroughly conversant with the functioning of Japanese private firms that are neither joint-stock companies nor individually owned companies, I believe that their behavior differs little from that of typical private firms, as discussed in the two preceding sections. For example, life insurance companies organized as mutual companies and those organized as joint-stock companies seem to show no marked differences, apart from differences in their formal procedures, in the appointment of directors, remuneration to executives and employees, management policies, investment behavior, and so on (see Chapter 6).

In the case of agricultural or consumers' cooperatives or mutual companies, even though these are not joint-stock companies and pursue objectives other than earning profits, it is desirable from the point of view of the members of the cooperatives or mutual companies, of the management, and of the employees that the firms develop and grow steadily. To facilitate the growth of such firms it is necessary to obtain revenues exceeding costs and to accumulate a large part of the surplus as retained earnings.

The growth of such firms requires funds. A part of these funds can be supplied through borrowing, but creditors will not be willing to lend to a firm unless it is earning sufficiently high profits (defined broadly) or at least has prospects for such profits, and unless increased ,retained earnings will match increased borrowings. Furthermore, in order to raise the morale of the management and employees and to reward their efforts, a part of the "broadly defined profits" must be distributed to them in accordance with the firm's performance.

It is true that firms which are not joint-stock companies do not have to make payments corresponding to dividends in joint-stock companies (in most cooperative societies, however, dividends are paid on the funds contributed by the members, though at low rates) and hence the outflow of funds can be smaller to that extent. But these firms cannot raise funds by issuing new capital stock or convertible bonds, so that they must depend to a greater extent on retained earnings for "owned" funds necessary for their growth.

From the above considerations one may conclude that, in the contemporary Japanese environment, the behavior patterns of collectively owned firms differ little from those of joint-stock firms.

The Chinese Firm (I): Present Conditions

Putting aside agriculture (or the rural sector) for the time being, let us look at the nature of Chinese firms in urban areas (the "city economies"), especially industrial (manufacturing) firms. According to *Gendai Chugoku Keizai Jiten* (The Handbook of the Contemporary Chinese Economy), the organizational forms of people-owned, i.e., state-owned (and state-run) industrial enterprises in China encompass what is called in Chinese "gongchang" (factory), "zonghe gongsi" (composite factory), "gongsi xintai" (company firm), "zhuanye gongsi" (specialized company), "lianhe gongsi" (allied company), and "jinji lianheti" (economic union). Among these forms "gongchang" (often written simply "chang") is the most basic form and numerically the most prevalent one.[23]

I have not been able, as yet, to form a comprehensive and concrete image of a typical manufacturing firm in China: how it is managed, what functions it performs, and what its pattern of income distribution is. For those of us who are accustomed to a system of the firms like the Japanese type, with clear demarcation between firms and the firms and administrative organizations, it is extremely difficult to comprehend a Chinese firm. My understanding of the "gongsi xintai" and "jinji lianheti" is especially poor. Despite these limitations, I shall put forth my limited understanding of Chinese state-owned industrial enterprises, especially "gongchang" or "chang," although it may be criticized as arbitrary, and make a preliminary attempt to compare the Japanese and Chinese situations.

1. Nature of the "gongchang"

As is clear from the *Gendai Chugoku Keizai Jiten*, "chang" ("gongchang") is the most basic form of Chinese state-owned industrial firms. Most of the "lianheti" or "gongsi xintai" firms are no more than a loose combination of these "gongchang" and, therefore, are substantially different from a decision-making unit like a Japanese firm.

My first impression of a typical Chinese "gongchang" is that it is an entity engaged in producing a specific product or in carrying out a specific production process (e.g., an electric power station) and, more often than not, located at a specific site or within a particular area.

That is, generally, it is not an entity with plural establishments at various places around the country (or even abroad), as is the case with Japanese firms. Most of the larger "gongchang" are controlled either directly by one of the 12 industrial ministries of the State Council (e.g., the Ministry of the Machinery Industry [now the Committee for the Machinery Industry] or the Ministry of the Spinning and Weaving Industry), or by the industrial bureaus of the provincial-level governments (provinces, special cities (Beijing, Shanghai, Tianjin), or autonomous regions), or jointly by the two.[24]

It appears that some of the "gongchang" are fully or partially controlled by a national-level "gongsi" or the "zong gongsi" (general company), or by a "fen gongsi" (branch company) at the provincial level, but so far such "gongsi" have had the character of an administrative organ rather than that of a firm. If one is to find a counterpart of a "gongchang" in Japan, it is obviously a "factory" of a firm rather than a "firm" as far as its functions are concerned. That is, it corresponds roughly to one of several factories controlled by a Japanese firm.

Attempts have been made recently in China to give a degree of autonomy to the firm, and efforts to expand the scope of this autonomy are also under way. The emphasis placed on the development of firms as vigorous economic entities in the resolution adopted at the Third Plenum of the 12th Central Committee on October 20, 1984, points to a momentum for further steps in this direction. Despite these efforts at providing the "gongchang" with wider autonomy, the degree of present autonomy or the degree of autonomy expected in the near future is rather limited. The autonomy allowed the firm appears to be generally within the following bounds. (The situation, however, is in a state of flux, given the policy to further extend autonomy, and differs depending on the sector, region, and even individual "gongchang." Presented below is a broad outline of the author's interpretation of conditions prevailing in the period 1983–1984.)

(a) The amounts of individual products to be produced. Earlier, targets set by higher authorities were followed, but recently the "gongchang" have been allowed to make adjustments within a small margin.

(b) The sale and pricing of excess outputs after delivery of the allotted production target of a product. The price determined through negotiations with the buyer, called the "negotiated price," is constrained to be within the fixed margin of 10 to 20% above or below the official price.

(c) Investment in plant and equipment out of retained profits, depreciation allowances, and bank borrowings. A large part of the profits is still to be paid to the government as taxes and other payments, leaving little to be retained within the firm. Since expenditures for experimental production of new goods, employees' welfare, and bonus payments to the employees are also made out of retained profits, only a small proportion is available for investment in plant and equipment. As for depreciation allowances, the asset life used in computing depreciation allowances has been quite long (25 to 33 years). Although this life span seems to have been shortened somewhat in recent years, since a part of the depreciation allowances is collected by the government, the fund available for investment purposes, at the discretion of the firm, is very small.

(d) Purchase of materials. A major proportion of basic materials under state control is still allotted to the firm by higher authorities. Autonomy in this area pertains to the purchase either of already decontrolled commodities or, if the commodities are still controlled, of those materials to be used for excess outputs produced for free sales.

(e) Payment of bonuses to and rewards and penalties for the employees. The basic wage structure, grading of individual employees, regulation of wage raises, total wage payments inclusive of bonus payments, etc., are either completely determined by the government or kept within strict limits. In this regard, the wage system of state-firms in China resembles that of government employees or employees of major public corporations and enterprises in Japan.

That the Chinese "gongchang" is hardly equipped with essential functions necessary for playing a role similar to that played by the Japanese firm in a competitive market mechanism based upon private enterprises can be easily seen by enumerating the functions that are not carried out (or barely carried out) at the "gongchang" level. The "gongchang" does not engage in the following types of activities— or, if it does, only to a very limited extent: that is, the firm's autonomy is quite restricted. Generally speaking, the "gongchang" does *not* possess managerial autonomy in the following areas:

(a) Research and development.

(b) Development or introduction of new products.

(c) Marketing. A large part of sales goes to state trading organizations at a price determined in advance by higher authorities. Recently, the "gongchang" have been allowed to sell a part of their output freely. This type of free sales, however, is conducted either at the location of the "gongchang" or at some other specified location. Full-fledged marketing activities, such as establishment of multiple sales outlets, opening of new markets, and development of new products, new types of services, and sales techniques conforming to consumers' needs as revealed through organized market surveys, are still largely lacking.

(d) Export of products and import of raw materials. All exports of manufactured products must go through "the export-import 'gongsi' " set up for each individual product area. To import necessary materials and equipment, one must apply to higher authorities and if the approval comes through, imports can be made through the import organizations. This implies, for example, that when raw cotton was still imported, a spinning and weaving factory had to purchase raw cotton in an amount, at one time, to be used for a period of half a year, since the foreign exchange allocations for import were made only once every 6 months. This is extremely inefficient as it requires huge inventories of raw materials to be held at each factory. The individual "export-import 'gongsi' " seems so far to have functioned more as an administrative unit than as a firm.

(e) Expansion or contraction of employment, recruitment or dismissal of workers, and determination of their salaries.

(f) Technological collaboration or joint ventures with foreign firms.

(g) A large expansion in production facilities.

(h) Construction of a new plant in a geographical location different from the original one, or establishment of sales outlets.

(i) Mergers and joint ventures with other firms, acquisition of subsidiaries, or setting up of new ones.

In short, the degree of managerial autonomy now given (or expected to be given in the future) to the Chinese "gongchang" amounts, in comparison to the situation in the Japanese manufacturing industry, to no more (or even less) than the degree of autonomy given to a single plant within a firm.

In the case of Japan, large firms often adopt the so-called division system under which several plants producing the same or similar products are controlled by a division (*jigyo-bu*) or a "general division" (*jigyo honbu*), and give such divisions (or "general divisions") a fairly high degree of autonomy. The degree of autonomy granted to the Chinese "gongchang" is far below that given to the division (or "general division") of a Japanese firm.

2. Is the "gongchang" a firm?

The "gongchang" is in the forefront of industrial production in the Chinese economy, and it is a unit of economic accounting as well.[25] Its basic function, however, is to execute routine productive activities and meet the production targets set by the planning authorities. The

Chinese "gongchang" does not play a central role as a decision-making unit in industrial production. It does not make decisions on what are thought to be fundamental and important items of the firm's management in Japan, i.e., decisions related to R&D, product development, investment planning, marketing, personnel affairs, etc., referred to above as the functions of the head office of the firm, or decisions on much simpler matters such as the determination of yearly and monthly production levels, purchase of materials, salary structures, wage raises, and employment levels. In other words, the Chinese "gongchang" can hardly represent a "firm" in the accepted sense of the term.

If the Chinese "gongchang" does not act as the decision-making body for production activities, corresponding to the firm in Japan, what sorts of institutions in China are responsible for making the important managerial decisions which are made daily, monthly, and annually by a firm's management in Japan? Do the higher authorities in China possess the attributes of a firm?

Summing up my tentative impressions of this question, it appears, first, that generally authorities of a rank higher than that of the "gongchang," i.e., the industrial ministries of the State Council, national-level "gongsi" or "zong gongsi" under them, or the industrial bureaus at the provincial level, are also mainly preoccupied with quantitative expansion of routine production activities and perform only to a greatly limited extent functions which correspond to those performed by the head office of a Japanese firm such as planning and decision making with respect to R&D activities in new areas, product planning, demand forecasting, investment, and marketing. The vertical compartmentalization of the industrial ministries of the State Council by product category seems to be a major obstacle in this respect. The fact that firms under the jurisdiction of local governments (including some very large firms in terms of the number of employees) are confined within administrative divisions like provinces, special cities, cities, and prefectures also impedes the firms' business activities.

Second, the higher authorities are basically administrative organizations and are not responsible for profits or losses arising from their decisions; also, they do not enjoy the benefits resulting from the profits. That is, these administrative organizations cannot play the role of the firm in its accepted meaning.

Third, because of these limitations, the relationship between decisions taken by higher authorities regarding R&D, investment, marketing, and so on, and the profits, which are the economic result thereof, is necessarily diluted. That is, higher authorities tend to overemphasize simple quantitative targets such as the levels of output for products already in production (especially output levels of basic materials like steel, cement, coal, electricity, and products related in one way or another to these materials, or the level of consumption of energy) and to pay little attention to economic costs, benefits, and efficiency.

Fourth, basic decision-making powers, with respect to economic activities related to industrial production, are vested in higher authorities which are not responsible for profitability, because they are administrative organizations. These organizations are not "economic accounting units," and by definition, take no responsibility for the economic consequences of their decisions.[26] The "gongchang," which is an "economic accounting unit," on the other hand, has a very limited say in the important decisions related to its own economic activity. This divestiture of decision-making powers from economic accounting units constitutes one of the most important and fundamental weaknesses of Chinese industry.[27]

In sum, according to my impression, there is no entity in China that may be called a firm, at least not in the accepted sense of the term.

3. Two examples

I will cite two examples of Chinese firms which were instrumental in forming my views as set forth above.

(a) *An automobile plant in Changchun City.* The First Automobile Factory in Changchun City, which I visited in 1984, was the largest automobile factory in China and was then one of only two automobile factories under the direct control of the Ministry of Machinery Industry of the State Council. This factory had been producing the same Jiefang (liberation) model of truck since it was established in 1956 with technical assistance from the Soviet Union. The truck was equipped with a 110-hp gasoline (not diesel) engine which was much larger and heavier than the diesel engines of the same horse power in use in Japan and other developed countries. This engine was based originally upon a Ford truck engine of the 1940s. A new, 140-hp engine was being developed in this factory, and a model change was expected in the near future. Continued production of exactly the same model of an automobile for over 30 years without a model change is utterly inconceivable in Japan or in any market economy where firms must compete with each other. Following the Sino-Soviet confrontation in 1960, all Soviet technical assistance was discontinued and all Soviet technicians were recalled. Yet over 70–80% of the machine tools in use in the factory in 1984 seemed to be Soviet-made, and they had been used for over 30 years without being replaced. This indicated that both at the level of the First Automobile Factory and at the level of its supervising organization, the Ministry of Machinery Industry, some of the basic functions of a firm (R&D, product development, deployment of new machines (transfer machines, NC machine tools) for raising productivity, automation of the production process, energy conservation, etc.), which must be performed by the management, had generally been neglected.

(b) *A communications equipment factory in Shanghai.* I visited a factory that was manufacturing communications equipment in Shanghai in the same year (1984). This factory had comparatively greater managerial autonomy than the First Automobile Factory. It employs 2700 blue-collar and 400 white-collar workers and is engaged primarily in the production of radios and radio–tape-recorders as well as wireless radio equipment for civilian use. I was told that this was a strategic (experimental) plant in the Shanghai area for testing the effect of expanding the degree of a firm's autonomy and that it had been given wide-ranging freedom of action in recent years. This product field is characterized by fast technological progress, quick product changes, and keen competition. Because consumers prefer superior products, unpopular products end up in accumulated unsold stock. Hence a factory responsible for production in this field must exhibit the attributes of a firm to a greater extent than the First Automobile Factory.

Despite this, even at the time of my visit, when a greater degree of managerial autonomy was being granted to the factory, most of the important items for the firm's managerial decision, in the Japanese perspective, were decided upon by higher authorities or required their approval. The Shanghai City's Bureau of Instruments Industry and Bureau of Prices, and the East China First-Class Wholesale Station were the supervising administrative organizations immediately above this plant, and they in turn were supervised by the Ministry of Electronics Industry and the Ministry of Commerce of the State Council.

The degree of managerial autonomy granted to this factory can be outlined as follows:

(i) The plant engaged in R&D activity to a certain extent, but the kinds of products to be produced were dictated by the higher authorities.

(ii) Until recently, the production plan had been determined entirely by the higher authorities, but a part of the production plan in 1984 was now prepared by the plant, on the basis of demand conditions, and submitted to the higher authorities for approval.

(iii) The same was true of product pricing as well. The sales price, once fixed, could not be changed.

(iv) A large proportion of raw materials used could now be requisitioned from the open market, but steel, aluminum, copper, and lumber were still rationed, and the factory received allotments.

(v) Whereas earlier the factory had been required to sell its entire output to the wholesale station, about 20% of its production had been sold by the factory itself in recent years. This was sold on a commission basis by shops in Shanghai or other provinces. Selling in this way was somewhat more advantageous than selling to the wholesale station because the factory received the wholesale margin set by state authorities. Its products were not exported.

(vi) Though the basic wage structure was regulated by the government, recently the factory had been allowed to distribute 13% of any increase in profits over the previous year as additions to basic wages, salaries, and bonuses to its employees.

(vii) In order to expand its operations, the factory was considering formation of a "jinji lianheti" with a few plants in Shanghai or other provinces which had encountered business difficulties.

(viii) Before the economic reforms, the factory had no power with respect to technical collaboration with foreign firms and purchase of equipment from abroad, but now it could consider such possibilities. In practice, however, the process involved was quite cumbersome; a number of steps were required before approval for entering a contract is given.

My overall impression from the above description was, first, that even with the expansion of the managerial autonomy granted to this factory in recent years, it amounted to no more than the autonomy given to a factory within a Japanese firm. Second, one might ask, "Were the higher authorities carrying out the functions of the firm?" The answer is that, due to their administrative nature, the higher authorities performed the essential functions of a firm involving R&D, planning for new products, collaboration with foreign firms, nationwide marketing, opening up of export markets, and the like only to a limited extent.

4. The Chinese economy without firms

In Japan, economic controls were maintained extensively during and after the Second World War. The bureaucracy was compartmentalized vertically into bureaus and divisions each of which was responsible for narrowly defined industries or products, and regulated productive activities of the firms down to the details regarding the type and price of products and raw materials, production levels, quantity of materials used, etc. In the case of military procurement or other government procurement, private firms were ordered to produce battleships, aircraft, rolling stock, etc., and the military (the Army and the Navy) or other government agencies supervised the private firms engaged in such production. Furthermore, under the "planned shipbuilding" policy carried out by the Ministry of Transport in the postwar period, the government took the lead in formulating plans for expanding the Japanese merchant marine fleet and implemented the plans by directing the private shipping and shipbuilding firms.

In Japan, however, there existed the head offices of the private firms, which mediated between the government supervisory authorities and the factories and dockyards, the actual production units. Despite the extensive controls, planned production, and government orders discussed above, they were able to some extent to carry out the functions of a firm. That is, these firms continued to pursue profits, to ensure their own existence and growth, and endeavored to raise productivity, improve technology and products, and reduce costs. Even under a system of extensive controls or government procurement, these firms were in a competitive relationship with each other and, in the long run, the firms with superior managerial skills were able to persist and grow by improving their technologies and productivity and accumulating profits, while the firms with low managerial efficiency and stagnating technology fell into oblivion.

The firm's head office normally does not limit itself to a single product, nor is it an economic entity with production activities limited to a single location. It is a diversified entity interested in the development of a wide range of products with its business activities spread widely over the country and even abroad. Most large-scale Japanese firms set up a "division" (or "general division") for each major product group and grant it a certain degree of autonomy. Such firms can survive beyond the rise and fall of particular products by diversifying into new areas and new markets.

As against this, there are no entities in the Chinese economy corresponding to firms in Japan (see Fig. 1, boxes containing question marks). As a result, there is no economic entity dealing with functions (a) to (f) listed in Section II as the functions of the head office of a Japanese firm or with functions regarding (a) to (i) in this section, which were found to be lacking in Chinese firms. It would be inappropriate to assert that the Chinese economy lacks these functions entirely. At present, however, the general tendency in various industries reveals that these functions or items have been attended to and implemented only to a very limited extent, both at the level of administrative organization and at the "gongchang" level.

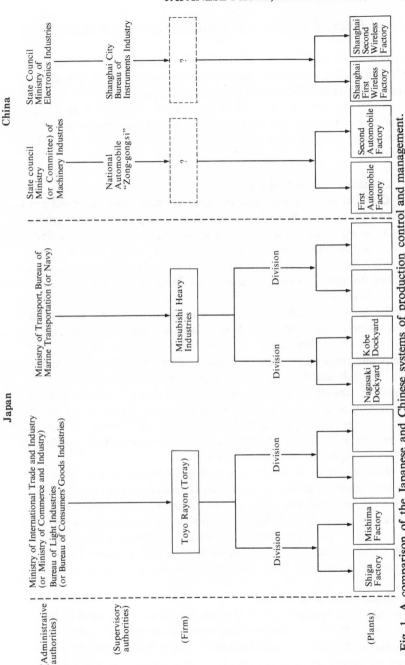

Fig. 1. A comparison of the Japanese and Chinese systems of production control and management.

The Chinese Firm (II): Essential Problems for Reform

Private firms participating actively and vigorously in a highly competitive market mechanism were the major driving force behind the rapid economic development of postwar Japan. Whether the Chinese economy can develop smoothly or not depends, in my view, to a large extent on whether or not a competitive market mechanism and vigorous firms can be developed within the framework of a socialist economy.

1. Creation of full-fledged firms

In China today, creative and imaginative individuals (farmers) and small but vigorous firms ("cunban" firms, cooperatives, and private firms) in agriculture and rural industry are already actively participating in a competitive market mechanism. The central problem to be resolved for the success of structural reforms of the Chinese economy is how to create vigorous, full-fledged firms in the state-owned industrial sector.

The Japanese—and Chinese, as well—word for "firm" consists of two Chinese characters roughly translated as "plan" or "undertake" and "work" or "business." In other words, a firm is an entity that plans and implements some new ideas related to productive activity. The English word "enterprise" also encompasses connotations of planning, ambitious venture, and progressiveness.[28] Thus a firm is thought of as an entity undertaking new activity. Hence, it is difficult to characterize the present Chinese "gongchang," which is engaged in repeating routinized productive activities, endeavoring merely to expand the quantity of outputs, as a firm.

What should be done to create such a full-fledged firm in the state-owned industrial sector (or the urban economy) that is endowed with essential functions for carrying out technological progress and innovations? It is difficult for me to provide a satisfactory answer to this question given my limited knowledge of prevailing conditions in the Chinese economy, especially in the area of administration and management of firms. I can only offer a few thoughts on the problem.

2. Organization of new firms

An individual "gongchang" in present-day China is too small to function as a firm. It is necessary to combine a number of "gongchang" producing the same or related products, or the "gongchang" in a common or similar technology area, to form a single firm, and establish a nuclear management body which performs the functions of a head office. Such a firm, controlling several "gongchang," should be granted a sufficient degree of autonomy.

It is difficult to say how many "gongchang" in which areas should be combined, to form a single firm. Formation of excessively large firms, without regard for the actual state of managerial and organizational capabilities and the feelings of solidarity among the employees concerned, can result in emergence of "diseconomies of scale" in management. It may also give rise to monopolistic abuses. It would be necessary to ensure conditions of effective interfirm competition in each product area and in each region. In view of these considerations, it will be practical to keep the size of the firms relatively small initially and, as businesses become well established and markets expand, to consider further reorganization depending upon conditions prevailing then.[29]

The establishment of the competitive price mechanism that we have in mind should be restricted to ordinary manufacturing, retail and wholesale trade and several other industries, however. Areas of social overhead capital (or infrastructure), like trunk line transportation, communications, electricity, gas, and water supply, are not expected to be run on the basis of competitive principles. Furthermore, even in Japan, large-scale regional development programs, industries with substantial economies of scale, and high-technology industries have been conducted as a public or semi-public sector under government control, in many ways quite differently from ordinary manufacturing industries which are conducted in the private sector. In Chinese economic development, too, the role of the competitive market mechanism in these areas is expected to be quite different from that in other areas.[30]

A high degree of autonomy, appropriate for conducting functions of a head office in a proper firm, viz., autonomy with respect to choice of products to be produced, introduction of new products, production planning, product pricing, research and development, investment, sales activities, collaboration with foreign firms, export and import, etc., must be granted to the firm thus established. This would, however, have to be implemented in step with the development of a price mechanism (market conditions). Establishment of firms with extensive rights to self-determination may be initiated in areas where such firms can stand on their own relatively easily, and for firms for which a responsible managerial group can be formed. Hence, the formation of full-fledged firms can only proceed in phases.

3. Equity capital and its ownership

For the establishment of a full-fledged firm, it is necessary to determine the assets owned by it, as well as their value (though a valuation of assets always involves a number of difficult problems); prepare its balance sheet; record the proportion of equity capital in the total assets; and determine the owners of the firm's equity capital, who would correspond to the shareholders of a joint-stock company.

In line with the socialist principle of "ownership by the whole people," the owners or the "shareholders" of the newly created firm must be organizations of "public" character. Initially, the "shareholders" could be the industrial ministries of the State Council that supervise industries; provincial, municipal, prefectural, "zhen," and "xiang" governments; various banks; or other state firms. These "shareholders'" as in the case of the Japanese joint-stock firms, should be given power to decide whether to continue or close the firm and to rule upon important organizational changes, appointment and dismissal of principal executives, and disposal of profits. They should also participate positively in decisions at times of major business difficulties and in formulation of reorganization plans in such circumstances. In normal circumstances, however, the executives, appointed (or approved) by the owners, should have the power to deal with all matters of the firm's activity.

In their capacity as owners, the state authorities (or industrial bureaus of provincial governments, banks, etc.) can, if they are not satisfied with the firm's management, ask for an explanation from the managers and hold consultations with them. They can also demand changes in managerial policies or request deployment into new fields of business. Moreover, they can replace the management with a new set of executives and set the basic directions for future business activities. The owners of the firm, however, cannot intervene in details or provisions of contracts (including labor contracts) that the firm enters into nor nullify existing contracts. Interference by the owners in everyday business activity is not conducive to smooth functioning of the firm. Furthermore, they cannot ask for information about those parts of contracts relating to technologies or contracts which are commercial secrets. Also, retiring executives should be sworn to secrecy about the firms' commercial secrets. It is the management as a group, not the owners, that runs the business or enters into contracts on behalf of the firm. Since the shareholders of the joint-stock company, or the government authorities in the case of China and public enterprises in the case of Japan, cannot be the central figure responsible for management of the firms, they should refrain from playing an active part in the formulation of contracts entered into by the firm; in my view, this is essential for the managerial autonomy of a firm.

4. Distributive structure of the firm

The firm must pay dividends to the owners, in proportion to their share in the owned capital, out of profits exceeding a certain minimum rate which would depend upon the level of profits. This, then, accrues to the state, local governments, or other state-owned firms as their incomes. This gives support to the principle that these firms are owned "by the whole people." Therefore, to ensure proper distribution of profits, it is essential that a proper evaluation of the assets of the firm be made at the time it is established.

The remainder of the profits, as retained earnings, may be used for investment in the firm or appropriated, in part, to employee welfare funds or bonuses.[31] It would be appropriate to require the owners' approval regarding the disposal of profits. The wage and salary scheme of the employees of each firms should be liberalized gradually, and should gradually be left to the autonomous decisions of each firms' management. Highly profitable, fast-growing firms should be allowed to pay higher wages (including bonuses) than low-efficiency, stagnant firms. Though such measures are already under way, further liberalization should be carefully phased in, depending upon the performance of individual firms. If it is not, the result could easily be excessive wage rises. As a new group of specialized executives with managerial talent and a longer time horizon emerges and leads management toward stable development of the firm, excessive increases in wages would be restrained.[32]

5. Principles of firm behavior

What sort of behavior will be expected of Chinese firms established in the manner described above? It is believed that, under certain conditions, the behavior of these new firms would differ little from that of typical Japanese firms as discussed in Sections II and III (Part I). That is, the management and the employees of the new firms, given a high degree of autonomy, would pursue profits and endeavor to increase productivity and technological progress by engaging vigorously in research and development, investment, marketing, and financial activities. The growth and development of the firm would depend a great deal on the accumulation (retention) of a fairly high proportion of its profits.

A large number of cooperative firms ("cunban" firms and others) in Chinese villages have already embarked on such a path of development.[33] It should, therefore, be possible to expect similar progress in state-owned industries in the urban sector.

One of the necessary conditions for such progress is that a firm's employees develop a sense of participation in its management and have an incentive for active participation in raising productivity and in pursuing profits. A sort of egalitarianism generally practiced in Japanese firms and the seniority promotion system involving periodic salary raises and transfer of posts[34] may prove to be a useful management model for China.

6. Government control of firms' activities

As a large number of firms, with substantial managerial autonomy as described above, are established and as they behave as independent economic agents within the emerging competitive market mechanism, measures to control and coordinate activities of these firms from the viewpoint of the national economy, different from those which have been followed up to now, would be required.

Namely, from the viewpoint of national economic planning or from the viewpoint of developing a particular region or industry it would be necessary for economic policy (planning) authorities to encourage or discourage activities in a particular field. Furthermore, depending upon prevailing macroeconomic conditions, it may become necessary to cool down overheating of investment activity and inflationary price increases, or to adopt measures to bring the economy out of stagnation and counter unemployment (including what is called "job waiting"). For such purposes, recourse should be had to all the options available in an economy like that of Japan, such as tax measures, fiscal investment and loans policy, monetary policy, and the like (recently referred to as "economic levers" in China). The Chinese planning authorities, moreover, are in a far stronger position to affect allocation of investment funds than the Japanese government. Finally, the government authorities, as owners of the state-owned firms, are in a position to advise, guide, and direct them.

One of the important problems to be resolved as the competitive market mechanism becomes established in China is related to the control of monopolies, cartels, and other restrictive business practices. At present, China does not need such controls since the government interferes pervasively in all aspects of firms' activities. However, as firms are given extensive functional autonomy and, making use of this autonomy, begin to pursue maximum profits, monopolistic behavior and abuses could become an important economic problem and a legal framework to counter them would be necessary.

Competitive Price Mechanisms in Japan and China

If reform of the economic system in China takes the course outlined above, and builds up a competitive market mechanism that leads to steady development in the Chinese economy, in what ways would such a "socialist" competitive market mechanism differ, in terms of its functional role in the national economy, from the competitive market mechanism based on private entrepreneurs as it developed in Japan?[35] We conclude our discussion in this paper by briefly answering this question.

(a) *Large firms*. If the Chinese economy develops along the lines stated above, the large-firm sectors in the Japanese and Chinese economies would differ very little. In both economies, specialized professional managers would hold decisive powers in important business matters. They would receive high incomes (and other rewards in kind) and maintain a social status befitting their role. A major proportion of the gross profits of the firm would be paid to the government in taxes or other payments (similar to the corporate income tax, the local government's enterprise tax, the property (real estate) tax, and social welfare contributions, etc., in Japan), while in both economies a large part of the remainder would be retained within the firm for investment and research and development expenditures. Another part would be used for additional payments of wages, salaries, bonuses, and other benefits to the managers and employees.

The major points of difference would be: (1) In China the government, in its capacity as the owner of the firm, could intervene directly in management when firms are experiencing serious financial difficulties, when new firms are established, or when necessary for implementing a national economic plan. (2) In Japan, on the other hand, there are some owner-managers, though they are now very few in number; dividends are paid to individual shareholders, some of whom may be very wealthy; and shareholders can obtain large capital gains on their shares when the firm is exceptionally successful.

Still another point of difference may be that the proportion of the non-competitive "public sector," within the large-firm sector, is expected to be much higher in China than in Japan for a long time. But if we look at the much larger proportion accounted for by the Japanese public sector than by its counterparts in other "capitalist" countries from the early Meiji to the late 1920s (in Japan it included even a major part of the steel industry), we may consider it a difference in degree, not a difference arising out of the institutional setup of the economic system.

(b) *Medium- and small-scale firms.* In the sector of medium- and small-scale firms, the share of cooperatively owned firms, such as cooperative associations, is small in Japan. A large number of small "capitalists" flourish there. In contrast, a large proportion of the Chinese medium- and small-scale firms are either state owned (controlled) or cooperatively owned (particularly "cunban," "xiangban," and "zhenban" firms). However, a small number of privately owned firms (owned by individuals or by a small group of individuals) already exist in China as well, and in rural areas their number has rapidly increased recently. The owner-managers of the medium- and small-scale private firms can be described appropriately by the term "capitalists," but they are not necessarily rich people who exploit workers and live extravagantly. Though some of them have higher incomes than the managers of large firms, their living standards, in both Japan and China, are generally more frugal than those of the managers of large firms or high government officials, and their social status is much lower. This can be explained, at least in Japan, by the fact that a significant proportion of their incomes (including dividend income) must be reinvested for the expansion of their firms. The privately owned medium- and small-scale firms have been an important element in the sustained development of the Japanese economy. The "cunban" and other cooperative firms in China are expected to play a similar, increasingly important role.

(c) *Financing of firms.* With regard to financing of the firm sector, differences between Japan and China, for the large-scale as well as the medium- and small-scale firms, will be diminishing gradually. For financing investment they will depend on retention of profits, depreciation allowances, borrowing from financial institutions, and issuance of corporate bonds and new stocks. In the case of externally raised equity capital, that is, the issuance of new stocks, however, subscription by individuals would not be allowed in China. The proportion under the direct control of government authorities in the investment financing of the firm sector or the degree of such control will be greater for China than for Japan.

(d) *Savings.* Savings of an economy are composed of (1) household savings; (2) retentions by firms; and (3) public sector savings, including that of the central government. This is true for China as well as Japan. Of these, (1) is mobilized for investment purposes in China mainly in the form of deposits with the People's Bank of China (recently Chinese Industrial and Commercial Bank), or purchases of government bonds by households.

(e) *Land ownership.* In China agricultural land is under cooperative ownership while a large proportion of urban land is owned by the state. This situation differs markedly from that in Japan, where land is generally privately owned. However, large landlords are nonexistent in Japan, in urban land holdings[36] as well as in agriculture, and the farmers own the land they till. In China, on the other hand, agricultural land is collectively owned either by the villages (production brigades earlier) or by production teams (small communities within the village) and farmers are given exclusive rights to use the land under their cultivation for a period extending over 15 years. Land is salable property in Japan and a number of landowners have accumulated huge wealth through a rise in land prices; many farmers have also shared in this bounty.[37]

In an economy like that of Japan, capital gains in land and shares are incomes resulting from transfer of assets. There are no real goods and services corresponding to such capital gains, which are the result of productive activities and constitute GNP. Hence, these capital gains are not important to the functioning of the national economy, as they are only marginally related to annual economic activity (investment in plant and equipment, for example).

(f) *Dissemination of information.* Freedom of speech and freedom of the press are guaranteed by the Constitution in Japan and a large number of private firms including newspapers and publishing houses are engaged in collection, analysis, arrangement, and dissemination of information and opinions. As against this, no such private firms exist in China and dissemination of information is rigidly controlled. It appears that the executives and the employees of firms do not receive necessary information on even the most mundane matters. This is an important difference between the Japanese and the Chinese economic systems at present, and it constitutes a serious handicap for the Chinese economy in promoting competition, encouraging technological change, and raising productivity. When the advanced industrialized countries are now advancing toward the so-called "age of information" society, continued strict control of information dissemination by the state or party organs would be quite disadvantageous at least in economic terms.

This problem, however, is more political than economic in nature, and it would be inappropriate to discuss it here.

These are some of the major differences between the "socialist" type of competitive price mechanism of China as it is expected to develop in the future and the price mechanism based on private enterprise as it has developed in Japan.

This chapter is an abridged version of a two-part article, "Japanese Firms, Chinese Firms: Problems for Economic Reform in China," published in *Journal of the Japanese and International Economies*, Vol. 1 (1987), pp. 31–61 and 229–47. An earlier Japanese version was published in *Gendai Chugoku no Keizai Shisutemu* (China's Economic System Today), edited by Sogo Kaihatsu Kiko (NIRA) (Tokyo: Chikuma Shobo, 1986).

Notes

1. It is true that the government played an important role in the postwar industrial development of Japan, but this role was primarily in the form of facilitating the development of a competitive market mechanism where the private firms could flourish. Japanese industrial policy, except for the immediate postwar period, played a very limited role in the so-called "high growth" period, and the development of industry was primarily led by the private sector. This has long been subject to lively controversy. For the reasons for my position see Chapter 6, below, and Komiya *et al.*, 1984, esp. the Introduction and Chaps. 1–4.

2. A comparative study of Japan and China regarding the role of the medium- and small-scale firms in the process of economic development could provide fruitful insights into the Chinese economy and suggestions for its future development strategy.

3. My view of the modern firm, in this respect, is greatly influenced by Joseph A. Schumpeter.

4. To give a more or less accurate account of this point, it is necessary to examine and survey the organizational charts of some typical large firms, but as it is not possible to go into such detail here, I must limit myself to presenting summary statements.

5. For such an interpretation of the modern firm (and the functions of the head office), see Penrose, 1959; Komiya, 1975, Chap. 10.

6. See Aoki, 1984a, b, to which this section of the present paper owes much.

7. A similar trend is, however, observable in a few American firms as well.

8. See Nishiyama, 1983.

9. The case of companies in a parent–subsidiary relationship is, however, another story. For 100% subsidiaries or more than 50% subsidiaries it is normal to follow the overall directions set by the parent company.

10. According to a recent questionnaire survey, a large proportion of company presidents responding to it believe that prices of the stocks of their companies should be far above the currently quoted prices. (See *Nikkei Kaisha Joho* [Nikkei Directory of Corporations], 1985, No. 1.) This is because company presidents do not feel endangered by potential takeover raids. Such a response is out of question in the United States, where takeover bids abound.

11. This is an attribute of large firms in postwar Japan, which was not observed in the prewar period.

12. Needless to say, newly raised funds, in addition to retained earnings, are utilized for these purposes.

13. In a simplified model where the number of employees is assumed to be increasing at the same rate as the growth in profits, as an extreme case, the employees do not gain anything from the growth of the firm and thus become indifferent to growth (since growth requires expenditures out of profits). However, this result, and the model behind it, is unrealistic. In general, the management, representing the employee group, is expected to be more growth-oriented than large stockholders like financial institutions.

14. It is a difficult question to consider what discount rates (time preference) the stockholders, employees, and managers, respectively, apply to future incomes and what risk preferences they have. But there is no doubt that the management has a much longer time horizon than the stockholders in Japan The time horizon of institutional investors is considered to be much longer (perhaps varying between 2–3 years and 5–10 years) than that of individual stockholders (sometimes only a few weeks, and perhaps usually 1–2 years), but for the management it may be as long as 20, 30, or even 50 years. The reason why many managers often hesitate to invest in direct investment ventures (joint ventures, etc.) abroad restricted to a period of 10–15 years by the government of the host country, even though there may be a possibility of renewing the contract, is that their time horizon is normally far longer than 10–15 years.

15. It is assumed that the negative effect of a rise in the number of employees is exactly balanced by benefits like faster promotions.

16. This also applies to what is called "intermediate recruitment," that is, recruitment of employees who are not newly graduating from school but are in their late twenties, thirties, or forties, in the rapidly expanding firms, and to withdrawal (exit to other firms) from stagnant firms.

17. Some institutional investors like life insurance companies, however, sometimes find it necessary or preferable, for institutional reasons, to receive a certain proportion of the returns on investment in the form of dividends rather than capital gains. In their capacity as large stockholders, these institutions tend to request payment of dividends amounting to a certain proportion of the total profits.

18. The mechanism by which the benefits from the rapid growth of a firm are partly reaped by its employees (or their families) has also been evident in China recently, with regard to employment opportunities. A number of relatively large firms are now establishing the so-called "fuwu gongsi" (service companies), which are somewhat similar to related subsidiaries in Japan, and provide employment to the family members (especially the so-called "job-waiting youth") of their employees. Legally, these "fuwu gongsi" are cooperatively owned, not state-owned, firms. Some employees of these "fuwu gongsi" have been transferred from the parent companies, and some seem to maintain their status as employees of the parent, state-owned firms.

19. Keeping the above points regarding the pattern of income distribution within a firm in mind, there would be little conflict of interest between the stockholders, the management, and the employees when the firm is growing steadily, as is clear from the abstract discussion in the text. A conflict of interest arises, however, with respect to time preference for present and future

incomes (and also with respect to stability of future employment and job opportunities after retirement) and the degree of steepness of the hierarchical structure of the management and the employees. A conflict of interest also exists in relation to dismissals when the firm encounters financial difficulties, to a merger with or absorption by another firm (which could lead to a reduction in management and executive posts and, in the case of the absorbed firm, unsympathetic treatment within the new firm), or to regional reshuffling of employees resulting from construction of a new factory. Even though beneficial to the stockholders, these may represent a disadvantageous and difficult proposition for the adversely affected employees.

20. Organizational patterns of the Japanese public enterprises, their present conditions, and their problems may give important insights into and suggestions for the economic restructuring now proceeding in China. (See Okano and Uekusa, 1983).

21. In Japan, there are a relatively small number of well-known unlisted large firms (joint-stock companies), e.g., Idemitsu Kosan, Yoshida Kogyo, Suntory, and Takenaka Komuten.

22. The reasons for this lie in the postwar reforms to democratize the Japanese economy (breaking up of the "zaibatsu"), heavy inheritance and income taxation, inability of owners to supply enough capital to maintain their share of ownership given the high rate of growth of the firm, and the fact that firms with strong family ties are at a managerial disadvantage within the Japanese business environment.

23. *Gendai Chugoku Keizai Jiten*, 1982, pp. 433–436. There are also non-state-owned firms which are engaged in industrial activities. That is, (i) the former "sheban" firms run by people's communes which were transformed into either what is called "xiangzhen" firms run by "xiang" (village) or "zhen" (town) governments or cooperative firms; (ii) the former "duiban" firms run by production brigades which were transformed into "cunban" firms run by "cun" (village or hamlet) committees; (iii) private or cooperative firms established and run by farmers individually or in a group; and (iv) foreign-owned firms (joint-venture or 100% owned).

24. Smaller state-owned "gongchang" are often controlled by the city, prefecture, "zhen," or "xiang" governments. Firms under the supervision of "zhen" and "xiang" governments include some of the former "sheban" and "duiban" firms.

25. Though the "gongchang," or the "lianhe gongsi," are the "economic accounting units" where cost accounting is done for each product, the managers of the Chinese "gongchang" seem on the whole to have little interest in the profit situation of their "gongchang" or in the profitability of each product. The firm in Japan prepares and publishes its financial statement annually, and even the lowest-rank employees of a factory know about its profit situation or the profitability of each product (costs and selling price) of their firm and factory. This increases the sense of participation among the employees. In China, often the managers of a "gongchang" know the annual amount of output quite well but when asked about profits or the amount of investment, not infrequently they say either that they do not know or that it is a secret. It is obvious that there is a problem regarding the dissemination of information. [This situation has changed rapidly under the economic reform

in the latter half of the 1980s, as the managers and employees become more concerned with the profits of "gongchang."]

26. If production targets in a field under the control of a particular administrative organization are not fulfilled or if stocks accumulate because of poor sales, naturally the responsibility of the authorities in charge will be questioned. But for the administrative organizations there is wide latitude for excuse and there are ways to evade accusation. In any country, administrative responsibility is rarely made unambiguous.

27. According to the Resolution of the Central Committee mentioned earlier, the defect of the present Chinese economic system can be found in the lack of vitality of firms and, hence, "reinforcement of vitality of firms, especially the state-owned large- and medium-scale firms, is one of the most important problems to be resolved through the reform of the economic system."

28. "Entrepreneur" in French or "Unternehmung" in German has a similar meaning. The origin of the English word "firm," on the other hand, is quite different.

29. Whether to restrict the location of the factories of a firm within a single province (or special city) or to allow it to establish factories in provinces other than the one in which its head office is located would have to be carefully considered from the viewpoint of the national policy of regional development for China.

30. The capacities of railway transportation and energy supply are perhaps the two most important bottlenecks now constraining the development of the Chinese economy. The essential part of transportation facilities (electricity and gas supply facilities, pipelines, a part of coal transportation facilities) and a part of energy supply facilities belong to social overhead capital, and one cannot rely upon the market mechanism, based on competition among firms, for adequate capacity of such facilities. But in shortage-prone areas, the price mechanism can be used to restrain demand by raising the prices of outputs (coal prices, electricity tariffs, transportation fares) substantially, although not to a level which would equate demand and supply. Also, a part of the earnings from higher prices can be used as investment funds for resource development, expansion of facilities, and research on energy conservation.

31. This is already being implemented at "gongchang" in China.

32. In Japan, too, a tendency to pay unwarrantedly high salaries and other remunerations to employees is observed among some local governments. In view of this possibility, the government is rather tightly controlling salary levels in public corporations and other government enterprises.

33. The success of some of the "private firms," started and run by individual farmers or by groups of farmers in recent years, is remarkable. Some of them employ a large number of workers, as mentioned later. This phenomenon is a sort of "revival of capitalism," and would have to be controlled within a certain limit if the "socialist" principles are to be upheld. For example, it would be necessary to transform private firms above a certain size into some form of cooperative firms.

34. By going through this system of regular promotions in salaries and upward shifts in posts, the employees of a Japanese firm are trained and

accumulate experience, knowledge, and skills needed for higher posts and develop a wide perspective regarding the overall activity of the firm as well as its environment.

35. Many people call the Japanese economy a "capitalist" economy but I do not consider this characterization to be appropriate. This is because it is not necessarily an economy organized by capital (to begin with, it is not easy to pinpoint what people mean by "capital") or capitalists, or centered on capital, nor is it an economy of which private ownership of "capital" is the decisive characteristic.

36. In the case of forests, however, large landholdings still exist.

37. In China, too, when the farmers' landholdings were requisitioned for public works or industrial use in recent years, it appears that the "production teams" or the "villages" (or, formerly, "production brigades") were compensated by cash payments and that, moreover, the farmers who lost their landholdings totally or partially were offered employment opportunities. Farmers in the vicinity of big cities have become richer than urban employees since their incomes reflect, in part, the imputed rents on their landholdings, the prices of which are rising rapidly. This phenomenon corresponds to large capital gains resulting from a steep rise in land prices, enjoyed in recent years by Japanese farmers in the vicinity of big cities.

References

Abstract of Chinese Statistics (1984). Beijing (in Chinese).

Aoki, M. (1984a). *Gendai no Kigyo* (Modern Firms). Tokyo: Iwanami Shoten.

Aoki, M. (1984b). *The Co-operative Theory of the Firm.* New York/London: Oxford University Press.

Chinese Academy of Social Sciences (1982). *Gendai Chugoku Keizai Jiten* (Handbook of the Contemporary Chinese Economy). Tokyo/Beijing: Nihon Soken Shuppan and Chinese Academy of Social Sciences Press.

Ishikawa, S., ed. (1984). *Medium- to Long-term Prospects of the Chinese Economy.* Tokyo: Nitchu Keizai Kyokai.

Komiya, R. (1975). *Gendai Nihon Keizai Kenkyu* (Studies on the Contemporary Japanese Economy). Tokyo: University of Tokyo Press.

Komiya, R. (1984). "Keizai Hatten no Senryaku: Sengo Nihon to Chugoku ni tsuite no Hikaku Kosatsu" (Strategy for Economic Development: A Comparative Study of Postwar Japan and China), in *Proceedings, Japan-China Academic Exchange Symposium on Economics*, May.

Komiya, R., M. Okuno, and K. Suzumura, eds. (1984). *Nihon no Sangyo Seisaku* (Japan's Industrial Policy). Tokyo: University of Tokyo Press. English version published as *Industrial Policy of Japan* Orlando: Academic Press, 1988.

Mori, K. (1984). "Conditions of the Urban Labor Force." Chapter 4 in Ishikawa (1984).

Nishiyama, T. (1983) *Datsu Shihonshugi Bunseki* (Away from Capitalism: An Argument). Tokyo: Bunshindo.

Okano, Y., and M. Uekusa, eds. (1983). *Nihon no Ko-kigyo* (Public Enterprises in Japan). Tokyo: University of Tokyo Press.

Penrose, E.F. (1959). *The Theory of the Growth of the Firm.* Oxford: Black-well.

Tachi, R., R. Komiya, and H. Uzawa, eds. (1984). *Chugoku Keizai: Asu e no Kadai* (The Chinese Economy: Its Problems for the Future). Tokyo: Toyo Keizai Shimposha.

CHAPTER 6

THE LIFE INSURANCE COMPANY AS A BUSINESS ENTERPRISE

I. Introduction

As a "Japanese enterprise," the life insurance company has a number of features that arouse one's curiosity. Moreover, it occupies a distinctive position in the Japanese economy. First, life insurance companies possess great importance from the point of view of the "ownership structure" of Japan's enterprise sector. Life insurance companies' share in the ownership of the current aggregate value of the stock of all listed companies is 12.8%. This is smaller than the share of banks (22.8%), but the number of life insurance companies is also smaller: even prior to 1988, when the "*sogo* banks" (mutual savings and loan banks) were converted to ordinary commercial banks, there were more than 80 financial institutions formally called a "bank," and only 25 life insurance companies incorporated under the Japanese law.[1] The stockholdings of the higher-ranking life insurance companies, per company, are in relative terms extremely large.

Among the stockholders, all the aforementioned banks and non-financial corporations (with a share of 30.1%), are almost all joint-stock companies themselves,[2] issuing their own stock, the great majority of which is owned by other joint-stock companies. In contrast to this, the 16 companies that constitute the bulk of the life insurance business are not joint-stock companies but mutual companies. If we look at the "ultimate" owners of Japan's corporations by netting out the interlocking stock ownership among the joint-stock companies, considering the portion of each joint-stock company owned by another stock company as belonging to the latter's stockholders, then mutual life insurance companies as a class, alongside individuals, would have the largest component in the ownership of the joint-stock companies.

I believe that it is a two-fold mistake to call an economic society

233

like contemporary Japan. a "shihonshugi shakai" (capitalist society). First, since "capitalism" is not a principle or a doctrine, but instead refers to a system or process having a certain function, and in this resembles a mechanism, metabolism, or organism, the Japanese word *shihonshugi* (capital-ism; the doctrine of capital) is a mistranslation. It should be translated *shihonsei* (capital system). Second, in the modern Japanese economy both "capital," in the sense of control over general purchasing power over a certain period of time, and the "capitalists," in the sense of those who possess capital have played only a limited role.[3] In present-day Japan it is only in the medium- and small-enterprise sector that "capitalists" in the original sense of the word—that is, those who provide "capital" and bear the full risk of business under their own management—are really active. During the 40-odd years since World War II, "capitalists" have virtually vanished from Japan's big-business sector; in place of the former big capitalists, life insurance companies have enhanced their positions as enterprise owners. If one takes the view that the ownership of capital is accompanied by control over it, then 16 mutual life insurance companies are the most powerful "controllers" of Japan's big business sector.

Second, should not the fact that many of Japan's life insurance companies are organized not as joint-stock companies, but as mutual companies, arouse the interest of researchers concerned with the theory of the firm? Excluding the foreign-owned life insurance companies established since 1975, sixteen of Japan's twenty long-established life insurance companies are mutual companies, and four are joint-stock companies. Legally, the two organizational forms of enterprise co-exist. As enterprises, how do they differ in structure and in behavior?

Economists who specialize in the theory of the firm or, more broadly, in economic theory may say that a special enterprise such as the mutual life insurance company is not a matter of concern for them. However, in economics (in which, unlike many fields of the natural sciences, experimentation is extremely difficult) observation and theoretical analysis of phenomena, especially those phenomena which look exceptional and special, have great significance in testing and verifying the theory, just as in astronomy, geophysics, or meteorology. Without efforts to undertake these kinds of observation and analysis, economics cannot be a science.

The life insurance business is complex and has various peculiarities; it is not easy to achieve even a general understanding of it. It is not the purpose of this chapter to deal with the life insurance business in general. The goal of this chapter is to investigate the special structural features, management objectives, and behavior of the life insurance companies that stand at the apex of the ownership structure of Japan's big business sector in the sense described above. In particular we are interested in the mutual life insurance company as an enterprise or as "a Japanese enterprise."

The subsequent sections of this chapter will take up the following topics. In Section II the special structural features of the mutual life insurance company, which differs from the joint-stock company as an enterprise, are explained. Sections III and IV discuss how the surplus of the mutual life insurance company, which is the result of its business activity, is divided up among dividends to "members" (insurance policyholders), employee salaries and bonuses, internal reserves, and so on. A discussion of what the mutual life insurance company is thought to be trying to maximize is included as well.

Section V describes the life insurance enterprise organized as a joint-stock company. Section VI discusses the relationships between large Japanese coorporations, in which the life insurance company is a major stockholder, both with regard to the former as a stockholder and in other respects. The seventh and final section includes the principal conclusions summarized and suggestions, drawn from the facts and analysis presented here, which I believe to be important in further studying the theory of the firm and the Japanese enterprise in general.

II. Structural Characteristics of the Mutual Company

What are the special structural characteristics of the life insurance firm which is organized as a mutual company? Employees and executives of Japanese life insurance mutual companies have characteristics more or less similar to those of other large Japanese corporations.[4]

The role of top management and boards of directors in mutual life insurance companies differs little from that in other large Japanese corporations which are organized as joint-stock companies. Of the members of top management, the president and chairman, and a very few senior directors around them play a major role in decision-making in important matters relating to the management of the enterprise. The board of directors is normally no more than a formality, and rarely is a vote taken or a real discussion held.

Directors are selected and appointed by a process in which the board of directors draws up a draft, which is then confirmed by the approval of a "members' delegates' meeting." Practically all the directors of every life insurance company have worked as employees of that company for many years; there are only few "outside directors" on the board. Formally, selections and appointments to such posts as president, chairman, vice-president, managing director, and executive director are carried out by election from among the members of the board of directors. In reality, nominations to these posts are decided by a very small number of senior directors, the principal of whom is the president. All these arrangements are virtually the same as in the average large Japanese corporation.

The meeting of members' delegates
Legally, the mutual company's highest decision-making body is the "meeting of members' delegates," and in this it differs widely from the joint-stock company. The "members" of the mutual life insurance company are those who hold life insurance contracts with that company: the company's insurance policyholders. Formally, the mutual life insurance company is a corporation established by a group of 100 or more people gathered together who need life insurance and collect an "originating fund" for the purpose of cooperative, mutual assistance with regard to insurance. Legally, the "general meeting of all the members" is the highest decision-making body, but the meeting of members' delegates can substitute for the general meeting. All of Japan's mutual life insurance companies have delegates' meetings rather than members' general meetings. Out of an enormous number of members, 50 to 150 are selected as "members' delegates." A nominating committee for members' delegates selects the candidates and places notices in the newspapers. If no more than a certain number of members raises objections to the selection, the slate is appointed. Members of the "nominating committee" are selected when the board of directors recommends candidates to the members' delegates' meeting, and the latter approves these recommendations.

Thus, at some sacrifice of detail and precision, one may put the matter very simply as follows: the members' delegates' meeting selects the directors, the board of directors selects the nominating committee for candidates for the members' delegates' meeting, and this committee selects candidates for members' delegates, forming a triangular circle. Of the three, the one that actually plays a decisive role is the board of directors (or the leading members among them such as the company president).[5] The members' delegates or the members of the delegates' candidate nominating committee participate in the company affairs only marginally. This is true from both the point of view of delegates and members and that of the company. The extent to which they entrust their own fate to the vicissitudes of the company, or the degree to which they feel concerned with it, is extremely slight in comparison with, first of all, the full-time directors and the company's employees, who are as a matter of fact represented by the directors. Moreover, with the exception of accountants, lawyers, and other specialized professionals, for the great majority of the members' delegates it is difficult to understand the management of a life insurance company, which differs considerably from other non-financial corporations. In particular, the mutual company's financial affairs, its extremely complex financial statements, and its methods of distributing dividends to members are matters handled by means of broad resolutions of the members' delegates' meetings.

The members' delegates' meeting deliberates on (i) the appointment of directors, (ii) the appointment of the members of the nominating committee for members' delegates, (iii) the disposition of surplus funds, (iv) the allocation of dividends to members, and several other matters. Customarily, however, while very few delegates fail to attend the meeting, the meeting is concluded within an hour or so, with no objections. This is a striking contrast to the general meetings of stockholders of prominent joint-stock companies. Some sessions of these meetings have lasted quite a long time—sometimes longer than ten hours—since the revision of the Commercial Code a few years ago.

Labor unions

The labor unions of life insurance companies employees are no different from those of Japan's other major enterprises in that they are organized on a company-by-company basis, whether they are mutual companies or joint-stock companies. However, the fact that there are companies with two or three unions rather than just one as in most other companies is a special feature of labor unions in life insurance companies. When there are two unions in one company, they are organized separately as a union for "internal personnel" (office workers) and a union for "external personnel" (sales representatives); when there are three, the external personnel of a company are divided up into two categories and a union is organized for each. Most recently the trend has been toward a decrease in the number of unions as internal and external unions have merged. Moreover, the federation of internal employees unions (formed in 1946) and the federation of external employees unions (formed in 1949) united in 1969 to form the only industrial union in the life insurance field, Seiho Roren (National Federation of Life Insurance Workers' Unions).

III. Distribution of Dividends to Members and the "Convoy Approach"

What kinds of economic goals is the mutual type of life insurance company pursuing? What is it acting to maximize? There is no mistaking the fact that mutual life insurance companies are "firms," so one may ask how microeconomic theory—and in particular "the theory of the firm"—answer these two questions?

From the legal standpoint, and also from the standpoint of simplified abstract economic theory, one might say that the goal of the mutual life insurance company is to minimize the cost to the insurance policyholders, who are the "members" of the company and are provided with insurance services; however, when one looks at the "basic management goals" of mutual life insurance companies, while they of course declare they are acting "on behalf of the policyholders/contractors," at the same time such goals as "broadly promote the public welfare," "improve the lives of employees," and "progress and development of the trade" are enumerated. The "management goals" of joint-stock life insurance companies include such phrases as "the policyholder first" (does this imply "stockholders second"?) and "'trinity' management of the policyholders, stockholders, and employees, as a single entity." When one judges by the yardstick of economic theory, one gets an impression of a kind of obscurantism in this sort of declaration by the insurance companies.

Distribution of surplus: dividends to members

To an economist, the "surplus" in the broad sense—that is, the results a mutual life insurance company obtains from its business activities— is distributed in the following four forms:

(1) Dividends to the insurance policyholders who are "members" of the company.

(2) A portion of the salaries and bonuses of employees and executives, that portion which exceeds the standard compensation for those engaged in the same kind of work.

(3) Contributions to social welfare undertakings and certain kinds of excessive internal expenditures.

(4) Retained profits.

Let us first consider "dividends to members." The mutual company's "funds" were redeemed long ago, and the return of profits to the policyholders, who are presently the "members," takes the form of payments of "dividends" to them. These dividends are determined in an extremely complex manner, based on the type of insurance, number of years elapsed since the beginning of the insurance contract, and many other factors. Due to the Ministry of Finance's so-called "convoy approach" policy and the cartel-minded proclivity of the insurance trade, insurance premiums to be paid by the policyholders at the time of the contract and other prescribed times are determined in such a way that there are few differences from company to company. However, the dividends to members (policyholders) is high in insurance companies that show good business performance and small in companies that perform poorly. This means that there are differences in the real cost of insurance for the policyholders, depending upon the performance of the companies with which they hold insurance policies.

Dividends are paid in various ways: some dividends are paid to certain policyholders every year; some are paid when the insurance is terminated (upon death or maturity). Dividend arrangements are extremely complex and difficult to understand for outsiders. As an example, however, when endowment (old age) insurance covering a period of 20 to 30 years comes to maturity, a company that has good business performance pays a special expiration dividend of 600,000 yen on an insurance policy of one million yen (hence the policyholder receives 1,600,000 yen), while at companies with poor performance only a small special dividend of this kind is paid. (These figures are fictitious since they vary widely depending on the time when payments into the insurance fund begin and on the number of years over which payment continues.) A difference of this kind does appear to exist.[6]

Each company offers a great many types of insurance, and the various arrangements of dividend payments to members are quite complicated. It is very difficult for an outsider to compare the dividend payments of the various companies. To my knowledge, there are no published materials that bring together and compare dividend rates. Thus, hardly any life insurance policyholders know whether the dividend rate on their own insurance policy compares favorably or poorly with the dividend rates on insurance of exactly the same type offered by other companies.

Moreover, not only is there a dearth of information on dividends; since life insurance companies are not listed on the securities exchange, they are not required to publish documents equivalent to the Financial Report on Securities of listed companies. In the case of listed (joint-stock) companies, various financial ratios representing the companies' performance in each financial period such as return on equity, ratio of operating expenses to sales, liquidity ratio, and so on, are computed and analyzed by securities analysts, but no such ratios representing business performance are computed, nor has any financial analysis ever been made for mutual life insurance companies.

Characteristics based on customers' simultaneous roles as owners

If there were no difference in the insurance premiums among all the life insurance companies but large differences in the dividend rates paid to members for the same kind of insurance, then customers would gradually move to the company(s) that paid the highest dividend rates.

Accordingly, if there were an adequate flow of information among customers (insurance policyholders) about the dividend rates paid to members by all the mutual life insurance companies, then differences in dividend rates among the various companies would not, in the nature of things, long continue.

There is a peculiarity here which arises from the structural characteristics whereby the "member," who is an "owner" of the mutual life insurance company, is at the same time a very "footloose" customer. Considering the matter theoretically, since in a competitive market a situation in which there are large differences in the "real" prices of the goods and services sold cannot long continue, in the case of business insurance, large differences in the "real" cost to the policyholder—that is, differences in the insurance premium minus the dividends—among mutual-type companies operating in a competitive market cannot long continue either. That is, if there are differences in the "real" cost of insurance, the member/customer sooner or later will move to a company with better performance offering the same insurance service at a lower price. The company that performs poorly will lose its members (customers), it will run into business difficulties, and the company's very existence will be threatened. This is how the selection process for the survival of the fittest is supposed to work in a competitive market.

In the case of joint-stock companies, differences in the business performances of enterprises appear as differences in earnings on equity capital, and this is reflected in such things as the dividend rate of stock and share prices. This produces differences in the cost of raising capital and exerts a certain amount of influence over the company's rate of growth, but since the stockholders and the customers are separate entities, differences in rates of returns on equity capital do not immediately result in increases or decreases in the number of customers.

For example, even if the rate of return on equity capital for Toyotas were far higher than for Nissan automobiles, this would hardly be a matter of concern to a consumer considering buying a car. The consumer, who is primarily concerned with quality, design, after-purchase service, and price, decides to buy a car which fits with his own needs and tastes, and which he can afford. Where durable goods such as automobiles and electric home appliances are concerned, there may be consumers who shun the products of manufacturers whose business performance deteriorates badly and gives rise to uncertainty over its future ability to provide reliable after-purchase service, but to the purchaser of non-durable goods and services, such matters are totally beside the point. Even among buyers of durable consumer goods, it is a rare customer who examines manufacturers' financial statements before making purchases.

In contrast to this, since the average life insurance contract is of long duration, and, moreover, since in the case of mutual life insurance companies a customer holding an insurance policy is at the same time an "owner" of the company and receives part of the "surplus" as "dividends to members," it is to his or her advantage to have a life insurance contract with a mutual life company with outstanding financial performance and large internal reserves. It would be rational behavior for a customer (or an organization) to make a life insurance contract only after investigating the financial performance of life insurance companies, particularly the internal reserves of each of the mutual companies and, if possible, their "hidden reserves." In this regard, there is a sharp theoretical difference between mutual life insurance companies and the joint-stock companies in such industries as manufacturing and banking. A discussion of life insurance that fails to take this fact into account makes a fundamental error.

Agricultural and fisheries cooperatives are firms which take a form similar to mutual life insurance companies in that the "owner," a member, is at the same time a customer. However, the mobility of members of these cooperatives is comparatively limited for geographical reasons, and each cooperative is not competing keenly to win customers who are at the same time owners as in the case of life insurance. The consumers' cooperative society, particularly the so-called "regional consumer co-op," resembles the mutual life insurance company in the sense that the customer, who is at the same time an owner, is "footloose." In places where several regional consumer cooperatives are competing in the same area, like those in the vicinity of Tokyo and in the Osaka-Kobe area, or in areas where consumers can go to ordinary (non-cooperative) retail stores, I would think that it would be quite difficult to revive a co-op once it has begun to show poor business performance and its membership has begun to decline.

The conventional view of the "convoy approach"

The so-called "convoy approach," in which government controls and administrative guidance ensure that there is no difference among banks' interest rates on deposits, service charges, and other fees, and no differences among insurance companies' premiums, characterized postwar banking and insurance in Japan until recently. However, if one takes dividend payments to "members" into account, price competition has not been ruled out among the mutual life insurance companies. In spite of the use of the phrase "convoy approach" in banking and insurance alike, there is a decisive difference between banks and casualty insurance,[7] where the organizational form of the enterprise is—or predominantly is—that of a joint-stock company, and life insurance, where mutual companies are dominant. In banking and casualty insurance, differences in management performance under the "convoy approach" are reflected in differences in returns on equity, earnings per share, and stock prices, or changes in any of these; in mutual life insurance companies, in contrast, differences in the business performance of individual companies are in principle reflected, at least to some extent, in differences in the dividend payments to the members, who are essentially the customers. In view of such an important difference, the following popular notions concerning life insurance are fundamentally mistaken, in my view:

(a) In postwar Japan, the Ministry of Finance implemented the so-called "convoy approach," in the life insurance business as well as in other financial businesses, and a *de facto* insurance rate cartel has been in operation, restricting price competition.

(b) Under the "convoy approach," even the companies with the poorest business performances do not fall into financial difficulties; instead, they are protected in such a way that they are always able to gain a new lease on life.

(c) It is said that in the life insurance industry there are substantial "economies of scale" and that the larger the size of a life insurance company, the greater its efficiency. But since the "convoy approach" attempts to protect the smallest, and hence weakest, companies as well, "the top companies in the business wind up getting fatter and fatter."[8]

It would be difficult to rigorously demonstrate that notions like the above are erroneous, but the general situation can be surmised from a comparison of all the life insurance companies.

Comparison of several management indices among insurance companies

From readily available statistics on life insurance companies a few simple indices are computed and compared for 20 life insurance companies which are said to have been operating under the protection of the Ministry of Finance's "convoy" policy, and the results are shown in Table I. For all the life insurance companies in Japan, excluding (partly or wholly) foreign-owned companies, which are all recent entrants into the industry, I compared three kinds of indices: (1) the rate of increase of total assets for the last two, five, and ten years; (2) the ratio of each company's "premium income" received from policyholders to dividends paid out to policyholders; and (3) each company's ratio of total assets at the end of the fiscal year to the "surplus for the current year."

First, when differences in total assets (1) among the 20 life insurance companies are compared, the largest exceeds the smallest by a factor of roughly 140 to 1, a large difference indeed. A look at the rate of increase in total assets for the last two years shows that the average rate for the 20 companies was nearly 50%, a very high rate indeed, but the five fastest-growing companies in terms of total assets are those ranked (in order) 16th, 13th, 10th, 11th, and 9th in total assets (end of 1987). When the period over which growth rates are compared is extended to five years and ten years, average growth rates of assets are again very high, at 129% for the last five years (thus, total assets more than doubled in five years) and 365% for the last ten years. However, the top four companies in terms of growth rates, for both the five-year and ten-year periods, ranked between 10th and 16th in total assets in 1987. They are relatively small compared with the largest companies, with one-seventh and one-twenty-sixth of the total assets held by the top company in 1987.

These facts clearly show that the simplistic notion that "the top companies get fatter and fatter" is entirely mistaken. Next, with regard to column (2) of Table 1, "premium income" is insurance premiums received from policyholders in return for insurance services of future annuity payments. "Dividends" are, as stated above, that portion of the surplus arising from the company's business operations which is distributed to the "members"—that is, the policyholders. The ratio (2) depends on a variety of factors, such as the type and term structure of the insurance policies in force which each company has contracted. If a large number of policies have just been written, this ratio will be low. But it will tend to be high if the insurance for which the company has contracted has high rates of maturity or termination, if there are ample internal reserves for each type of insurance policy in force, if many long-term insurance contracts are maturing, and if the company is paying out large special dividends at maturity. Yet in a company which has a high value for the ratio for (2) over a period of many years, the policyholders are getting insurance at low cost and the company is achieving outstanding performance on their behalf.

The "surplus" which is the numerator of the ratio for (3) corresponds to "net profits" (after taxes) for a joint-stock company. In the case of insurance companies, the lion's share of the "surplus" (over 99% in most companies) is transferred to the reserves for dividends to policyholders, while a very small portion is allocated to bonuses to officers (for example, at Nippon Life Insurance Co. the articles of incorporation stipulate that this amount is to be 5% or less of the surplus, while the amount actually allocated is around 0.03%) and several voluntary reserves and other funds. Accordingly, from the standpoint of the "members" of a mutual life insurance company, the ratio for (3) is an index of how efficiently each company is using its total assets,[9] which are the joint property of the members. It can be seen as an index similar to the "rate of returns on equity" for joint-stock companies.

Table 1 is no more than a very simple comparison of the business performance for each of the life insurance companies based upon readily available statistical data which anyone can use. Even from such a simple comparison, the following points are clearly observed:

(i) There are considerable differences in the business performances of life insurance companies as measured by (3), the ratio of surplus to total assets, and there are considerable differences among the companies in terms of (2), the ratio of insurance premium income to dividend payments, as well. Even if we suppose that all the companies' insurance premium rates are the same because of the cartel under the "convoy approach," for individuals or groups considering newly contracting life insurance, there is an appreciable difference in the real cost of insurance services, depending on the company with which one contracts insurance, or at least there is a possibility that such a difference would arise.

(ii) When a company has a high ratio of surplus to total assets (3), there is a tendency for its premium-to-dividend ratio to be high as well. When the former is low, the latter tends to be low, too.

(iii) No particularly close relationship is discernible between the size of the company, as measured by total assets, and the surplus to total assets ratio. The six companies with the highest ratios of surplus to total assets over a period of three years ranked 7th, 17th, 13th, 15th, 9th, and 14th (in that order) in terms of size. There are some large companies with low surplus to gross assets ratios, as well as some very small companies which rank high on this ratio.[10]

IV. Salaries, Internal Reserves, and a Behavioral Hypothesis

From these facts it is clear that the popular notion regarding the "convoy approach" introduced above is fundamentally mistaken.[11] In the following I will comment on major items other than payments to "dividend members" to which the "surplus in the broad sense" arising out of the business activities of a mutual life insurance company is allocated namely, (a part of) of salaries and bonuses of employees and officers, internal reserves, and so on. Based on these and what I stated in the previous section, I will present a simplified hypothesis about the behavioral principles of the mutual life insurance company.

Interfirm differences in salary levels

What sparked my interest in the life insurance industry, while I was thinking about Japanese companies, was a column in a newspaper I saw a few years ago, which reported that a university graduate employed by Nippon Life, from the time he joined the company immediately after graduation until he retired at around the age of 60, received in excess of ¥400 million in salary and bonuses from the company. This is a very large amount, larger than the comparable lifetime earnings figures for even most of the largest corporations listed in the first section of the stock exchange. I do not remember the exact details, and although a lump-sum retirement payment was obviously included in the calculation, the article did not explain the details of calculation, for example regarding pensions or social insurance, or the method of conversion of future payments to current values. Nevertheless, it seems to be common knowledge, not only in the life insurance business, but among large company employees in general, that Nippon Life salary levels are very high.

As shown in Table 1, Nippon Life is by far the largest of the 20 life insurance companies: there is a difference of 140:1 in the size of total assets between Nippon Life and the smallest life companies, and a difference in the level of annual surplus of 300:1. In the banking business, banks are classified into city and regional banks; moreover, mutual loan and savings banks and *shinyo kinko* (credit mutual companies) carry out the same business as banks in their respective local areas. In contrast, in the life insurance business, all companies are nationwide, and there is no significant difference in the content of employees' work. Despite this, there are large differences in salary levels within the insurance business. It can be inferred that the industry

Table 1.
Ratio of Dividend Payments to Total Assets, Rate of Growth in Total Assets and Insurance Premium Revenues, and the
Ratio of Surplus to Total Assets for Each Life Insurance Company (%)

(1)
Total assets and their rate of increase

Company^a	Total assets at the end of 1987 (¥trillion)	Rate of increase 1985–1987(%)	Ranking by rate of increase 1985–1987	Ranking by rate of increase 1982–1987	Ranking by rate of increase 1977–1987
1. Nippon	18.16	44.1	10	11	10
2. Dai-Ichi	12.50	49.7	7	6	7
3. Sumitomo	10.49	50.1	6	5	6
4. Meiji	6.80	48.8	8	8	8
5. Asahi	5.74	40.3	12	14	14
6. Mitsui	4.39	43.0	11	12	9
7. Yasuda	3.67	39.0	16	13	11
8. Taiyo	3.18	35.3	17	18	16
9. Chiyoda	2.60	52.1	5	10	12
10. Toho	2.55	72.3	3	1	5
11. Kyoei*	1.90	57.0	4	4	1
12. Dai-Hyaku	1.48	39.6	15	16	15
13. Daido	1.47	72.9	2	3	2
14. Fukoku	1.33	47.8	9	9	13
15. Nihon Dantai*	1.12	40.0	13	7	3
16. Nissan	0.70	89.2	1	2	4
17. Tokyo	0.53	32.5	19	19	17
18. Heiwa	0.27	35.0	18	15	20
19. Daiwa	0.14	40.0	13	17	18
20. Taisho*	0.13	30.0	20	20	19
(Average)	(3.96)	(47.2)			

Table 1 (continued)

Company[a]	(2) Ratio of dividend payments to premium revenues, and rankings by this ratio				(3) Ratio of surplus to total assets and rankings by this ratio			
	1987 (%)	1987 Rankings	1986 Rankings	1985 Rankings	1987 (%)	1987 Rankings	1986 Rankings	1985 Rankings
1. Nippon	12.0	6	6	5	3.74	9	11	5
2. Dai-Ichi	12.9	2	7	7	3.70	10	8	12
3. Sumitomo	10.4	9	11	9	3.61	12	13	15
4. Meiji	11.0	7	8	9	3.49	13	12	13
5. Asahi	12.8	3	5	6	3.87	6	8	14
6. Mitsui	12.3	5	4	1	3.84	7	8	11
7. Yasuda	12.6	4	2	2	4.65	1	1	1
8. Taiyo	4.6	20	20	20	1.84	19	19	19
9. Chiyoda	10.3	11	3	2	4.40	2	5	10
10. Toho	9.2	12	16	16	2.80	15	15	8
11. Kyoei*	9.1	14	13	12	3.62	11	7	7
12. Dai-Hyaku	5.7	17	18	18	2.33	18	18	18
13. Daido	8.1	15	15	13	3.94	5	2	2
14. Fukoku	10.6	8	10	8	3.84	7	6	4
15. Nihon Dantai*	10.4	9	9	14	4.09	4	4	5
16. Nissan	4.8	18	12	11	2.51	17	14	8
17. Tokyo	13.5	1	1	4	4.24	3	3	3
18. Heiwa	7.2	16	16	17	2.76	16	17	17
19. Daiwa	9.2	12	14	15	2.99	14	16	16
20. Taisho*	4.7	19	19	19	1.59	20	20	20
(Average)	(10.9)				(3.62)			

Sources: Insurance Research Institute, Insyuaransu: Seimei Hoken Tokei-Go (Insurance: Life Insurance Statistics Issue), various issues. Data are for all life insurance companies (20 companies), except recent entrants.

a Asterisks indicate joint-stock companies. The others are all mutual companies. In the case of joint-stock companies, "surplus" is the sum of "profits" (after taxes) and the amount transferred to the reserves for dividend payments to policyholders.

has a "graduated structure" whereby, with Nippon Life at the top of the list, wage levels rise with the size of the company, and probably also with the excellence of its performance.

There is no published information available on the salary levels of individual companies, but judging from what I have heard from life insurance industry executives, mid-level employees and labor union leaders, wage levels for "internal personnel" (those for "external personnel" will be discussed later) differ considerably with a company's position in the industry, whether it belongs to the top group, comprising the two leading companies (Nippon and Dai-Ichi) and the other major companies, the middle group, or the lower group. For example, there seems to be a difference of two to four million yen in the average annual income of a 45- to 55-year-old employee of department manager rank, between top and mid-level companies.

Although I have not yet been able to obtain published information on the life insurance companies, while examining so-called "model wages" data, I came across data on Tokyo Marine and Fire Insurance Co., Ltd., the top casualty insurance company, and Taiyo Fire Insurance, which belongs to the lower-ranking group of casualty insurance companies. According to this source, at Tokyo Marine and Fire in 1988, the average annual income (model salary for scheduled working hours including bonuses) of a 45-year-old section chief, a university graduate with 23 years' continuous service in the company, was approximately ¥13.4 million, while it was ¥8.8 million, at Taiyo Kasai, less than two thirds the level at Tokyo Marine. The annual income of a 35-year-old employee who is a high-school graduate with 17 years of continuous service in the company was ¥5.65 million at Tokyo Marine and Fire, while at Taiyo Kasai[12] it was ¥3.92 million, less than 70% of the former. When I showed these data to a number of people in the life insurance business, they remarked that the situation in life insurance was "pretty much the same."

It has often been asserted recently that, for workers engaged in the same type of work, wage differences between Japanese companies are not very great, but "model wages" data for scheduled working hours for each company show at a glance that such an assertion is false.

By collating various sorts of information, and making some theoretical inferences, we can see that mutual life insurance companies and their core employees ("internal personnel") bear out my previous assertion that "large Japanese corporations possess to a high degree the characteristics of worker-managed enterprises where the employees share in (part of) the profits."[13]

Special characteristics of "external personnel"

While employees share in the distribution of the profits in a wider sense, there is a striking difference between "internal" and "external" personnel. A large portion of salaries of "external personnel" (sales representatives) is based on a commission system, varying in proportion to, or in accordance with, sales performance. This "commission system," like the dividend rates discussed above, are extremely complex, and it is difficult to make comparisons between companies. Yet a number of people knowledgeable about life insurance told me that external personnel at the top companies such as Nippon or Dai-Ichi do not necessarily enjoy the highest salary levels.

External personnel at life insurance companies are treated, like most female employees of large Japanese corporations, as if they existed in a "grey zone," midway between male white-collar workers, who are under the umbrella of the lifetime employment and seniority promotion systems, and temporary part-time workers, who are not. Perhaps they more closely resemble part-timers. Close to 90% of external personnel in the life insurance industry are women, and their income depends largely on individual sales performance, not much on length of service or seniority. Their average length of employment is only six to seven years; two-thirds of them retire within two years, and a large number of new sales reps join each year.

It is no exaggeration to say that the only employee group in the life insurance business that fully shares in the "surplus," in a broad sense, are the non-transient internal personnel—in other words, the male, white-collar, long-service employees (plus a very small number of long-term outsiders).

Retained profits

If we adopt the "convoy approach" to the life insurance business, which holds that even poorly performing companies must be protected from going out of business, then it is undesirable for large differences to arise in the dividends paid to members (policyholders). In life insurance companies that perform particularly well, a considerable proportion of the "profits" in a broad sense, are distributed to the employee, and the remaining part is either retained or used for donations and other purposes The larger life insurance companies have established grant-making foundations that support social welfare, science, and culture, and the sizes of donations to these organizations seem to vary greatly with the size of the company. The headquarters buildings and directors' offices of the top life insurance companies are palatial, while those of mid- and lower-level companies are more modest.

If a company with outstanding business performance retains a large proportion of its "profits" in the broad sense, then, in a joint-stock company, the stock price rises in accordance with this portion, and the stockholders who are the "owners" of the company receive the profits immediately.[14] But in a mutual company this effect does not come into play, and there is no way for the members, who are the "owners," to receive the benefit corresponding to the profits retained. In businesses like life insurance, where insurance payment obligations fluctuate due to the phenomenon of random occurrence, it is thought to be an essential condition of stable management for the company to have sufficiently large retained profits.[15]

It is probably not appropriate for a life insurance company to cut back hard on retained profits so as to increase dividend payments to the members. An increase in retained profits, however, should lead to further improvement in business performance since, generally speaking, profits in subsequent terms will increase by the amount of investment income on the retained profits.

However, although people in the life insurance business tend to emphasize large differences in the size of retained profits and so-called "hidden reserves" as a major factor behind the differences in performance between companies, I would guess that this factor has had limited influence recently. The total assets of life insurance companies are increasing rapidly: 56.3% of the ¥80 trillion total assets of the life insurance industry represents a net increase over the last five years, and in gross terms even more new money has flowed into the industry during the same five years. With such a high growth rate and the influx of funds from new members, I would expect a rapid "watering down" in the ratio of "hidden reserves" to total assets (at book value). What is meant here by "watering down" or "dilution" is a lowering of the ratio of retained profits (and "hidden reserves") to total assets (or owned capital). I think the notion that the life insurance companies have vast "hidden reserves" has to be considerably qualified at times like the present, when there is a very rapid influx of new money into them.[16]

In joint-stock companies, the "dilution" of owned capital means a situation disadvantageous to existing stockholders, because issuing of new stock at market prices has proceeded too fast or because share prices are too low at the time of new stock issues to new stockholders. But in the mutual life companies, a situation similar to the "dilution" in a joint-stock company can arise if the influx of new money is too fast—in other words, if there is a rapid increase in the number of new members participating to some degree in the distribution of profits arising from existing retained profit (including hidden reserves). This may be thought of as a sort of "brake" which operates to control growth: when a mutual life company grows too fast, its business performance suffers. In an enterprise such as a mutual life insurance company, then, there exists a mechanism which we might describe as an "automatic brake on rapid growth." Even in theoretical terms, therefore, in the life insurance business, the tendency for "the top companies in the business to get fatter and fatter" cannot continue for long.

What do mutual life insurance companies seek to maximize?
A behavioral hypothesis

Let us return to the question posed above: "What is a mutual life insurance company acting to maximize?" It is clear from the above that the members, who have a high level of mobility, have no systematic means of ensuring that managers try to maximize benefits to them exclusively, and that no such system can be devised.

For example, suppose that a top life insurance company wishes to make a huge donation of funds to establish a foundation, which may have great social or scientific significance but which brings practically no benefit to the members. If it were possible to obtain direct votes from members, corresponding to their "share" (though, in contrast to a joint-stock company, this is difficult to define), on whether to use the funds in this way or to increase dividends to members by an equivalent amount, the majority of members would probably want to have the dividends increased, but there is no means for the members to enforce their will against the policy of the management.[17]

However, it is probably not true to say that the interests of the "members" are largely ignored by the management. The managers and employees of a life insurance company benefit from its steady growth, and to bring this about they must always give adequate compensation to the "members" who are at the same time its customers, distribute to them dividends equivalent to or higher than those of rival companies, provide good service, and steadily increase the number of customers. To do this, they must also secure competent external personnel. No mutual life insurance company can grow unless in this way it rewards its customers and increases their numbers.

Although it is no more than a hypothesis in a highly simplified abstract model, we can think of a mutual life insurance company as deciding on its rate of growth and on the number of new "core" employees to employ each year, in such a way as to maximize the lifetime income of the "core" employees, based on a distribution system under which a considerable portion of the profits (in the broad sense) are distributed to the members/customers and the remainder to the employees (principally internal personnel) and officers, and subject to various conditions such as the recruitment of those relating to external personnel.

Translated into a theoretical model, from a static point of view, the management of a life insurance company acts so as to maximize the per capita income of the "core" employees, and therefore sets employee recruitment at a level where the average productivity and marginal productivity of their labor are equal. From a dynamic point of view, it acts so as to maximize the current value of the cumulative lifetime earnings those employees can expect. Under a theoretical model where an enterprise maximizes the per capita income of its employees, the amount of capital it uses is determined so as to make productivity of capital equal to the price of capital on the outside capital market. Applied to the mutual life insurance company, this means that a company determines the amount of funds it receives from the "members" (policyholders), and therefore the number of new insurance contracts, on the basis of the expected rate of return which they can earn by investing the funds in capital markets, and the rate of dividends to the "members" of other companies in the life insurance business. Namely, it determines the amount of funds under its control so as to maintain the expected rate of returns on the funds at a level no lower than, and if possible a little higher than, the expected yield on investment and dividend rates of other companies.

V. Joint-Stock Life Insurance Companies

Excluding companies which are recent entrants into the business, all of which are joint-stock companies, there are currently 20 Japanese life insurance companies, of which 16 are mutual and four are joint-stock companies. Of these four, Nihon Dantai Seimei, which started out mainly as a group insurance company but now also sells individual insurance policies, has a slightly different management policy from the other life insurance companies, while Heiwa and Taisho are extremely small, ranking 18th and 20th in the industry in terms of size of total assets. Kyoei was originally a reinsurance company but was reorganized after World War II, and established in 1947 as an ordinary (not reinsurance) life insurance company. At that time many joint-stock life insurance companies affiliated with the old *zaibatsu* were reorganized as mutual companies at the direction of the Allied Occupation Forces GHQ, but I have no accurate information as to why Kyoei started out as a joint-stock company rather than a mutual company.[18]

Kyoei Seimei is now a mid-ranking life insurance company and has the joint-stock form, but its actual business operations seem to resemble closely those of a mutual company. First, the company is capitalized at a mere ¥90 million, less than one twenty-thousandth of the value of its total assets. Since dividends to stockholders were held down by Ministry of Finance "administrative guidance" to less than 10% (annual rate) of the capital stock, until these accounted for no more than ¥9 million a year. This was clearly an extremely small amount compared to total expenses, and even compared to after-tax profits (approximately ¥1.5 billion in 1987), which are legally owned by the stockholders. In addition, more than 99% of the total value of the company's annual "ordinary profits" and "special profits" (after deduction of special losses) is transferred to an "insurance policyholders' dividend reserves," compared to which "current profits" on the capital account are extremely small.[19] Kyoei Seimei's largest stockholder (25%) is a foundation established by donations from Kyoei. This foundation provides a training program for life insurance employees in Southeast Asia, and its board of directors is similar to the council of a mutual company, in terms of lineup and actual rules. Obviously, joint-stock life insurance companies have no meeting of "members' delegates," but they pay out insurance policyholders' dividends on almost all insurance, and in this respect are little different from mutual companies.[20] It is not clear what sort of policy joint-stock companies have regarding the distribution of profits and insurance policyholders' dividends. The "current profits" accruing to the stockholders that appears on Kyoei Seimei's profit-and-loss statement was less than one four-hundredth of the "amount transferred to the insurance policyholders' dividend reserves" in 1988.

The insurance policyholders of a joint-stock life insurance company are not the "owners" of the company, unlike those of a mutual company, but the company must still look after their interests well; otherwise it will not be able to attract new customers. In turn, the members of a mutual life insurance company are legally the "owners" of the company, yet they do not seem to enjoy any significant economic advantage over the policyholders of a joint-stock life insurance company. This is an interesting point to bear in mind when we consider the question of "ownership" in the present-day world of big business.

In Japan, partly because of the administrative guidance of the Ministry of Finance, there is not very much difference between joint-stock and mutual life insurance companies, but it is not correct to say that there is no difference at all. Joint-stock life insurance companies, though they are "joint-stock" in name and stockholders do have some authority, have virtually no capital on their accounting books and distribute practically no dividends to stockholders. Yet, considering the possibility of further financial deregulation and the lifting of restrictions on dividends to stockholders, the value of the stock of any joint-stock life insurance company is probably quite high.[21] The five new companies which have recently entered the life insurance business, including Seibu Alllstate and Sony Pru Co, have capital stock of ¥5–8 billion each.

In terms of total assets and premium income, these five new companies are smaller than Heiwa and Taisho, belonging to the smallest group among the 20 established life insurance companies and capitalized at ¥100 million each. It would not be surprising if their stocks rose to 50–100 times their par value. Also the benefits the large stockholders of joint-stock life insurance companies have obtained through such means as capital subscription to affiliated companies cannot be ignored.

VI. Life Insurance Companies as Stockholders

As we have seen, Japanese life insurance companies are very important stockholders of large corporations. Nihon Seimei is the largest stockholder in more than 100 companies listed in the first section of the Tokyo Stock Exchange, and even mid-level life insurance companies are major stockholders, ranking among the top ten in a large number of listed companies.

There are a number of aspects to the relationship between life insurance companies and the corporations in which they hold stock. In most cases, the life insurance companies are not simply stockholders but also lenders of funds, and particularly of long-term funds. The relative importance of loans in the total asset management of life insurance companies is said to have declined sharply in recent years. Nevertheless, they still account for 39.2% (end of 1986), a larger proportion than stocks (17.9% in 1986; but this is mostly at book value). In negotiable securities, life insurance companies are major buyers of privately placed bonds, which are close in nature to long-term loans. If stockholding or the lending of funds (particularly long-term) brings with it "control" of the company in question, life insurance companies could be said to "control" a large number of corporations to the extent of their stockholding and lending. At the same time, as mutual companies, they themselves issue neither stocks nor bonds and rarely borrow funds, so that they are subject to no such "control" by other companies. Among the members' delegates of a mutual life insurance company are quite a few presidents and other executives of companies of which the life insurance company is a major stockholder or to which it makes loans. It is hardly likely, however, that such delegates would take a critical stance towards the management of a life insurance company at the meeting of members' delegates.

As a matter of fact, however, the life insurance companies' control over—or, to define it a little more strictly, their voice in—the corporate management of companies in which they are major stockholders or to which they loan funds generally seems to be extremely limited. The voice of the life insurance companies which are major stockholders has, up to now, been far weaker than that of the banks, or at least that of the "main" banks, as they are called by businessmen in Japan. There have been far fewer corporate directors who were formerly directors or employees of life insurance companies than those who were formerly with banks. This is perhaps because banks act as the channel for the inflow and outflow of short-term corporate funds, so that they would take on an advisory, or even a management, role in the corporation, whereas life insurance companies have hardly had anything to do with short-term corporate finance or fund management.

Slight changes seem to have occurred in these areas over the last ten years or so. Factors such as the declining growth rate of the national economy, the trend towards a surplus of corporate funds, and the diversification of financing methods, due to financial liberalization and internationalization of finance, have led to a remarkable decline in the "control" of banks over corporations. Furthermore, there have been increasingly strong demands and pressure from overseas, particularly the United States, for the Japanese government and businesses to adopt a more open policy towards corporate takeovers, and there have been an increasing number of takeover attempts and purchases of stocks by "invaders" within the country, from Hong Kong and elsewhere. This has resulted in a mood of growing anxiety over take-overs among the managers of smaller corporations listed on the stock exchange. Under these circumstances, life insurance companies, which are considered stable stockholders by corporations, are seen as being increasingly important.

The relationship between life insurance companies and individual corporations (including banks) is also influenced by the fact that corporations are important customers of the life insurance companies in group insurance and corporate pension funds, and the life insurance companies compete keenly with each other (for pension funds, they also compete with trust banks) to obtain corporate customers. If an insurance company were to treat a corporation in a high-handed manner in its capacity as a stockholder or lender, the corporation could well retaliate in its capacity as a customer.[22] There are very few cases of a single life insurance company being the only major stockholder in a company without any other life insurance companies or trust banks on the list of its major shareholders.

The life insurance company and the phenomenon of the corporate group (keiretsu)

I would like to touch on the relationship between life insurance companies and the phenomenon—or product of the imagination—known as the *keiretsu* or corporate group. All the top life insurance companies in Japan are mutual companies, and, as we have seen, they neither borrow funds from other financial institutions nor issue bonds. Hence, if we define a company as belonging to a *keiretsu* or corporate group on the grounds that its stocks are held by other companies in the group, and that it borrows funds from the core financial institutions in the group, no life insurance company can be said to belong to any *keiretsu* group. However, it is common knowledge in the Japanese business world that not only the life insurance companies with prewar "zaibatsu" names such as Sumitomo and Mitsui life insurance, but also Meiji (Mitsubishi group), Yasuda (formerly Yasuda *zaibatsu*, now in the "Fuyo" group centered around Fuji Bank), and Asahi (formerly Furukawa *zaibatsu*, now in the Dai-Ichi Kangyo Bank group) do in fact all belong to particular corporate groups. By contrast, Nihon Seimei, the largest Japanese life insurance company, and Dai-Ichi Seimei, one of the three companies that were organized as mutual companies before World War II, are not considered as belonging to any particular corporate group.[23]

Though life insurance companies may be said to belong to one of the old *zaibatsu* groups, so far as the ownership relationship is concerned there is no reason to consider Sumitomo Life, for example, as dependent on the Sumitomo Group. The special relationships between the life insurance companies and the companies in their respective groups derive primarily from historical roots. In any case, life insurance companies are not in a position to be forced to do business that might be disadvantageous to them under pressure from other companies in the group.

The insurance companies listed above which are affiliated with prewar "*zaibatsu*" groups were originally joint-stock companies, with their stock held by the head office of the old *zaibatsu* or by other companies in the *zaibatsu* group, so that they really were under the "control" of the *zaibatsu*. But with the dissolution of the *zaibatsu* by the Allied Occupation Forces after World War II, they were recognized as mutual companies. In addition, companies that were originally "conscription insurance" companies, like Toho, Dai-Hyaku, Daiwa, and the other major life insurance companies,were also reorganized into a mutual company form as business got off to a new start from its demolished position in the period immediately after World War II. The Occupation Forces GHQ, on the grounds that most of the large life insurance companies in the United States and Britain were organized as mutual companies, decided to change the form of life insurance companies from joint-stock to mutual as part of its policy to democratize the Japanese economy and to reduce as much as possible any remaining *zaibatsu* influence.

In the lists of stockholders of those companies which belong to the group descending from the old *zaibatsu*, we frequently find the names of a life insurance company, a trust bank, and a bank belonging to the same group. However, such lists nearly always contain the names of other trust banks and life insurance companies, especially Nihon Life and Dai-Ichi Life, as well.

In companies belonging to a group descended from the prewar *zaibatsu* the life insurance company from the same group perhaps has a dominant position in group insurance and company pension funds, as well as personal insurance. In such a situation, however, the life insurance company affiliated with the group will probably have to offer conditions, in terms of premiums and services, as good as or even superior to those of its rivals. It is unlikely that a company would sign group insurance and pension contracts with an affiliated life insurer that were even slightly inferior in terms of premiums and services, solely because the latter belongs to the same group. Today business dealings between corporations within a *keiretsu* group are essentially "arm's length" transactions.

For many large corporations, life insurance companies are both major stockholders and very important lenders of funds (particularly long-term funds), but this does not give the life insurance companies any strong "control" over the corporations in the big business environment of Japan today. Instead, the relationship is generally one between entities with equal status. The life insurance company in its role as a major shareholder—and as an important lender of funds—intervenes or speaks out regarding the management of the company of which it is a shareholder only in exceptional circumstances, such as serious financial difficulties.

VII. Conclusions

In this chapter, we have considered a certain special form of private enterprise, the mutual life insurance company, from the points of view of the theory of the firm and the economic analysis of the Japanese firm. My own understanding of the life insurance business is still incomplete, but the main purpose of this chapter is not to discuss the life insurance business per se but, by looking at the special form of business enterprise represented by the mutual life insurance company, to shed light on the characteristics of the Japanese firm and the theory of the firm.

In the following I will summarize the main conclusions of this chapter, and in addition draw attention to some of the inferences to which the analysis in this chapter leads us, since they are significant for the study of the theory of the firm and the problems of the Japanese firm in general.

First, concerning who actually "controls" corporations—that is, who makes the important decisions on the management of a firm and actually participates in these decisions—it perhaps goes without saying that although we cannot ignore the legal principles which dictate who should control the firm, they are not the decisive factor. Whatever form a firm takes, the people who "control" it are generally (1) those who possess professional knowledge of business management in the field the firm specializes in and (2) those who have a large stake in the firm, or share large risks with the firm. An average individual stockholder who is not the owner-manager of a joint-stock company, a member or "members' delegate" of a mutual life insurance company, or in the majority of corporate stockholders of a joint-stock company, lacks both conditions (1) and (2) and therefore can exercise little real "control" over the company despite being a nominal "owner."

Second, the people who do possess conditions (1) and (2) and actually "control" a Japanese firm are the managers and "core" employees with long records of continuous employment, from whose ranks the succeeding generation of managers will be chosen. This is equally true for both joint-stock and mutual companies.

Third, the system is such that a part of the "profits in a broad sense" is distributed not only to the members of management but also to these core employees, which works as an incentive spurring the management and employees to greater efforts. This is why the Japanese corporate system functions with a high level of efficiency. My view is that large Japanese corporations exhibit to a considerable degree the characteristics of the labor-managed firm, where the core employees share the profits, and this also seems to apply well to mutual life insurance companies and their core employees (internal personnel).

In the "golden age" of the capitalist system, the "captains of industry" combined the roles of capitalist and manager, put up the stakes and ran the business, taking all the fruits of the enterprise for themselves, as well as all the losses. In the world of big business today, however, where running a company requires substantial funds and a high level of professional knowledge, such an old-fashioned capitalist system is not only incompatible with notions of democracy and equality, but cannot function efficiently for other reasons as well. Japan's big-business system, characterized by lifetime employment and seniority principles, seems to provide a rather skillful solution to central problems of large-scale corporate management: the problems of stake, control, and incentives, as discussed above.

Fourth, due to the fact that the Ministry of Finance's "convoy approach" (under which the Ministry tries to protect even the weakest firms from going out of business) has resulted in a *de facto* cartel in the financial sector, including the life insurance business, it has come to be a widely held popular belief that the top companies in the business wind up getting fatter and fatter. This belief is basically mistaken however, in the case of life insurance. In the case of mutual life insurance companies, in which the policyholders are at the same time the owners, differences in business performance between companies are ultimately reflected in the real costs borne by, and profits passed on to, the members. Hence cartels in the true sense of the word cannot be maintained over the long term in the life insurance business. Furthermore, rapid growth of a mutual life insurance company results in the dilution of retained profits and hidden reserves, because of the special structural characteristics of mutual companies. Hence, theoretically, the phenomenon of "the top companies in the business getting fatter and fatter" would not arise, and this is confirmed by statistical data. If we look at performance over the last 5–10 years, all the companies with the highest growth rates and best performance are mid-ranking or lower in the industry in terms of size, and not the largest ones.

Fifth, Japanese life insurance companies are major stockholders in a large number of corporations, and also lenders of funds, particularly long-term funds, to corporations, but these same corporations are customers of the life insurance companies for group insurance and corporate pensions. In the present-day Japanese big business environment, where there is always keen competition, insurance companies have only a very small voice in the management of companies of which they are major stockholders, barring the exceptional circumstances of a company facing grave financial difficulties or "invasion" by a takeover raider.

Sixth, in the Japanese big business sector, the "owners" of a large company, whether joint-stock or mutual, are hardly able to exercise any control over the management of the company, yet their interests are by no means treated lightly. The principal mechanism that guarantees the interests of stockholders and members is not the legal mechanism of the stockholders' general meeting or the meeting of members' delegates, but, first, disclosure of the company's financial condition, and, second, the "market mechanisms" of the capital markets and supply and demand for insurance services. What exerts the decisive influence on the distribution of the "profits in a broad sense" within the company is, in the case of a joint-stock company, the question of whether fund raising on the capital markets necessary for the growth of the company can be carried out smoothly and advantageously. In the case of a mutual life insurance company, it is the question of whether new insurance policyholders can be recruited steadily. What frightens the managers of a large corporation and its core employees is not so much critical and hostile comments at its general stockholders meetings or meetings of members' delegates as the "whip" of the markets, both the market for its products and services and the capital market. For the mutual life insurance company, as for a joint-stock manufacturing company, the "market whip" threatening management is the double whip of the market for insurance services, which combines the product market and the capital market.

This chapter is an English version of Chapter 18 of *Nihon no Kigyo* (Japanese Enterprises), edited by Ken'ichi Imai and Ryutaro Komiya (Tokyo: University of Tokyo Press, 1989).

Notes

1. Five of those insurance companies are foreign-owned companies incorporated under the Japanese law, which were established after 1975 and which are still small. In addition, there are five foreign corporations which have branches doing business in Japan.

2. Exceptions are *shinyo kinko* (credit mutual companies), agricultural and fishing cooperatives, consumer cooperatives, and agricultural and industrial cooperative banks, but their shares are very small.

3. See Komiya (1989), p. 352.

4. See Chapter 4.

5. There are also mutual companies which, in addition to these organs, have "board of trustees meetings," but these do no more than such things as express their opinions on company management and have no decision-making power or authority.

6. As an example of a report on this point, the *Asahi Shimbun* of December 12, 1988, states: "When there is a special dividend which is the payout of capital gains, the difference widens still further, and as for special dividends on insurance which has been in force 10 years or more since the inception of the contract, in 1987 15 life insurance companies paid out amounts equivalent to 60% of the insured amount at maturity, whereas some other companies were able to pay out only 25%."

However, I have heard the view that the several "higher-ranking" companies have adopted a policy of setting their dividend rates at virtually the same levels, and that only a small number of companies have dividend rates different from those of the majority. Still the fact remains that the real costs of insurance to policyholders differ among insurance companies. Moreover, as a result of different business performance, the latent possibility that this will in due course be reflected in differences in dividend rates always exists. In the case of joint-stock companies in manufacturing, it is extremely difficult for all the companies in the same industry to maintain identical dividend rates over the long term, even if it is not difficult to form a product price cartel in an oligopolized field (or, if a cartel should be illegal, to practice price leadership, a practical equivalent of a cartel).

7. However, even among the indemnity insurance companies there are two mutual companies.

8. Items (a), (b), and (c) are seen rather widely, first of all in Japanese economic and business journalism, and even among those engaged in the financial and life insurance business.

9. Since, due to their special characteristics as enterprises, short- and long-term borrowing of capital of life insurance companies was in fact hardly ever approved until recently, and since bonds are rarely issued even today, insurance premium income from policyholders (and the earnings on the use of those revenues) are the only source of funds for mutual life insurance companies' total assets, apart from the "original funds" which were redeemed long ago.

10. When Spearman and Kendall's test for rank order correlation is performed on (a) the rankings for scale and for the surplus assets ratio and

on (b) the rankings for the premium to dividend payments ratio and for surplus to the total assets ratio, tests for each of the years from 1985 to 1987 all show no significant correlation even at the 10% level for (a), while (b) was significant at the 1% level.

11. There are a number of problems with a simple comparison of management indices such as that in Table 1: total assets tend to be larger in companies with a high ratio of those insurance policies which have savings elements than in companies with a high ratio of insurance policies covering only a short period with no element of savings, and as a result the ratio of surplus to total assets tends to be higher in companies of the latter type. But the facts stated here are, I believe, still adequate to show the fallacy of notions such as (a), (b), and (c).

12. Source: Industrial Labor Research Office (1988).

13. Neither the assertion quoted here nor its applicability to mutual life insurance companies has yet been definitely proven. In elementary particle theory, there are numerous examples of theorists putting forward bold hypotheses which are verified some years later through observation and experiment. The statement made here with regard to mutual life insurance company salary levels is for the time being no more than a hypothesis, based on theoretical inference and analogy.

14. This is what the famous "dividend theorem" of Franco Modigliani and Irwin Miller tells us.

15. From this point of view, it is thought to be rather difficult for new companies to enter the life insurance business unless they bring some kind of "innovation" to the industry. If a mutual company has already established itself in the life insurance business, a new customer who purchases a new insurance policy with that company receives some benefits from the retained profits and "hidden reserves" accumulated in the company from the premiums paid both by past policyholders and by existing policyholders unconnected to himself or herself. This means that, as each policy expires, the company does not pay out the whole of the retained profits associated with that policy. The new entrant in the insurance business, by contrast, has neither retained profits nor "hidden reserves."

If all the individual life insurance companies reward members poorly, however, taking excessive profits without returning them adequately to members, and if the dividend rates of all of them are unreasonably low, it should not be difficult, for example, in such fields as group life insurance for seven or more promoters to recruit more than 100 members, establish a mutual company, and start a group life insurance business to, for example, provide group life insurance to some group (say, university and high school employees) nationwide. The fact that this has not been done probably attests to the keen competition among the existing life insurance companies and the high level of efficiency with which they are managed. Also, though it is not touched on in this chapter, we cannot ignore the competition from postal life insurance and mutual aid insurance operated by agricultural, fishermen's and consumers' cooperative associations and workers' mutual aid societies.

16. In the last 3 or 4 years, due to a sharp rise in real estate and share prices, the phenomenon here referred to as "dilution" has probably not come to the surface much in spite of a large influx of funds to life insurance com-

panies. However, there is no doubt that the proportion of retained profits and "hidden reserves" in total assets should be lower in companies where the influx of new money has been rapid than in companies where it has been slow.

17. Even assuming that the majority of the members could exert definite control over the management by some means or other, so that the company was managed according to the majority wishes of its members, it would probably be poor strategy to depress the salary levels of employees (and managers) to a level that was clearly lower than that of other insurance companies just in order to increase dividends to members. The employees and managers would lose incentive for the work and management of the company, and there would be a serious danger that the company would be unable to attract and train talented people.

18. According to the company's account of its history, while procedures were under way to set up the company in a mutual form, it was suddenly changed by GHQ directives to a joint-venture company, whereupon approval was granted; but the circumstances surrounding the change are not very well understood even by Kyoei's management. See Kyoei Life Insurance Co., Inc., (1963), pp. 80–101.

19. Since Taisho Seimei and Heiwa Seimei do only a small volume of business, levels of capital stock and dividends are in a slightly higher ratio to other items of account, but they are still very low.

20. However, Heiwa Seimei and Nihon Dantai Seimei, which are joint-stock companies, issue "insurance without dividends" for certain types of insurance products.

21. None of these companies is listed on the stock exchange.

22. A newspaper article published after the original version of this essay was completed states that in March 1988 Asahi Life Insurance disposed of part of the stock it held in the Industrial Bank of Japan, and that subsequently the bank reduced the Asahi Life share in group insurance for its employees (*Asahi Shimbun*, Aug. 9, 1988). Asahi Life, for its part, probably judged that the benefit of shifting the funds from the extremely low-yield bank stocks elsewhere would more than make up for its losses on group insurance contracts.

23. It seems to be generally assumed that Nihon Life belongs to the "Sanwa Group" since its president is a member of the "presidents' meeting" of that group. But I am skeptical about whether a "Sanwa Group" as such exists in the first place (see Komiya, [1988] no. 3, p. 62, note 2; Komiya [1989], pp. 137–38); in addition, Nihon Life does not seem to have close relations with many companies said to belong to the Sanwa Group.

24. At one mutual life insurance company, I was told that, on one occasion when its financial performance turned out to be poor for some time, salary rises were restrained and bonuses kept low, for several years until performance recovered and the company was once again able to pay salaries and bonuses comparable to those of other companies of similar size. If this kind of thing does occur frequently, the core employees of a mutual life insurance company may be said to have a larger stake in the company than the core employees in a joint-stock company. In a joint-stock company, if performance temporarily worsens, it is possible to report lower net profits and reduce dividend payments to stockholders, without necessarily losing

long-standing customers. Whereas in a mutual company, if the dividends paid to members, who are at the same time the customers, are visibly reduced, there is a danger of adverse effects on sales of new insurance contracts. Hence, the management must be very cautious about reducing the dividend payments, or even just admitting that the company's performance has deteriorated. Since it is probably not possible and/or advisable to cut remunerations to sales representatives, the core employees of a mutual company are likely to shoulder a greater burden.

References

Komiya Ryutaro, (1988). "Structural and Behavioural Characteristics of the Japanese Company," in *Economic Essays*, Tokyo University, vol. 54, nos. 2 & 3 (July, October). Reproduced as Ch. 3 of Komiya, (1989).

Komiya Ryutaro (1989). *Gendai Chugoku Keizai: Nichu no Hikaku Shisai* (The Contemporary Chinese Economy: A Comparative Study of China and Japan). Tokyo: University of Tokyo Press.

Kyoei Life Insurance, Inc., (1963). *Kyoei Life: A History*. Tokyo: Kyoei Life Insurance, Inc.

Industrial Labor Research Office (1988). *Model Wage Data: 1989*. Tokyo: Industrial Labor Press.

Industry and Government

CHAPTER 7

ECONOMIC PLANNING AND INDUSTRIAL POLICY

I. Economic Planning in Japan

When people speak of "economic planning" in Japan they usually have in mind the national economic plan prepared by the Economic Planning Agency once every two or three years. Yet in my view these national plans are not so much a "plan" in the usual sense of the term, and are not as important as they appear at first. Those who are not well informed about economic policymaking in Japan might think that the Japanese government largely follows its medium-term (usually five years) national economic plan when making annual or day-to-day economic policy decisions. In fact, this is not the case. In recent years especially, the national economic plan is becoming less and less relevant to actual economic policy, at least so far as macroeconomic and sectoral quantitative indices are concerned.

This does not mean, however, the Japanese economy is run without much governmental planning. The Japanese government intervenes widely in individual sectors, industries, or regions, and there is much planning on industry as well as regional bases. Many of the plans in individual fields appear to be quite effective in channeling resources into particular industries or regions.

In the following two sections of this chapter, Japan's national economic planning, regional planning, and planning for individual industries will be discussed. In the last section a few concluding remarks will be made.

National Economic Plans

The multiplicity of plans and the reasons for underestimation
The multiplicity of Japan's national economic plans is perhaps well

known. During the eighteen years from 1955 to 1973, the Japanese government announced seven medium- or long-term national economic plans. Table 1 gives a brief summary of these plans.

Some of the Japanese words appearing in these plans are rhetoric without much substantive meaning and are difficult to translate into English. Even so, the words in Table 1 still indicate what Japanese plan-makers considered the most important policy goals at the time of preparing each plan, and reflect the changing atmosphere of economic policymaking in postwar Japan. In the early postwar years, the emphasis was on industrial growth, saving, investment, and export. Later the priority shifted to "balanced growth" (whatever that means), price stability, and international cooperation, and more recently, welfare, quality of life, and environment have been included among most important policy goals.

The natural question will be raised why there are so many national economic plans. An immediate answer is that although each of the plans listed in Table 1, except the ten-year National Income Doubling Plan, covered about five years, after its introduction the actual rate of growth surpassed the planned rate substantially, especially in the case of earlier plans, and planning indices became obsolete within a year or two after implementation.[1] Especially in the case of Plans II, IV, and V, the actual level of private investment in plant and equipment by far surpassed the planned targets. Later an unexpected rapid increase in exports and huge balance-of-payments surpluses were the main factors which made the plan obsolete very quickly. Also, rapid and unexpected changes in the socioeconomic as well as external conditions made it necessary to change the policy goals declared in the national economic plan.

Why then have Japan's national economic plans persistently underestimated the rate of growth, at least until around 1970? First, in the period immediately after the war, most Japanese were not confident not only of the future of the economy but also of the nation and themselves. The prewar level of per capita real income was regained only around 1955: of the nations which fought World War II, severely defeated Japan took the longest time to recover from war destruction. The target rate of growth of 5% given in the Five-Year Plan for Economic Self-Support, the first official economic plan, was severely criticized as too optimistic and as unrealistic by intellectuals, journalists, and leaders of nongovernment parties. Such a criticism was not unrelated to a Marxian view of "monopoly capitalism," according to which the world capitalist system, which entered the period of "a general crisis of capitalism" in 1930, was bound to fall into stagnation and could not continue to grow without undergoing a proletarian revolution or at least a drastic social reform.

Second, having experienced unusually high rates of growth for some time immediately after the war, still an overwhelming majority of knowledgeable Japanese did not believe that such high rates would continue to prevail. Especially those who belonged to the older generations (those who finished university education before the war) continued to criticize the target rates of growth in national economic plans as overly optimistic well into the mid-1960s.[2] It was argued that a high rate of growth was possible in the reconstruction period because capital expenditures to repair war-damaged plant, equipment, and social overhead capital could raise GNP very quickly, whereas after the reconstruction period the increase in GNP could be achieved only by substantial new net investment and/or technological progress.

Another argument was that the Japanese economy was in a catching-up process immediately after the war, making use of a large backlog of new technologies developed in the United States and Europe during the war. Once such a backlog was exhausted, technological progress in Japan would be slowed down.

Pessimists also emphasized the balance-of-payments constraint. They thought that Japan's exports could not continue to grow indefinitely at a much faster rate than the total volume of world trade, and therefore the rate of growth of Japan's raw material and fuel imports, vital for Japan's industrial growth, would be restricted.

Looking back with the hindsight of today, it is obvious that the majority, including the plan-makers, underestimated not only the growth potential of the Japanese economy, but also the adaptability of the economy to changing circumstances and the resultant structural changes. The national economic plans predicted more or less correctly the directions of the changes in the industrial structure, the industrial distribution of the labor force, and the composition of exports, but almost always underestimated the extent of such changes.[3]

Contents of a national economic plan

To facilitate the understanding of the nature of national economic planning in Japan, I will briefly describe the contents of the 1973–1977 *Basic Economic and Social Plan*. The Plan is published as a government document of about 170 pages, and consists primarily of two components. The first two tables of the Plan, reproduced here as Tables 2 and 3, summarize these two components. Table 2 give the plan's targets for various items in each of the four major planning areas. For example, under the heading of "creation of a rich environment"

Table 1
Summary of National Economic Plans: 1955–73

Name of Plan	Planning period and date of publication	Planned and actual real rates of growth (percentage)	Objectives of Plan	Major policy problems to be solved
I. Five-Year Plan for Economic Self-Support	1956–60; December 1955	5.0; 9.1	Economic self-support (meaning growth without U.S. aid); full employment.	(a) modernization of productive capacity, (b) development of international trade, (c) increased domestic supply (of raw materials), and (d) economy in consumption (increased savings).
II. New Long-Range Economic Plan	1958–62; December 1957	6.5; 10.1	Maximum growth; improvement of living standard; full employment.	(a) Strengthening of industrial base, (b) expansion of heavy and chemical industries, (c) promotion of exports, and (d) increased supply of savings.
III. National Income Doubling Plan	1961–70; December 1960	7.2; 11.0	Same as in Plan II, above.	(a) Investment in social overhead capital, (b) modernization of national industrial structure, (c) international trade and cooperation, (d) betterment of human capabilities and advance-

Table 1 (continued)

ment of science and
technology, and
(e) mitigating the so-called
dualistic structure² and
increasing social stability.

IV.	Medium-Term Economic Plan	1964–68; January 1965	8.1; 11.0	Correction of distortions (arising out of rapid economic growth).	(a) Modernization of low-productivity sectors, (b) efficient use of labor force, and (c) improvement in the quality of life.
V.	Economic and Social Development Plan	1967–71; March 1967	8.2; 12.0	Development toward a balanced and enriched economy and society.	(a) Price stability, (b) economic efficiency, and (c) advancement of social development.
VI.	New Economic and Social Development Plan	1970–75; May 1970	10.6	Establishing a humane economy and society through balanced economic development.	(a) Improved economic efficiency through international specialization, (b) price stability, (c) promotion of social development, and (d) maintenance of proper rate of growth and cul-

Table 1 (continued)

Name of Plan	Planning period and date of publication	Planned and actual real rates of growth (percentage)	Objectives of Plan	Major policy problems to be solved
				tivation of the basis for further development.
VII. Basic Economic and Social Plan	1973–77; February 1973	9.4	Enhancement of civil welfare; international cooperation.	(a) Creation of a rich environment, (b) ensuring a comfortable and stable civil life, (c) price stability, and (d) international cooperation.

Sources: Japan Economic Council, *Economic Planning in Japan* (in Japanese) (Tokyo, 1969); and Japan, Economic Planning Agency, *The Basic Economic and Social Plan, 1973–77* (Tokyo, 1973).

^aThe dualistic or dual structure of the Japanese economy refers to the coexistence of modernized big business, on the one hand, and more or less traditional, labor-intensive small business and small-peasant agriculture, on the other. The disparity in wage rates between the big-business and small-business sectors is generally considered a reflection of the dualistic structure of the Japanese economy.

(see the column for "major policy problems to be solved" in Table 1), the target levels for improvement in air pollution, water pollution, city parks, etc., are stipulated. Similarly target levels are given under the other three broad planning objectives, "ensuring a comfortable and stable civil life," "price stability," and "international cooperation."

Later in the Plan, the policy measures required for achieving each target are explained. But the explanation given in the Plan is largely qualitative rather than quantitative, and sometimes quite vague. Rhetorical and euphemistic words difficult to translate, or almost meaningless words such as "take necessary measures," "promote coordination," "consider improving such and such," appear repeatedly. Moreover, on important policy issues hotly debated currently, the Plan often avoids indicating the future directions of government policy. For example, on the problem of the price of land, which has been rising very rapidly recently and causing social unrest among the urban population, the Plan says little beyond what has already been said. On the price policies of public corporations such as national railways and on the problems of cartels and resale price maintenance, all of which are considered by many Japanese as the crucial areas for policies to curb inflation, the Plan spends several paragraphs, but says almost nothing meaningful. Or, while emphasizing very strongly international cooperation and avoidance of protectionism, the Plan says nothing about Japan's own agricultural protection. But, as explained later, the national economic plan under Japan's present institutional setting is bound to be elusive on such specific policy issues.

Table 3 gives what is called by the Plan a "profile" of the Japanese economy in 1977. Here the figures in 1977 for GNP (in current and constant prices) and its components, the balance of payments, the price deflator for household consumption, the ratio of taxes and other obligations to national income, and several other items are given. These figures are backed up by more detailed figures in later tables and an appendix of the Plan, which are based upon extensive macroeconometric simulation studies. The appendix of the Plan gives detailed national income accounts and an industry breakdown of output and employment in 1977. It is the failure of this part of the earlier national plans to predict the future course of the economy accurately enough that caused the large discrepancies between actual and planned figures within a few years after the introduction of the Plan, and quickly made the Plan obsolete. Earlier plans gave these figures as "planned" or "targets," but in recent plans these figures for the terminal year of the planning period are labelled "predicted" or "estimates."

Table 2

Targets of the Basic Economic and Social Plan, 1973–77

Area	Item	Targets to be reached in 1977
I. Creation of a Rich Environment		
1. Preservation of environment	Air pollution due to sulfur oxides	(a) Environmental quality Standards more stringent than those presently in force shall be established to avoid adverse effects on human health. (b) In the Big Three Bay Areas[a] the amount of discharge shall be reduced to about half of the 1970 level.
	Water pollution	(a) At least the present water quality standards or the provisional targets shall be met during the period of the plan, with a view to restoration of a situation of no adverse effects on health or living environment by 1985. (b) In the Big Three Urban Areas[b] the BOD[c] discharge load will be reduced to about one-half of the 1970 level.
2. Living environment facilities	City parks	4.7 sq.meters per capita (estimated figure for 1972, 3 sq.m.; goal for 1985, 9 sq.m.).
	Sewerage systems	Service to 42% of the population (estimated figure for 1972, 19%).
	Disposal of refuse Human wastes	Within areas covered by plans: 100% sanitary disposal in 1975 (estimated figure for 1972, 87%).
	Combustible refuse	100% disposal in 1980 (estimated figure for 1972, 81%).
3. Nationwide transportation and communications network	Super express railways (*Shinkansen*)	Extension to total length of approximately 1,900 km. in operation (construction target by 1985, about 7,000 km.).
	National expressways	Extension to total length of approximately 3,100 km. in operation (construction target by 1985, about 10,000 km.).

Table 2 (continued)

Area	Item	Targets to be reached in 1977
	Telephone installation	Catching up with backlog demands.
4. Improvement of agricultural and forest environments	Agricultural land	Doubling of hectarage which supports highly efficient farming (approx. 1.2 million ha. in 1972).
	Reserve forests	Designation of 10 percent more reserve forest area (6.9 million ha. in 1972).
II. Ensuring a Comfortable and Stable Civil Life		
1. Social security	Ratio of transfer income to national income	8.8% (estimated figure for 1972, 6.0%).
	Pensions*d*	
	Employees' Pension Plan	From 1973, a standard monthly pension of ¥50,000, with further improvements thereafter.
	National Pension Plan	A level commensurate with that of the Employee's Pension Plan.
	Non-contributory Old Age Pension	¥5,000 a month in 1973, ¥10,000 a month in 1975, and further improvements thereafter.
	Social Welfare facilities	Expansion of facilities so as to accommodate all of those elderly bedridden people, the seriously mentally or physically handicapped, and others who need care.
2. Housing	Publicly financed housing	Construction of four million new units.
	Housing developments	Early completion of large-scale "New Town" housing developments and other smaller projects already under way in the Tokyo and Osaka metropolitan areas covering approximately 30,000 ha. (to accommodate a total population of about four million), and commencement of other new projects.

(Table 2 continued)

Area	Item	Targets to be reached in 1977
3. Work week and retirement	Five-day work week	Promote general adoption by employers.
	Raising of compulsory retirement age	Promote general adoption of compulsory retirement at age 60 (presently 55).
4. Education and sports	Educational facilities	Improvement of facilities for kindergarten, primary, and secondary compulsory education, and higher education. To establish at least one medical school (or Faculty of Medicine in a university) in every prefecture.
	Community sports facilities	Provision over a period of about 10 years of readily accessible sports facilities such as athletic grounds, gymnasiums, swimming pools, playgrounds, etc.

III. Price Stability

	Consumer prices	Average annual rise of not more than 5%.
	Wholesale prices	Stability: at most a moderate, unaccelerated rise.

IV. Promotion of International Cooperation

	Balance of payments	Equilibrium in the basic balance (balance on basic transactions) within three years.
	Economic aid	Early realization within the period of the plan of a flow corresponding to 1% of gross national product (GNP).
	Official development assistance	Raising its ratio to GNP to a level comparable to those of other countries by an early date, attainment of the international goal of 0.7% over a longer period, and improvement of the terms and conditions of assistance.

Source: Table 1 of *The Basic Economic and Social Plan 1963–77*, pp. 15–17, with a few changes in wording.

*a*The Big Three Bay Areas: areas along Tokyo Bay, Osaka Bay, and the northern part of Ise Bay.

Apart from the large discrepancies in the past, some academic economists are critical of the procedure by which the estimates in recent national economic plans were derived. Although the general framework of the macroeconometric model used in the projection was made public, the procedure in deriving the predicted figures for 1977 was not. Only a few of the values for exogenous parameters and policy variables used in the predictions are explicitly given in the Plan (see Table 3). It is difficult, therefore, for outsiders to evaluate the overall validity of the predictions. The premises under which the predictions are made should be made public, according to the criticism. Especially in the case of the estimates for price deflators, some doubts have been entertained as to compatibility with other estimates: it is generally thought that for an obvious political reason the government chose artificially low figures for the rate of price increase.

Process of plan-making
To clarify the nature of Japan's national economic plans, it is necessary to describe the process by which the plan is prepared and announced.

The formal process is that first the Prime Minister requests the Economic Council to prepare a national plan, and then the Council presents its report to the Prime Minister. In the case of the latest plan, Prime Minister Kakuei Tanaka requested the Council in August 1972 to prepare "a new long-term economic plan which aimed at enhancement of civil welfare and promotion of international cooperation, in view of rapid changes in the domestic and external circumstances."

The Economic Council is an advisory committee reporting to the prime minister, and consisted in 1972 of about thirty members outside of the government. Its overwhelming majority were presidents and chairmen of big corporations and ex-government officials.[4] Its *Basic Economic and Social Plan* was reported to the prime minister in February 1973, and at the Cabinet meeting a few days later the Plan was formally adopted without any modification "as the guiding principle for managing the national economy during fiscal years 1973 through 1977."

---

[b]The Big Three Urban Areas: the part of the Kanto Area along the coast, the Tokai coastline, and the Osaka–Kobe area.

[c]BOD: biochemical oxygen demand; an index of water pollution.

[d]The Employees' Pension Plan covers employees in larger establishments, and the National Pension Plan covers those not included in the Employees' Plan: self-employed and their family workers, day laborers and workers in very small establishments. (Footnote supplied by the author.)

Table 3.
Profile of the Economy in 1977[a]

	1970		1977		1973–77	1961–70
	Actual figures	Percentages	Estimates	Percentages	Average annual rate of increase (percentage)	Average annual rate of increase (percentage)
I. Given Conditions and Policies						
Labor force (persons)	51,700,000		54,100,000		0.8	1.3
Government fixed capital formation (1965 prices)	¥5 trillion		[b]		15.5	13
Government transfers to households (current prices)	¥3 trillion	(percentage of national income, 5.3)	¥12 trillion	(percentage of national income, 8.8)	22.0	18
Private investment for pollution control (1965 prices)	¥0.2 trillion		¥2 trillion		34.1	
II. Profile of Economy						
Gross national product (1965 prices)	¥58 trillion		¥105 trillion		about 9	11
Gross national product (current prices)[c]	¥73 trillion	100	¥183 trillion	100	14	16
Personal consumption expenditures	¥38 trillion	51	¥95 trillion	52	14	15
Government fixed capital formation	¥6 trillion	9	¥23 trillion	13	18	18
Private plant and equipment investment	¥15 trillion	20	¥28 trillion	15	11	17
Private housing investment	¥5 trillion	7	¥17 trillion	9	20	22
Exports of goods and services and factor income re-						

ceived from abroad (less) Imports of goods and services and factor income paid abroad	¥9 trillion	12	¥21 trillion	11	14	17
	¥8 trillion	11	¥19 trillion	10	17	16
Balance of payments on current account[d]	$2.4 billion		$5.9 billion		not more than 5	5.7
Personal consumption expenditure deflator[e]	132		187			
Deflator for private inventory stocks[e]	109		126		about 2	1.4
Ratio of social insurance premiums to national income (percentage)	4.6		7.3			
Tax and non-tax (social insurance premiums, etc.) obligations (as percentage of national income)	21.7		f			
Balance of government revenue and expenditure (current prices)	0		−¥6 trillion[g]			

Source: Table 2 of *The Basic Economic and Social Plan, 1973–77*, with a few changes in wording.

[a] All figures are for the fiscal year, April 1 to March 31.
[b] Cumulative amount of investment between 1973 and 1977: ¥90 trillion (1973 prices), including Okinawa.
[c] Figures in 1977 include Okinawa Prefecture. Elsewhere Okinawa has not been included unless otherwise noted.
[d] Difference between receipts and payments on current account; positive figure indicates a surplus.
[e] Index figures with 1965 = 100.
[f] The Plan envisages a 3% increase from 1973 to 1977.
[g] Negative figure indicates a deficit.

The above might give an impression that the Economic Council or its members are responsible for preparing the plan. In reality, it may be said without much exaggeration that the Council members' involvement in plan-making is minimal. In the first place, the Council has many subcommittees. The total number of members of these subcommittees amounted almost to two hundred in the case of the latest plan. They are again dominated by corporate executives and ex-government officials. Preparation and deliberation of the plan were done mainly at meetings of these subcommittees. The Council itself met only a few times: usually it simply approves whatever is prepared by subcommittees or by the secretariat. Membership on the Council is largely honorary. After all, most members are very busy men with their own business or profession and can afford little time to study national economic problems carefully. The last point also applies to the members of the subcommittees.

Hence, it is only natural that the secretariat for the Council, the Economic Planning Agency (EPA)—or more precisely its Bureau of Comprehensive Planning—dominates the process of plan-making. In addition to the officials of EPA, officials of various ministries and agencies attend the meetings whenever matters on which they have jurisdiction are discussed. Together with officials of the EPA, they act as the secretariat of subcommittees: they collect necessary materials, prepare documents, and draft plans. Indeed, the ministries and agencies have a very strong voice on subjects relevant to them.

It might be asked what happens if the opinions of the members of the Council or its subcommittees are opposed to those of government officials. Such a conflict rarely happens. All members know that the officials of ministries and agencies have virtual vetoes, and do not waste time fighting against them. To begin with, the EPA selects as members of the Council or its subcommittees only those who will behave well, that is, those who cooperate with government officials. It is easy to recruit cooperative and more or less capable members, since being a member of the Council, one of its subcommittees, or any other governmental committee carries some public (rather than professional) prestige, although pecuniary remuneration is negligible. Also, for those outside of the government, the access to information is often an important advantage drawn from being a member of a government committee.

The nature of the national economic plan

The two components of Japan's national economic plan mentioned above must be distinguished in discussing the nature of the plan. On the one hand, the national plan is a compilation of current opinions on economic policy issues, and to the extent that the planning targets for specific policy aims (see Table 2) reflect the conclusions which have been reached by the various councils and ministries having jurisdiction over them, such targets in the plan are more or less thought of as something to be achieved through governmental efforts during the planning period. But since such planning targets are discussed and set by the respective councils and ministries first, and since the national plan is simply a collection of such planning targets independently arrived at with little attempt at coordination and elimination of inconsistencies among targets, it is misleading to consider the national plan as setting binding policy targets in individual policy areas.

On the other hand, the national economic plan gives "estimates" for macroeconomic variables such as the rate of growth of real GNP, its components, the balance of payments, the price indices, and so on during the planning period. This part of the plan is a prediction or a long-term forecast, as reliable or unreliable as a long-term weather forecast, of the future state of the economy, with some flavor of wishful thinking added.

The national economic plan is not binding: nobody feels much obliged to observe, or be responsible for, the figures given in the plan. This is especially true of estimates for macroeconomic variables (in Table 3), but is true also of planning targets for specific policy aims (in Table 2). The Ministry of Finance, the most powerful government ministry in economic policy matters, has not been enthusiastic about rigid economic planning, and for understandable reasons. Other government offices too have considered the national economic plan as primarily a forecast rather than a rigid plan which must be followed faithfully. I will explain the reasons why the national plan has been considered as nonbinding, first in regard to the private sector, and then in regard to the public sector.

Private sector. Past macroeconometric experience shows that it is difficult to predict variables pertaining primarily to the private sector with any accuracy for planning purposes beyond the time span of six months or at most one year. Two major sources of error in macroeconometric prediction are (i) changes in the economic structure over time, or the failure of behavioral equations in the macroeconometric model used to give good estimates for the future, even when exogenous variables to be given from outside the model are correctly predicted; and (ii) errors in predicting exogenous variables. My general impression is that for private investment in plant and equipment, certain categories of inventory investment, and price deflators, errors due to (i) are substantial; whereas for exports and the balance of payments, the main source of error is (ii).

The fact that errors of type (i) have been substantial, indicates that we do not yet know the mechanism of the economy accurately enough for the purpose of planning. Private firms in contemporary Japan are still a fertile source of energy and creative initiative, and their activities can often be unpredictable.

Suppose, for example, that in one year private investment in plant and equipment in a certain sector rises sharply beyond the "planned" level. Should private investment then be restrained, and if the answer is yes, by what means? At least in Japan, in most cases the government does not know whether it is desirable from a national economic point of view to restrain such an unexpected rise in private investment beyond the "planned" level. The government may tighten the money supply if it expects overall inflationary pressure to develop as a result of a general rise in private investment. Or it may intervene in a particular sector if an obvious excess capacity situation is foreseen as a result of too high a rate of investment there. Generally speaking, however, the "planned" figures in the medium-term national economic plan have never been considered as binding targets according to which the government should regulate the variables pertaining to the private sector.

In addition to unexpected developments from within the Japanese economy, there are errors of type (ii), that is, errors in predicting exogenous variables. From a planning point of view, the international economic conditions that will surround Japan several years ahead are especially difficult to predict. Unpredictable changes in world economic conditions can affect substantially the course of an economy, such as the Japanese, heavily dependent on international economic relations.

For these reasons the Japanese government has not paid much attention to the national economic plan when making short-run policy decisions affecting the private sector. Its macroeconomic policies, fiscal and monetary policies in particular, are determined primarily by considering the levels of domestic effective demand and employment, the balance of payments and movements of price indices. When the government steers fiscal and monetary policies watching these macroeconomic indicators, it can naturally end up with overall and sectoral growth rates which are quite different from those given in the medium-term plan, and discrepancies accumulate as time goes by.

It must also be noted that for many variables pertaining to the private sector, the government may not really have at hand policy instruments which can be used to correct effectively the actual course of these variables when they deviate from their "planned" course. Just consider, for example, Japan's huge balance-of-payments surpluses in the last few years, and how difficult and painful it has been to reduce them. Another example is price inflation: not only in Japan but in many countries of the world governments are having great difficulties in restraining the rise in prices.

Public sector. It might be asked whether the government follows the plan at least with regard to variables pertaining to the public sector: what is the use of the plan if the government itself does not feel obliged to observe, for example, the planned level of its own public investment in individual fields?

There are several reasons why even the planned levels of variables pertaining to the public sector are not closely followed by government ministries and agencies, except possibly at the very beginning of the planning period. First, when the actual GNP, the level of private investment, the balance of payments, and so on differ substantially from their predicted levels, it is meaningless or even harmful to stick to the plan only so far as the public sector is concerned. To do so will destroy the balance between the public and private sectors.[5]

Second, the government budget and "investment and financing plan" are voted upon by the National Diet on a rigid annual basis. Only in very special cases does the Diet allow the government to make commitments on capital expenditures beyond the fiscal year. In a democratic society, the Diet and the government budget should respond to the changing needs of its citizens, and the principle of annual deliberation of the government budget has never been challenged. In particular, the parties opposing the government party are against long-term commitments and planning, in the hope that they will win power in the next election and will change economic policies drastically.

Third, the Ministry of Finance, and especially its Budget Bureau, the most influential government office in the matter of economic policy, has a tradition of economy in, and non-commitment to, public expenditures. Officials of the Budget Bureau always try to economize and curtail public expenditures in the face of other ministries' and agencies' requests for appropriations. Budget officials think that if the Ministry of Finance once in some way commits itself to a long-term expenditure plan, it would be difficult to cancel or reduce the expenditures for a certain item previously agreed upon in the plan, whereas there will always be requests for new or additional appropriations when circumstances change. Thus according to their view a long-range plan for government expenditure or public investment will give rise to an expansionary bias or a tendency for "increasing fiscal rigidity" which they want to avoid.[6]

Also, not only do officials of the Ministry of Finance have an inclination to dislike long-term fiscal planning, but long-run planning is really difficult in regard to certain fiscal expenditures. Certain items in the budget, such as rice-price supports, national medical insurance, price and investment policies of national railways, social security and welfare programs, and national defense plans, have long been difficult political issues, and are very hotly debated during the process of budget compilation every year. Anyone who knows the political conflicts on these issues can understand that it is really difficult to make a long-run quantitative plan for these expenditure items.

Forecast rather than planning

Thus nobody considers the national economic plan as a rigid, binding plan which must be followed by the government. When the Ministry of Finance makes decisions on the annual budget, the Bank of Japan on money supply, and the Ministry of International Trade and Industry (MITI) on industrial policies, they pay little attention to the national economic plan. There is not much substance in the national plan which can be usefully referred to when government ministries and agencies make important policy decisions in their respective fields. Or putting it differently, it appears that government ministries and agencies other than the Economic Planning Agency tend to try to incorporate in the national economic plan as little as possible of those elements which they consider may bind them rigidly and undesirably in the future.

Therefore, Japan's national economic plan should be interpreted as a long-term forecast, with some flavor of wishful thinking by the planmakers, as far as its quantitative aspects are concerned. Interpreted in this way, it is not surprising that the government publishes a five-year national plan as often as once every two or three years. This is similar to a long-range (one to three months) weather forecast announced once or twice a month.

The reason for the national plans and their effects on growth

If the national economic plans have not been intended to regulate the variables pertaining to either the private or the public sector, one might ask, first, what is the reason for or the use of such plans—what functions are they supposed to perform—and second, what their effect is upon Japan's economic growth.

My immediate reaction to the first question is that in a democratic society in which various political forces of different strength are at work, the existing institutions such as economic plans, the tariff system, and price controls—or the government agencies responsible for them—are not always performing useful functions from the viewpoint of the economy or the society as a whole. Quite often they are established, or continue to exist, as a result of politically influential groups acting in their own interests, or simply as a political compromise between powerful pressure groups. This is quite different from the situation in which a single optimizing entity makes consistent, rational decisions. A democratic society cannot be supposed to behave always consistently and rationally, as an individual or as an enterprise might be.

Moreover, illusions, misunderstandings, and wrong theories, sometimes willfully cultivated and exploited by certain groups to their advantage, often play an important role. Therefore, one must not suppose that there is always a good "reason" for the existing economic plans or that they always perform some useful functions for the society.

In the period immediately after the war, the Japanese public's confidence in the functioning of price mechanisms was at a low point, and great hopes were entertained for national economic planning. Once the Economic Planning Agency was established, it became very difficult to curtail its personnel or to change its name to "forecasting" or "research," instead of "planning"—not to speak of abolishing it. The EPA and plan-making became a convenient platform for information exchanges among government ministries and between the government and the private sector, although national economic planning has turned out to amount to little more than forecasting.

From the private sector's point of view, there is little reason to object to the present arrangement. The big businesses obtain information through their representatives participating in the plan-making process. Nongovernment political parties are strongly against the national economic plans published by the Conservative government, because of the growth-oriented, pro-business bias of the plans, but they are not against economic planning as such, for obvious ideological reasons.

Turning now to the question of the effects of the national plans on economic growth, it seems to me that what is called the "announcement effect" of the national economic plans might have been quite substantial, especially in the case of the "Income Doubling" ten-year plan in 1960. However, the announcement effect would have depended not so much on the contents of the plans as on the government's political will, expressed in the plan, to give a top priority to

industrial growth. It is sometimes argued that indicative planning
would promote growth by reducing uncertainty and business risks
through information exchanges. But apparently this has not been the
case in Japan, as earlier national economic plans persistently underestimated both the growth rate and structural changes substantially,
and therefore one cannot say that uncertainty was reduced much by
economic planning.

The Income Doubling Plan was much publicized by the then Prime
Minister Ikeda, and probably carried a considerable propaganda
effect. It looked more or less plausible and prompted private firms to
invest more boldly than before. For some time after its publication,
it became fashionable among larger companies to publish their own
overall long-term management plan for a five- or ten-year period. When
making companies' plans, the national or sectoral rate of growth was
taken for granted, so to speak, and each company added a plus factor
to the industry average rate of growth, hoping for an increasing market
share for itself. But here again in practice few companies paid much
attention to their long-term plan in making actual investment decisions,
since most such plans turned out to underestimate growth potentials.
Shortly afterwards, long-term management planning went out of
fashion.

Thus the Income Doubling Plan may be said to have had a considerable impact on Japan's growth in the early 1960s. However, what was
important was not so much the contents of the national plans as the
political will to promote industrial growth. Even without national
plans, if the government would have made clear its willingness to promote growth, and fiscal, monetary, and industrial policy measures for
that purpose, almost the same effect would have been obtained. The
situation would then have been similar to West Germany in postwar
years.

Japan's national economic plan thus amounts to little more than a
long-range forecast. Yet this does not mean that the Japanese economy
is an overwhelmingly free market economy run without much governmental planning. In fact, the government intervenes extensively in
particular industries and markets, but governmental planning or policy
is primarily organized on an industry or sectoral basis. Before turning
to this question, however, I shall discuss briefly Japanese regional
plans, which are similar in important respects to national plans.

Regional Plans

Regional planning is quite extensive in Japan. Roughly speaking there are at least three different kinds of regional plans. First, there have been long-term nationwide regional plans concerned with regional distribution of population, industries, and national income. The National Comprehensive Development Plan published in 1962 and the New National Comprehensive Development Plan published in 1969, both prepared by the Bureau of Comprehensive Development of the Economic Planning Agency, are two overall regional plans hitherto adopted by the government. The 1969 Plan, for example, gives projections of income and population for seven major regions of Japan in 1985, on the one hand, and describes those policies affecting regional distribution of population and industry which are deemed desirable by plan-makers, on the other. Plans of this type are similar to national economic plans in character: that is, a combination of forecasts, wishful thinking and prevailing opinions. For each region the 1969 Plan lists almost indiscriminately all kinds of measures which are supposed to be desirable from a regional development point of view: public investment in roads, railroads and port facilities; modernization of agriculture; development of dairy farming, fishery, forestry, manufacturing, and the tourist industry; and prevention of pollution, investment in housing, and so on. But the Plan gives almost no figures at all, except a very rough regional breakdown of national income and population, nor does it commit the government in any way.

Second, in certain types of the central government's regional programs, (i) certain areas are designated as covered under the program, and (ii) special incentives, such as tax relief and low-interest loans from government financial institutions, are given to private firms in the areas, or to firms which will build new plants in the areas. Also, (iii) special grants or funds from the central government are allocated to local governments within the areas, and (iv) priority is given to the areas covered by the program in central government investment in roads, port facilities, railways, industrial water supply, and other social overhead capital.

For example, under the "New Industrial Cities Program" introduced in 1962, fifteen areas out of more than forty applications from all over Japan were designated as "new industrial city" areas, and measures (ii) through (iv), which were supposed to promote industrialization, were adopted. One "new industrial city" area usually comprised several cities and towns, and fifteen such areas were selected as new areas for immediate industrial development. For this type of plan the Economic Planning Agency has the final responsibility, but the Ministry of Finance, Ministry of Local Governments, MITI, and the local governments concerned participate in the planning process.

This type of plan includes fiscal measures (ii), (iii), and (iv), and whether they are successful or not in promoting regional development as planned,[7] the government is committed to implement the plans at least to some extent, and it appears that some plans are often effective in channeling resources to particular regions. Private enterprises and population are often attracted by incentive measures and public investment in infrastructure, but usually it is not easy to separate their effects from other factors in regional development.

Third, there are programs involving only the central government's assistance to the local governments. For example, under a program begun in 1970 to assist communities suffering from a rapid decline in population, any town or village losing more than 10 percent of its population in a five-year period is eligible for special grants-in-aid or low-interest funds from the central government.

The above are examples of nationwide regional programs. There are also regional plans for particular areas in which the central government participates. Proliferation of regional planning has reached such a stage of overlap that the overall total area covered under various regional plans authorized by the central governments is said to be several times the total area of Japan.

It may be mentioned in this connection that in Japan public finance of local governments (prefectures, cities, towns, and villages) is highly integrated with that of the central government. Its Ministry of Finance and Ministry of Local Governments are in a very powerful position to influence local governments' finance, and the degree of fiscal autonomy of local government is very limited.

II. Japan's Industrial Policy?

The term "industrial policy" was until recently seldom used in English, and while found somewhat more often in Continental Europe, was not too familiar even there. It is safe to say that the term is also of relatively recent vintage in Japan. There is today an Industrial Policy Bureau within the Ministry of International Trade and Industry (MITI), but even within MITI the term was not widely used until around 1970. Prior to that time, various facets of industrial policy were discussed in terms of industrial rationalization, the rationalization of firms, industrial structure and its modernization, a new industrial system, industrial reorganization, and the like.

In the past I defined industrial policy as "government policies taken in order to change allocation of resources among industries or the level of some economic activity of the constituent firms of an industry. In other words, industrial policy aims at increasing production, investment, research and development, modernization or restructuring in some industry or industries, and decreasing them in other industries. Protective tariffs and excise taxes on luxuries are "classical" examples of policies under this definition."

I now feel that this definition needs to be broadened and amplified.

When examined logically from the standpoint of economic theory, several points can be made concerning what is labeled in the press and in government circles as industrial policy. First, the "industry" of industrial policy is in most cases assumed to be manufacturing and hence does not include agriculture, construction, services,[8] or transportation. Electric power and other energy-related sectors are under the purview of MITI, however, and thus are commonly included as objects of industrial policy. It is normally unclear whether mining is to be considered an object of industrial policy.[9]

Next, if we look at the "policy" part of industrial policy, we can group its content into several categories:

(1) Policies that affect the allocation of resources to industry, including

(a) Items that affect the infrastructure of industry in general, such as the provision of industrial sites, roads and ports, industrial water supplies, and electric power,[10] and

(b) Items that affect inter-industry resource allocation.

(2) Policies that affect industrial organization, including

(c) Items aimed at regulating the internal organization of particular industries, such as industrial restructuring, consolidation of firms, output restrictions, and the adjustment of output and investment, and

(d) Items affecting cross-industry organization, such as small and medium enterprise measures.

Of these groupings, (b) is what would be thought of as industrial policy in the narrow sense of my original definition, while the guiding principle of (d) in postwar Japan was the prevention and elimination of "excess" competition (leaving aside for the time being what is implied by this term). I cannot find a clear guiding principle behind small and medium enterprise policy, but my strong impression is that it consists of *ad hoc* measures of varying content adopted under the political pressures faced in a parliamentary democracy, without any apparent ideal or theoretical basis.[11]

The Economic Case for Industrial Policy

Current industrial policies are directed toward various goals, many of which are noneconomic. The classification of what constitutes economic and what constitutes noneconomic is inevitably in part subjective. The term "economic" will be used in a narrow sense henceforth. Thus it will be held that, for example, measures to promote local industries and aid regional development, measures to restrain consumption of alcohol and luxury goods, and measures designed to increase the self-sufficiency of certain goods for national security reasons are all noneconomic. Such noneconomic policies are obviously quite wide ranging. The focus of this chapter will be on industrial policy undertaken for narrowly economic reasons. In addition to policies for the above noneconomic goals, policies aimed at redistributing income or shifting population among regions will not be directly examined.[12]

In the following subsections, I will briefly discuss the theoretical underpinnings of industrial policy and examine postwar debates and practices, limiting myself to policies that are undertaken for reasons specific to conditions in particular industries, and that are designed to affect the allocation of resources among industries.

Theoretical basis

If we confine our attention to those policies aimed at intervening in interindustry resource allocation, we can define, from the standpoint of economic theory, the content of industrial policy to be those policies that fall under areas (a) and (b) above: namely, those interventions which are to cope with what are called "market failures," that is, failures of the market mechanism or price mechanism in allocating resources efficiently. Subject to certain conditions, the market, that is, the price mechanism, has proven capable of playing a very substantial role in the efficient allocation of resources; nevertheless, it fails under certain conditions or in the face of certain types of problems, leading to a less-than optimal allocation of resources. I believe the central function of industrial policy (narrowly defined) is to prevent possible market failures or to compensate for them as they occur.[13]

Once it is agreed that industrial policy may be necessary in the face of such market failures, the following four problems must be considered.

1. What sort of conditions will be recognized as constituting market failures?

2. What sort of policy measures are appropriate in response to the various types of market failure?

3. While it is true that markets may fail, the government may fail too. How are "government failures or policy failures" to be dealt with?

4. In most cases, industrial policy measures incur costs, including budgetary outlays, and are also accompanied by side effects. These cannot in practice be ignored, thus the policy benefits and the various costs must be weighed. How is this to be done? It certainly cannot be said that the government should always intervene whenever there is a market failure.

All of these are difficult problems, and there is much room for divergence of opinion on each of these points, even among informed and disinterested observers. Yet, discussing industrial policy in terms of "market failures" enables the use of terms familiar to economic analysis, such as the presence of economies of scale and externalities, the elimination of monopoly, the criteria for promoting infant industries, the promotion of research and development and technical change, the building of infrastructure, the dealing with uncertainties in the course of economic development, and the control of environmental pollution.

In the period immediately after World War II, however, the officials who were responsible for industrial policy in Japan, along with a group of academic economists who were close to them, did not accept the basic approach to industrial policy outlined above, at least in public pronouncements. Thus they refused to examine industrial policy in terms of the concepts of economics. Instead they argued that Japan, as a country with little land, few natural resources, and a large population, obviously had to have an industrial policy, or that to "catch up" with the industrialized nations of the west or to improve the international competitiveness of Japan's industry required industrial policy.

In contrast, from the perspective of economic theory, differing resource endowments, being a latecomer, or undergoing reconstruction from war does not in itself constitute a market failure; witness in this regard the case of West Germany after World War II. As is clear from the cases of Hong Kong and Singapore, with little land and dense populations it may be better to rely on the operation of the price mechanism, which may in fact lead to faster industrialization. I therefore do not think that such reasons as mentioned above in themselves provide a case for policy intervention.

In any event, until about the mid-1970s, it was hard in Japan to have a dialogue between academic economists and policymakers about industrial policy, while even among academics and economic writers it took a long time for the common theoretical base given here to be accepted. There was little in common between the arguments of those who studied from the standpoint of economic theory and those of the older generation who operated in the "prehistoric" period.[14]

Policy versus practice

While there may have been a big gap between economic theory and the "leitmotif" of industrial policy (or the ideology of the policymakers) in the period immediately after World War II, at the same time there also was a large gap between the ideology of the policymakers and the slogans they used on the one hand, and the policies they actually implemented on the other. To illustrate this, let me briefly summarize the rationale and practice of industrial policy, dividing the postwar era into three subperiods.

Reconstruction era

During the period immediately after the war, the main tasks for industrial policy were held to be reconstruction and achieving economic independence. The themes of this era included (1) the priority production system, (2) the promotion of "basic" industries,[15] (3) the supplying of "basic" raw materials at low and stable prices, and (4) the encouragement of exports. These themes reflect the dregs of prewar and wartime economic thinking with its emphasis on wartime economic controls and planning, such as the "materials mobilization planning." The influence of the Soviet Gosplan model on prewar and wartime "progressive" bureaucrats and scholars seems to have been carried over into this period. There is room to doubt, however, the economic rationality of these policies or the way of thinking that they reflected, even given the economic chaos that then prevailed.[16] It would be an interesting project to investigate this question more deeply.

In any event, for a considerable period after the end of the war, even as late as 1962, examples of prewar and wartime economic thinking can easily be found. One such example is the Petroleum Industry Law with its presumption of pervasive direct government controls for the purpose of "providing for a stable and inexpensive supply of oil." Such a law reflected the strong influence of wartime government materials planning, though another contribution was the memory of the oil embargo placed on Japan by the United States and its allies, one of the causes of Japan's entry into World War II. There was no likelihood, however, of any particular market failures for petroleum products in the 1960s, and I do not believe there was any necessity for government intervention and controls.[17]

I think there was not much of a gap between the ideology or slogans of industrial policy and the policies that were actually carried out during the early postwar period. In a system that incorporated more or less direct controls, industries thought "important" or "basic" were provided with subsidies and low-interest finance and were given priority in import allocations. The authority of the responsible government departments was strong at the time, and not a few businessmen were heard to mutter that they could not manage to get even simple things settled without daily visits to the Ministry of International Trade and Industry.[18]

High-growth era

During the period of rapid economic growth, the ideology of the formulators of industrial policy was symbolized by the slogans "building heavy and chemical industry" and "improving the industrial structure." Within manufacturing, a "vision" was drawn up that proposed actively fostering industries that met the dual criteria of experiencing a rapid increase in productivity and producing goods with a high income elasticity of demand.[19] It is exactly this type of thinking that typified the "prehistoric" era I characterized above, for if goods are produced by an industry in which rapid productivity increases are occurring and for which the income elasticity of demand is high, then the industry will grow on its own. Hence there is no reason why, due to these two criteria, such an industry should be made a particular object for promotion by the government.

It was during this period that a considerable gap developed between the policies that were actually implemented and the ideology or guiding principles (or at least the slogans and catch phrases) of the formulators of industrial policy. For example, government officials had no intention of promoting industries such as tourism, supermarkets, and fast-food restaurants, however well these industries satisfied the above criteria.

I believe rather that industrial policy in Japan generally aimed to develop industries that government officials—with the backing of public opinion—felt Japan should have; the above criteria for industrial policy were extraneous rationalizations. After the war, the industries that policymakers or the general public felt Japan should have were iron and steel, shipbuilding, a merchant marine, machine industries in general, heavy electrical equipment, and chemicals. Later on they added automobiles, petrochemicals, nuclear power, and the like, and recently industries such as computers and semiconductors have been added. One might inquire why the Japanese people wanted these industries in particular, but policymakers had to attach some sort of rationale, and often this was not easy to do. In sum, I believe that the government promoted exactly those industries that most people felt the country had to have. Of such industries, about the only one to date that has not been firmly established in Japan is the aircraft industry.

To give a specific example, for the protection of shipping and shipbuilding, planned shipbuilding has been continued over many years for such stated reasons as rebuilding the merchant fleet, expanding fleet capacity, saving foreign exchange, improving the invisible trade balance, and so on. In the late 1960s, I was asked by officials in charge of the shipping and shipbuilding industries for an appropriate rationalization for planned shipbuilding at a time when the balance of payments was no longer in deficit but was instead showing increasing surpluses. The policymakers, and those related to the various industries were working on the assumption that such policies should be continued, and they were only concerned that it was proving difficult to come up with a rationale for the policies that would obtain public acceptance.

On the other hand, during the period of rapid growth and into the next period, quite a few new industries developed, many of which achieved remarkable success in exporting worldwide. Early on they were the industries that produced such goods as sewing machines, cameras, bicycles, motorcycles, pianos, zippers, and transistor radios. From the middle of the 1960s on, the list included the manufacturers of color television sets, tape recorders, magnetic recording tape, audio equipment, fishing gear, watches and clocks, calculators, electric wire, machine tools, numerically controlled machine tools, textile machinery, agricultural machinery, insulators, communications equipment, ceramics, and robots. These industries developed with little dependence on protection and promotion policies. The majority of the firms in these growth industries started from almost nothing after the war or at most were very small firms. They developed on their own without particular benefits from industrial policy measures. It would undoubtedly be the executives of these firms who would disagree most vehemently with the statement that industrial policy in Japan was extremely strong, systematic, and comprehensive. Given a chance to speak, they would proclaim that they had succeeded on their own, through strenuous labor in the face of great difficulties, and not because of government favors that in fact seldom came their way.

What, then, were the sort of industries that policymakers and public opinion believed it was desirable for Japan to have? This is a very difficult question, but my impression is that the industries that those who formulated policy wanted Japan very much to have and to which they devoted much effort in protecting and fostering were those that involved an element of national prestige. It seems that the desired industries were those that met the following two general requirements. First, they had to be the industries, symbolic of industrial might, that had already been developed by countries more advanced than Japan: "modern states" from the Meiji period to the early post-WWII years, "advanced countries" in the period of rapid growth, and "technologically leading nations" from the 1970s on. The industries themselves were seen as ones that Japan could develop with a greater or lesser amount of effort (meaning protection and promotion). Second, these industries had to have a certain size, so that the theme of their development could garner people's attention, that is they had to have "news value" both domestically and internationally. Industries that met these two criteria gained the attention of policymakers as candidates worthy of protection and promotion policies.[20]

One could think of the following industries as meeting these two criteria: iron and steel, machinery, heavy electric machinery, ocean transport, shipbuilding, air transport, petrochemicals, nuclear power, aircraft manufacturing, computers, and integrated circuits. In contrast, many of the export industries listed above, which showed spectacular development after the war, did not meet either of these two requirements, regardless of whether they fulfilled the requirements of high income elasticity and rapid productivity growth (which are in themselves dubious as criteria). The camera, bicycle, watch, tape recorder, and magnetic tape industries are good examples in that they did not have much attractiveness as objects for promotion and protection in terms of public appeal and consequently did not receive much emphasis.

During the period right after the war policymakers possessed a fair amount of leverage over industries and private firms through their power of approval of import licenses, foreign capital inflows, and technology import (patent and knowhow licensing) permits; the use of Japan Development Bank loans; and the designation of special tax measures. During the rapid growth era the leverage of the government disappeared gradually, or at least its importance declined drastically, with the liberalization of import and capital movements—direct investment, joint ventures with foreign firms, and technology imports. Thus despite wide coverage in the press and the pervasiveness of various catch phrases, throughout this period the reality of industrial policy was that intervention declined in importance and the price mechanism and the autonomous decisions of enterprises under competitive pressure came to play the central role in allocating resources among industries.

Since the oil crisis

As the 1970s unfolded, the interventionist and direct control coloration of the thinking of the formulators of industrial policy began to recede, and gradually a critical attitude toward policy excesses and a more positive view of the price mechanism became prevalent. In this period, trade and direct foreign investment were liberalized, tariff and nontariff trade barriers were lowered, and the economies of the advanced nations became more tightly integrated. With this development, foreign criticism of the artificial protective policies of the Japanese government heightened. Thus the gap between economic theory and bureaucratic ideology rapidly lessened.

But it still remains unclear what the thinking is behind the concept of raising the "knowledge-intensity" of Japan's industry put forth by the Industrial Structure Council. Will such knowledge-intensive and high-technology industries develop by themselves, or is policy intervention in the form of artificial protection really crucial? And if protection and promotion are required, through what policy tools can this actually be accomplished? Furthermore, fashion design, information-processing software, the advertising industry, and management consulting are knowledge-intensive industries, but it does not seem that the industrial policy authorities feels they should be promoted. They are not the kind of industries that either policymakers or the public think of as enhancing national prestige and hence requiring artificial promotion.

In addition, during this period more and more industries have been turning to the government for industrial "adjustment assistance." These industries are not limited to agriculture and mining, but include manufacturing industries in decline or suffering under comparative disadvantage in the face of high wage and energy costs or depressed markets for their goods on a worldwide basis. Examples include all types of textiles, nonferrous metal refining, and shipbuilding. In terms of the fiscal burden of industrial adjustment assistance and protection from import competition, the relative weight of declining and internationally uncompetitive industries in industrial policy has been increasing since the high-growth period. The most prominent examples of industries in decline are coal mining, textiles, ocean transport and shipbuilding, nonferrous metals, and petrochemicals. I believe that the direct and indirect cost of backward-looking policies to help such industries has, since the high-growth era, exceeded the cost of resources devoted in a forward-looking way to the development of new, promsing industries.

Excess Competition

In Japan, from the end of the war through today, one guiding principle for the formulators of industrial policy with respect to intra-industry organization has been the prevention of excess competition. Even now one finds in newspapers countless times the statement that a given measure is being used, or should be used, to prevent excess competition. But in terms of economic theory, most of the arguments put forward in debates on excess competition are unclear on the damage done and on the necessity for government intervention to prevent it. Hardly any participants in these debates have bothered to explain with any degree of clarity what they mean by excess competition. One of the few attempts to define excess competition by those who stress the need to prevent it is that of Yoshihiko Morozumi. According to Morozumi, "'excess' competition is competition such that the losses to the national economy exceed the gains that arise from that competition."[21] But his definition is little more than a tautology and the meaning of "loss" or "gain" to the "national economy" is vague. It cannot be said that this definition has much substantive content.

It is sometimes claimed by economists who are critical of the idea that the "excessive" competition of J.S. Bain (1968) is relatively close to the bureaucrats' use of "excess" competition.[22] Briefly, Bain's use of the term refers to a condition in an unconcentrated industry in which the majority of firms earn little profit or even operate at a loss, the transfer of productive resources (principally labor) to other uses and exit by constituent firms is not rapid, so that low profitability or losses continue for a long time.

This industrial organization concept differs, however, in two important aspects from the excess competition of Japanese practitioners. First, the Japanese term literally means "more than appropriate," and as symbolized by Morozumi's discussion of gains and losses to the national economy, the normative sense of the term is dominant and reflects the user's value judgment that the condition referred to is not desirable. In contrast, Bain's excessive competition refers to an objective phenomenon for purposes of analysis, and does not reflect in itself a value judgment. Furthermore, in spite of the strong value judgment reflected in the Japanese use of excess competition, the value premises on which the judgment is based is never made clear. The lack of content of phrases such as "gains or losses to the national economy" is a characteristic trait of debates over excess competition by policymakers and industry represen tatives.

Second, the term "excessive competition" in Bain's sense refers to a competitive, unconcentrated industry with a large number of firms, such as the numerous small coal mines of West Virginia in the United States or the weaving sheds run as a self-employment sideline by many small farmers in Japan. In Japan, however, the term "excess competition" has been used in conjunction with demands for the lessening of competition in all sorts of industries, not only in unconcentrated industries. Such industries include competitive oligopolies, concentrated tight oligopolies, industries in which market prices are unregulated, and publicly regulated industries (such as domestic scheduled airline service).

There is much dispute among academic economists on how to deal with the phenomenon of excess competition. But it is safe to say that in general economists, especially those specializing in industrial organization, feel this concept has no analytic value. They thus tend to be dubious of, or hostile to, the demands that accompany the use of this term by government officials or business executives.

The *genkyoku* system

In Japan there is a strong tendency for a *genkyoku*, the ministerial bureau, division, or section under whose jurisidiction a given industry falls, to want its industry to be orderly and well organized and for there to be no disturbances of any kind. I venture to say that the notion of excess competition is related to the Confucian concept of appropriate elder/younger relations. In other words, there seems to be a tendency for the government officials in charge of an industry to feel that the ideal situation is one in which an industry is composed of only a few firms whose market shares are stable and whose rankings in terms of sales, profits, and number of employees are unchanging. The reason should be fairly clear. When there is strong competition, some firms go bankrupt or at any rate clear losers appear, and they and third parties who suffer losses go running to the government to ask for aid and succor. It is the bureaucrats who then suffer in turn, in trying to clear up the mess. In such situations, bureaucrats may have to answer questions in the Diet or face the examining eye of the press about what is going on and how they could have permitted such a situation to arise in their domain. Thus government officials have no desire to see excess competition, or, for that matter, competition in any form, arise in their jurisdiction. They would much prefer for a stable order to be maintained in which all firms make a reasonable profit and in which "junior" firms respect their "elders." Thus officials have tried to see to it that, whenever possible, measures are instituted that assure that none of their firms get into trouble, that their firms remain profitable, and that their industry is not faced with the specter of import competition or the entry of foreign firms.

In order to exclude excess competition, the officials in the *genkyoku* for an industry have come to think it desirable, when possible, to reorganize an industry or to consolidate firms. Countless examples from many industries can be given in which the *genkyoku* has raised the banner of reorganization and consolidation, and for which it has provided incentives in varying degrees. Likewise during recessions, when prices tend to decline and firms to run in the red, officials come to think it desirable for prices to be maintained as much as possible so that no firm will go bankrupt. Thus, there is a need to implement some sort of pricing agreement, recession cartel, output restriction, production controls, orderly investment program, or the like—or at least so it is often claimed. It is not surprising that there are policies for which it is almost impossible to find any positive benefit from an economic perspective, yet about which the responsible bureaucrats are enthusiastic and raise a fanfare. One example of this is the reorganizing of industry through large-scale mergers, such as that of Fuji Steel and Yahata Steel (to form Nippon Steel) or of the Dai-Ichi and Kangyo Banks (to form Dai-Ichi Kangyo Bank).

Even the Ministry of Finance, which is relatively liberally oriented with regard to economic policy, tends in its capacity as a *genkyoku* to be intent on restraining price competition. For example, the Ministry has long controlled the retail prices of alcoholic beverages under the provisions of the Liquor Tax Law and continued to regulate bank deposit interest rates, insurance premium rates, issuing terms for bonds, and fees for securities transactions, *de facto* or *de jure*.

This preference for upholding the existing "Confucian" order, the striving to maintain and extend authority over industry, the xenophobic tendency to exclude foreigners, is not limited to MITI (though recently MITI has changed). It also can be found in the Ministry of Finance, the Ministry of Health and Welfare (pharmaceuticals), the Ministry of Transport (shipbuilding, ocean transport, airlines, and all types of surface transport), the Ministry of Agriculture, Forestry, and Fisheries (food processing along with all types of agriculture, forestry, and fisheries), and elsewhere.

Among these ministries, MITI was the first to pay heed to the argument presented by academic economists, switching to policies that place more emphasis on the workings of the price mechanism and the role of interfirm competition. MITI's policies also reflect a change in thinking that emphasizes closer international economic relations rather than an orientation toward a closed economy, viewing favorably the implications of freer trade and foreign direct investment in Japan. Thus the statement that "industrial policy consists of the policies formulated and implemented by MITI"[23] is artfully and teasingly put, but not quite accurate. Rather, it should be phrased that "in postwar Japan, industrial policy consists of the policies pursued by the various *genkyoku* of the government."

Industrial policy and antitrust policy

The predilection of the *genkyoku* bureaucrats for limiting competition and restructuring—that is, for encouraging mergers, vertical and horizontal firm groupings, and interfirm operating agreements—is fundamentally at odds with antitrust policy. Thus the various ministries, and in particular MITI, have from time to time come into direct conflict with the Fair Trade Commission (FTC), which is responsible for antitrust policy. Antitrust policy was initially imported from the United States during the postwar occupation, in conjunction with the dissolution of the *zaibatsu*. Antitrust, did not fit well, however, with the Japanese tradition of emphasis on the status quo, the harmony of the Confucian order. In the pre-World War II era and continuing throughout the war, the government had been guiding the formation of cartels. Thus it was not surprising that in the Japanese situation attempts to implement policies to foster competition did not easily take root, representing as they did a 180-degree turn in excluding cartels and interfirm collusion. From the 1950s through the mid-1960s, during the heyday of industrial policy, antitrust policy on occasion collided head-on with the predominant Japanese, *genkyoku* approach, and in general, the antitrust policy authorities (the FTC) were the loser. Since then antitrust policy has gradually begun to gain acceptance, but it is not as yet firmly rooted and able to fulfill its appointed role.

Effectiveness of restrictions on competition

Based on the record, if one asks whether in seeking the prevention of excess competition and the restructuring of industry the relevant bureaucracies have had effective policies with great success, the answer has to be more no than yes. An oft-used example is that of the automobile industry, which at first MITI sought to limit to one firm, and failing that two, with the final target set at "at most" three firms. They were unable to do this, and at present there are no less than seven "independent" passenger car manufacturers in Japan (not including firms formally affiliated with one of these). There was in fact vigorous competition in most industries in postwar Japan, and as a result of widespread competition, there was growth and decline and birth and death among firms. This lively competition was in fact one of the most important sources of vitality for the Japanese economy.

What, then, were the reasons for this vigorous competition, which implies that in spite of weak antitrust policy and the strong inclination of the government ministry responsible for an industry to control competition, policies seeking to maintain the "proper" order did not generally succeed? My opinion is that while in general the government and the leading firms in an industry, together with the leaders of the official industry policy councils and advisory committees, favored the limitation of competition and the restructuring of industry, the rank-and-file firms in an industry, new entrants, and the banks and related industries that were pushing these latter firms did not favor restructuring or policy intervention by the government. Rank-and-file firms were always seeking opportunities to eat into the market shares of the top firms, while purchasers of an industry's products desired competition within the industry. Perhaps the antitrust policies of the FTC and the academic economists who argued for the fostering of competition had some influence as well. From the beginning of the 1960s, when extremely rapid economic growth and the transition to an open economy commenced, it came to be thought natural that in the midst of vigorous competition, firms brimming with innovative ideas should grow, leaving behind stagnant firms clinging to the old order.

Furthermore, restructuring, especially mergers and takeovers, seldom went smoothly. One reason is that, in the presence of lifetime employment practices, firm mergers—as with the abolition of a feudal domain during the Tokugawa era—often were accompanied by tragedy. Not only the managers of a firm, but the employees as well, would be willing to undergo hardship for a considerable length of time when their firm ran into difficulties, fighting for their independence, and seeking new avenues of development to preserve their firm's existence.

Industrial Policy Formation

Through what process were decisions relating to industrial policy made in Japan? There are almost no empirical studies of this question based on questionnaire surveys or other data. I had previously attempted to describe this decision process, based on my own limited observations, scattered interviews, press reports, and the like.[24] The reaction of those involved in policy making after the publication of my account was that as a description of the decision-making process through the 1960s it was on the whole on target. Below I will summarize the situation in the 1960s, based on my earlier work, and will try to indicate ways in which things changed in the 1970s.

Through the end of the 1960s

During this period the Diet played almost no role in setting industrial policy. The opposition parties might proclaim that the government was ignoring national welfare in the interest of production, or decry that policies favorable to big business and monopoly capital were being implemented, but they showed almost no concern with the detailed contents of proposed industrial policy measures. Almost all laws were drafted by the bureaucracy, and those that the government sought to have passed in general went through successfully, without amendment.

Those groups whose influence was substantial in the formulation of industrial policy on the government side were the *genkyoku*—the bureaus, divisions, and sections within the various ministries and agencies responsible for particular industries—and the bureaus and divisions that mediated between different parts of a ministry and different ministries. On the private side there were the various industry associations, and in an intermediate role were the various industry councils and advisory committees that formally are part of the government. In addition, two more groups had perhaps some influence, the *zaikai*, a group of corporate executives,[25] and the banks and financial institutions that supplied funds to industry. It was in general quite unusual for only one of the above groups to have a predominant influence regarding a given decision. Thus the decision-making game of setting industrial policy consisted of the above players trying to convince each other as to the proper policy position, to realign their respective goals, or even at times to strongarm their opponents. The fighters in these battles will be described in greater detail below.

1. *The* genkyoku *and the mediating bureaus.* The actor that played the predominant role in the formation of industrial policy in Japan

was the *genkyoku*, the section of the bureaucracy within the government that had the primary responsibility for developing and supervising policies for a given industry. Then, as now, each industry had one associated *genkyoku*. This system is rather similar to the organization of the industrial bureaucracy in socialist countries and seems to have no direct counterpart in the other advanced Western countries.

Overall MITI is the single most important *genkyoku* ministry within the Japanese government. In 1970, among its nine bureaus, five were *genkyoku* bureaus: the Heavy Industries Bureau, the Chemical Industries Bureau, the Textile and Light Industries Bureau, the Coal and Mining Bureau, and the Public Utilities Bureau. Internally a bureau is subdivided into divisions and then into sections, the majority of which are in turn responsible for one or another part of the relevant industry; these can be termed the *genkyoku* divisions or sections. For example, within the Heavy Industries Bureau could be found, among others, sections for iron and steel, industrial machinery, electronics and electrical machinery, automobiles, aircraft, and rolling stock.

Sometimes *genkyoku* bureaus are called vertical because each specializes in an industry or industries, but within MITI there also are four horizontal bureaus that specialize in problems that cut across industries. In 1970, these were the International Trade Bureau, the Trade Promotion Bureau, the Enterprise Bureau, and the Safety and Environmental Protection Bureau. These, together with the Ministerial Secretariat, occasionally had ideas of their own and took the lead in formulating policy, but they also played coordinating roles within MITI and among *genkyoku*.

It should be remembered that even within manufacturing, MITI was not the only *genkyoku* ministry. As noted previously, the Ministry of Agriculture, Forestry, and Fisheries had responsibility for the various food and beverage processing industries, along with the industries obvious from its name. Pharmaceuticals were overseen by the Ministry of Health and Welfare, while shipbuilding was the bailiwick of the Ministry of Transport. And last, not only were banking, insurance, and securities part of the domain of the Ministry of Finance, but so were beer, sake, and other alcoholic beverages.

Each *genkyoku* was responsible for drawing up policy relating to its industry or industries. For example, the *genkyoku* bureaus and sections of MITI were first responsible for drawing up and implementing various industry laws, such as the Petroleum Industry Law (1962), the Machine Industries Law (1956),[26] and the Electronics Industry Law (1957).[27] Second, the *genkyoku* drew up proposals for (1) making available special tax provisions for a given industry (that is, tax incentives), (2) changing tariff rates, (3) measures to free up imports, and (4) measures to permit direct investment in the industry by foreign firms. Third, in terms of transactions between foreign and domestic firms, each *genkyoku* was responsible, prior to the liberalization of capital transactions, for approving (5) patent and technology agreements and (6) joint ventures. Each *genkyoku* bureau or section was also (7) the authority for the issuing of licenses for industries such as petroleum refining, shipbuilding, and electric utilities, where new capacity was regulated. Finally, the *genkyoku* at the section or bureau, or sometimes the ministerial, level had a deciding voice in the allocation of Japan Development Bank and other government financial institution funds.

The proposals drawn up by the *genkyoku* bureau or section for items (1) through (6) were first considered and coordinated with other policies at the ministerial level. They were then passed on to the Ministry of Finance (MOF). In the case of (1), they would go to the Tax Bureau; for (2) and (3), to the Customs and Tariff Bureau; and for (4) through (6), to the International Finance Bureau. These MOF bureaus had within the government the overall responsibility for coordinating policy, while legal details would be overseen by the Cabinet Legislation Bureau. Without some overriding reason, however, it was very hard to change proposals at the Ministry of Finance or cabinet levels that had been decided on or formally requested by another ministry. Finally, the Fair Trade Commission, which was responsible for antitrust policy, was another prominent agency in the formation of industrial policy. Its existence was largely ignored in the 1950s, but throughout the 1960s its relative status within the bureaucracy was increasing, albeit slowly.

2. *Industry associations.* As counterparts to each of the various *genkyoku* were major industry associations, which numbered in the hundreds, such as the Japan Iron and Steel Federation, the Japan Automobile Manufacturers Association, and the Shipbuilders Association of Japan, as well as numerous minor associations at the narrower industry level. In general they worked in close cooperation with the relevant *genkyoku*, but the nature of the relationship varied in each case. From the standpoint of the industry or its major firms, whose presidents served as chairmen of the association on a rotating basis, the main purpose of an association was to work with the *genkyoku* to see that the government adopted policies favorable to their industry or at least toward the major firms. At times there were confrontations between the associations and the *genkyoku*, and at times the associations themselves were divided internally. In addition, in industries

dominated by smaller enterprises, firms were often unable to effectively organize themselves and so relied on the *genkyoku* for assistance.

Immediately after the war, the government took the leading role in the interaction of the *genkyoku* and the associations, with there being a strong tendency for the government to propose policies that it felt desirable and then try to pull the industry into line. As time passed, the balance of power shifted toward the industry groups, so that the *genkyoku* ministry or agency came to play more of a mediating role. Later on the *genkyoku* took into consideration the express interests of the industry (or at least its leading firms), organizing these interests and interacting on the basis of them with other sections, bureaus, and ministries on the industry's behalf. As to the industry associations themselves, many of them consisted of nothing more than friendly gatherings or forums for exchanging information with others in the industry. While they might engage in a little lobbying, the majority of the associations probably had relatively little influence on either outsiders (the government and politicians) or insiders (individual, especially dissident, firms).

(3) *Policy councils (shingikai)*. A system of using *shingikai* on major policy matters has gradually come into use in postwar Japan. These are consultative bodies whose deliberations are referred to in the process of policy formation, and whose principal members are private individuals, including former bureaucrats. In the case of MITI there were in 1970, for example, 27 different councils and advisory committees (*chosakai*), of which 15 were for industrial policy issues, serving formally to advise the Minister on each of their respective areas. The Industrial Structure Council advised on industrial policy in general, and there also were councils, among others, for machinery, petroleum extraction, coal mining, and promoting electronic data processing, aircraft, and energy. The members of these councils are formally nominated by the Minister of MITI and therefore tend to include those individuals thought useful by MITI bureaucrats. The majority thus consists of industry leaders, *zaikai* members, and former bureaucrats, with there being in addition very small numbers of scholars (academics), journalists (from newspapers), and others.

These councils tend to be criticized as being captive to the ministry, and certainly the bureaucrats work to see that deliberations come out to reflect their opinions. In practice, however, it is not the case that only things desired by the ministry are reflected in the groups' reports, for on issues that directly affect the interests of firms, industry representatives do speak out strongly. In fact, on such issues, the councils take on the coloration of a forum in which parties can adjust proposals to reflect their joint interests. Thus proposals that are passed through these councils, that is, that have been negotiated to reflect vested interests, can be afterwards implemented relatively smoothly, at least in terms of the industries represented on the relevant councils. In this sense the *shingikai* process is one explicitly democratic development in postwar Japanese government.

One point that needs to be emphasized regarding such councils is their role in the exchange of information and obtaining consensus on policy matters. I have previously expressed an opinion to the effect that, whatever the defects in the postwar Japanese approach to industrial policy, forums such as these have been a very effective means for the collection, exchange, and dissemination of information on industry and as such have contributed greatly to postwar economic growth.[28] My view remains unchanged.

Post-1970 developments

The above description applies to the policymaking process during the heyday of Japanese industrial policy, but there appears to have been some developments since then. First, the trend has been to the increasing importance of the horizontal bureaus within MITI (in 1983, these were the International Trade Policy, International Trade Administration, Industrial Policy, Industrial Location and Environmental Protection Bureaus, and the Ministerial Secretariat) relative to the vertical bureaus (in 1983, the Basic Industries, Machinery and Information Industries, Consumer Goods Industries Bureaus, and the Agency of Natural Resources and Energy). Cases in which the horizontal bureaus took the initiative in proposing policies increased greatly relative to those in which the initial movers were the vertical bureaus.

Second, this meant that the *genkyoku* had less of a role in formulating policies for their industries' benefit; the major policy issues are ones that cut across many industries or across industrial policy or economic policy as a whole.[29] For MITI, examples of such issues would be responding to trade disputes with other countries, pollution and energy problems, dealing with industrial relocation and adjustment assistance in declining industries, and promoting high-technology industries. Those concerned refer to this as a change of MITI from an "industries" ministry to a "policy-issues" ministry. There has thus been a gradual transition in the character of industrial policy from its initial emphasis on infant-industry protection and the promotion of particular industries to a well industrialized country standpoint in which industrial policy is one facet of general economic policy. It is this sort of transformation that is reflected in the rise of the horizontal bureaus. Here MITI has been the first to change among those ministries that have a *genkyoku* role. It would probably not be an exaggeration to say that MITI has undergone such a change 5 to 10 years ahead of the Ministry of Agriculture, the Ministry of Health and Welfare, the Ministry of Transport, and the *genkyoku* parts of the Ministry of Finance.

Third, the influence of the ruling Liberal Democratic Party and its members over industrial policy has increased somewhat. The number of ruling-party politicians with detailed knowledge of industrial policy, the tax system, and budget making has increased, as has the importance of geographically concentrated small- and medium-scale manufacturing industries as a source of votes, including textiles and other stagnant industries that are crying out for protection. This trend is probably not unconnected with the prevailing atmosphere of political conservatism. In the face of these trends and the demands for fiscal reform, the role of the Ministry of Finance as a mediating agency has declined and has been supplemented by the Policy Committee of the party in power, with its growing number of members who have experience in ministerial or vice-ministerial posts.

Fourth, the number of *shingikai* associated with MITI has increased slightly to 32, and they have come to play an ever greater role as forums for the exchange of information. But overall, apart from the content of industrial policy itself, there has not really been that much change in the process of policy formation.

III. Some Additional Remarks

The problem of equity

As explained in Sections I and II, the process of decisionmaking about industrial policies in postwar Japan is, first, organized predominantly on an industry-by-industry basis, and, second, dominated by the officials in the *genkyoku* offices and representatives of the industries in question. This means that individual industries' interests or producers' interests tend to be promoted more or less in disregard of the interests of other groups affected by such policies and industrial development.

An example is the disregard of harmful effects of environmental pollution in the 1950s and 1960s. In spite of warnings by quite a few people, the government officials in charge of industrial policies tended to belittle the harmful effects of pollution until around 1970, when environmental pollution caused by industries reached very serious and almost unmanageable dimensions.

Consumers' interests have also been largely ignored. A famous representative of the steel industry once said that steel was the nation, meaning that anything good for the steel industry was good for the nation. Although they have never said so blatantly, until recently the *genkyoku* officials have often behaved as if they consider that anything good for the industry which they supervise is good for the country. Not only the interests of consumers in the sense of households, but also the interests of users of the products of the industry in question, have received little attention. For example, users of electronic computers were asked to cooperate with the government's protective policy to develop Japan's own computer industry. Various councils on industrial policies have always been dominated by producers' interests. The *genkyoku* offices, which are formally supposed to supervise their respective industries, often act as an advisor, a protector, or a deputy for them.[30]

Another dimension of the problem of equity is that Japan's industrial policies tend to favor leading firms in the industries concerned. When the government makes plans or rations quotas, the usual criterion as to each firm's share is the past record. Thus industrial policies or planning tend to freeze the status quo in regard to the relative shares of individual firms. Industry associations and councils which play important roles in the process of industrial policy making are dominated by presidents and chairmen of the leading firms having the largest shares in the respective industries. Industry associations, councils, and the *genkyoku* offices spend much time trying to persuade all the firms in the respective industries, in order to be fair and impartial and to avoid criticisms that policies or planning are unfair or partial, but usually the individual firms' shares change little. This means that if industrial policies of the postwar Japanese type are implemented effectively they tend to suppress new entrants and aggressive expansion of smaller but more vigorous firms. At least, the changes in the relative shares of firms are moderated by government intervention.

Also, for the same reason, the system of industrial policies is often incompatible, at least in principle, with antitrust policy. The former emphasizes mutual persuasion, collaboration, and mergers among firms, whereas collusion and mergers in restraint of competition must be prosecuted under the latter. In fact, MITI was often in conflict with the Fair Trade Commission in the 1950s and early 1960s, when the system of industrial policies was in its heyday.

State monopoly capitalism?

Some Marxian economists have argued that the system of industrial policies is, a scheme whereby the government and capitalists collaborate to exploit workers and the public at large. Although the Marxian argument of "state monopoly capitalism" cannot be dealt with easily, a few relevant points may be noted.

First, the ownership and management of firms are probably more thoroughly separated in postwar Japan than in most other countries, including the United States (see Chapter 4). Only a very few of the large companies are run by owner-managers. Generally, salaried executives rather than capitalists dominate the management of big business. They pay less attention to profits and lay more emphasis on growth of the firm than managers in other countries, so long as the profit rate is higher than a certain minimum considered as acceptable to the industry. This is one of the reasons why Japanese firms compete to invest very heavily, even with borrowed funds. Both the government offices in charge of industrial policies and the management of firms are manned overwhelmingly by middle-class intellecturals who are graduates of a few leading unversities. They are managers, administrators, and technocrats, and do not think that they themselves are "capitalists," or capitalists' agents, nor that they are serving the interests of wealthy capitalists.

Second, most industries where the government has intervened extensively, such as iron and steel, shipbuilding, shipping, petroleum refining, chemicals, petrochemicals, and electric power, have been characterized by a low rate of profit throughout the 1960s. Their profit rates have been substantially lower than the average for manufacturing industry. Because of lively competition, government assistance in various forms to these industries has largely been passed on to the purchasers—some of them foreigners—of their products or services. As a result of industrial policies favoring them, these industries and firms have grown and their wage rates have risen rapidly, but their profit rates have remained relatively low.

Third, Japan's ruling Conservative government has been closely associated with the interests of big business and the relatively rich, and has done many things which are considered to be favorable to them and little if anything which was opposed by them. However, the functioning of the highly competitive market mechanism of the postwar Japanese economy is such that big businesses cannot retain for themselves all or most of the benefits of industrial policies which are supposed to be favorable to them. Smaller firms have grown about as rapidly as big ones, and the degree of industrial concentration remains largely unchanged. It appears that in the process of rapid economic growth two counteracting forces are at work, one increasing the advantages of large-scale production and marketing, the other creating new openings and opportunities within the economy for new and smaller firms to develop and prosper. Apparently these two forces have been more or less balanced so far.

Another point which may be mentioned here is that income distribution in postwar Japan is relatively equal. Although reliable statistical data on income distribution are scarce, and international comparison of income distribution is extremely difficult both in practice and conceptually, it appears that income is more nearly equally distributed in Japan than, say, West Germany or France. There is no doubt that Japan's income distribution is now much more nearly equal than in prewar years. This is due to the land reform, *zaibatsu* dissolution, and the once-for-all capital levy enforced immediately after the war, on the one hand, and on the other high progressive income as well as inheritance taxation in the postwar years.

Historical background and applicability in other countries

The system of industrial policies in postwar Japan is closely related to the tradition of "strong government," or the dominant and pervasive role played by the government in Japan. As is well known, since the Meiji Restoration in 1868 the Japanese government has been the main driving force in Japan's industrialization and modernization. The Meiji government was organized by samurai of lower strata of a few leading anti-Tokugawa feudal clans which overthrew the Tokugawa Shogunate and won the civil war. Between 1868 and 1890 the Meiji government organized the national army and navy based upon a national conscription system, established the Bank of Japan and a commercial banking system, introduced a compulsory education system, a national postal system, a system of local governments, and so on. Thus the Meiji government took all kinds of measures to change a feudal country divided into nearly three hundred clans into a modern nation-state. Yet during this period there was no popularly elected national Diet or Congress.

The first national Diet was elected in 1890, but in this election only about one percent of the population was given the right to vote. Throughout the prewar years suffrage was expanded only gradually, and the power of the Diet to check the government (administration) remained very weak, constitutionally as well as in practice, until World War II. In prewar years, therefore, the Japanese government was more or less an absolutist government, nearly omnipotent in pursuing whatever policies it chose. The traditions of free enterprise and economic liberalism were almost nonexistent in prewar Japan. Businessmen were generally viewed as a social group whose status was lower than that of government officials or the military.

During World War II and the period immediately after the war, extensive direct controls were a necessity, as in many other countries. This led to further extension of government intervention in industries and markets. The decontrol process after the war was much slower in Japan than in other countries. The Allied Occupation enforced a series of democratization measures, a drastic and successful land reform, less thoroughgoing but still quite effective dissolution of the *zaibatsu*, and the introduction of an antitrust law. Also, the constitutional status of the Diet in regard to the government budget and economic policies was substantially strengthened. Yet, the extensive involvement of the government in economic affairs, its powerful position vis-à-vis the private sector, its close relationship with business, and the public attitude toward the government-business relationship were not affected much by the democratization measures.

The elaborate system of industrial policies in postwar Japan must be understood in the light of this historical background. It would not be easy, and might be impossible, to introduce Japanese-type industrial policies and planning in countries with much different cultural and political traditions.[31]

This chapter is based upon the author's contribution, "Planning in Japan," in *Economic Planning, East and West,* Morris Bornstein, ed. (Cambridge, MA: Ballinger, 1975), and "Josho" (Introduction) in *Nihon no Sangyo Seisaku* (Japan's Industrial Policy), Tokyo: University of Tokyo Press, 1984. An English translation of the latter, *Industrial Policy of Japan,* was published in 1987 by Academic Press (Tokyo & San Diego).

Notes

1. How the plan underestimated the growth rate may be illustrated by the fact that if the "ambitious" (according to the criticisms at the time of its announcement) National Income Doubling Plan had been carried out as planned, the real GNP in 1970, the terminal year of the Plan, would have been only about 70% of its actual level.

2. Osamu Shimomura, Tadao Uchida, Hisao Kanamori, and I were among the minority optimists.

3. Hence it is a mistake to think that the Japanese government intentionally underestimated the growth rate in order to boast about the overfulfillment afterwards. Not only the government but also the majority of Japanese under-

estimated the growth and structural changes, and those critical of the government often did so more than the plan-makers.

4. Eighteen members were from big business (most of them presidents or chairmen of firms); four, previously high-ranking government officials; five, academics (four of them professors emeriti, that is, retired from universities); and two, labor union representatives. Even this distribution is more diversified than the situation before: at the time of the Medium-Term Economic Plan (1965), of thirty members of the Council all were executives of big business or ex-government officials, except two professors emeriti.

5. This is what actually happened to some degree. As a result of an unexpectedly high rate of growth of the private sector in the 1960s, the public sector in general was lagging behind, and public investment in social overhead capital and public policies against environmental pollution in particular were very inadequate.

6. This is also the reason why Ministry of Finance officials purposely try to underestimate the rate of economic growth in the government's annual economic outlook, which is the basis for the government budget. If a high rate of growth is expected, tax revenue will also be expected to increase substantially, the income-elasticity of tax revenues being greater than unity. This will invite bolder requests for appropriations as well as for tax relief. Obviously such purposeful underestimation is not a rational step in planning if a single optimizing body is going to make a plan. But since the budgetary process is essentially a political game, the attempt to underestimate tax revenues may well be rational from the viewpoint of Ministry of Finance officials, who want to leave something in reserve in order to avoid inflationary developments in the face of irresponsible pressure groups demanding big public expenditures and tax relief.

Incidentally, in recent years the government's budget bill has never been modified by the Diet. What is submitted by the Cabinet is always passed by the Diet, so that the real budgetary process is in preparing the government's budget bill.

7. For example, a few of the "new industrial cities" have not been successful in developing as industrial centers.

8. Among service industries, however, those that are closely linked to the development of a manufacturing industry, such as computer software or telecommunications, may well be considered as objects of industrial policy, as may the distribution systems for certain manufactured goods.

9. In English the word "industry" can refer to broad groups of firms producing similar items, as in primary, secondary, and tertiary industries, as well as specifically to manufacturing. In the latter usage, it is not always clear whether construction, electric power, and mining are included.

10. It is probably necessary to include the formulation and implementation of the Japan Industrial Standards (JIS) codes, safety guidelines, and other standards in this category.

11. The following argument may be worth considering. A strong and diversified small enterprise sector is important as one base for a political and/or economic democracy. In addition, small firms that are full of creativity are an important element for the advancement of industry. Therefore, it is beneficial to somewhat protect or encourage small enterprises. There have been, however, few discussions that introduced this point of view in advancing theoret-

ical arguments for the protection and promotion of small enterprises. Very recently, a considerable amount of attention has been paid to "venture businesses" and policies to promote such firms. It would thus make sense to carry out economic analyses of the impact of promoting promising smaller enterprises, such as has been done by the Investment Development Corporations in Tokyo and elsewhere.

12. For actual industrial policy, however, the goals are not always clear. Publicly stated goals may be ambiguous, and it is not uncommon for there to be a gap between purported and actual goals. Furthermore, policy measures and programs that are actually implemented represent the compromises over many years in adjusting the interests of losers and gainers, so that their policy aims become hard to discern. Thus the decision to limit the discussion to industrial policies undertaken for narrowly economic goals represents a fairly severe restriction from the viewpoint of economic analysis.

13. Another possible role for industrial policy is to improve a country's terms of trade internationally. This, however, is disadvantageous to trading partners, and except when the firms in the trading partner country are monopolist or oligopolists, such policies impose a burden on resource allocation from the standpoint of the world as a whole.

14. The majority of the people who were active in the Industrial Structure Council belonged to the "prehistoric" period, including the three giants of the era, Hiromi Arisawa, Ichiro Nakayama, and Miyohei Shinohara. The works of Yoshihiko Morozumi [1973] and Nobuyoshi Namiki [1973], who were at one time in charge of industrial policy in MITI, also belong to the era. Much as their opinions may diverge on the four key issues raised above, the younger generation has come to use a common vocabulary based on economic theory in their analyses. For example, the majority of the younger generation has taken a critical stance toward the strong control aspects of the current Petroleum Industry Law and to the permit system for shipbuilding, which requires a government license for each new ship to be built.

15. There was no clear attempt made to define what sort of industry was a "basic" industry, but in the immediate postwar period it came to refer to industries such as coal mining, electric power, iron and steel, and ocean transport, as well as shipbuilding.

16. For example, as was the case with West Germany, if the exchange rate had been set at a level that would have permitted maintaining a balance of international payments without much difficulty, it would not have been necessary to undertake policies to stimulate exports or to lower the prices of raw material inputs for the production of export goods. Again, as production takes place to eventually meet final consumption demand, there seems to be little rationality of in general favoring the production of |investment goods and intermediate inputs over that of consumer goods.

17. See Imai, 1969.

18. A story that illustrates this point is that of the firm Toyo Rayon, which introduced the then-revolutionary new product of nylon into Japan. Demand far exceeded supply, and many businessmen hoping to purchase a supply were observed going daily to the firm's headquarters in the Muromachi district of Tokyo. Toyo Rayon thereby earned the nickname "the MITI of Muromachi."

19. In the subsequent period, two additional criteria were added: (1) that

there be a strong linkage effect to other industries and (2) that there be employment generation. The economic basis for these additional criteria, however, is not clear. Suppose that industries are ranked according to their total labor intensity by using input-output analysis to attribute total costs to labor and other primary inputs. Does the employment generation criterion then imply that the industries that are more labor-intensive should be promoted over those that are less so? What about those industries that satisfied only two or three of these four criteria? Should they be considered candidates for favorable treatment under "industrial structure" policies? There was no clear answer.

20. One other point of view was that, in an industry that was internationally close to a monopoly or a collusive oligopoly and where well-established firms thereby earned high profits, Japan should have nurtured new firms strong enough to lower the monopoly price or to share in the monopoly profits. Color film, automobiles, heavy electrical equipment, and large-scale computers may be examples of such industries.

21. Morozumi, 1973.

22. For some of my own earlier thinking on this subject, see Imai et al. (1972), pp. 248–256.

23. Kaizuka, 1973, p. 167.

24. Komiya, 1975, pp. 208–211.

25. It is not clear who belongs to the *zaikai*, but it refers in general to those top corporate executives who are well informed about economic or policy affairs. They are constantly conferring with one another in various forums, and they play the role of spokespersons for major companies. In general, those thought of as members have prominent positions in the associations that represent big business interests. As a matter of fact, they do not, however, have the power attributed to them by the press or in popular thinking, and I believe that as time progresses their influence has lessened.

26. Officially, the Law on Temporary Measures for the Promotion of the Machinery Industry.

27. Officially, the Law on Temporary Measures for the Promotion of the Electronics Industry.

28. Komiya, 1975, p. 22.

29. Note that from the start there was little criticism of MITI, in contrast to the Ministry of Finance, as being only a conglomeration of independent bureaus and not a "ministry" (though this criticism is exaggerated).

30. In the early 1960s a young official in one of the *genkyoku* divisions of MITI told me that he sometimes felt as if he were a financial manager for companies which were under the supervision of his division, since much of his time was spent in negotiating on loans for the companies with other MITI offices and the Japan Development Bank.

31. A necessary condition for Japanese-type industrial policies to succeed is the existence of a bureaucracy capable of planning, implementing, and administering complicated policy systems. There must be an abundant supply of honest, intelligent, and dedicated bureaucrats. It may be noted that there have been very few cases in which high officials in charge of industrial policies were involved in bribery. For government officials it does not pay to receive bribes. For one thing, acceptance of bribes is severely punished, and also, although their salaries are surprisingly low, government officials are under

the lifetime employment scheme, and high officials can take prestigious and well-paid jobs after retirement from the civil service.

References

Imai, Ken'ichi (1969). "Sekiyu Seisei" (Petroleum Refining), in Niida and Ono, 1969, pp.159–200.

Imai, Ken'ichi, Hirofumi Uzawa, Ryutaro Komiya, Takashi Negishi, and Yasusuke Murakami (1972). *Kakaku Riron* (Price Theory). Tokyo: Iwanami Shoten.

Kaizuka, Keimei (1973). *Keizai Seisaku no Kadai* (Problems of Economic Policy). Tokyo: University of Tokyo Press.

Komiya, Ryutaro (1975). *Gendai Nihon Keizai Kenkyu* (Studies of the Contemporary Japanese Economy). Tokyo: University of Tokyo Press.

Morozumi, Yoshihiko, et al. (1973). *Sangyo Taisei no Sai Hensei* (Reorganization of the Industrial System). Tokyo: Shunjusha.

Namiki, Nobuyoshi (1973). "Kigyokan Kyoso to Seisaku Kainyu" (Interfirm Competition and Policy Intervention), in Shinohara and Baba, 1973, pp. 35–51.

Niida, Hiroshi, and Akira Ono, eds. (1969). *Nihon no Sangyo Sohniki* (Japan's Industrial Organization). Tokyo: Iwanami Shoten.

Shinohara, Miyohei, and Masao Baba, eds. (1973). *Sangyo Seisaku* (Industrial policy). Vol. 3 of *Gendai Sangyo Ron* (Modern Industry). Tokyo: Chikuma Shobo.

CHAPTER 8

JAPAN'S MACROECONOMIC POLICIES DURING THE TWO OIL CRISES

The drastic rises in oil prices brought about by the two oil crises of 1973–74 and 1979–80 severely affected the Japanese economy. When one compares the new burdens placed on major industrialized countries by these oil-price rises, in terms of the increase in oil-import bills relative to GNP, Japan bore the largest burdens along with the United Kingdom (the first oil crisis only) and Italy.

Although the influences on the Japanese economy from the two oil crises were severe and extensive, Japan quickly sloughed off the direct inflationary effects and stagflation accompanying these crises, in comparison with other industrialized countries. This is particularly true in the case of the second oil crisis. Consequently, Japan's macroeconomic performance received widespread international attention in the late 1970s and the early 1980s.

Section I of this paper reviews macroeconomic developments in the Japanese economy over the decade following the first oil crisis. In order to identify factors behind this relatively good macroeconomic performance, Section II analyzes Japan's labor maket, trends in productivity, and the balance of payments. Section III examines Japan's monetary and fiscal policies during the same period and attempts to evaluate their effects.

I. A Review of Macroeconomic Developments in Japan: 1973–82

In this part we shall review briefly how the Japanese economy was affected by external shocks generated by the two oil crises, how it went through the adjustment process, and how Japanese macroeconomic policy coped with inflation and depression following the oil crises.

Period 1: 1973–75

As a result of the first oil crisis, which broke out in the fall of 1973, the prices of crude-oil imports in Japan soared by May 1974 to about four times the prices prevailing in the first half of 1973. The resulting income transfer to oil-producing countries amounted approximately to 14 billion dollars in 1974, a huge sum representing about 3.1% of Japan's GNP in that year. This oil-price rise pushed up supply costs extensively and accelerated inflation. At the same time, on the demand side, the rise in oil prices brought about a decline in aggregate demand as would an increase in indirect taxes not accompanied by a simultaneous increase in government expenditure.

Unfortunately for Japan, the first oil crisis occurred at the last stage of a rapid expansion which began in the fall of 1972. In the middle of 1973 the level of production activity was beyond the normal level compatible with a reasonable degree of price stability, and inflation was already running at a high rate (see Figures 1 and 2). From the macroeconomic point of view, there was widespread excess demand. Centering on the "Plan to Reconstruct the Japanese Archipelago," the government greatly expanded fiscal expenditure in 1972 and 1973, and at the same time the Bank of Japan adopted an excessively easy money policy. As a result, business conditions became buoyant rapidly

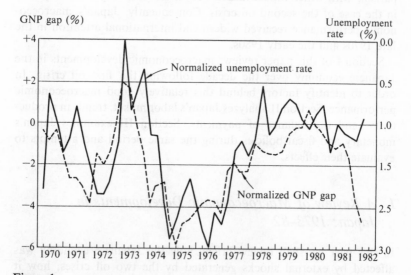

Figure 1

GNP gap and "normalized" unemployment rate.

Source: See Notes 1 and 2. The negative value of normalized GNP gap indicates excess capacity.

after the latter part of 1972, and inflation accelerated as well. From the beginning of 1973, a tight-money policy was adopted. The rate of increase in money supply ($M2 + CD$) began to decrease from the beginning of 1973, but remained more than 20% until the outbreak of the oil crisis (Figure 2). It appears that even if the oil crisis had not occurred, the Japanese economy was approaching the end of a shortlived, steep boom around the spring of 1974.

Because the first oil crisis occurred when aggregate demand exceeded the normal level in relation to supply and the inflation rate was already high, the inflationary impact was especially severe. The rapid price increases before and after the oil crisis generated strong and persistent inflationary expectations and fears of future supply shortages. A unique characteristic of this period was a widespread buying spree by consumers not only of oil-related products but also of consumer goods in general such as soap, toilet paper, soy sauce, and sugar. In addition, from the fall of 1972, speculative transactions of stocks and real estate became brisk as did inventory investment by firms in raw materials. Strong inflationary expectations were clearly strong throughout the Japanese economy.

In 1974 the Japanese economy was confronted with three difficulties. The first was high inflation. In February, 1974, wholesale prices rose

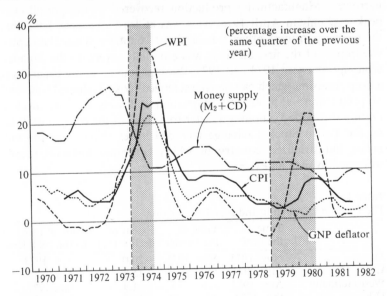

Figure 2
Money supply and inflation rates.
Source: Bank of Japan, Keizai Tokei Nenpo (Economic Statistics Annual).

37% over the level a year earlier. Consumer prices, from the spring of 1974 until November 1974, continued to be 24–25% higher than the previous year. Moreover, at the time of the first oil crisis the labor market was very tight (see Figure 1), and firms' profits, swollen by inflation, were much higher than expected. Employers were still optimistic about their ability to pay higher wages. Hence, in the spring of 1974, wages rose about 33% compared with a 25% increase in the consumer price index for the twelve months ending in April 1974. The rise in wages further spurred inflationary expectations. The Japanese economy appeared trapped in a vicious inflationary wage–price spiral.

The second difficulty was the rapid decline in the level of productive activity. As a result of the depressive impact of the oil-price rise and tight-money policy, productive activity, especially in manufacturing, declined rapidly. Output of the Japanese manufacturing industry fell throughout 1974, and reached a trough in March 1975 20% below the peak level. As shown in Table 1, this was the largest decline among major industrialized countries.

Real GNP continued to decline from the middle of 1974, and the growth rate relative to the same quarter of the previous year did not turn positive until the beginning of 1975. The gap between normal and actual GNP remained large during 1974 and was only gradually narrowed. Manufacturing production recovered to the pre-oil crisis peak level only in April 1978. This was at least one year later than the recovery in most other industrialized countries. Thus the depressive impact of the first oil crisis was especially severe on the Japanese economy. Between 1974 and 1977, the Japanese economy experienced a deep recession which can be characterized by an L-shaped time path of production: a protracted stagnation following a sharp decline. During this period, about a quarter to a third of the companies listed on the Tokyo Stock Exchange recorded losses. Japan was the only major industrialized country in which corporate financial records worsened to such an extent.

Table 1
The Peak and Trough in Industrial Production

	Time of the peak	Time of the trough	Extent of decline (%)	Time of recovery to the peak level
Japan	Nov. 1973	Mar. 1975	−20.0	Apr. 1978
U.S.	June 1974	Mar. 1975	−15.3	Aug. 1976
West Germany	Aug. 1973	July 1975	−11.9	Jan. 1977
U.K.	Oct. 1973	Aug. 1975	−11.0	May 1977
France	Aug. 1974	May 1975	−14.9	Sept. 1976

Source: OECD, Main Economic Indicators.

The third difficulty was the drastic worsening of the balance of payments on current account and the weakening of the yen exchange rate. In 1973, Japan's balance turned into a deficit because of the overheating of the domestic economy and the quadrupling of oil prices. In 1974 exports rose on a volume basis by 18% and on a dollar value basis by 50% compared with the previous year, partly offsetting the increase in the value of imports, yet the current account turned into a record deficit of 4.7 billion dollars.

Because of pessimism as to the future of the Japanese economy, ongoing inflation, and large continuing deficits on current account, the yen exchange rate depreciated substantially. These accelerated domestic inflation, creating a vicious circle. In the second half of 1974, however, domestic demand began to stagnate, and the decline in imports contributed to the improvement of the current-account balance. By the end of 1975 there was almost a balance in spite of stagnating exports.

In response to accelerating inflation in 1973, Japan's monetary policy was tightened, and with the outbreak of the oil crisis, it was tightened further. As a result of the extremely tight money policy, the rate of increase in money supply ($M2$) over the previous year declined sharply from more than 25% in the second quarter of 1973 to 11% in the second half of 1974 in the face of high inflation. Thus, real money supply turned negative in 1974.

As the level of industrial production fell, the supply–demand situation for various basic materials changed from excess demand to excess supply, and pressures for price increases were diminished. In the second half of 1975, the rise in wholesale prices over the previous twelve months fell to zero, and the rise in consumer prices was approaching a one-digit level. It appears from Figure 3 that inflationary expectations generated in the period before and during the first oil crisis had largely subsided by the beginning of 1975.

A major event which enabled Japan to terminate the wage–price spiral more quickly than other major industrialized countries was the outcome of the 1976 spring labor offensive. The spring labor offensive, or "*shunto*" in Japanese, is an annual event in the Japanese labor market. The word "*shunto*," literally meaning "spring struggle," describes a series of negotiations between labor unions and employers on the annual wage hikes in each industry or company. In Japan the wage level (as a matter of fact monthly salaries in most cases rather than hourly, daily, or weekly wages) are raised annually, and the amount of the raise is negotiated every spring. The overall rate of increase resulting from these negotiations, called the "*shunto* rate,"

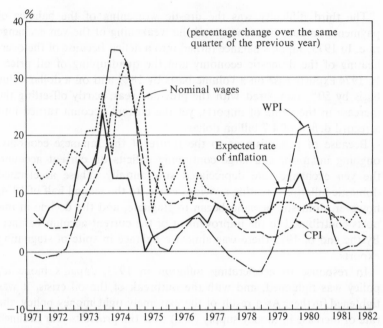

Figure 3
Movements of price indices in the first and second oil crises.
Source: Same as Figure 2.

plays a decisive role in determining the extent of annual wage increases in the Japanese economy. In 1973 and 1974, the *"shunto* rate" greatly exceeded the increase in the consumer price index, but in 1975, they were roughly the same, and in 1976, the former was restrained to a level below the latter. As a consequence, the rise in real wages in manufacturing industries turned negative (-1.7%) for the first time since labor–management relations were normalized shortly after World War II (Table 2). This outcome contributed greatly to easing the inflationary expectations following the first oil crisis.

The background of the low 1976 *"shunto* rate" may be briefly described as follows. The government, in the hope of restraining wage increases, publicly pledged to bring down the rate of increase in the consumer price index to a one-digit level by March 1976. This pledge became the focus of the political confrontation between labor (and opposition parties supporting labor unions) which demanded large wage increases and the government which gave top priority to overcoming inflation. Consumer price increases relative to the level a year

Table 2
The Rate of Increase in Wages

		1973	1974	1975	1976	1977
					(% rate of increase over the previous year)	
1)	Rate of increase in wages as result of spring labor offensive	20.1	32.9	13.1	8.8	8.8
2)	Changes in the consumer price index (in April of every year)	9.5	25.0	13.5	9.5	8.7
3)	Changes in nominal wages (manufacturing)	23.8	31.4	15.1	7.5	9.1
4)	Changes in real wages (same)	10.8	5.7	3.0	−1.7	1.1
		1978	1979	1980	1981	1982
1)	Rate of increase in wages as result of spring labor offensive	5.9	6.0	6.9	7.7	7.0
2)	Changes in the consumer price index (in April of every year)	4.1	2.7	8.5	5.2	2.8
3)	Changes in nominal wages (manufacturing)	5.8	4.5	6.4	6.6	4.1
4)	Changes in real wages (same)	1.9	0.8	−1.5	1.6	1.4

Sources: Ministry of Labor, and Bank of Japan.

earlier came down to 9.3% in February and 9.0% in March of 1976. Thus, the government pledge was barely fulfilled in time.

One reason why the 1976 "*shunto* rate" was modest may be that economists convinced some labor leaders that, from a macroeconomic viewpoint, excessive wage increases would lead to an acceleration of inflation that would substantially reduce real wages later. Market forces were the main reason for the low wage increases in the 1976 *shunto*, however, First, as mentioned earlier, inflationary expectations had subsided, and with business conditions worsening employers could not raise wage rates. Second, as is shown in Figure 1, from the second half of 1974 until 1976, there was a conspicuous easing in the labor market almost without precedent in recent years. As a consequence, labor unions were confronted with the choice between substantial wage increases and/or employment as the main target of *shunto* strategy. They could not afford to continue to press their demands for large wage increases only.

To cope with the worsening employment situation in 1975, the government introduced a new subsidy system for "employment adjustment." Under the system the government paid part of the salary of redundant workers who, instead of being discharged, were on stand-by at home waiting to be called back by employers. Those covered by the new system totalled 23,990,000 man-days in fiscal 1975, which indicates the substantial easing in the labor market. Union members did not like being on stand-by with consequent reduction in incomes and preferred secure employment to large wage increases.

Period 2: 1976–78

Severe inflation started before the first oil crisis and accelerated after. Then inflation subsided. As a result of the tight-money policies, inflationary expectations had largely gone away. Throughout this period, prices remained largely stable: the rate of increase in the wholesale price index even turned negative for a time, due partly to the appreciation of the yen exchange rate. However, aggregate demand in the Japanese economy was stagnant, and industrial activity remained at a low level. There were larger-than-normal inventories and excess capacity in many industries. Unemployment and other forms of underutilization of labor remained at high levels.

Throughout this period of low-demand pressure, structural adjustments were taking place in the Japanese economy. The industrial structure was changing from one which depended heavily on low oil prices to one which could cope with high oil prices. In other words the outputs of industries with high dependence on energy such as steel, nonferrous metals, chemicals, and pulp and paper were falling or stagnant, and investment in plant and equipment in these industries was sluggish. Growth in output and investment in industries with low dependence on energy, on the other hand, such as precision machinery, electronics, and electrical machinery, was high (see Section II).

Accompanying the movement towards an industrial structure characterized by low dependence on energy was a widespread effort in every industry to conserve energy. As a result, energy conservation in Japan proceeded rapidly.

Throughout this period, the Japanese economy faced, on an aggregate level, insufficient demand and excess supply capacities. This

Table 3
Private Investment in Plant and Equipment: 1974–81

(%, on a real GNP basis)

	1968–73 average	1974	1975	1976	1977
Rate of increase	14.0	−4.8	−5.5	0.7	2.5
Ratio to GNP	18.0	17.8	16.4	15.7	15.2
	1978	1979	1980	1981	1982
Rate of increase	6.5	11.9	8.1	5.6	1.8
Ratio to GNP	15.4	16.4	16.9	17.2	17.0

Source: Economic Planning Agency, Kokumin Keizan Keisan Nenpo (National Income Accounts Yearbook).

can be seen in Figure 1, which shows the normalized GNP gap and unemployment rate.[1]

To investigate why this low-demand-pressure continued throughout this period, let us look at the major elements of aggregate demand separately. First, investment in plant and equipment of private enterprises was stagnant because many industries had excess capacity (Table 3). Although new investment was required for energy conservation, environmental protection, and labor-saving rationalization, the general tendency of excess capacity in many industries dampened new investment. It was not until 1978 that investment finally began to recover, centering on industries having low dependence on energy.

Second, household consumption was stagnant since the rate of increase in real wages was sharply reduced compared with the period before the first oil crisis. Furthermore, consumption was affected by the savings behavior of the household sector. The oil crisis revealed to many Japanese the vulnerability of the Japanese economy to external shocks. This, together with anxiety over unemployment and earlier retirement, caused the savings ratio to rise noticeably (see Table 4). The rise in savings ratio during these years was observed in other industrialized countries as well, but the trend was most conspicuous in Japan.

Similarly, the level of housing construction fell considerably from the pre-oil-crisis level (Table 5). When people feel optimistic about the future, they build or purchase new houses and make large consumption expenditures (on consumer durables, vacations abroad, etc.). After the oil crisis, pessimistic views about the future of the Japanese economy, especially about employment and the rate of increase in income, caused a slowdown in housing construction and large consumption expenditures.

After the first oil crisis, the government budget posted large

Table 4
Household Savings Ratio: 1974–81

(%)

	1968–73 average	1974	1975	1976	1977	1978	1979	1980	1981
Savings/ dispos- able income	18.2	23.7	22.1	22.4	21.0	20.6	18.7	19.2	19.8

Source: Same as Table 3.

Table 5
Private Housing Construction: 1974–81

(%, on a real GNP basis)

	1969–73 average	1974	1975	1976	1977
Rate of increase	14.8	−12.7	2.5	8.8	1.7

	1978	1979	1980	1981	1982
Rate of increase	6.6	−1.0	−9.4	−2.6	−1.0

Source: Same as Table 3.

deficits. On the one hand high inflation from 1972 to 1974 caused substantial increases in the salaries of government employees and social security expenditures. Deficits of the Japan National Railways, the National Health Insurance Program, and the National Farm Price Support System were also aggravated by inflation. Consequently government expenditures increased greatly. On the other hand, government revenues did not increase proportionately, partly because a bold tax cut amounting to "one trillion yen" was implemented in the 1974 fiscal year, and partly because corporate tax revenues declined sharply as a result of deep depression. The deficits of the central government as a percentage of GNP, which had been less than 1% before 1974, increased sharply and reached almost 5% in 1977–78. This percentage was the second highest among the major industrialized countries. Because the government deficits had reached such a high level, many felt it unwise to expand government expenditure further to stimulate the economy.

When the inflation rate declined to a low level, there were calls for a further easing of monetary policy. However, monetary authorities, in the light of the inflation experience of 1972–74, continued to be cautious in adopting expansionary measures.

In this continuing low-demand-pressure situation, export increased substantially. It is a characteristic of the Japanese economy that export increases in a recession and pulls the economy out of recession. Such a phenomenon, called an "export drive effect" of recession in Japan, was observed several times in the 1950s and 1960s under fixed exchange rates. A strong "export drive effect" was observed in 1975–78, under floating exchange rates. This is discussed in more detail in Section II. Increased export was a leading force in Japanese economic growth during this period. The export drive effect turned the current account balance into record surpluses of 10.9 and 16.5 billion United States dollars, respectively, in 1977 and 1978. These surpluses, in turn, created bilateral trade friction between Japan and the United States, as well as between Japan and European countries, and heightened criticisms of Japanese economic policy from abroad.

Period 3: 1979–82
At the end of Period 2, just as domestic demand was beginning to recover, the second oil crisis occurred. This second round of large increases in oil prices had yet another serious impact on the Japanese economy. Period 3 is the time during which the Japanese economy adjusted to the impact of the second oil crisis.

Through the second oil crisis, the price of crude oil imports to Japan rose 2.8 times, and the increased cost of oil imports resulting from this price rise as a percentage of GNP was roughly comparable to that in the first oil crisis. In contrast to the first oil crisis, however, the overall impact on the Japanese economy of the second oil crisis was smaller.

The inflationary impact of the second oil crisis on Japan was considerably less severe than that of the first. The peak rate of inflation in terms of the wholesale price index (WPI), reached in April 1980, was a 24% rise over the twelve months, and gave the impression that the economy was experiencing vicious inflation once again. But the overall rate of increase in WPI is misleading unless one looks at major categories of goods covered by WPI separately. The price increase of raw materials peaked in March of 1980 with a 73.7% rise over the previous year level—nearly the same extent as at the time of the first oil crisis. But prices of intermediate materials and those of finished products exhibited much smaller increases than they did during the first oil crisis (see Figure 4). The fact that during the second oil crisis oil prices and other oil-related components of WPI rose sharply but domestic components did not is reflected in the stability of the GNP deflator. It rose only gradually and moderately in 1980–81.

Inflationary expectations did not become widespread during the

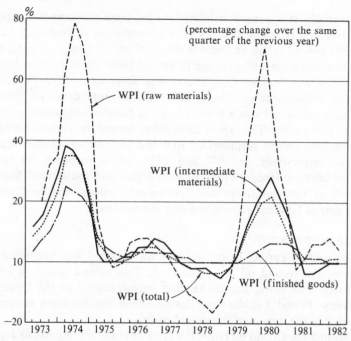

Figure 4
Wholesale price index for major categories of goods.
Source: Same as Figure 2.

second oil crisis. An index of inflationary expectations calculated using questionnaire data from the EPA's *Shohisha Doko Yosoku Chosa* (Survey of Expectations on Consumer Trends) rose to 25% in the fourth quarter of 1973 but reached only about 14% in the first quarter of 1980 (see Figure 3). At the time of the first oil crisis inflationary expectations became widespread mainly because of the rapid inflation preceding the oil crisis, both in Japan and the world. In 1979–80, because prices and the money supply in Japan were stable prior to the second oil crisis, inflationary expectations did not become widespread.

One reason that inflationary expectations were not as high at the time of the second oil crisis as they were in the first oil crisis is the difference in the supply and demand conditions. When the first oil crisis occurred, excess demand was present in many sectors of the Japanese economy, whereas during the second oil crisis excess capacity existed in many industries. Consequently, producers were unable to push up their prices to meet the increase in their costs resulting from higher oil prices.

Another reason for a much lower rate of inflation when the second oil crisis occurred may be concerned with lessons learned from the first oil crisis. The Bank of Japan swiftly tightened monetary control in response to the rise in oil prices. Producers and labor unions were generally restrained from pushing up prices and wages. Consumers did not cause buying sprees as they did at the time of the first oil crisis.

The depressive effect of the huge income transfer to OPEC countries was relatively mild in 1979–80 for a variety of reasons. First, between 1979 and 1981 demand for investment in plant and equipment in the private sector was rising, because excess capital stocks present after the first oil crisis had been reduced and existing plant and equipment had aged. Also, there was an increase in demand for new investment for energy conservation, for the production of energy-saving goods, and in labor-saving rationalization. Second, the steady increase of exports until the fall of 1981 contributed to stabilizing the aggregate demand. On the other hand, because of stagnant or declining real wages and increased real tax burdens, personal consumption and demand for housing construction continued to be sluggish. Third, at the time of the first oil crisis the Bank of Japan had to tighten money supply drastically to wipe out inflationary expectations, even at the high cost of a sharp decline in the real GNP. Since money supply before the second oil crisis was not excessive, such a drastic monetary tightening was not necessary.

While oil prices were raised almost four times in three months at the time of the first oil crisis, they rose gradually over nearly two years through the second oil crisis. In Japan the price of imported crude oil per barrel rose from 13.6 dollars at the end of 1978 to 38.5 dollars in the spring of 1981. The inflationary effect of this gradual oil-price increase on prices in general lasted a much shorter period than the inflation following the first oil crisis. The wholesale price index was nearly stabilized in the spring of 1980. The peak rate of increase in the consumer price index over the previous year was 9%, recorded in September 1980.

Let us now look at the balance of payments. Expansion of domestic demand, together with the lagged effects of substantial appreciation of the yen during 1977–78, turned the current-account balance into a deficit of 4 billion dollars (at an annual rate on a seasonally adjusted basis) in the second quarter of 1979. The deficit on current account peaked at a sizable 18 billion dollars in first quarter, of 1980, but the deficit had been largely eliminated by first quarter 1981.

As far as the immediate impact on its own economy is concerned, one may say that Japan came out of the adjustment process initiated by the second oil crisis by the second quarter of 1981.

Industrial production in Japan rose fairly steadily throughout the second oil crisis until the spring of 1980. The summer of 1980 witnessed a slight decline in production, and since then the level of production has fluctuated but has shown a moderate upward trend. In contrast to the first oil crisis, the depressionary impact of the second oil crisis on Japan's productive activity was mild.

In contrast to Japan, the influences of the second oil crisis on other major industrialized countries were protracted. In many countries, the second oil crisis caused prolonged acceleration of inflation, worsening of the balance of payments, increased unemployment, and stagnation of industrial production. Although world inflation now appears to have subsided, unemployment in many countries reached a level unprecedented in postwar years. As the world recession continues to deepen, these depressionary trends have caused Japanese exports to decline from the autumn of 1981, casting a shadow over the Japanese economy and widening the GNP gap once again.

II. The Labor Market, Productivity, and the Balance of Payments

Direct impacts on the Japanese economy from the two oil crises in terms of income transfer induced by the oil price rise were among the largest of major industrialized countries. The first oil crisis occurred when inflation was already accelerating in Japan. The crisis further accelerated inflation, and the decline in output was greater and more protracted than in most countries. Nevertheless, after the immediate adjustment period of the first oil crisis, Japan's macroeconomic performance was better than in most other countries. Also, the adverse effects of the second oil crisis on inflation, unemployment, and the balance of payments were much smaller in Japan than in other major countries. In the remainder of this paper we shall consider factors behind Japan's performance. In Section II, the characteristics of the Japanese labor market which appear to be relevant to price performance and industrial productivity will first be explored.[2] Next, factors behind Japan's balance-of-payments performance will be considered. In Section III the role of monetary and fiscal policies in Japan's macroeconomic performance will be considered.

The labor market

Real wage flexibility. Two factors can be pointed out as having contributed to Japan's price performance. First, in Japan, the strength of labor unions in pushing up wages in the process of inflation is much weaker, in our view, than in other countries, especially when the labor demand is sluggish. Consequently, it is less likely that Japan would fall into a wage–price spiral. Wages, or at least real wages, appear quite flexible. The second factor is the high rate of increase in industrial productivity. This enables firms to raise wages without giving rise to inflationary pressures and at the same time to carry out investment in plant and equipment and in R&D for improving productivity still further. Before analyzing the latter issue, let us first examine why wage-push inflationary pressures from labor unions are weak in Japan.

In Japan, annual increases in nominal wages are largely dependent on business conditions prevailing at the time of the spring labor offensive (*shunto*) mentioned earlier. In times of recession when business performance is poor, the rise in wages is bound to be modest. As an example, a modest rise in wages in the 1976 *shunto* negotiations has already been cited. In 1976, and also in 1980, wages rose less than consumer prices, dampening inflationary expectations.

Figure 5 shows for the period 1964 to 1982 (1) the annual "*shunto* rate," (2) the ex post nominal wage increase (excluding service sector), and (3) the rise in real wages calculated by subtracting the rise in the consumer price index from the rise in actual nominal wages. As can be seen, these figures fluctuate considerably from year to year. In a boom year, or in the year immediately thereafter, the *shunto* rate tends to be high, and in an unexpectedly good year the rate of increase in total wages including bonuses and overtime pay exceeds the *shunto* rate considerably. But in a year of recession, the *shunto* rate becomes modest, and the ex post rise in wages falls short of the *shunto* rate. At the time of the second oil crisis the worsening of the terms of trade contributed substantially to a decline in real wages.[3]

Thus, annual wage increases in Japan are sensitive to economic conditions. The following regression analysis explaining annual wage increases, based upon quarterly data for 1970–1982, indicates that nominal wages are influenced by labor-market conditions as well as by prices and labor productivity:

$$\dot{W}_t = -4.1347 \, U_t + 0.9100 \, (\dot{P}_{t-1} + \lambda) + 6.6598$$
$$(-3.0585) \quad (11.0535) \quad (2.2492)$$

$\dot{W}_t$ = the rate of increase (over the level of one year ago) in nominal wages in manufacturing industry.

$\dot{P}_t =$ the rate of increase in the GNP deflator.
$U_t =$ the unemployment rate for the heads of households.
$\lambda =$ the trend rate of increase in labor productivity in manufacturing industry.
$R^2 = 0.877, D.W. = 1.945$
(Figures in parentheses are t values.)

The above regression indicates that the unemployment rate for heads of households has a large impact on wages. A 1% change in this unemployment rate brings about a 4% decrease in the rate of wage increases.[4] Since the annual wage increase is negotiated between employers and labor unions every spring, and moreover bonus payments in December (and June in some firms) are also negotiated each time (as well as the flexible adjustment of overtime pay), the time lags between price or unemployment variables and wages are short. It means that business and general economic conditions are reflected in wages fairly quickly. In periods of recession when the labor market is slack, wages do not rise to any great extent; and the possibility that pressures from wage-push will initiate a wage–price spiral is small.

Employment practices: three groups of employees. In Japan wage increases are quite sensitive to labor-market conditions and to current and prospective profits, and change flexibly in response to business conditions. This contrasts with Europe and North America, where until recently wage increases have tended to be less responsive to conditions in the labor market or to general economic conditions. We shall now consider characteristics of the Japanese labor market which differ substantially from those of Europe and North America.

To understand the factors behind the flexibility of wages in Japan, it is useful to classify the Japanese labor force into three major groups by type of employment.

First, there are those employees, both blue- and white-collar, who are employed under the lifetime employment (or commitment) (*shushin-koyo*) system. After graduating from school, a worker belonging to this group is immediately employed by a company where he remains nearly until the end of his working career.[5] Secondly, there are self-employed or those engaged in family businesses. Finally, there are marginal or peripheral employees who do not fall under the lifetime-employment umbrella.

In earlier times the lifetime-employment practice was primarily for white-collar employees in large enterprises and in the public sector, but after World War II the practice spread to blue-collar workers and to workers in small and medium businesses as well. Workers in this category are typically married (or soon to be married) males and are the principal income-earners of the households. Females in this category are still a minority. A majority of workers organized into labor unions are in this category.

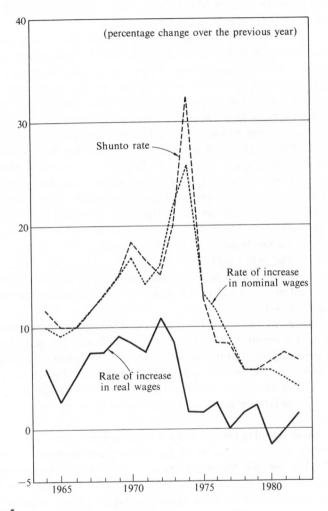

Figure 5
Shunto rate and other wage indices.
Sources: *Shunto* rate (the average rate of increase in nominal wages agreed on by employers and labor unions as a result of the "spring labor offensive" negotiations) is from the Ministry of Labor. Rates of increase in nominal and real wages are from Bank of Japan, *Keizai Tokei Nenpo* (Economic Statistics Annual).

Workers in the second category, those self-employed or in family businesses, have been traditionally represented by workers in agriculture, but they have been important in commerce and manufacturing as well. Although the percentage of workers in agriculture has declined from 28% in 1960 to 10% in 1980, workers in this category are still an important part of the labor force.

The third category, marginal workers, consists of young unmarried females, married females, males with relatively little formal education, and those who have moved out of agriculture. Also in this category are agricultural workers who leave agriculture during off-season and workers who have left a family business either temporarily or permanently. Of these latter workers, some, particularly males, find their way to the lifetime employment system or start their own business. Mobility of these marginal workers is high, and the duration of employment under a given employer is short. Few marginal workers are members of labor unions. Larger firms employ marginal workers as temporary workers, workers on loan from other smaller firms, or part-time workers. In boom times, this type of employment by larger firms expands, but even at such times marginal workers employed by large firms are rarely admitted to labor unions.

Thus, a relatively small portion of the Japanese labor force is organized into labor unions. As a consequence, the wages of marginal workers are much less than the wages of workers under the lifetime employment system.

The wages of the workers in the third group are determined by supply and demand in the labor market and hence are quite flexible. The wage component of the income of the second group is also flexible. The workers in the second and third groups generally get what they earn in the market; they are in no position to enforce the wage push even when the labor market and business conditions are tight.

Labor union organization and wage determination
The wages of the workers under the lifetime employment system are also flexible for the following reasons. Although a large majority of workers under the lifetime employment system belongs to labor unions, organization of labor unions in Japan differs radically from that of Europe and North America. In Japan, labor unions are organized on an enterprise basis, separately for each firm or establishment.[6] Hence, while the number of unions in the United Kingdom is less than 500 and in the United States less than 200, in Japan the number of legally independent labor unions is more than 34,000 (see Table 6).

Table 6
Some Statistics on Labor Unions in Major Countries

		Japan	U.S.	U.K.	West Germany
Ratio of union	1970	34.9	27.0	48.6	36.2
members to total	1978	32.6	23.6	57.6	40.9
number of workers					
(%)		30.5(1982)		58.1(1980)	42.0(1981)
Number of labor		34,163	174	462	n.a.
unions		34,200(1981)		438(1980)	

Sources: Ministry of Labor and elsewhere.

Labor unions organized on a firm-by-firm basis are common in Japan because of the tradition of the lifetime employment practice. The level of wages and salaries differs firm by firm, with prosperous, high-profit, growing firms paying higher wages than low-profit, stationary firms. Permanent employees receive bonus payments once, twice, or four times a year which amount, on an annual basis, to three-to-eight months of their salaries. The amounts of the bonuses depend largely on the firm's profits.[7]

A firm and its permanent employees have many interests in common. For members of a labor union organized on a firm-by-firm basis, it is most desirable that their firm earn high profits and grow rapidly, since their wages and bonuses will be increased and they will be promoted rapidly to higher posts. For the firm to grow it must keep a high rate of investment in plant and equipment and in R&D, and this is possible only when certain levels of dividends and retained earnings are maintained. Annual wage increases are negotiated industrywide to some extent during the *shunto*, but final wage determination is always settled at the individual-firm level. For a union organized on an enterprise basis, it is not good to enforce a wage policy that greatly reduces the firm's profits, because the firm is the goose that lays the golden egg for union members.

From the firm's perspective, in the long run, permanent employees represent more important assets than customers and stockholders. The division of ownership and management in large firms in Japan today has progressed farther than in any other country. Large corporations owned by specific families are few in Japan. The president and executives are usually chosen from among employees of the corporation who have worked for the corporation continuously for thirty or forty years after graduation from high school or college. It is not going too far to say that under the Japanese lifetime employment system, a firm's regular employees are the firm itself.

Under the Japanese employment system, an overwhelming majority of outstanding engineers, middle-management staff, and skilled workers remain in the same firm for their lifetime. If a firm discharges these workers during a recession, it would be difficult to rehire a competent, professional, skilled productive labor force after the recession ends. Therefore, a firm treats its permanent employees well in all aspects, such as working conditions, bonuses, promotions, wages, and job security. If it does not, it will not be able to recruit competent new employees.

Japanese unions nevertheless exert significant influence on wages. In a firm that earns high profits, employees always get the lion's share. Because the interests of the firm and its permanent employees have much in common, unions always have an interest in the survival and growth of the firm. It is not true that there are few strikes in Japan. But in the private sector most strikes are "ceremonial" and last only a few hours or possibly a day. Labor–management relations generally deteriorate only in the public sector, or when financial conditions of a firm in the private sector are so aggravated that the firm has to discharge even permanent employees.

The reasons why the level of employment does not change much through booms and recessions should now be obvious. Dismissals of permanent employees take place only when the firm encounters severe financial difficulties. For the same reason businesses are cautious about increasing the number of permanent employees in booms. Firms take on permanent employees only when they expect to maintain such employment in the long run. Adjustments to short-term fluctuations in labor demand are made through extending or cutting back overtime work, or through part-time workers, temporary workers, and workers on loan from other companies. When it becomes necessary for a firm to reduce the number of permanent employees, it will do so by not replacing those retiring, or by transferring redundant workers to other plants or divisions, or to affiliated companies which need them.

Employment performance: low unemployment rates. Let us now examine more closely factors behind Japan's consistently low rate of unemployment. Japanese employment practices and the labor-market characteristics are responsible in many respects for Japan's low unemployment rate relative to other developed countries. The practice of not discharging employees during a recession is one of the reasons, as mentioned above. Another important reason is the widespread existence of self-employed workers and marginal or peripheral workers. Many of these members of the labor force do not appear in the unemployment statistics, as they are not considered "entirely unemployed

millions

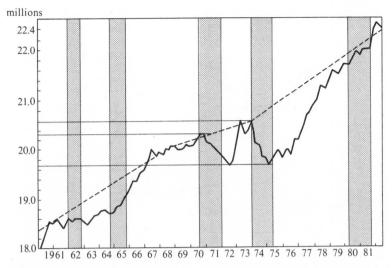

Figure 6
The size of the female labor force.
Source: Shimada (1981).
Note: Shaded areas are periods of recession.

persons." Haruo Shimada (1981) and his collaborators have shown persuasively that the size of the female labor force, namely, the number of women employed plus women counted as "entirely unemployed" increases in boom times, and contracts sharply in recessions (Figure 6).

To analyze this tendency more precisely, we have regressed the labor force participation rate,[8] separately for male and female, on (1) the unemployment rate for the heads of households, which is taken as a proxy variable for the employment condition, (2) permanent income of households,[9] and (3) transient income. The sample period extends from the first quarter of 1970 to the second quarter of 1982. The results are summarized as follows.

For *males*, when the employment condition worsens, the labor-force participation rate drops slightly. Also, a rise in permanent income causes a decline in labor-force participation. However, when transient income increases, the labor-force participation rate rises.

For *females*, results from using Shiller-type lags on the unemployment rate of household heads indicate that when the employment condition worsens, the labor-force participation rate declines at first. However, when an adverse employment condition continues, females search for jobs, thus increasing the female labor-force participation

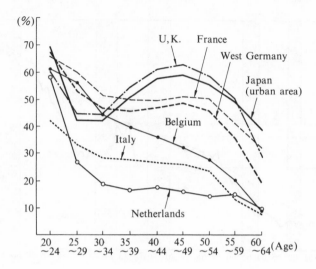

Figure 7
Labor force participation rate for females by age (Japan, 1975; EC countries, 1977).
Source: Koike (1980).

rate. A rise in permanent income of households brings about a decline in the female labor force. In contrast to males, however, when transient income increases the female labor-force participation rate declines. As pointed out by Koike (1980), Japan's female labor force is one of the highest among major industrialized countries. There are a number of difficulties in comparing internationally the female labor force, but according to Figure 7 Japan belonged, as early as 1970, to the countries having the highest labor-force participation for females between ages of 40 and 60. Most of these female workers in Japan, however, are marginal workers. Their wages and job security are low, and their length of continuous employment in a given firm is short (Figures 8 and 9). Until at least the late 1970s female workers tended to drop out of the labor market and to withdraw into their households during times of slack labor demand.

The preceding discussion indicates that the statement that Japan's performance in relation to unemployment is conspicuously good by international standards requires qualification. Certainly the Japanese practice of not discharging permanent employees in times of recession supports workers' incomes and contributes to economic and social

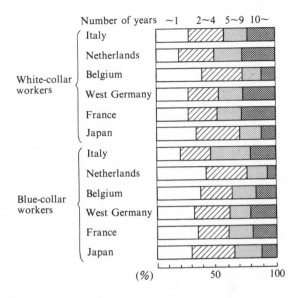

Figure 8
Composition of female work force by number of years of continuous employment (Japan, 1973; EC countries, 1972).
Source: Same as for Figure 7.

stability. Nevertheless, in such times, there is a large body of underemployed labor, and the "real" unemployment rate may be said to be higher than the statistics show. Also this practice of Japanese firms leads to much extended overtime work in boom times, constraining the free time of permanent workers.

Japanese unemployment statistics do not count as unemployed those people who are paid even for one hour's work during the week in which the employment survey is conducted. In family businesses, those who work over one hour but receive no pay are also counted as employed. This results in disguised employment, counting workers who are nearly unemployed as employed. Also, in Japan both the minimum wages enforced by labor legislation and the level of unemployment compensations are low relative to average wages. Those not in the labor force (neither employed nor searching for jobs) and marginal workers who receive low wages and/or work only for a short time in Japan may well be included in unemployment statistics in countries where minimum wages and unemployment compensations are higher.

Table 8
Energy Costs and Trend Rates in Production Indices for Manufacturing Industries

(%)

	Energy costs as a proportion of output value		Output		Production capacity		Fixed capital formation		Labor productivity	
	1973	1979	1968~73	1975~81	1968~73	1975~81	1968~73	1975~81	1969~73	1976~81
Machinery	n.a.	n.a.	12.3	11.4	13.2	3.8	5.7	18.5[a]	12.8	14.3
General	0.9	1.2	9.5	9.0	17.6	1.5	4.4	13.2	10.3	10.8
Electrical	0.6	0.9	14.7	15.7	12.1	4.2	4.5	23.6	16.0	18.0
Transport	0.8	1.2	12.7	5.5	12.6	4.8	7.2	17.0	12.5	6.4
Precision	0.6	0.8	10.7	26.3	5.8	12.8	n.a.	n.a.	11.0	25.8
Metal products	1.2	1.7	12.2	3.7	5.4	1.5	n.a.	n.a.	11.6[b]	5.2
Petroleum and coal products	3.8	3.6	12.6	-0.6	14.9	0.4	n.a.	n.a.	9.6	0.4
Textiles	1.7	3.7	5.6	0.6	2.8	-1.4	11.1	2.2	9.9	5.0
Chemicals	4.2	5.6	11.3	6.7	12.6	2.2	-1.5	-0.8	12.8	8.5
Nonferrous metal	2.8	5.7	10.4	5.5	13.0	1.3	1.8	8.0	11.5	8.4
Steel	5.8	7.7	9.8	3.2	11.3	2.3	0.2	-9.6	15.9	6.2
Pulp and paper	3.8	7.8	8.4	3.7	7.2	0.9	8.3	-0.4	13.1	7.2
Nonmetalic mineral products	6.6	12.0	8.4	4.1	8.8	1.9	n.a.	n.a.	10.0	6.8

Source: Economic Planning Agency, Economic White Paper for 1982. Trend rates are average rates of increase at annual rate.
[a] Total of general, electrical and transport machinery.
[b] 1971–73.

in oil prices were immediately shifted to prices of intermediate materials and finished products, contributing to the progress of energy conservation.

It is not easy to explain why the increase in productivity in Japanese manufacturing industries was higher than in other countries. Two factors may be pointed out here, however, to provide a partial answer. First, investment in plant and equipment in the private sector as a proportion of GNP is higher in Japan than in other countries. As stated in Section I, in the recession following the first crisis, this proportion dropped; but after 1978, investment in plant and equipment began to pick up. From an international perspective, Japan's private-sector capital formation was exceptionally high throughout the 1970s. This continued high rate of capital formation obviously contributed to increased labor productivity and advanced energy conservation.

Another important cause of Japan's high rate of productivity may be labor–management relations. Labor unions and individual workers are generally cooperative with employers on the production process and accompanying personnel transfers.

As an example, of the industrial robots in use in factories around the world, 70 to 80% are used in Japanese factories. Most robots in Japan are used to substitute for workers whose jobs are most unpleasant or difficult, such as welding, painting, handling high-temperature materials, rinsing materials in acid or alkaline solutions, and soldering integrated circuits.

In countries where labor unions are organized by kinds of jobs, such unions attempt to make it difficult to replace workers by robots. For instance, welders' unions will try to ensure that their jobs are not replaced by welding robots. In industry-wide labor unions also, similar opposition to the introduction of robots occurs if those workers originally employed as welders are discharged when welding robots are introduced.

In Japan, in contrast, a corps of blue-collar workers is employed by a firm as general workers under the lifetime commitment umbrella. After being employed they undergo training for several weeks or months, and then each worker is assigned to a specific job. For a young worker under the lifetime employment system, being assigned to an unpleasant, difficult job can bring a great deal of hardship. Hence, both the firm and workers involved investigate the best way to replace jobs by robots. When robots are so introduced, workers released from unpopular jobs receive additional training within the firm and are transferred to more desirable jobs. As far as permanent employees are concerned, most of them benefit directly from rationalization or

production but redundant labor as well. Marginal costs are quite low. Since domestic demand is stagnant and domestic sales are sluggish, firms look to foreign markets as outlets for their products and attempt to increase exports; i.e., the export-drive effect is observed.

Thus, since the middle of the 1960s, both movements of exports and imports have tended to improve the current account balance in recessions. Because the Japanese economy fell into an unusually deep recession following the first oil crisis, the export-drive effect was particularly strong. These exports pulled the Japanese economy toward recovery until 1977.

The export-drive effect in 1976–78 was less pronounced than in earlier times when Japan's share of world exports was smaller. Japan's share in the total world exports of manufactured goods has risen steadily, and reached 11–13% in 1976–78. Japan was no longer a "small country" in world trade. Also, after 1970, business fluctuations in the world economy had become synchronized. Hence, the Japanese export drive centering on manufactured goods in the face of the world recession increasingly caused trade friction, especially in the areas where Japan's share had become high such as automobiles, steel, video tape recorders, and machine tools. Through voluntary export restrictions on some of these products, export was curtailed. Because of stagnating world demand and export restrictions, the export-drive effect on the recession in Japan has not been as pronounced as earlier.

III. Monetary and Fiscal Policies

Let us now examine the role played by monetary and fiscal policies in the macroeconomic stabilization of the Japanese economy in the decade following the first oil crisis.

Monetary policy

In order to evaluate the monetary policy, let us consider the following four phases. Phases one and two are the periods preceding, and immediately after, the first oil crisis. Phase three covers 1975–78, when prices were largely stabilized and the Japanese economy faced sluggish demand. Finally, phase four concerns responses of monetary policy to the second oil crisis.

Monetary conditions prior to the first oil crisis. As shown in Figure 11, "detrended real money supply $(M2 + CD)$" expanded excessively in 1972 and 1973. The period 1971–72 witnessed a breakdown of the old Bretton Woods System. The yen-dollar parity which had been set

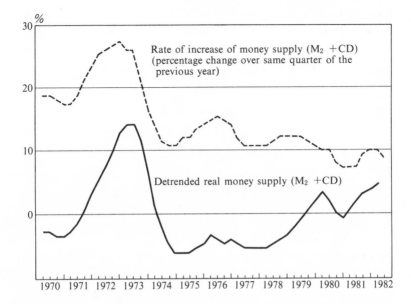

Figure 11
Detrended real money supply.
Source: Same as Figure 10. Detrended real money supply is defined as de-
viation from the trend of money supply deflated by GNP deflator.

and supported at a level of 360 yen to the United States dollar since
1949 was discarded, and the yen appreciated to 308 yen to the dollar.
This large appreciation of the yen led many Japanese to fear a serious
recession. For this reason, monetary policy was eased and the money
supply greatly expanded (Komiya and Suzuki, 1977).

From the fall of 1972, the Bank of Japan took a tightening stance
through the use of "window guidance." Early in 1973 the required
reserve ratio against bank deposits was raised, and the official discount
rate was raised in the spring. But these produced little effect in tightening the money supply until late in 1973. The detrended real money
supply did not decline until the fourth quarter of 1973. In September,
immediately before the first oil crisis, wholesale prices stood about
20% above the level of the same period in the preceding year, and
inflation was further accelerated after the outbreak of the oil crisis.
Yet the detrended real money supply remained more than 10% above
the trend level in the third quarter of 1973.

The first oil crisis occurred at a time when excessive money supply
had created rapid inflation and aggregate demand exceeded supply
capacity. All this resulted in aggravated inflation.

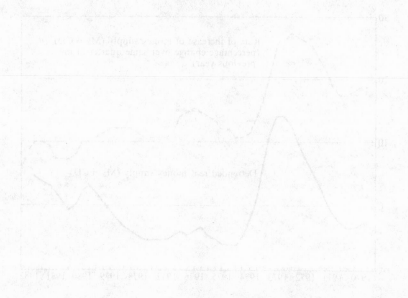

Table 11

Changes in the Discount Rate and the Reserve Ratio: 1979–80

Discount Rate		Reserve Ratio	
April 1979	3.5 → 4.25%		
July 1979	→ 5.25		
December 1979	→ 6.25		
February 1980	→ 7.25		
March 1980	→ 9.0	March 1980	1.625 → 1.75
		April 1980	→ 2.0
August 1980	→ 8.25		
November 1980	→ 7.25	November 1980	→ 1.75

Source: Same as Table 9.

second oil crisis started, the Japanese economy was undergoing a gradual recovery due mainly to a rise in domestic demand in late 1977. However, underutilization of capacity and labor persisted in many industries. Consequently, the Bank of Japan was confronted with a difficult choice in coping with the massive rise in oil prices. The Bank chose to give priority to price stability over a higher level of productive activity. Thus, in order to prevent the rise in oil prices from stirring up inflation again and especially from pushing up wages and other domestic factor prices, a tight money stance was firmly adopted.

From the first quarter of 1979, the Bank of Japan again restrained bank lending through "window guidance" and adopted a precautionary tight money policy to control inflation. From April 1979 until March 1980, the official discount rate and the required reserve ratio were raised several times, and "window guidance" was further strengthened (Table 11).

In the process of economic recovery led by expansion in domestic demand beginning in the latter half of 1978, the rates of increase in various indices of money supply went up considerably. However, as monetary policy shifted to tight money after the outbreak of the second oil crisis, the rate of increase in the money supply in 1979 did not exceed that of 1978. As a matter of fact it actually began to decline gradually from the second quarter of 1979 (see Figures 2 and 11).

Indices of import prices and wholesale prices peaked at yearly rates of increase of 85% (1st quarter 1980) and 22% (2nd quarter of 1980), respectively. The peak rate for the GNP deflator was only 4.8% (1st quarter of 1981), which was not much different from the level in the low-demand-pressure period 1976–78. In this regard, the second oil crisis was quite different from the first.

The Bank of Japan gave top priority to price stability, having learned from the experience of the first oil crisis, and was successful in overcoming strong inflationary pressures coming from the rise in oil prices. Also, wide recognition by the public at large, as well as by those responsible for economic policies, of the necessity of price stability as a critical condition for economic growth and social stability contributed to an appropriate monetary policy.

In order to stabilize prices, a stable money supply was viewed by the Bank of Japan as an important intermediate target. The Bank now considers that in view of the fairly long and complicated time lag in the effect of an increase in the money supply on aggregate demand, the money supply should not be increased excessively even in the early stage of a recovery when the GNP gap is still large.

But the Bank of Japan's use of money supply indices as an operating target of monetary policy is considerably different from that of the Federal Reserve Board in the United States. From the third quarter of 1978, the Bank of Japan has been making quarterly announcements of the expected money supply. Unlike the Federal Reserve Board which announces the target range of the money supply up to a year ahead, the Bank of Japan's approach has been primarily a forecast of the rate of increase in the money supply for the next quarter over the previous year, based upon trends in business conditions and in prices, and the current stance of monetary policy. The Bank uses the projection as a yardstick to analyze factors causing differences between the predicted and realized values of the money supply.

In projecting and also in implementing monetary policy, the Bank of Japan emphasizes a wider and more stable definition of money (M_2 + CD) than M_1, which is used by the Federal Reserve.

As for other monetary variables, although it is not true that the Bank of Japan totally disregards interest rates as monetary policy variables, neither before nor after the first oil crisis did the Bank of Japan attempt to stabilize the nominal or real interest rates at particular levels or within particular ranges. One of the circumstances which led to the stress on money supply indices as a more important intermediate variable for monetary policy than interest rates may be the fact that not all interest rates are entirely flexible in Japan.

Interest rates in the short-term money markets in Japan, such as call-money rates, "gensaki" rates (yield of bonds traded on repurchase agreements), bank-bill discount rates, and CD rates, have become flexible recently; yet interest rates on bank deposits and bond rates at the time of floatation are still regulated de facto, if not de jure. Hence, interest rates in the banking system, including lending rates, tend to be more or less rigid rather than fully flexible.

Therefore, when strong tight-money policy was called for, as it was

the strong built-in stabilizing effect of increased tax revenue, caused the real-demand effect of the government sector to turn negative for a short time in the first quarter of 1974.

The fiscal policy stance announced by the Ministry of Finance and other officials at the beginning of 1974 was a very tight one, but there were several loopholes in the restrictive policies. The 1974 fiscal year budget announced at the end of 1973 included reductions of personal income and other taxes totalling 1.8 trillion yen, an unprecedented figure. Preparations for this reduction of personal income tax and other taxes had been made in view of the high inflation then prevailing, but in light of later developments the timing of this huge tax cut was unfortunate (Komiya, 1976).

Another loophole was the supplementary budget for 1974 which increased government expenditure for that fiscal year substantially. This increase was necessitated by adjustments in social welfare expenditures and the salaries of government employees to compensate for losses due to inflation.[13]

Because of these loopholes, the index for the demand effect of the government sector in nominal base exhibited an increase between 20–40% from the second quarter of 1974 until the third quarter of 1975.

In 1975, the fiscal policy stance was somewhat confused. The government had promised publicly to bring down the high inflation rate to a one-digit level by March 1975 (see Section II). Also, it was clear that the government deficit was increasing rapidly, and government officials felt that a further increase would create greater difficulties. On the other hand, because of the strong deflationary impact of the oil crisis, there were calls for expansionary fiscal policies. These conflicting demands created confusion.

Fiscal policies in the low-demand pressure period. In the low-demand pressure period 1976–78, tax revenues were low, on the one hand; on the other hand it was difficult to keep such items of government expenditures as salaries of government employees, social welfare programs, national health insurance payments, social insurance payments, and subsidies to government corporations from rising. Hence, the government deficit grew rapidly. The dependence on borrowing by the central government, defined as a proportion of the total expenditure in the general account of the central government financed by bond issues, climbed from 11% in 1974 to 25% in 1975 and 29% in 1976.

In 1976, wariness about government deficits was heightened, and a policy to keep the dependence on public debt below 30% was announced. Measures to raise minor taxes and to restrain government expenditures were implemented. As a result, the index for the demand effect of the government sector in both real and nominal terms was much lower in 1976 than in 1975.

After the middle of 1976, foreign governments charged that Japan achieved recovery through a sort of "beggar-thy-neighbor" policy and asked the Japanese government to increase domestic demand. In the 1977 and 1978 fiscal years, considering these criticisms and requests, the Japanese government abandoned its principle of keeping the debt dependence ratio below 30%, and adopted fiscal measures to stimulate the economy. In 1978, domestic demand, especially private-sector investment in plant and equipment, which had been stagnating since the first oil crisis, began to pick up. First expansionary fiscal policy and later private investment led the Japanese economy to recovery. In 1978 and the first half of 1979, exports were not the driving force in recovery, partly because of the appreciation of the yen (Figure 10).

The second oil crisis and thereafter. The 1979 (initial) budget was mildly expansionary. Central and local government investment expenditures were 20% larger than in the previous year. At the beginning of 1980, part of the expenditures appropriated in 1979 were postponed to the 1980 fiscal year. The stance of policies in fiscal 1980 was moderately restrictive. Also, the increase in tax revenues due to inflation brought about by the oil crisis exerted a strong built-in stabilizing effect.

The overall demand effect of the government sector was restrictive in both real and nominal terms in 1979 and 1980. The fiscal policies helped to curb inflationary expectations and to prevent so-called "homemade" inflation.

Evaluation of fiscal policy. How would one evaluate these developments in fiscal policy from the viewpoint of macroeconomic stabilization? Our first impression is that counter-cyclical fiscal policy during highly turbulent times such as the 1970s and early 1980s was in any sense difficult to carry out. A fairly long period is required from the recognition of the necessity for discretionary fiscal policy, through the adoption and implementation of such policy, to the final effects upon the private sector and GNP. The appreciation of the yen brought about by the breakdown of the old Bretton Woods system, the two oil crises, rapid inflation, the deepest depression since World War II and world wide depression all worked against a smoothly working discretionary counter-cyclical fiscal policy.

Second, the built-in stabilizing effect of fluctuations in tax revenues appears to have been quite strong in the period immediately preceding the first oil crisis and also in the inflationary periods following both oil crises. Also, in 1975–76 a sharp decline in corporate tax yields acted as a stabilizer, at least through its direct impact on effective demand.

Third, it is not clear how fiscal policy can be used as a stabilizer in the face of external shocks which greatly reduce effective demand on the one hand and accelerate inflation on the other.

Finally, although it is relatively easy to increase fiscal expenditures, it is difficult to reduce these expenditures or even to prevent them from increasing later. It takes time to persuade those concerned that reductions are necessary. Political opposition to such reductions is always strong. Thus, the adoption of retrenchment policy tends to be delayed. From a middle-to-long-term perspective, fiscal policies were continuously expansionary from 1971 to 1975 and resulted in the large cumulative government deficits today. Confronted with the huge accumulated government debts for the above-mentioned reasons, it will be difficult for Japan to use fiscal policy as an effective countercyclical instrument in the near future.

Conclusion

In Japan, rapid inflation following the first oil crisis had been largely contained by 1975–76, primarily by a drastically restrictive monetary policy. Milder inflation following the second oil crisis had on the whole been successfully overcome by the early 1980s. In the period from 1975 to the present, Japan's performance in regard to inflation, unemployment, the balance of payments, and productivity increase has been better than in most industrialized countries. Especially after the second oil crisis, many other countries experienced high inflation and unemployment, whereas Japan's inflation and unemployment rates remained at a low level.

It is not easy to identify the main factors on which Japan's performance was based. This paper has examined various factors which are thought to be related to Japan's good macroeconomic performance.

Because Japan's labor market is heterogeneous, unemployment in an open, clearly identifiable form is smaller than the real degree of underutilization of labor, including disguised unemployment. The labor force participation rate fluctuates considerably responding to business conditions, and the labor force shrinks in recessions. Hence, during recessions, unemployment statistics do not rise as much as they would in other countries where unemployment takes primarily an explicit form. Thus, unemployment has so far not become too serious a social problem in Japan.

In Japan, real wages are sensitive to supply and demand in the labor market. Hence, in times of recession, wages do not exert an upward pressure on costs. In other industrialized countries, because of the strong wage-push pressure exerted by labor unions, the phenomenon of a wage–price spiral is widely recognized. Even when the inflation rate in Japan was very high, as during the first oil crisis, the real wage-price spiral phenomenon did not occur.

The uniqueness of the wage determination mechanism in Japan is closely related to labor union organization, which is on an enterprise-by-enterprise basis. A firm's management and the labor union organized by its employees have many interests in common. If a firm earns a high profit, the wages of employees rise and bonuses are large. In recession, when a firm is not doing well and expectations for the future are not bright, the rise in wages is restrained. It is primarily through this mutual awareness that tight money policy in Japan has a strong restraint on prices.

Labor unions organized on an enterprise-by-enterprise basis are also important in contributing to Japan's productivity increase, conspicuously higher than in other countries. Since the first oil crisis the Japanese industrial structure has swiftly adjusted to high energy costs, and energy conservation has progressed fast both in individual industries and in the economy as a whole. Labor unions generally cooperate with the management in the productive process: replacing workers by robots, introducing new products, opening up new areas of business, and redistributing labor. It is largely in their own interests to do so, as union members are usually guaranteed job security under lifetime employment practices and their incomes increase.

In Japan exports decline in booms and the balance of payments on current account turns into deficit, whereas exports increase and the balance of payments becomes surplus in recessions. This has been observed since the end of the 1950s, and the tendency of exports to increase in recessions has been called the "export-drive effect" of a recession. It contributes not only to restoring the balance on current account but also to the stability of aggregate effective demand. However, the relative importance of Japan in the world economy has increased substantially, and this, along with the fact that many major countries simultaneously fell into a deep depression after the first oil crisis, has caused "trade friction" between Japan and other major industrialized countries. Thus, the export-drive effect of the recession is weakened.

Concerning the role of monetary policy, the Bank of Japan, having learned a lesson from excessively easy money and rapid inflation at the time of the first oil crisis, first adopted a severe tight money policy and then a policy of cautiously stabilizing the money supply. These were successful in winding down inflationary expectations and contributed to price stability after 1975. In the recession of 1975–77, the Bank of Japan did not shift to an explicit easy-money policy, as in previous recessions, and excessive liquidity was not built up during the low-demand-pressure period from 1975 to 1978, contrary to what happened in 1971–73. Here lie the main reasons why Japan's macroeconomic performance in the face of the second oil crisis was better by far than in 1973–75. Fiscal policy was also moderately restraining in 1979–80.

The prices of oil-related products rose after the second oil crisis, but the general price level did not; the GNP deflator was extremely stable in 1979–81. "Homemade" inflation did not occur as in 1971–73. The impact of the two oil crises on the Japanese economy was quite different, depending on whether or not excessive liquidity had been built up by high money supply or inflationary expectations were already rampant before the outbreak of the crisis.

The review of fiscal policies from the first oil crisis to the present indicates the great difficulty in the successful use of discretionary fiscal policy for stabilization purposes under contemporary turbulent circumstances. A positive factor has been the built-in stabilizing effect of tax revenues from personal income and corporate taxes. Also, fiscal policy during the second oil crisis was better managed than at the time of the first oil crisis.

Since 1975, the government in Japan has been running huge deficits. Government debt and the debt of government corporations have increased enormously. There is as yet no clear solution to restoring a reasonable balance in government finance. It seems that an effective use of fiscal policy as counter-cyclical measures cannot be expected in the near future.

In the ten years following the first oil crisis, Japanese economic performance was better than that of most other industrialized countries. Nevertheless, the present outlook for the Japanese economy is not bright. The Japanese economy is now undergoing a recession induced by the stagnation of world economy. How quickly the Japanese economy can recover from this recession seems to depend much on the world economic recovery.

This chapter was co-authored by Kazuo Yasui, who was then with the Bank of Japan. It originally appeared in Volume 20 of the Carnegie-Rochester Conference Series on Public Policy, published in 1984 by North-Holland.

Notes

1. "Normalized GNP gap" is calculated as the ratio of actual real GNP to the level of real GNP which is high enough but does not accelerate inflation (what we call "normalized GNP"). Normalized GNP was derived from the following estimated Cobb-Douglas equation by substituting the labor force under the normal economic condition and the corresponding operating ratio for actual values.

$$\ell n \frac{Y}{E} = a\ell n \frac{K \cdot OCR}{E} + b\ell n V + \ell n\theta \cdot \frac{P_e}{P} + dt$$

Y : Real GNP
E : Labor input (man-hours)
K : Total capital stock
OCR : Operation ratio index for manufacturing industries
V : Vintage of capital
θ : Ratio of oil consumption to real GNP
P_e : Price index of imported oil
P : GNP deflator
t : Time trend variable

2. In Japan the official rate of "complete" unemployment does not necessarily reflect the actual labor-market condition for the reasons explained in Section III. Labor-force participation rate especially declines in recessions, contributing to relatively low unemployment rate in official statistics. Therefore, the normalized unemployment rate is calculated as the ratio of actual number of workers employed to the normal size of the labor force which corresponds to the normalized level of real GNP using the equation for the labor-force participation rate estimated separately for male and female workers.

3. In this regard, Shinkai (1981), quoting a position paper of one of the labor union's national centers, stated that union leaders even considered the worsening in the terms of trade when making their wage demands, and demanded a lower rate of increase in real wages than the growth rate of real GNP.

4. The rate of unemployment of household heads may reflect not only the strength of labor supply and demand forces but also business conditions in general. Overtime pay is an important component of wage bills. Overtime pay increases in booms, and decreases in times of recession. The value of the coefficient on U_t probably reflects this.

5. These workers may be transferred to an affiliated company for a few years on an "on-loan" basis during their career and on a permanent basis towards the end of their career. Yet they are by and large under the lifetime employment umbrella.

6. There are exceptions to this. The Japan Merchant Marine Union is organized on an industry-wide basis. Also, there are cases in which workers employed by one firm are organized into two or more unions. On the other hand, large firms which are not unionized are not uncommon.

7. This tradition dates back to the Tokugawa period for white-collar workers, and has spread gradually to blue-collar workers since the early 1930s. The lifetime employment practice for blue-collar workers became well established only after World War II.

8. The labor force participation rate is defined as those participating in the labor force (those employed those plus "entirely unemployed") divided by the total potential labor force.

9. Permanent income has been represented by the average real wages of the past three years.

10. Recently it is becoming popular even among very small businesses employing only a few workers to use, for example, welding robots. This is because it is now becoming difficult to hire workers who are willing to take welding jobs in such small businesses.

11. Until the middle of the 1960s machinery imports increased much during booms because of the rise in prices and the lengthening of the delivery time of domestic machinery producers, and exhibited the same cyclical pattern as described in the text.

12. Portions of these profits were not real, but nominal due to insufficient (in real terms) depreciation allowances.

13. In Japan, the fiscal year lasts from April to March. The central government budget is compiled in December or January and voted on in the Diet between January and March. However, to cope with changing economic conditions, a supplementary budget (or sometimes two) is usually prepared, voted and implemented during the last part of the fiscal year. The increased government expenditures necessitated by unexpected inflation referred in the text were common to both the central and local governments. Welfare benefits and the salaries of central and local government employees are largely uniform throughout the country.

References

Carlson, J.A. and M. Parkin (1975). "Inflation Expectations", *Economica*, **42**: 123–38.

Koike, K. (1980). "Female Labor Force Participation Rates and Wage Difference Between Male and Female—An International Comparison" (in Japanese), *Contemporary Economics*, **35**: 33–44.

Komiya, R. (1976). "The Causes of the 1973–74 Inflation" (in Japanese), *Keizaigaku Ronshu*, **42**: 2–40.

Komiya, R. and Y. Suzuki (1977). "Inflation in Japan", in L. Krause and W.S. Salant (eds), *Worldwide Inflation: Theory and Recent Experience*. Washington, D.C.: Brookings Institution.

Shimada, H. et. al. (1981). *Japan's Labor Market Mechanism* (in Japanese). Tokyo: Economic Planning Agency.

Shinkai, Y. (1981). "Terms of Trade, Wages and Foreign Exchange Rates in Japan" (in Japanese), *Economic Journal of Osaka University*, **31**: 1–29.

CHAPTER 9

ECONOMIC POLICY MAKERS IN THE JAPANESE GOVERNMENT

In Japan one cannot discuss the role of the economist in government, since there is not one professional economist employed as such by the government of Japan. The employment practices and personnel policies of the Japanese government, or any other large institutional employer in Japan, are quite different from those of countries with European traditions. Two distinctive characteristics peculiar to Japan in regard to the role of the economist in the government are: firstly, there is no profession called economist in Japanese society; second, large organizations in Japan, whether government ministries, banks, or corporations, are run by generalist administrators or managers who work in most cases in one organization for their entire careers and reach the top positions after occupying many different posts in the organization.

There is no word in the Japanese language which corresponds exactly to "economist" in English. The term *keizai-gakusha* means "academic economist," that is, a professor or scholar who teaches and/or does research in economics at a university or a research institute. Although a graduate from the School of Economics of a university receives a bachelor's degree in economics (*keizai-gakushi*) and is referred to as a graduate of the Economics School or "economics graduate," these graduates cannot be said to constitute a recognized profession. Neither in government nor business employment is a graduate in economics treated as a professional economist, nor, indeed, as one significantly different from a graduate from a School of Law, Management, Commerce, or even Literature. Master's or doctor's degrees are conferred on those who have studied economics and fulfilled the requirements of the new system of graduate education started in 1949. But most of those entering a Graduate School of Economics choose to become academic economists, researchers in research institutes, or school teachers, and very few go into public service or the business world, because there is no demand from the government or business for candidates with advanced degrees in economics.[1] A Japanese ministry or agency is run by a relatively small number of elite generalist administrators, and there are few senior-rank positions for professional specialists of any kind in the government. The same is true of the central bank, commercial banks, and big corporations in general.

As compared with industrialized countries with European traditions there are distinctive features in the recruitment and promotion process of high-ranking officers in charge of economic affairs in the Japanese government:

(i) a highly competitive examination when they are first employed on their graduation from colleges;

(ii) the so-called "lifetime employment" practice within a single ministry or agency;

(iii) extensive on-the-job training throughout their careers; and

(iv) steady promotion year by year on a seniority basis, up to positions near to the very top.

In the process of promotion according to the seniority principle the generalist administrator holds a series of different posts in a wide range of areas.

A corollary of the lifetime employment practice and the seniority principle in promotion is that government and academic society constitute two separate worlds, as far as the interchange of personnel is concerned, although academic economists and the economic policymakers interact in several ways. There is no opportunity for outsiders to enter government service as permanent employees, except at the time of graduation from schools. Thus the civil servant's career is completely separated from that of a professor of economics, political science, or international relations. Unlike the practice in the United States and other countries, in postwar Japan prominent academic economists have never occupied important positions in government or the central bank; nor have highranking officials become professors in leading universities after retiring from government service.

Because elite administrators or managers serve essentially in the same ministry or corporation for a long time—up to thirty to forty years—such an organization in Japan is a solid, independent, and cohesive body, maintaining a degree of solidarity and consistency over time. Anyone who occupies a responsible position in such an organization highly values harmony, solidarity, and consensus within the organization.

Japanese people try very hard to achieve full consensus inside an organization. Under normal conditions a decision within a tightly knit organization must be unanimous; a majority decision, however small the minority, is considered a sign of lack of solidarity. Hence a decision on a major issue by voting must be avoided as far as possible in any well-developed Japanese organization, such as a ministry, a political party, the board of directors of a corporation, or a faculty or the senate of a university.

This tendency towards consensus and solidarity among the elite administrators belonging to a ministry or agency may explain why the Japanese bureaucracy has a strong tradition of non-partisanship and political neutrality.

Historical Background

The characteristics of the Japanese bureaucracy briefly described above were already well established before World War II. Nor is government intervention in private economic affairs a new phenomenon in postwar Japan: ever since the Meiji period the government has intervened extensively in private activities for economic and other policy purposes in order to industrialize and modernize the then backward Japanese economy and society.

However, economic issues have become much more important in politics and government policy in postwar Japan. The military, which had great political influence in prewar years, collapsed at the end of the war and disappeared from the political scene. But the bureaucracy was able to maintain its broad continuity from the prewar period, despite extensive democratization measures under the American occupation immediately after the war.

In the early postwar years, the most important national objective on which the government concentrated its effort was "economic independence," meaning growth and balance-of-payments equilibrium without foreign aid. "Export or die" was a popular slogan in those days. Thereafter, "the high rate of economic growth" was given a high priority in government policies. Thus, economic problems and the social problems related to these objectives became among the most important policy issues in postwar Japan.

About 1955, when the national economic plan was prepared and published for the first time, government officers first began to pay attention to economics and economic theory. Initially only a small group of officers in the agency responsible for national economic planning (the Economic Planning Agency, EPA) concerned themselves with economics. In practice in those early days the officers making the key economic policy decisions were not concerned with economics or the national economic plan.[2] Interestingly enough, a high percentage of the pioneers in EPA were graduates from the School of Engineering—partly, perhaps, because Marxian economics was the dominant school in economics in the leading Japanese universities during the early postwar period, with only a few exceptions, such as Hitotsubashi University. It was only after about 1960 that contemporary non-Marxist economics began to be taught on a full scale at the University of Tokyo, which continued, as in prewar years, to produce a large proportion of high-ranking government officials.

Prime Minister Hayato Ikeda's Income Doubling Plan, published in 1960, was an epoch-making event in postwar Japanese economic and political history in several respects, including its impact on the role of economics in economic policymaking. This plan was based upon the original ideas of Osamu Shimomura, then an officer in the Ministry of Finance, who deserves great credit for bringing economics and economic theory into politics and the bureaucracy. Since then, Keynesian macroeconomics, the Harrod-Domar theory of growth and business cycles, national income accounting and macroeconometric models have been widely discussed and rapidly disseminated in government and the business world. During the recession which began in 1965, the balanced-budget principle upheld in the postwar years was formally abandoned by a law enacted in 1966, and Keynesian fiscal policy began to play a major role as a countercyclical measure.

Throughout the latter half of the 1960s and the 1970s Japan's international economic relations with other major countries became increasingly close. The Japanese government played a much more active role in IMF, GATT, and OECD than earlier, reflecting Japan's growing importance in the world economy as a result of Japan's "economic miracle." The number of cooperative economic projects as well as conflicts with other countries has been increasing, and Japan's status in international conferences has been rising. Consequently the Japanese government's top officials have been obliged to take a growing interest in international economic affairs and adopt an economic approach to them.

However, despite these trends the government ministries' and agencies' demand for professional economists has not increased. As in earlier days, the prevailing Japanese bureaucratic tradition has subordinated the professional specialists, so that almost all the career officers in government are treated as general administrators rather than specialists or professionals. As in other countries, new university graduates trained in contemporary non-Marxist economics have joined ministries and agencies concerned with economic affairs. Older officers in those organizations have also tried to learn the subject, and incentives have been provided to encourage this re-education process. Nevertheless, this only means that a certain amount of knowledge of economics, especially macroeconomics, has become recognized as a common-sense requirement for top-level officials in charge of economic affairs. It does not mean that the government has wanted to employ professional economists as such, in the European or American sense of the term.

Economists within the Japanese Government

As already mentioned, there is no word in the Japanese language corresponding to "economist" in English, and there is no socially recognized economics profession.[3] All the government's economic affairs are managed by elite generalist administrators.

Although the word *kancho-ekonomisuto* (economist in the government) is sometimes used in Japanese, it refers only to a very few highly competent people who are prominent in economic forecasting, planning, and research within the government and frequently express their views on economic prospects and macroeconomic problems.[4] They appear to be influential in governmental decision-making, both because they occupy key posts and because they display excellent judgment on macroeconomic trends and policy issues. Sometimes their personal acquaintance with the Prime Minister, ministers, or the president or governors of the Bank of Japan may be a crucial determinant of their influence on economic policy.

Generally speaking, however, personal specialist capability as an "economist" is not much appreciated in Japan. In practice, an official's rank or position and his ability to mobilize his staff resources are usually the decisive factors. We shall therefore focus our attention on those posts in the government which are especially important in the decisions on economic policy. These include most of the senior posts in the Ministry of Finance (MOF), the Ministry of International Trade and Industry (MITI), and the EPA, which are the three foremost among ministries and agencies in charge of economic affairs; also the Bank of Japan (BOJ), which does not belong to the government but is in charge of monetary policy; and the Ministry of Foreign Affairs,[5] which has many senior posts more or less concerned with the government's economic policy.

Most of the occupants of these posts are highly intelligent and capable men, who are generally quite knowledgeable about economic affairs under their jurisdiction. In practice they often play the role of an economist. In addition, there are a few senior posts dealing primarily with economic problems in such government offices as the Ministry of Agriculture, Forestry and Fisheries, Ministry of Transport, the Ministry of Construction, the Ministry of Welfare, the Ministry of Labor, and the Fair Trade Commission.

Those who occupy these posts have varied backgrounds, except that almost all have been what is called a "career officer" in the ministry or agency in question. All are basically "generalist" administrators, diplomats, or central bank officers; none is a professional economist. They are influential in the economic policymaking process not because they apply advanced knowledge of economics or economic theory to the issues under consideration, but because they have wide experience as generalist administrators and can react promptly to new problems and changing circumstances, mobilize the information, knowledge, and capabilities available among their subordinate staff, and build up a consensus among those concerned through deliberate persuasion and skillful negotiation. In making judgments on any given issue they must take many factors into account: economic, legal and political aspects, precedents, relations with other ministries and agencies, and public opinion and sentiment. Indeed, given the existing climate of opinion in the Japanese bureaucracy any attempt on the part of a high official to parade his knowledge of advanced economic theory or to discuss current issues primarily or exclusively in economic terms, in the manner of a professional economist, will probably provoke negative reactions. Most of the career officers performing economist functions do not wish to be regarded as economists. They know that they may in future be transferred to non-economic work and appreciate that there are better career opportunities for generalist administrators in higher posts both within and outside the ministry or agency. There are, however, some exceptions to this generalization, for recently a few specialists have left the EPA to become university professors or join research organizations and, anticipating such a move, may have been glad to be known as economists.

The Recruitment Process

Every year the Personnel Agency conducts National Government Officers Examinations to select candidates for government positions. The examination system, which started in 1949, includes written examinations of various categories, and each ministry or agency must select and interview its own prospective employees from one of the lists of candidates prepared by the Personnel Agency, which releases the names and records of those who passed the written examinations in the respective categories. Some are employed in the main office of each ministry or agency, while others go into one of the regional branch offices.

Those wishing to become a "career officer" (or simply "career," as they are known) actively involved in the process of economic policy-making in the MOF, the MITI, the EPA, or elsewhere must first pass in the senior level (*jokyushoku-koshu*) examination, and then be interviewed in the main office of one of these ministries or agencies. Once employed, they are promoted annually according to a given pattern, at the fastest speed permitted by Personnel Agency Regulations, and they eventually occupy most of the key government policy-making posts.

The Ministry's other head-office staff are either hired directly after passing the medium- or junior-level examination, or are transferred from a regional branch office—in the case of the MOF, for example, a regional tax office or a regional financial office—after several years of distinguished service. Such persons are sometimes called "non-career" officers even though they also serve on a lifetime, seniority-principle basis. Some very capable "non-career" officers are promoted to the Division Director level in the main office.[6]

Within the senior level there are various categories of examinations such as administration, law, economics, civil engineering, etc. (in 1978 there were 28 such categories of examinations altogether). In each case the written examination is comparable to that set for university graduates. Most of those wishing to become career officers in economic ministries or agencies are graduates from the Schools of Law or Economics.[7]

The senior-level examination in law or economics is highly competitive, and in recent years only 1 in 40 has passed (see Table 1). Most of the successful candidates have first-class academic records in a few leading Japanese universities, so that the government can choose its career officers from among very capable graduates.

However, it is inappropriate to regard an applicant who has passed

Table 1

Results of the Senior-level Written Examination for Career Government Officers (*jokyushuku-koshu*)

	Total	Law	Economics
Applicants, 1977	48,514	8,729	5,060
Those passing	1,206	240	89
Applicants, 1978	55,992	10,630	5,826
Those passing	1,311	245	89

the economics examination and is hence eligible for interview as an economist. Under the current Japanese system, specialized undergraduate education in economics lasts only about two years (before 1953 it was three years), since the first two years of college education are devoted to general cultural education. Hence, on their employment they have only an elementary knowledge of economics. Moreover, the personnel officers of the ministry or agency in question who conduct the interviews do not expect the candidates either to possess or to acquire the advanced knowledge of economics required by a professional economist.

As Table 2 shows, recently the MOF and the MITI have annually employed about 25 administrative "career" officers each from among the successful candidates at the senior-level examinations, and EPA about 8. They are selected mainly because of their potential ability or general personality and, second, according to the distribution of the new vintage of career officers in any given year in terms of such factors as the schools from which they graduate and their backgrounds—urban, provincial, etc.

In the case of the MOF, in recent years about a fourth to a third of new career employees every year have passed the economics examination.[8] Before 1963, and especially in prewar years, most of the MOF's career officers were law graduates, and the share of economics graduates was no more than 10 percent (the prewar recruitment system was somewhat different from the present one). Apparently the MOF has recently attached greater importance to the economics examination as a source of new recruits.[9] The MITI personnel policy is similar to that of the MOF, but the share of those passing the economics examination is somewhat higher. In addition to those counted in Table 2, the MITI hires about 20 new "engineering" career officers every year who have passed various subdivisions of the senior level engineering examination. They later occupy senior posts in the ministry's research-oriented offices or laboratories under MITI.

Besides the three government offices listed in Table 2, successful

Table 2
Number of Administrative Career Officers Newly Employed by the MOF,
MITI, and EPA: 1960-78[a]

	I. MOF		II. MITI		III. EPA	
Year	Total	Econ. exam.	Total	Econ. exam.	Total	Econ. exam.
1960	17	1	18	6	4	2
1961	18	5	19	4	3	3
1962	21	3	23	8	4	4
1963	20	1	22	4	5	4
1964	20	5	24	8	5	5
1965	20	8	21	6	7	2
1966	22	1	18	5	9	6
1967	23	7	18	6	7	6
1968	22	10	19	9	7	4
1969	21	6	23	8	9	8
1970	22	6	19	9	10	9
1971	23	5	22	6	10	9
1972	24	8	18	6	7	5
1973	17	9	21	7	7	4
1974	27	9	21	9	9	7
1975	27	6	26	12	7	5
1976	25	7	25	11	8	7
1977	23	6	23	9	8	6
1978	26	8	26	8	7	7

[a] "Total" refers to the number of career officers newly employed in each year and "Econ. exam." to those among them who passed the economics examination. Comparable figures for all kinds of officers newly employed in each year are not available. The total number of all officers in the service of the MOF, MITI or EPA is as follows:

	MOF	MITI	EPA
1970	15,895	7,755	570
1978	15,421	6,591	512

The above figures refer to the respective ministries proper, and do not include those in the Internal Revenue Agency, Printing Bureau, and Mint Bureau under the MOF, nor those in the Agency of Industrial Science and Technology, Patent Agency, Small and Medium Enterprise Agency, and Resources and Energy Agency under the MITI. The total number of career officers in the service of the MOF, MITI, or EPA in a year is not available either, but since they normally serve twenty to thirty-five years after being employed, it would not be far from the mark if one multiplied the average figure in Table 2 for each ministry by 25.

economics candidates are sought by the Ministries of Construction, Transport, Home Affairs, Agriculture, Forestry and Fisheries, Labor, and Health and Welfare and by the Fair Trade Commission, Defense Agency, and Agency for Environmental Protection. However, each of these offices usually employs only from one to three recruits, sometimes none at all. An overwhelming majority of the administrative career officers of these ministries and agencies have passed the law examination.

Although the Bank of Japan is responsible for monetary policy its officers are not government officials. While its employees do not come under the National Government Officers Examination System, its personnel policy is closely parallel to that of the MOF or MITI. The BOJ hires about 25 to 30 new graduates every year as its career officers, of which the proportion of economics graduates (including a few in Commerce and Management) is approximately 60%, the rest being overwhelmingly law graduates. Nevertheless the BOJ does not consider economics graduates as professional economists, either actual or potential. However in recent years it has begun to foster a new breed of central-bank economists by sending a very small number of promising young career officers to graduate schools in the United States and elsewhere, afterwards frequently placing them in research-oriented posts in the Research or Statistics Bureau, or the recently established Institute for Monetary and Economic Studies. Roughly half of the present executive governors and directors general of the BOJ are recent economics graduates. Three out of eight post–World War II presidents have been economics graduates, although none of them has ever been considered a professional economist.

Promotion and Functions

We shall now discuss how career officers in charge of economic affairs are promoted year by year within a ministry, and what kind of work or functions they perform at each stage. We shall focus on the Ministry of Finance, the office most influential on economic affairs, but mention other offices as necessary.

First years in the Ministry

A freshman career officer entering MOF is usually first assigned to a division dealing with relatively generalized and/or coordinating work in a bureau such as the General Affairs Division, the Research Division, or the Archives and Documents Division in the Minister's Secretariat (*Kanbo*). This is in order to enable him or her to learn about the ministry's activities and become familiar with the annual cycle of its administrative operation. Here he serves for two years as an apprentice and undergoes basic training such as preparing documents, processing statistical data, or accompanying and helping a senior officer in negotiations with other offices within or outside of the ministry.

When a freshman is allocated to a particular division, no attention is paid to the kind of examination he passed or the school he graduated from. Thus an economics graduate may be assigned to a section dealing mainly with legal affairs, or a law graduate to a section performing economic or statistical analysis. Once a young man has succeeded in the highly competitive entrance examination and entered MOF as a career officer, he is now an integral part of the MOF family, and his academic background ceases to be a significant attribute.

In the third year, five or six out of the annual crop of about twenty-five career officers are sent abroad for two years' graduate work in Economics or Business Administration (usually two to the United States, two to France, one to England, and one to Germany). All the rest are withdrawn from administrative assignments and attached to the Minister's Secretariat as an "economic theory (economics, as a matter of fact) trainee" for one full year's schooling in economics (see Appendix A). Thus nowadays even if a career officer is not an economics graduate, he will have had a fairly extensive basic training in economics either at home or abroad. The BOJ and MITI have similar but less extensive in-service training programs, with the main emphasis on economics.

After finishing the "economic theory training" program or graduate study abroad, the MOF's career officer becomes a section chief (*kakari-cho*) for two years, and for the first time performs real administrative duties requiring a fair amount of judgment. This will be during his fourth and fifth years in MOF (i.e. fifth and sixth years for those who have studied abroad). However, he does not make final decisions by himself, but follows the instructions of his immediate senior officer, an assistant director (*kacho-hosa*).

Director of an Internal Revenue Office

The MOF career officer is next assigned for one year as director of a local office of the Internal Revenue Agency. As the director of a small office in a local town or city he is expected to learn how to make judgments and decisions, and above all, how to exercise leadership. At the same time he must become familiar with the reality of a local economy, and learn how the MOF administration becomes involved with the common people. He will be in charge of some fifty to sixty subordinates, many of them older, some much older than himself and with far longer service in tax administration. He will also prepare himself to become a senior government officer by making formal and informal contacts with influential local personalities such as business executives, politicans, and local government administrators. This is a unique on-the-job training program for the career officer in MOF, which is an essential part of its long tradition, though it somewhat resembles the training of a French *inspecteur des finances*. Thus about 20 to 25 out of the 506 local Internal Revenue Offices (in 1978) throughout Japan are headed by such young career officers (aged 28 to 30) each year. As the result of this experience, they are said to mature greatly both personally and as administrators and leaders.

Other ministries also send their career officers to their local offices or posts in prefectural governments outside the central government. In the case of BOJ, after a year's work in its main office a freshman career employee is assigned to one of its twenty or so local branches for two years. This is considered a very useful way of enabling a young career employee to learn how the central banking system operates on a local scale.

Assistant Director

After service as a director of a local Internal Revenue Office, a career officer returns to the MOF's main office and becomes an assistant director (*kacho-hosa*) in a division, and an active participant in the policymaking process. Some of the career officers are sent or seconded to other ministries or agencies for one to three years, working there temporarily on what is called a *shukko* basis (see Appendix B).

A career officer's period of service as assistant director is usually about ten years, i.e. approximately from ages 30 to 40. During this period he changes his post approximately every two years, so as to occupy about five different assistant-director posts successively, normally in different bureaus.[10] In this phase he is expected to develop his general administrative ability, his capacity to respond promptly to a new situation, to negotiate effectively, to take leadership in reaching a consensus among those concerned, and to be knowledgeable—or to appear knowledgeable—about the matters within his jurisdiction. Needless to say, he must first be able to understand what is happening in the area in which he operates, and to make a sound judgment, whatever kind of job he is assigned to.

In the Japanese bureaucracy it is considered undesirable for the career officer to specialize in any single field or to judge a matter only from a particular point of view, whether legal or economic. In order to participate actively in the policymaking process he should form a well-balanced judgment, taking full account of both the economic and non-economic aspects of a situation. Furthermore, he should use common sense, sound logic, and simple language when expressing his views in a group discussion, so that other career and non-career officers can understand without difficulty.

Almost all the MOF's policy plans are first prepared by an assistant director. When a certain policy decision is necessary, the assistant director in charge is called upon to prepare a basic document, which should deal, as concisely as possible, with the historical background, relevant statistical data, legal aspects of the issue under consideration, merits and demerits of possible policy changes, the arguments for and against them, and a final conclusion.

When the original draft is completed, possibly with some revisions by the director of the division, it is submitted to a formal meeting of the bureau (*kyoku-gi*). The director general and other high officers of the bureau, as well as officers of other bureaux concerned, discuss the issue and the prepared document from every conceivable point of view. The drafter of the basic document must be able to answer promptly and clearly any question raised and to respond to opinions expressed at the meeting. If there remains any room for doubt, the document and the policy plan it embodies will not be approved at that stage. This involves a very severe test of the ability of the assistant director in charge.

When a new policy has successfully passed the "test" of the bureau meeting, it usually becomes MOF official policy. However, if the issue is very important or, more especially, if two or more of the bureaux concerned are in disagreement, the matter will be submitted to the office of the vice-minister or minister. In such a case, the officers of the Minister's Secretariat and the bureaux concerned will be called to a formal meeting of the ministry (*sho-gi*).

Division Director to Director General

When the period of his service as assistant director is completed, an MOF career officer either becomes the director of one of its regional offices for two to three years, which is somewhat similar to service as director of a local Internal Revenue Office in earlier years but at a higher level, or goes abroad to a Japanese embassy as a financial attache for three to four years. Then he returns to the main office and becomes the director of a division (*ka-cho*). In the Japanese bureaucracy a division directorship in the main office is considered a post much superior to the division directorship in a regional office, although they have the same title. This is also true of the *kyoku-cho* (director general), and of other supervisory posts. A career officer usually serves for two years as director of a particular division, and normally holds three different division-director posts successively. Beyond this he will usually become director general (DG) of a regional branch office, or occupy some equivalent post, for one to two years.

Since there is only a limited number of director-general posts in the ministry's head office, differentiated treatments start at this stage among career officers in the same class year, who have all been promoted more or less alike up to this point. Some retire from MOF after serving as DG of a regional office.

When an officer returns to the main office of MOF he ascends the final steps of the ladder to deputy DG and DG of a bureau. If a deputy DG is promoted to DG, it normally occurs within the same bureau, although a bureau DG may be transferred to an equivalent post in another bureau.

It is a tradition of the Japanese bureaucracy that only one person from a class year can become vice-minister, the highest civil service post in a ministry, since the minister is a politician. All the rest of the class quit the ministry when one of their classmates becomes vice-minister. This is true of any ministry or agency. Thus none of the career officers of a ministry is older than its vice-minister, who has usually been around 55 years old in recent years, although the average age was considerably lower before World War II.[11]

The retirement from the MOF of career officers belonging to a particular class year usually begins when they reach the deputy DG level, or sometimes even earlier. At that stage some retire from MOF and take up a position in a government institution or a private company, particularly a commercial bank, securities company or insurance company. After having retired from the post of vice-minister or DG, or a lower post, quite a few former government officers have become politicians, especially a member of Parliament, but sometimes governor of a prefecture or mayor.

The role of non-career officers

Thus in the Japanese bureaucracy the career officer is promoted step by step for about thirty to thirty-five years as a generalist administrator and to remain in a specific field for a long time or become a specialist in a certain area is to impair one's promotion possibilities. This does not, however, apply to non-career officers. Some posts require highly technical and/or specialized knowledge and experience in any ministry, for example, those in charge of computer work or census analysis. Such posts are usually occupied by distinguished non-career officers who are quite often treated as specialists in a particular field, and even encouraged to become such, unlike career officers.

This tendency is especially strong in MOF's budget and taxation bureaux. Indeed, the ministry has many non-career specialists who have worked in a single bureau for ten to twenty years, and their specialized knowledge and experience are very highly appreciated. It is generally recognized that no budget bill or tax law can be prepared satisfactorily without extensive work by non-career specialists. Some distinguished non-career officers have become division directors in the main office, or DG's in regional offices. Many more have become director of an Internal Revenue Office in their home town, a highly respected position in a local community, after serving fifteen to twenty years in the ministry's and/or Internal Revenue's main offices. However, none of these non-career officers ever specializes as an economist. They are experts on specialized practical matters such as tax laws, bank inspection, financial affairs of local governments, administration of customs tariffs, and so forth. They are neither economists, statisticians, nor lawyers. Career officers have a much better knowledge of economics or economic theory, and basic documents on economic policy issues submitted to the bureau meetings are almost always prepared by career officers.

The Role of Research Divisions

The government hires no professional economists or statisticians, for neither of these constitutes a recognized profession in Japanese society. Nor is this situation likely to change in the near future. Nevertheless, economics and economic theory are becoming increasingly important year by year in the bureaucratic process of economic policy-making. One consequence is that in almost every ministry the research divisions play a more and more important role in this process.

We shall again take the MOF as an example, one where there are now five independent research divisions[12] engaged in statistical and economic analysis, forecasting, and the investigation of academic literature, and scholarly and public opinion on matters under the jurisdiction of the bureau to which they belong. They also prepare basic data, analyses, or reports on issues under the bureau at the request of senior ministry officials or members of Parliament. Such requests have substantially increased lately.

The most influential MOF research division is the Research and Planning Division of the concerned Minister's Secretariat. It is headed by a deputy-DG-level officer who is the highest ranking deputy DG in the MOF, and its staff includes a division director, two under-directors (*sanji-kan*), a couple of assistant directors, a large number of career officers, and personnel working on a temporary, on-loan basis from commercial banks and other institutions. In terms of the number of its staff members it is nearly as large as a small bureau, and the functions it performs probably parallel those performed by economists in some other governments. Its staff analyze economic trends, compile statistics, and prepare economic forecasts. They closely follow news of economic affairs and press comments in both Japanese and foreign newspapers and economic periodicals, and collect and examine national and international economic forecasts published by private research institutes, foreign governments, and international organizations and academic studies useful in forming judgments on economic policy issues. They use their own macroeconomic model to analyze business trends and make economic forecasts. On the basis of this work they take the lead in formulating official views of the MOF on the business situation and prospects. The division frequently presents a report to the Minister of Finance, vice-minister, or other top officials and holds a briefing session with them, on business prospects and economic and industrial trends. When any MOF officer needs to quote officially any figure on the economic situation he must first check it with the Secretariat's Research and Planning Division.

Every Monday economic indicators and the analysis thereof prepared by the Research and Planning Division are presented to the ministry's Executive Meeting, comprising officers at and above the DG level. This has a pedagogical value, for the high officers of the MOF learn a great deal about current macroeconomic situations. Although the division's staff perform functions essentially identical to those of economists in some other countries, they do not individually have the professional economist's ability or formal qualifications. Instead, collectively, they play the role of economists. It often happens that none of the division's top officers is an economics graduate. They have perhaps acquired their knowledge of economics partly through the Economic Theory Training program, but primarily through on-the-job training since joining the MOF. They do not simply try to apply economic theory or economics directly, but they try to analyze economic problems from an administrator's viewpoint and seek solutions which are not only economically desirable but also compatible with the logic and conventional way of thinking commonly accepted within the MOF. Their thought processes have deep roots and are derived from the MOF's long history and accumulated experience. The research divisions of other MOF bureaus are smaller than that of the Minister's Secretariat, but they perform broadly similar economic functions.

However, it is difficult to evaluate the influence of these research divisions on economic policy decisions. Undoubtedly any statistics, facts, and opinions relevant to a policy issue are collected and examined carefully before making a decision, although the outcome is usually a delicate compromise between economic, legal, and political considerations.

The EPA's Research Bureau and Economic Research Institute, the MITI's Research Division of the Minister's Secretariat and Research Division in the Industrial Policy Bureau, and the BOJ's Research and Statistics Bureaux and newly established Special Research Department are all performing economist-type functions in their respective organizations. The MOF's *Monthly Research Bulletin, Monthly Fiscal and Financial Statistical Bulletin,* the BOJ's *Monthly Research Bulletin,* and several other publications of these research offices are among the economic periodicals most widely read by those who closely follow current economic developments in Japan.

The Power Structure and the Bureaucracy

The formal power structure

Viewed from a formal and short-term standpoint, the structure of authority in Japanese economic policy is highly concentrated. In principle, important economic policy decisions are made in the twice-weekly Cabinet meetings. The Cabinet has been a conservative, single-party body for thirty years and thus the Liberal Democratic Party (LDP) has the formal power, through the Prime Minister and his Cabinet members, to make all the economic policy decisions. In practice, however, frequent close contacts and negotiations take place beforehand between the ministries and agencies concerned, e.g. in vice-ministers' meetings, in order to prepare the ground for an agreement. It is no exaggeration to say that when a certain matter is placed on the Cabinet agenda the government has already made up its mind, and that these meetings merely represent a ceremonial confirmation and recording of the conclusion.

Parliament has formal authority on many important economic policy issues. The government budget must be authorized by Parliament, at least by the Lower House, and in order to implement the budget it is usually necessary to pass a number of new laws and amend even more existing ones. Such matters as tax reform, national bond policies, the prices of goods and services supplied by certain government enterprises, customs tariffs, and social-security benefits, all come under the authority of Parliament. Nevertheless Parliament has not recently played an important role in formulating Japan's economic policies because the ruling LDP has held a majority in both houses for more than thirty years. Consequently the government's budget bill and accompanying legislation have almost always received Parliamentary approval.[13]

What role, then, is played by the ministries and agencies in charge of economic affairs? In our view they are quite influential in Japanese economic policymaking, since they have superior accumulated expertise and access to information. Particularly the MOF, and especially its Budget Bureau, are the most influential bodies, for they are responsible for the government budget, and without the MOF's agreement it is virtually impossible to carry out any economic or other policy measure requiring government expenditure, regardless of the amount involved. Furthermore, the MOF often acts as a coordinator among ministries and agencies even where no direct public expenditure is involved.

The MOF is also influential on monetary policy, as the BOJ is legally under its supervision. The BOJ's President and Executive Governors are appointed by the Minister of Finance, and any revision of the reserve requirements ratio must be approved by him. The BOJ can legally alter the official discount rate by itself, but in practice it always consults the MOF's Banking Bureau in advance. It also has close contacts with the MOF on its lending and bond-purchase policies. On the other hand, the MOF is responsible for the foreign-exchange policy, and the BOJ is consulted by the MOF and deals in the exchange market as its agent.

The EPA is concerned primarily with economic forecasting, economic planning, and coordination of economic policies and has final responsibility for the government's annual economic prospect and for the medium-term national economic plan.[14] Its role in government is somewhat similar to that of the Research and Planning Division in the MOF's Minister's Secretariat. The EPA also sometimes plays an important role as economic policy coordinator on problems involving more than one ministry or agency, such as inflation, water resources, and regional development planning. With respect to the economic prospect, it often acts as a mediator between the bullish MITI and the bearish MOF.

The role of the government party
The foregoing remarks should not be taken as implying that Japanese economic policy is entirely controlled by the bureaucracy. On the

Table 3
Numbers of Members of Parliament Who Were Formerly Government Officers (1978)

| | Total members | Former government officers | |
		LDP	Non-government parties
House of Representatives	511	69	20
House of Councillors	252	47	20

contrary, the government party, the non-government parties, various pressure groups, public opinion, and academic economists all play their roles in the process of economic policymaking.

Considering the government party, since the LDP first held the majority in Parliament in 1948, its president has always been designated as Prime Minister, and eight out of the first fifteen Prime Ministers since World War II have in fact been former government career officers. Among these eight, three —Hayato Ikeda, Masayoshi Ohira and Takeo Fukuda, —were MOF graduates; Fukuda in particular kept in close contact with the "MOF family" of present and former MOF officers and was generally regarded as "strong on economic affairs."

As shown in Table 3, many members of Parliament, especially those in the LDP, are former government officers, in both the Lower House (Representatives) and the Upper House (Councillors).

Most of these LDP politicians are former career officers who retired from the civil service at the DG level or higher, whereas those of non-government parties include former non-career officers who have become leaders of government employees' labor unions.

The LDP's Political Affairs Research Committee (Seimu-Chosa-Kai) plays an important role in the policymaking process, as it is the formal party policy-formulating organ. It has a number of subcommittees corresponding to the respective ministries or agencies, where the party's substantive policymaking decisions are made. For example, from the MOF's policy standpoint, the LDP's Fiscal Sub-committee and Tax Policy Research Committee, both under its Political Affairs Research Committee, are the two leading LDP committees. Many of its executive members are very familiar with the MOF's affairs, and some are former MOF career officers or ex-Parliamentary Vice-Ministers of Finance.[15] The debate in the LDP's Tax Policy Research Committee is of major importance to the MOF. The Committee's annual discussion of tax reforms parallels that in the government's Tax Policy Research Committee, an advisory body reporting to the Prime Minister. As the Tax Bureau has a hard job to persuade the LDP committee members every year, it has a number of experts on "Parliamentary liaison."

In preparing the government's annual budget the assistant directors (*shusa*; MOF career officers in their 11th to 16th year) and the Budget Bureau's Budget Examiners (*shukei-kan*, who have division-director rank) start examining requests from individual ministries and agencies in early September. The negotiations and bargaining with other ministries or agencies continue until the end of November, when the Budget Bureau holds its annual "budget meeting." Then the negotiations go up to higher and higher levels, first between the other ministries' DGs and the deputy DG of the Budget Bureau, and subsequently between the other ministries' vice-ministers and the Budget Bureau's DG. Eventually the government's budget bill is finalized through negotiations at the ministerial level and consultation with the three top executives of the LDP. Assistant directors and budget examiners may pay some heed to petitions and appeals from all kinds of interest groups and requests from influential members of Parliament. But they try to be as neutral and independent as possible. Sometimes the budget bill is revised in negotiations between the Finance minister and the LDP's three top executives in order to reflect the party's policy, but the budget examiners usually anticipate and prepare for this in advance.

Generally speaking, the bureaucracy outweighs the government party in the economic policy planning and decision-making processes and when the LDP wishes to adopt a new policy in a certain area, its implementation would be impossible without full consultation with the ministries or agencies concerned. Therefore the LDP usually consults with the bureaucracy about the feasibility of any prospective new policy at a very early stage.

The principal officers in charge of Parliamentary liaison in the MOF are the secretary general and the director of the Archives and Documents Division, both of whom are members of the minister's Secretariat. They occupy key posts, and no policy is adopted in the MOF without their consent.

Non-government parties, pressure groups and public opinion

The non-government parties—from left to right, the Communist Party, Socialist Party, Komei Party, Democratic Socialist Party, and New Liberal Club, and a couple of other very small groups—seem not to be much interested in economic policy issues. Apart from the New Liberal Club, which recently split off from the LDP, these parties have not been in power in the past thirty years, and they have little chance of being so. Their ability to collect information, analyze economic conditions, and plan policies is necessarily limited, so they tend to concentrate on criticizing the government for what it does or fails to do.

Nevertheless, these parties do exert an important influence on the government's economic policy, for they are channels, together with the LDP, whereby pressure groups and the general public participate in politics. The government's majority has recently been much reduced and some Parliamentary standing committees are sometimes chaired by nongovernment party members. Under such conditions the LDP government tends to avoid submitting a bill which is bound to be strongly opposed by the non-government parties. Therefore the methods of negotiating with non-government party members of Parliament for the passage of each ministry's bills constitute an important part of the ministry's Parliamentary liaison work. Career officers at the division-director level and above often visit non-government party M.P.s in order to explain particular policy issues, to exchange views, and to solicit their support, or at least to ask them to refrain from strongly opposing the ministry's policy. Ministries and agencies generally assign some of their most competent career officers to this Parliamentary liaison work.

A party's policies on major current issues affect the number of votes it can collect at elections, including the general election, so that it is sensitive to popular sentiment in choosing its policy lines. Especially for the LDP, popular support from a wide range of social strata and interest groups is essential to the maintenance of its power. As a result, over the long run, pressure groups such as farmers, small enterprises, and specific industries exert considerable influence on economic policy decisions, through political parties, both non-government and LDP.

Nonpartisanship of the bureaucracy

Under the American Occupation immediately after the war a large number of politicians, businessmen, scholars, journalists, and military officers were "purged" from—that is, declared ineligible for—public or other socially prominent positions because of their active roles in World War II. But only a few civil government officials and almost no central bankers, whether in active service or in retirement, were purged then, and this may be taken as evidence of the nonpartisanship of high-ranking Japanese government officers. Although they maintain close contact with LDP politicians, and sometimes with non-government party politicians as well, they try to remain politically neutral as far as possible, especially with regard to the LDP *habatsu* (factions). Only in rare cases do the top civil servants lean towards any of them.[16]

How many high officers would be asked to resign if the LDP failed to hold a majority in the Parliament and a new Cabinet was formed? If the LDP still maintains a majority in a new coalition Cabinet there would probably be almost no change. If the Socialists and the Communists acquired power jointly and formed a two-party Cabinet, the situation may be somewhat different, but the new Cabinet would be able only to accelerate the retirement of senior officials, exclude a few strong dissidents, and promote those sympathetic or at least neutral towards them. Even under such a drastic Cabinet change the situation in Japan would be very different from that in the United States where many top positions of the bureaucracy are filled by what are called political appointees.

The consensus system
One of the prominent characteristics of the Japanese decision-making process lies, as already mentioned, in the high value attached to full consensus on any given decision. When a meeting is held to make a decision, it must normally be unanimous. Consequently much negotiation, discussion, and persuasion, both formal and informal, must take place before the meeting at which the final decision is made.

Within a ministry or company, there is a procedure called the *ringi* system. If a document proposing a certain policy measure is drafted by a person in charge, perhaps an assistant director, in a ministry, it goes step by step through the desks of director, deputy DG, DG and vice-minister, adding one signature at each stage. If it affects more than one bureau, the document gets numerous signatures as it goes through many desks in the bureaus concerned. In such a case, nobody knows when the decision was actually made or who was actually responsible for it. Any attempts to circumvent this consensus procedure will be likely to give rise to trouble at a later stage, since some of those who should have known of the decision will complain that they have not been consulted and have not yet endorsed it.

Any document sanctioned by a bureau DG goes to the Archives and Documents Division of the Minister's Secretariat and, after a careful scrutiny, is sent on to the Secretary General of the Secretariat and the vice-minister, and, if the matter is sufficiently important, to the minister. In this way the ministry's decision is finalized. When it is deemed necessary, the minister or other high officers will meet the Prime Minister to explain the ministry's view and to receive the latter's instructions or to obtain his approval. Furthermore, if the matter involves other ministries or agencies too, the responsible officers in all the divisions and bureaux concerned will endeavor to reach a consensus on it.

This consensual decision-making process is time-consuming, and even in Japan the system is workable only in a tightly knit organization where there are no important conflicts of interest or ideological differences, and where everyone considers himself an insider or a permanent, well-protected member of the organization. A loyal insider should always participate sincerely in the arduous process of consensus formation, although confrontation with outsiders may be unavoidable at some stage. In the process of economic policymaking, the Cabinet members, career government officers concerned, and LDP leaders are all insiders, and there should be no difference of views on important issues.

The Japanese type of consensus system appears inefficient because is takes so much time, and few dare to take active leadership when there is a sharp difference of opinion or a serious conflict of interest. But once the decision is made, all those concerned are willing to accept it and to cooperate in its implementation. Thus if one looks not only at the decisionmaking process itself, but views the whole process, including implementation of a decision, it can be said to work well.

The role of academic economists

In Japan those responsible for government economic affairs and the academic economists constitute two separate worlds as far as the interchange of personnel is concerned, apart from such special cases as the EPA's Research Institute or the Ministry of Agriculture's General Research Institute of Agriculture.

Some academic economists are appointed by the government as members of councils or research committees, advisory bodies which discuss economic policy issues and report to the Prime Minister or some other minister. For example, in 1979 among the councils and research committees related to the MOF, 2 out of 30 members in the Tax Policy Research Committee,[17] 5 out of 23 in the Public Finance System Council, 3 out of 33 in the Banking System Research Committee, and 2 out of 35 in the Customs Tariffs Council were professors (some of them emeritus) of economics. However, no academic economist participated in the Securities Exchange Council or in the Insurance Council (which had 13 and 28 members respectively). Moreover, generally speaking, these relatively few academic economists in government councils and research committees do not appear to play an important role in the various committees or councils, nor are these bodies influential in the economic policymaking process. They merely contribute to the exchange of views and to the persuasion of certain representatives of business interests.

Nevertheless it would be wrong to conclude that academic economists exert only a minimal influence on Japan's economic policy. Professors of economics express opinions and write articles in daily newspapers and non-academic weekly or monthly periodicals and appear on television discussing economic policy issues and economic prospects, much more frequently in Japan than in any other country. The government research divisions mentioned earlier, which essentially play the economist's role, always pay attention to relevant articles or the opinions of influential academic economists because these articles or opinions represent a sample of the public's opinion and sometimes have an impact upon public opinion. Similarly, some senior officials and ministers, and even the Prime Minister, have private contacts with academic economists' and take account of their views on important policy issues thereby short-circuiting the cumbersome formality of councils and research committees of the government. Indeed, these personal contacts may sometimes directly affect economic policy decisions because bureaucrats in responsible positions do not want to be criticized by well-known academics whose views may be cited in attacks on the ministry's policy in the mass media and parliamentary discussions.

There are practically no interchanges of personnel between the bureaucracy and the academic community, and only a small number each of government officers and academics meet informally and discuss economic policy issues frankly. Of course, practitioners and academics think in fundamentally different terms: politicians and civil servants tend to distrust academic economists because of their abstractness, ignorance of political factors, and unrealistic proposals; academic economists tend to look down upon practitioners because of their ignorance of economics, short-sightedness, and excessive concern with existing vested interests.

Even so, these two separate worlds still interact intensively, when viewed in a long-range perspective. Economics and an economic way of thinking have gradually been spreading into the government offices responsible for economic policy planning and implementation in postwar Japan. Keynesian macroeconomics, economic forecasting, and planning based upon macroeconomic models and input–output analysis have become a part of the standard equipment of civil servants in charge of economic affairs. For example, academic economists have exerted a considerable influence on the government's policy in the process of liberalizing trade and direct investment. It can be said that views of professors of economics and law have had an important effect on recent developments in antitrust policy. Also, monetary economics, which emphasizes the role of the money supply and a new approach to the balance of payments and exchange rates based upon monetary and asset balance analyses, now appears to be gradually spreading into the MOF, EPA, and BOJ.

Concluding Remarks

The role of the economist in government or business is merely one of many examples of the differences between Japan's culture and human relations and their counterparts in countries with European traditions. In Japan, there is no profession of economist or statistician. Government and other large organizations employ almost everybody on a so-called lifetime commitment basis, and career employees are promoted year by year according to the seniority principle. Collectively they form a hierarchical team and run the organization as generalist administrators or managers.

This does not, however, mean that the Japanese government can dispense with the functions which economists perform in other countries, for they are undertaken by teams headed by generalist administrators in the research divisions or elsewhere which are engaged in statistical and economic analysis, forecasting, and planning. As economic problems have become increasingly important among government policy issues, the research divisions and comparable offices in the Japanese government and the Bank of Japan have been playing an ever more important role in the economic policymaking process. Moreover, top government officials responsible for economic policy today have accumulated much more economic knowledge and become much more accustomed to thinking in economic terms than ten or fifteen years ago.

To outsiders the postwar performance of the Japanese economy appears to have been highly successful. Nevertheless, in comparing Japan with other industrialized countries, it is natural to ask whether the quality of Japan's economic policy would have been superior if the Japanese government had been able to hire good economists and had taken notice of their advice. It would obviously be unwise to answer such a hypothetical question in dogmatic terms, but on the whole, a limited affirmative reply seems warranted. However, in order to affect economic policy even slightly such economists would have needed to be able to speak the language used by bureaucrats and politicians and to cooperate closely with generalist administrators; few Japanese academic economists have been able to do this. Many academic economists are either too theoretical to be effective in government or are reluctant to leave their university posts, and in Japan there have been no professional economists outside the academic community.

Appendix A. MOF's Economic Theory Training Program

The content of the program, started in 1961, is shown for 1978 in the accompanying table.

Microeconomics	25 sessions[a]
Macroeconomics	20
Mathematics for Economics	35
Statistics	20
Econometrics	20
Input–Output Analysis	20
Public Economics	15
Monetary Theory	15
Public Finance	13
International Economics	15
International Finance	10
Seminars	60
Lectures on Special Topics	32
Total	300 sessions

[a]One "session" consists of three hours of lecture or seminar.

The main objective is to provide a basic training in economics for young career officers who have already undertaken some administrative work. Teachers are professors and younger scholars at such leading universities as Tokyo, Hitotsubashi and Keio. The course is generally considered very useful, especially for Law School graduates who have not hitherto studied economics seriously. The program obviously involves a considerable cost for the MOF, since the trainees are completely freed from administrative duties for one full year.

Appendix B. The Practice of On-loan Service

The practice of *shukko*, which may be translated as "on-loan service," is perhaps one of the peculiar characteristics of the Japanese bureaucracy, and indeed of Japanese employment practices in general. Once a person is employed by a ministry or a company as a permanent rather than temporary or part-time employee, whether white-collar or blue-collar, he or she usually serves in that organization until very near the end of his/her career. This is generally called the lifetime employment system. Sometimes, however, a career government officer may be transferred for a limited period of one to three years outside of his ministry or agency to a post in another ministry or agency, a government institution outside of the government proper, a local government or an international organization such as the IMF, IBRD, or OECD. Private companies also send their employees on a *shukko* basis to their subsidiaries, to joint-venture companies, or in the case of banks, to their customer companies.

The MOF regularly lends its officials, both career and non-career personnel, at various levels to the Ministry of Foreign Affairs, MITI, Ministry of Internal Affairs, EPA, Defense Agency, Environmental Agency, Fair Trade Commission, Prime Minister's Office, and many others. Originally such relatively new agencies as the EPA, Fair Trade Commission, or Environmental Agency had to borrow senior officers from ministries and elsewhere because they lacked suitable highranking officials of their own. The MOF also sends its officials to a large number of other government institutions and local governments, and even to a few semi-government/semi-private nonprofit bodies such as the Japan External Trade Organization (JETRO). In most cases, the MOF sends its officials successively to the same posts of other ministries, agencies, and other bodies. *Shukko* from the MOF also includes transfers to diplomatic posts abroad, which are under the Ministry of Foreign Affairs. A *shukko-sha* sent from the MOF then becomes a diplomat temporarily and works as a financial attache in charge of international financial and economic affairs abroad.

Other ministries or agencies also send their officials to the MOF, but the number of posts at higher levels in the MOF occupied by the 'outsiders' (*shukko-sha*) is very small. Some employees of commercial and long-term credit banks work in the MOF, EPA, and government financial institutions on a *shukko* basis for a term of about two years. Because government salaries are lower than those in the private sector, especially in banking, in such cases the difference is made up by the banks who lend the *shukko-sha*. From the banks' point of view the information, experience, and personal contacts gained during the *shukko* period justify the cost of sending their employees in this manner.

This chapter was co-authored by Kozo Yamamoto. It was first published in *Economists in Government: A Comparative Study,* edited by A. W. Coats (Durham, N.C.: Duke University Press, 1981) and at the same time in *History of Political Economy,* Vol. 13, No. 3 (Fall 1981).

Notes

1. The situation is different with respect to those having M.A. and Ph.D. degrees in Engineering or Natural Science, for whom there has recently been an increasingly brisk demand from large corporations. On the other hand, there are no schools in Japan which more or less correspond to a U.S.-type graduate school of Business Administration or Law School.

2. On economic planning in Japan, see "Economic Planning and Industrial Policy," Chapter 7 in this volume.

3. There is no Japanese word corresponding to "statistician" in English, nor a socially recognized profession of statistician in Japan. Socially recognized professionals in Japan (e.g. medical doctors, lawyers, accountants) undergo several years' post-graduate special training, are authorized or

licensed by the government, are employed or practice by themselves as professionals, and belong to coherent and influential national and regional associations.

4. Such former or incumbent officials as Hisao Kanamori (EPA), Saburo Okita (EPA), Osamu Shimomura (Ministry of Finance), Toshihiko Yoshino (Bank of Japan) in the past, and Takao Akabane, Yutaka Kosai, Isamu Miyazaki (all EPA), Yoshio Suzuki (Bank of Japan), and Masaru Yoshitomi (EPA) recently. Among them Okita is a graduate in engineering, Yoshino and Kanamori in law, Yoshitomi in liberal arts, and others in economics. To my knowledge only Kosai and Yoshitomi had a formal education in economics at the graduate level.

5. In the Ministry of Foreign Affairs, some career officers, that is those who passed the senior-level diplomatic service examination, are considered as especially "strong on economic affairs," having gone through many posts dealing primarily with international economic affairs, such as posts in the Bureau of Economic Affairs, Bureau of Economic Cooperation, and Permanent Delegations to OECD and to International Organizations in Geneva, and "economic" posts in other offices of the Ministry.

6. Thus the distinction between "career" and "non-career" officers in the Japanese civil service is similar to that between commissioned officers and other soldiers in the military service.

7. There are exceptions, however; for instance, in recent years the MOF normally selects one of the new career officers employed every year from among graduates in either natural science or engineering. The EPA also hires one or two Natural Science or Engineering graduates every year. They must first pass either the law, administration, or economics seniorlevel examination in order to be eligible for the interview, and quite a few do succeed! This indicates the level of knowledge in law or economics taught at the undergraduate level and required in the senior-level examination.

8. As already mentioned, the MOF also hires about one graduate in science or engineering every year, and he or she often comes out of the "economics" examination.

9. The number of career officers who occupied the posts above the Director General (kyoku-cho; DG) level in the MOF from 1960 through 1978 is 115, of which the number of graduates from Schools of Economics, including the prewar commercial college, similar to the German *Handelshochschule*, is only 13. An overwhelming majority of these 115 officers are graduates of the University of Tokyo. But former Prime Minister Masayoshi Ohira, is a graduate of Tokyo Commercial College (now Hitotsubashi University) and was employed as a career officer in the MOF under the prewar system. Former Prime Minister Hayato Ikeda was also an MOF career officer and graduated from the School of Law of Kyoto University. They quit the MOF after filling many high posts there, became politicians, were elected as members of Parliament, and then later became Minister of Finance and Prime Minister. Thus one does not have to be a graduate of the University of Tokyo in order to be successful as a career officer in the MOF.

10. The MOF's personnel policy seems to be changing somewhat in this regard. Previously, there were quite a few career officers called *shukei* (budget)-*batake* (or *bata*) or *shuzei* (taxation)-*batake*, meaning "grown up in Budget (or Taxation) Bureau," who have gone through many posts in the Bud-

get or the Taxation Bureau. *Shukei-batake* officers used to be considered the mainstay of the MOF, with *shuzei-batake* coming next. But until recently the MOF has tended to shift career officers around from one bureau to another, and not to foster many officers "grown up" in a particular bureau.

11. An exception to the above general rule takes place in the case of the Ministry of Foreign Affairs, where the vice-minister, who is always a career diplomat, is often appointed as ambassador to the United States, Russia, or China. A few other ambassadors could also be older than the Vice-Minister of Foreign Affairs.

12. The Research and Planning Division of the Minister's Secretariat was established in 1952, and Research Divisions of Budget, International Finance, Taxation, and Banking Bureau in 1962, 1971, 1976, and 1977 respectively. In other bureaus the research work is done by the General Affairs Division.

13. As far as the budget is concerned, there have been only two exceptions. In 1972, a part of defense expenditure was subtracted from the original budget bill because it included the cost of the Fourth Defense Plan, which had not yet been approved officially by Parliament. In 1977, the social-welfare expenditure was increased as a result of a compromise between the government and opposition parties on a reform of the national pension system.

14. For the meaning of national economic plans and planning, see Chapter 7 in this volume.

15. Each ministry or agency has three vice-ministers: the administrative Vice-Minister, who is the head of the ministry's career officers, and two Parliamentary Vice-Ministers, appointed by the Prime Minister from among Upper and Lower House members. The simple word "vice-minister" normally refers to the former of these two. In addition, one or two career posts next to the administrative vice-minister, such as *gaimukan* (MOF), *gaimu-shingikan* (MFA), *tsusan-shingikan* (MITI), are called Vice-Minister in English.

16. When a career officer serves as a personal (but official) secretary to, or as vice-minister under, a minister who is naturally a politician and belongs to a certain faction of the LDP, an intimate relationship may develop between them, and later the former may belong to the latter's faction when retiring from the civil service and going into politics.

17. This is an advisory body to the Prime Minister, and different from the LDP's Tax Policy Research Committee mentioned earlier.

Bibliography

There is no work dealing directly with the role of economists in the Japanese government, since there exists no economist in the government employed as such, as explained in the text. The following are works on the contemporary Japanese bureaucracy and/or policymaking process.

Craig, A.M. (1975). "Functional and Dysfunctional Aspects of Government Bureaucracy," in E.F. Vogel, ed., *Modern Japanese Organization and Decision-making*, (Berkeley: University of California Press.

Komiya, Ryutaro (1979). "Planning in Japan." In Morris Bornstein, ed., *Economic Planning: East and West* (Cambridge, Mass.). Reprinted in M. Bornstein, ed., *Comparative Economic Systems: Models and Cases*. 4th ed. (Irwin, Calif., 1979).

Ito, Daiichi. (1980). *Gendai Nihon Kanryosei no Bunseki* (An Analysis of Contemporary Japanese Bureaucracy), in Japanese. Tokyo.

Stockwin, J.A.A. (1975). *Japan: Divided Politics in a Growth Economy.* London: Allen & Unwin.

Tsuji, Kiyoaki. (1952). *Nihon Kanryosei no Kenkyu* (Studies on Japan's Bureaucracy), in Japanese. Tokyo (revised, 1969).

INDEX

advisory committees *(chosakai)*, 305
agricultural cooperatives, 206, 207
agriculture, protection of, 11, 13, 22, 34, 35-36, 37, 38-39, 43, 48-49, 53, 102-4
Aliber, R. Z., 145
"announcement effects," of national economic plans, 285-86
Anti-Monopoly Law, 161
antitrust policy, 15, 300, 308
Aoki, Masahiko, 198
Asahi Chemical Industry, 196
Asahi Mutual Life Insurance Company, 167, 256
Asia, Japanese direct investment in, 120, 121, 123, 130, 132-33, 139, 140, 141
automobile industry, 34-35, 301

Bain, J. S. 297, 298
balance of payments, 5-6, 17, 21, 22, 31, 40, 44, 72-73, 78-80, 120, 126, 321, 329, 344-46
Bank of Japan, 6, 310, 318, 349, 350-51, 357-58, 365, 370, 377, 378
banks, Japanese, 167, 206, 233, 255
Basic Economic and Social Plan (1973-77), 269-77
Baumol, William J., 198
biotechnology, 33, 187
Brazil, 98
Bretton Woods System, 4, 20, 69-70

Budget Bureau (Ministry of Finance), 283-84, 380
bureaucracy, structure and role of the Japanese, 14-15, 362-63, 367-75, 381-82
Burke-Hartke Bill, 11, 96

Cabinet Legislation Bureau, 304
capitalists, 162, 167-68, 181, 205, 233-34, 259, 309-10
cartels, 15, 259, 300
chemical industries, 5, 32-33
China, organization of businesses in, 208-22
chosakai (advisory committees), 305
collective firms, 205-8
Communist Party, 380
comparative advantage, 31-33, 46
competition, excess, 14-15, 289, 297-98, 299, 300-301
Confucianism, 298, 299
consumer cooperatives, 206, 207
"convoy approach," 239, 242, 243, 245, 249, 259
corporate behavior, Japanese: life insurance companies, 245-52, 258-60; and pursuit of growth, 176-79, 181-83, 188, 203; theories of, 159, 169-75 corporate structure, Japanese, 161-62, 184, 195-97
current-account deficits, 79-80; of the United States, 44, 50, 72-73, 78-79, 84-85, 87-90, 94, 95-96, 101

391